THE NEW
GOLDEN TREASURY
OF ENGLISH
VERSE

THE NEW GOLDEN TREASURY OF ENGLISH VERSE

chosen by
EDWARD LEESON

PAN BOOKS
in association with
MACMILLAN LONDON

ACKNOWLEDGEMENTS

The editor and publishers are grateful to the following authors, publishers and owners of copyright for giving permission to reproduce some of the poems which appear in this anthology.

From *Collected Poems* W. H. Auden, Faber & Faber Ltd; from *Collected Poems* John Betjeman, John Murray Ltd; Mrs Nicolette Gray and the Society of Authors on behalf of the Laurence Binyon Estate; *Report on Experience* Edmund Blunden A. D. Peters & Co. Ltd; from *The Poetical Works of Robert Bridges*, Oxford University Press; *Will It Be So Again?* the Executors of the Estate of C. Day Lewis, Jonathan Cape Ltd and the Hogarth Press; the Literary Trustees of Walter de la Mare and the Society of Authors as their representative; from *The Complete Poems of Keith Douglas* Oxford University Press; from *Collected Poems 1909–62* T. S. Eliot, Faber & Faber Ltd; from *Collected Poems* William Empson, Chatto & Windus; from *Collected Poems* Roy Fuller, André Deutsch Ltd; from *Collected Poems* Robert Graves; from *My Sad Captains* and *Moly* Thom Gunn, Faber & Faber Ltd; from *Collected Poems* the Society of Authors as the literary representative of the Estate of A. E. Housman, and Jonathan Cape Ltd; from *Lupercal* and *Crow* Ted Hughes, Faber & Faber Ltd; *Cities and Thrones and Powers* and *The Way through the Woods* Rudyard Kipling, the National Trust; *Recessional* and *Danny Deever* Rudyard Kipling, the National Trust, and Eyre Methuen Ltd; from *The Whitsun Weddings* Philip Larkin, Faber & Faber Ltd; Laurence Pollinger Ltd and the Estate of the late Mrs Frieda Lawrence Ravagli; from *Raider's Dawn and Other Poems* Alun Lewis, Allen & Unwin Ltd; from *Collected Poems* Hugh MacDiarmid, Macmillan Publishing Co. Inc. and Christopher Murray Grieve; from *The Collected Poems of Louis MacNeice*, Faber & Faber Ltd; the Society of Authors as the literary representative of the Estate of John Masefield; from *The Collected Poems of Edwin Muir* Faber & Faber Ltd; from *A Map of Verona* Henry Reed, Jonathan Cape Ltd; from *Collected Poems* Edith Sitwell, Macmillan; from *Collected Poems* Stephen Spender, Faber & Faber Ltd; from *The Poems* the Trustees of the Copyrights of the late Dylan Thomas, J. M. Dent & Sons Ltd and New Directions; from *Collected Poems* W. B. Yeats, Michael Yeats.

First published 1980 by Pan Books Ltd, Cavaye Place, London SW10 9PG
in association with Macmillan London Ltd

9 8 7

Selection, arrangement and all editorial matter © Edward Leeson 1980
ISBN 0 330 26165 7
Printed and bound in Great Britain by Cox & Wyman Ltd, Reading

CONTENTS

INTRODUCTION

IN POETRY, as Thomas Hardy observed, is 'concentrated the essence of all imaginative and emotional literature', and in every age the poets have provided some of the most sublime expressions of Man's genius and some of the most profound insights into the nature of human experience. For most of us, our first awareness of the English poetic tradition comes from exploring anthologies. For more than a century the character of English poetry anthologies has been moulded, directly and indirectly, and to a remarkable degree, by one man – Francis Turner Palgrave (1824–97), an exceptionally gifted Victorian man of letters who created *The Golden Treasury*, an anthology so distinctive that its influence has reached down to our own time.

The Golden Treasury was first published in 1861. As the book's full title makes clear, Palgrave made his selection from 'the best songs and lyrical poems in the English language', which he presented in four sections corresponding to what he considered to be the four poetic epochs from the middle of the sixteenth century to the middle of the nineteenth. Within each section Palgrave arranged the poems in a 'poetically-effective order' shaped by 'gradations of feeling or subject', rejecting a strictly chronological sequence since he believed it would inhibit his readers' enjoyment of the poems. *The Golden Treasury* quickly established itself as one of the most popular and most enduring of all anthologies; and it was subsequently reissued with additional poems chosen both by Palgrave himself and – after his death – by others, including Laurence Binyon and Cecil Day Lewis, who wisely remained faithful to Palgrave's original concept.

Palgrave's influence was immense. Ironically, although Palgrave himself was well aware that his selection of songs and lyrical poems was not representative of English poetry as a whole, *The Golden Treasury* was soon accepted as a basic canon of English poetry, receiving the final seal of approval at the turn of the century, when Sir Arthur Quiller-Couch came to compile *The Oxford Book of English Verse* – surely the best-known and best-loved of all English anthologies. Acknowledging the extent to which *The Golden Treasury* had helped to form the poetic taste of his generation, Quiller-Couch followed Palgrave in restricting his choice to the 'lyrical or epigrammatic', though he, too, had sometimes to confer the honorary status of 'lyrical poem' on pieces which did not really fall within his terms of reference. Indeed, save that Quiller-Couch introduced the chronological structure that Palgrave had carefully avoided, the two anthologies are identical in spirit and intention, and their supremacy has been long and absolute.

However, if poetry is to retain its vitality, and continue to grow and develop, we must make a fresh appraisal of past poetic achievement from time to time, admit new poets to the tradition and place the work of established poets in a fresh perspective. In the last quarter of the twentieth century an exclusively lyrical interpretation of the English poetic tradition no longer seems adequate. Developments as various as the impetus given to English poetry by the young American writers who arrived on these shores in the years immediately preceding the First World War, the influence of social and political awareness in the thirties, and the recent general growth of interest in medieval culture have all contributed to make us receptive to a wider range of poetic expression than was accessible to Palgrave's original readers. In 1972 *The New Oxford Book of English Verse*, edited by Dame Helen Gardner, was published. It was not a revision of Quiller-Couch's anthology, but a new selection. The scope of the anthology was wider than that of its predecessors: dialect poems were included; there were many extracts from long poems; and recent developments in English poetry up to the outbreak of the Second World War were taken into account, many twentieth-century poets being admitted to the canon. Nevertheless, the influence of Sir Arthur Quiller-Couch, and through him of Palgrave, was still clearly to be detected: the emphasis was still on the short lyrical poem and the descriptive set-piece. The time is surely right for attempting a new view of English poetry.

The New Golden Treasury of English Verse offers a more broadly based anthology of English verse than has hitherto been available in one volume. Embracing major English poets from the Middle Ages to the present day, it also includes dialect poetry, Border ballads and important translations. Many significant long poems have previously been represented – where anthologists have included them at all – only by extracts, thus taking on a life of their own out of context; they are here included in their entirety. Early English poetry receives more generous treatment than ever before, and major figures such as Langland, Gower, Henryson and Douglas make their first substantial appearance in an anthology of this kind. Dramatic verse has been excluded because it invariably suffers when wrenched out of its proper setting.

It is not the business of a collection such as *The New Golden Treasury* to be speculative, and the work of living writers in the middle of their career has been approached with caution; but, although time will undoubtedly modify our estimation of the handful of contemporary poets included here, the high quality of their writing has already ensured that their work will last.

Inevitably, an anthology spanning nearly eight centuries confronts the editor with formidable problems of presentation. Consistency is out of the question. Language develops and changes, and poetic diction along with it, and the editor has continually to make minor adjustments if, in Palgrave's words, he is to 'present each poem, in disposition, spelling and punctuation, to the greatest advantage'. In the early texts editorial intervention has been minimal; the current practice of partial modernisation is never satisfactory, and the poets are probably better served by a conservative text and ample annotation. The side-notes should help the reader who is unfamiliar with medieval verse to grasp the poet's meaning. With later texts a firmer editorial hand will be evident. In particular war has been waged on Excessive Capitalisation and on the apostrophe: thus *reveal'd* becomes *revealed*, and where the rhythm requires an extra syllable an accent has been inserted (*revealèd*). However, the apostrophe has not been replaced if modern pronunciation would automatically introduce an additional, unwanted syllable (*vig'rous*). Where a poem bears a title that is not the author's, but has been introduced especially for this collection, that title is printed inside square brackets. The aim has been clarity throughout, in the hope that as little as possible will stand between the reader and the poet. Modern texts are, of course, printed unchanged.

In compiling this anthology I have benefited from the advice and encouragement of many people. I should especially like to thank David Kewley of Pan Books and Richard Garnett of Macmillan for their faith in the book and for their patience during the agonies of its preparation; and Michael Schmidt and James Wright for their valuable suggestions. The final selection of poems remains my own. Lastly, I must acknowledge the assistance afforded by the London Library, whose seemingly inexhaustible resources never let me down.

EDWARD LEESON
January 1980

For my mother

ANONYMOUS

SUMER is icumen in –
Lhudë sing, cuccu!   *Loud: cuckoo*
Groweth sed and bloweth med   *seed: meadow*
And springth the wudë nu.   *leaves are on the trees now*
Sing, cuccu!

Awë bleteth after lomb   *Ewe: lamb*
Lhouth after calvë cu,   *Cow lows after calf*
Bulluc sterteth, buckë verteth,   *leapeth: farteth*
Murië sing, cuccu!   *Merry*
Cuccu, cuccu,
Well singës thu, cuccu –   *thou*
Ne swik thu naver nu!   *stop: never*

Sing, cuccu, nu! Sing, cuccu!
Sing, cuccu! Sing, cuccu, nu!

Thirteenth century

I SING of a maiden
That is makëless: *mateless, i.e. without equal*
King of alle kingës
To here sone she ches.   *She chose for her son*

He cam also stillë   *as silently*
There his moder was,   *Where*
As dew in Aprillë
That falleth on the grass.

He cam also stillë
To his moderes bowr,
As dew in Aprillë
That falleth on the flowr.

He cam also stillë
There his moder lay,
As dew in Aprillë
That falleth on the spray.

Moder and maiden
Was never non but she:
Well may swich a lady   *such*
Godës moder be.

Early fifteenth century

ADAM lay ibounden,
Bounden in a bond;
Foure thousand winter
Thought he not too long;
And all was for an appel,
An appel that he tok,
As clerkës finden   *scholars*
Wreten in here book.   *their*

Ne hadde the appel takë ben,   *Had not*
The appel take ben,
Ne haddë never our Lady
A ben Hevene Quen.   *Have been*
Blissèd be the time
That appel takë was!
Therfore we moun singen,   *may*
'Deo gracias!'

Fifteenth century

WESTRON winde, when wilt thou blow,
The smalle raine downe can raine?
Christ if my love were in my armes,
And I in my bed againe.

Early sixteenth century

JOHN GOWER

From CONFESSIO AMANTIS

THANNE is noght al mi weie in vein,	
Somdeil I mai the betre fare,	*Somewhat*
Whan I, that mai noght fiele hir bare,	*know*
Mai lede hire clothèd in myn arm:	*on*
Bot afterward it doth me harm	
Of pure ymaginacioun;	
For thannë this collacioun	*reflection*
I make unto miselven ofte,	
And seie, 'Ha lord, hou sche is softe,	*how*
How sche is round, hou sche is smal!	
Now woldë god I hadde hire al	
Withoutë danger at mi wille!'	*Freely*
And thanne I sike and sittë stille,	*sigh*
Of that I se mi besi thoght	*Because: devotions*
Is tornèd ydel into noght.	*turned into dalliance*
Bot for all that lete I ne mai,	*may not let pass*
Whanne I se time an other dai,	*occasion*
That I ne do my besinesse	
Unto mi ladi worthinesse.	*lady's*
For I therto mi wit afaite	*devote my attention*
To se the timës and awaite	
What is to done and what to leve:	*be done: be left*
And so, whan time is, be hir leve,	
What thing sche bit me don, I do,	*bid*
And wher sche bidt me gon, I go,	
And whanne hir list to clepe, I come.	*pleases to call*

WILLIAM LANGLAND

From PIERS PLOWMAN

[BELLING THE CAT]

WITH that ran ther a route of Ratons at ones   *crowd of rats*
And smale mees myd hem, mo than a thousand,
    small mice with them: more
Comen to a counseil for the commune profit.
For a cat of a court cam whan hym liked   *Because: pleased*
And overleep hem lightliche and laughte hem at wille
    pounced on them swiftly: caught
And pleide with hem perillousli and possed aboute.   *passed*
'For doute of diverse dedes we dar noght wel loke,
And if we grucche of his gamen he wol greven us alle,   *complain*
Cracchen us or clawen us, and in hise clouches holde   *Scratch*
That us lotheth the lif er he late us passe.   *let*
Mighte we with any wit his wille withstonde   *scheme*
We myghte be lordes o lofte and lyven at oure ese.'   *on high*
A Raton of renoun, moost renable of tonge,   *reasonable*
Seide for a sovereyn salve to hem alle.
'I have yseyen segges', quod he, 'in the Cite of Londoun   *seen lords*
Beren beighes ful brighte abouten hire nekkes,   *chains: their*
And somme colers of crafty werk; uncoupled thei wenden
Both in wareyne and in waast where hem leve liketh;
    warren: common: when they please
And outher while thei arn elliswhere, as I here telle.   *make trouble*
Were ther a belle on hire beighe, by Jesu, as me thynketh,
Men myghte witen wher thei went and hire wey roume.
    know: run away
And right so', quod that Raton, 'Reson me sheweth
To bugge a belle of bras or of bright silver   *buy*
And knytten it on a coler for oure commune profit   *attach*
And hangen it upon the cattes hals; thanne here we mowen
    neck: can tell
Wher he ryt or rest or rometh to pleye;   *rides, i.e. on the prowl*
And if hym list for to laike thanne loke we mowen
    play: we can watch
And peeren in his presence the while hym pleye liketh,

And if him wratheth be war and his wey shonye.'   *wary: shun*
Al the route of Ratons to this reson assented.

Ac tho the belle was ybrought and on the beighe hanged   *But when*
Ther ne was Raton in the route, for al the Reaume of Fraunce,
That dorste have bounden the belle aboute the cattes nekke,
Ne hangen it aboute his hals al Engelond to wynne;
Ac helden hem unhardy and hir counseil feble,
                              they were ashamed of themselves: feeble plan
And leten hire laboure lost and al hire longe studie.   *reckoned*
A Mous that muche good kouthe, as me tho thoughte,
                              seemed very shrewd: as they thought
Strook forth sterdely and stood bifore hem alle
And to the route of Ratons reherced this wordes: *spoke*
'Though we hadde killed the cat yet sholde ther come another
To cracchen us and all oure kynde though we cropen under benches;
                              creep
Forthi I counseille al the commune to late the cat worthe,   *So: alone*
And be we nevere so bolde the belle hymn to shewe.
The while he caccheth conynges he coveiteth noght our caroyne
                              rabbits: blood
But fedeth hym al with venyson, defame we hym nevere;
For bettre is a litel los than a long sorwe.
The maghe among us alle theigh we mysses a sherewe,
For I herde my sire seyn, seven yeer ypassed,   *father*
Ther the cat is a kitoun the court is ful elenge;   *Where: unhappy*
That witnesseth holy writ, whoso wole it rede:
Ve terre ubi puer rex est!
For may no renk ther reste have for Ratons by nyghte,
And many mannes malt we mees wolde destruye,   *men's*
And also ye route of Ratons rende mennes clothes
Nere the cat of the court that kan yow overlepe;
For hadde ye rattes youre raik ye kouthe noght rule yourselve. *own way*
I seye for me', quod the Mous, 'I se so muchel after,
Shal nevere the cat ne the kiton by my counseil be greved,
Ne carpynge of this coler that costed me nevere;   *talking*
And though it costned me catel biknowen it I nolde
                              money: I'd say nothing
But suffren as hymself wolde to slen that hym liketh,
                              kill what he liked

Coupled and uncoupled to cacche what thei mowe. *Leashed: unleashed*
Forthi each a wis wight I warne, wite wel his owene.'
What this metels bymeneth, ye men that ben murye, *dream means*
Devyne ye, for I ne dar, by deere god in hevene. *dare not*

GEOFFREY CHAUCER

From THE PROLOGUE TO THE CANTERBURY TALES

A KNYGHT ther was, and that a worthy man,
That fro the tymë that he first bigan
To riden out, he loved chivalrie,
Trouthe and honour, fredom and curteisie.
Ful worthy was he in his lordës werre, *war*
And therto hadde he riden, no man ferre, *farther*
As wel in cristendom as in hethenesse, *heathen lands*
And evere honourèd for his worthynesse.
At Alisaundre he was whan it was wonne. *Alexandria: taken*
Ful oftë tyme he hadde the bord bigonne *sat at head of table*
Aboven allë nacions in Pruce; *Prussia*

In Lettow hadde he reysèd and in Ruce,
  Lithuania: campaigned: Russia
No Cristen man so ofte of his degree.
In Gernade at the seege eek hadde he be *Granada: also*
Of Algezir, and riden in Belmarye. *Algeciras: Benmarin*
At Lyeys was he and at Satalye, *Lyas: Attalia*
Whan they were wonne; and in the Gretë See *Mediterranean*
At many a noble armee hadde he be. *expedition*
At mortal batailles hadde he been fiftene,
And foughten for oure feith at Tramyssene *Tremessen*
In lystës thriës, and ay slayn his foo. *three tourneys: always*
This ilkë worthy knyght hadde been also *same*
Somtymë with the lord of Palatye *Palathia*
Agayn another hethen in Turkye. *Against*
And everemoore he hadde a sovereyn prys; *superior reputation*
And though that he were worthy, he was wys,
And of his port as meeke as is a mayde. *disposition*
He nevere yet no vileynye ne sayde *coarseness*

In al his lyf unto no maner wight. — *no manner of man*
He was a verray parfit gentil knyght. — *perfect*
But, for to tellen yow of his array, — *dress*
His hors were goodë, but he was nat gay. — *ostentatious*
Of fustian he werèd a gypon — *wore: tunic*
Al bismotered with his habergeon, — *marked by: hauberk*
For he was late ycome from his viage, — *campaign*
And wentë for to doon his pilgrymage.

THER WAS also a Nonne, a Prioresse,
That of hir smylyng was ful symple and coy; — *demure*
Hire gretteste ooth was but by Seintë Loy; — *Eligius*
And she was clepèd Madame Eglentyne. — *called*
Ful weel she soong the servicë dyvyne,
Entunèd in hir nose full semely, — *Intoned: very pleasingly*
And Frenssh she spak full faire and fetisly, — *elegantly*
After the scole of Stratford attë Bowe,
For Frenssh of Parys was to hire unknowe.
At metë wel ytaught was she with alle: — *dinner*
She leet no morsel from hir lippës falle,
Ne wette hir fyngres in hir saucë depe; — *Nor: deeply*
Wel koude she carie a morsel and wel kepe — *knew how to: take care*
That no drope ne fille upon hire brest. — *fell*
In curteisie was set ful muchel hir lest. — *mind*
Hir over-lippë wypèd she so clene — *upper lip*
That in hir coppe ther was no ferthyng sene — *spot*
Of grecë, whan she dronken hadde hir draughte. — *grease*
Ful semëly after hir mete she raughte. — *reached*
And sikerly she was of greet disport, — *certainly*
And ful plesaunt, and amyable of port, — *of a friendly disposition*

And peynèd hire to countrefetë cheere — *took pains: imitate*
Of court, and to been estatlich of manere, — *dignified*
And to ben holden digne of reverence. — *worthy*
But, for to speken of hire conscience, — *tender feeling*
She was so charitable and so pitous
She woldë wepe, if that she saugh a mous — *saw*
Kaught in a trappe, if it were deed or bledde.
Of smalë houndës hadde she that she fedde
With rosted flessh, or milk and wastel-breed. — *white bread*

But soore wepte she if oon of hem were deed,   *one*
Or if men smoot it with a yerdë smerte;   *smote: rod: sharply*
And al was conscience and tendre herte.
Ful semyly hir wympul pynchèd was,
Hir nose tretys, hire eyen greye as glas,   *well formed*
Hir mouth ful smal, and therto softe and reed;
But sikerly she hadde a fair forheed;
It was almoost a spannë brood, I trowe;   *believe*
For, hardily, she was nat undergrowe.   *certainly*
Ful fetys was hire cloke, as I was war.   *Very fine: aware*
Of smal coral aboute hire arm she bar   *carried*
A peir of bedës, gauded al with grene,   *rosary: with green beads*
And theron heng a brooch of gold ful sheene,   *hung: very bright*
On which ther was first write a crownèd A,
And after *Amor vincit omnia.*

A SHIPMAN was ther, wonynge fer by weste;   *dwelling: far*
For aught I woot, he was of Dertëmouthe.   *knew: Dartmouth*
He rood upon a rouncy, as he kouthe,   *nag: as well as he could*
In a gowne of faldyng to the knee.   *coarse wool*
A daggere hangynge on a laas hadde he   *string*
Aboute his nekke, under his arm adoun.
The hootë somer hadde maad his hewe al broun;
And certeinly he was a good felawe.
Ful many a draughte of wyn had he ydrawe
From Burdeux-ward whil that the chapman sleep.

        Bordeaux: merchant
Of nycë conscience took he no keep.   *the finer feelings: heed*
If that he faught, and hadde the hyer hond,   *upper hand*
By water he sente hem hoom to every lond.
But of his craft to rekene wel his tydes,
His stremës, and his daungers hym bisides,
His herberwe, and his moone, his lodemenage,   *harbour: navigation*
Ther nas noon swich from Hullë to Cartage.   *such: Cartagena*
Hardy he was and wys to undertake;   *Bold: prudent in business*
With many a tempest hadde his berd been shake.
He knew alle the havenës, as they were,   *havens*
Fro Gootland to the cape of Fynystere,   *Gottland*
And every cryke in Britaigne and in Spayne.   *creek*
His barge yclepèd was the *Maudelayne.*   *called*

A GOOD WIF was ther of bisidë Bathe,
But she was somdel deef, and that was scathe. *somewhat: a pity*
Of clooth-makyng she haddë swich an haunt, *such: skill*
She passèd hem of Yprës and of Gaunt.
In al the parisshe wif ne was ther noon
That to the offrynge bifore hire sholdë goon; *church offering: go*
And if ther dide, certeyn so wrooth was she,
That she was out of allë charitee.
Hir coverchiefs ful fynë weren of ground; *kerchiefs: texture*
I dorstë swere they weyeden ten pound *weighed*
That on a Sonday weren upon hir heed.
Hir hosen weren of fyn scarlet reed,
Full streite yteyd, and shoes ful moyste and newe. *tightly*
Boold was hir face, and fair, and reed of hewe.
She was a worthy womman al hire lyve:
Housbondes at chirchë dore she haddë fyve,
Withouten oother compaignye in youthe –
But therof nedeth nat to speke as nowthe. *at present*
And thriës hadde she been at Jerusalem; *thrice*
She haddë passèd many a straungë strem; *foreign*
At Rome she haddë been, and at Boloigne,
In Galice at Seint-Jame, and at Cologne. *Galicia: St James's shrine*
She koudë muchel of wandrynge by the weye. *knew*
Gat-tothèd was she, soothly for to seye. *Gap-toothed: truly*
Upon an amblere esily she sat, *ambling horse*
Ywymplèd wel, and on hir heed an hat *Fully covered by a wimple*
As brood as is a bokeler or a targe; *buckler: shield*
A foot-mantel aboute hir hipës large, *foot-cloth: hips*
And on hir feete a paire of sporës sharpe. *spurs*
In felaweshipe wel koude she laughe and carpe. *knew how to: talk*
Of remedies of love she knew per chaunce, *undoubtedly*
For she koude of that art the oldë daunce.

From TROILUS AND CRISEYDE

THO gan she wondren moorë than biforn   *Then: began: before*
A thousand fold, and down hire eyghen caste;   *eyes*
For nevere, sith the tyme that she was born,   *since*
To knowë thyng desirèd she so faste;
And with a syk she seyde hym attë laste,   *sigh: said to him*
'Now, uncle myn, I nyl yow nought displese,   *will not*
Nor axen more that may do yow disese.'   *ask: displeasure*

So after this, with many wordës glade,
And frendly talës, and with merie chiere,
Of this and that they pleide, and gonnen wade
    amused themselves: passed on to
In many an unkouth glad and dep matere,   *strange: joyous: deep*
As frendës doon whan thei ben mette yfere;   *together*
Tyl she gan axen hym how Ector ferde,   *fared*
That was the townës wal and Grekës yerde.   *rod*

'Ful wel, I thonk it God,' quod Pandarus,
'Save in his arm he hath a litel wownde;
And ek his fresshë brother Troilus,   *also: bold*
The wisë, worthi Ector the secounde,
In whom that allë vertu list habounde,   *pleases to abound*
As allë trouth and allë gentilesse,
Wisdom, honour, fredom, and worthinesse.'

'In good feith, em,' quod she, 'that liketh me;
Thei faren wel, God save hem bothë two!
For trewelich I holde it gret deynté,   *truly: distinction*
A kyngës sone in armës wel to do,
And ben of goode condiciouns therto;   *qualities*
For gret power and moral vertu here
Is selde yseyn in o persone yfere.'   *seldom: one*

'In good faith, that is soth,' quod Pandarus.   *true: said*
'But, by my trouthe, the kyng hath sonës tweye –   *troth: two*
That is to mene, Ector and Troilus –
That certeynly, though that I sholdë deye,   *die*

Thei ben as voide of vices, dar I seye,
As any men that lyven under the sonne.
Hire myght is wyde yknowe, and what they konne.   *Their: can do*

'Of Ector nedeth it namorë for to telle: *no more*
In al this world ther nys a bettre knyght
Than he, that is of worthynessë welle;   *full*
And he wel moorë vertu hath than myght.
This knoweth many a wis and worthi wight.   *person*
The samë pris of Troilus I seye;   *excellence*
God help me so, I knowe nat swichë tweye.'   *such*

'By God,' quod she, 'of Ector that is sooth.
Of Troilus the samë thyng trowe I;   *believe*
For, dredeles, men tellen that he doth   *undoubtedly*
In armës day by day so worthily,
And bereth hym here at hom so gentily
To every wight, that allë pris hath he   *admiration*
Of hem that me were levest preysèd be.'   *most willing*

'Ye sey right sooth, ywys,' quod Pandarus;   *truly*
'For yesterday, whoso hadde with hym ben,   *whoever*
He myghte han wondred upon Troilus;   *wondered at*
For nevere yet so thikke a swarm of been   *bees*
Ne fleigh, as Grekës from hym gonnë fleen,   *fled*
And thorugh the feld, in everi wightës eere,
Ther nas no cry but "Troilus is there!"   *was not*

'Now here, now ther, he hunted hem so faste,   *them*
Ther nas but Grekës blood – and Troilus.
Now hym he hurte, and hym al down he caste;
Ay wher he wente, it was arayèd thus: *always: ordered*
He was hir deth, and sheld and lif for us;   *their: shield*
That, as that day, ther dorstë non withstonde,
Whil that he held his blody swerd in honde.

'Thereto he is the frendliestë man
Of gret estat, that evere I saugh my lyve,   *rank: saw in my life*
And wher hym lest, best felawshipë kan   *chooses: show*

To swich as hym thynketh able for to thryve.'
And with that word tho Pandarus, as blyve,　*quickly*
He took his leve, and seyde, 'I wol gon henne.'　*go hence*
'Nay, blame have I, myn uncle,' quod she thenne.

'What aileth yow to be thus wery soone,　*weary*
And namelich of wommen? wol ye so?　*especially: will*
Nay, sitteth down; by God, I have to doone
With yow, to speke of wisdom er ye go.'
And everi wight that was aboute hem tho,
That herdë that, gan fer awey to stonde,
While they two hadde al that hem liste in honde.

JOHN LYDGATE

From THE TEMPLE OF GLAS

WITHIN my bed for sore I gan me shroude,　*hid myself away*
Al desolate for constreint of my wo,　*agony: woe*
The longë nyght waloing to and fro,　*rolling*
Til attë last, er I gan taken kepe,　*before I knew it*
Me did oppresse a sodein dedeli slepe,
Within the which me thoughtë that I was
Ravysshid in spirit in a temple of glas –　*Transported*
I nystë how, ful fer in wildirnes –　*knew not: far*
That foundid was, as bi liklynesse,
Not opon stele, but on a craggy roche,
Like ise ifrore. And as I did approche,　*frozen ice*
Again the sonne that shone, me thought, so clere　*Against*
As eny cristal, and ever nere and nere
As I gan neigh this grisli dredful place,　*approached*
I wex astonyed: the light so in my face
Bigan to smyte, so persing ever in one
On everë part, where that I gan gone,　*wherever I went*
That I ne myght nothing, as I would,
Abouten me considre and bihold
The wondre hestres, for brightnes of the sonne;　*wonderful rooms*
Til atte last certein skyes donne,　*dark clouds*

With wind ichaced, have her cours iwent   *their*
Tofore the stremes of Titan and iblent,   *Before: sun's rays: obscured*
So that I myght, within and withoute,
Whereso I walk, biholden me aboute,
Forto report the fasoun and manere   *fashion*
Of al this place, that was circulere
In compaswise, round b'entaile wrought.   *adorned with sculpture*

ROBERT HENRYSON

From THE TESTAMENT OF CRESSEID

[THE COMPLAINT OF CRESSEID]

'O SOP of sorrow, sonkin into cair!
O cative Cresseid! For now and evermair   *wretched*
Gane is thy joy and all thy mirth in eird;   *earth*
Of all blyithnes now art thou blaiknit bair;   *deprived*
Thair is na salve may saif the of thy sair: *heal: thee: sorrow*
Fell is thy fortoun, wickit is thy weird;   *Cruel: destiny*
Thy blys is baneist, and thy baill on breird: *banished: sorrow grows*
Under the eirth God gif I gravin wer,   *if: buried*
Quhair nane of Grece nor yit of Troy micht heird!
        Where: have heard of me

'Quhair is thy chalmer wantounlie besene,
        chamber luxuriously adorned
With burely bed and bankouris browderit bene?
    handsome: coverlets beautifully embroidered
Spycis and wyne to thy collatioun,
The cowpis all of gold and silver schene;   *cups*
The sweit meitis, servit in plaittis clene,   *sweetmeats*
With saipheron sals of ane gud sessoun?   *saffron sauce: seasoning*
Thy gay garmentis with mony gudely goun;
Thy pleasand lawn pinnit with goldin prene?   *pin*
All is areir, thy greit royall renoun!   *behind*

'Quhair is thy garding with their greissis gay   *garden: her: walks*
And fresche flowris quhilk the Quene Floray   *which*
Had paintit plesandly in everie pane,   *flower-bed*

Quhair thou was wont full merilye in May
To walk and tak the dew be it was day,   *when*
And heir the merle and mawis mony ane;
                              blackbirds: thrushes: many a one
With ladyis fair in carrolling to gane,
And se the royall rinkis in thair array,   *folk*
In garmentis gay garnischit in everie grane?   *colour*

'Thy greit triumphand fame and hie honour,
Quhair thou was callit of eirdlye wichtis flour,
                              flower of earthly creatures
All is decayit – thy weird is welterit so.   *reversed*
Thy hei estait is turnit in darknes dour.
This lipper-ludge tak for thy burelie bour,   *leper-house: goodly*
And for thy bed tak now ane bunche of stro;   *straw*
For waillit wyne and meitis thou had tho   *choice: meat: rather*
Tak mowlit breid, peirrie and ceder sour: *mouldy: perry: cider*
Bot cop and clapper now is all ago.

'My cleir voice and courtlie carrolling,
Quhair I was wont with ladyis for to sing,
Is rawk as ruik, full hiddeous, hoir and hace;
                              harsh as a rook: rough: hoarse
My plesand port all utheris precelling,   *bearing: others: excelling*
Of lustines I was hald maist conding;   *most excellent*
Now is deformit the figour of my face –   *appearance*
To luik on it na leid now lyking hes.   *people*
Sowpit in syte, I say with sair siching,   *Drowned: sorrow: sighing*
Ludgeit amang the lipper leid: "Allace!"   *Lodging: leper folk*

'O ladyis fair of Troy and Grece attend
My miserie quhilk nane may comprehend,
My frivoll fortoun, my infelicitie,   *miserable*
My greit mischief quhilk na man can amend;
Be war in tyme – approchis neir the end –   *ready*
And in your mynd ane mirrour mak of me
As I am now; peradventure that ye
For all your micht may cum to that same end –
Or ellis war, gif ony war may be.   *worse*

'Nocht is your fairnes bot ane faiding flour;   *beauty: flower*
Nocht is your famous laud and hie honour
Bot wind inflat in uther mennis eiris;   *blown*
Your roising reid to rotting sall retour.   *rose-like red: shall return*
Exempill mak of me in your memour,   *memory*
Quhilk of sic thingis wofull witnes beiris.   *Who: bears*
All welth in eird away as wind it weiris: *wears*
Be war thairfoir – approchis neir the hour –
Fortoun is fikkill quhen scho beginnis and steiris.'   *she: stirs*

Thus chydand with hir drerie destenye,   *chiding*
Weiping scho woik the nicht fra end to end;   *lay awake*
Bot all in vane – hir dule, hir cairfull cry,   *dole*
Micht not remeid nor yit hir murning mend.   *remedy: mourning*
Ane lipper-lady rais and till hir wend   *rose: to: went*
And said: 'Quhy spurnis thow aganis the wall   *hurlest*
To sla thyself and mend nathing at all?

'Sen thy weiping doubillis bot thy wo,   *Since*
I counsall the mak vertew of ane neid –   *thee*
To leir to clap thy clapper to and fro,   *learn*
And leve efter the law of lipper leid.'   *live*
Thair was na buit, but furth with thame scho yeid   *help: went*
Fra place to place, quhill cauld and hunger sair
Compellit hir to be ane rank beggair.

WILLIAM DUNBAR

I THAT in heill wes and gladnes   *health*
Am trublit now with gret seiknes   *sickness*
And feblit with infermite: *enfeebled*
   Timor mortis conturbat me.

Our plesance heir is all vane glory,   *happiness*
This fals warld is bot transitory,
The flesch is brukle, the Fend is sle: *frail: Devil: cunning*
   Timor mortis conturbat me.

The stait of man dois change and vary,
Now sound, now seik, now blith, now sary,   *sick: sorry*
Now dansand mery, now like to dee: *dancing: die*
   Timor mortis conturbat me.

No stait in erd heir standis sickir;   *safe*
As with the wynd wavis the wickir   *willow*
Wavis this warldis vanite:
   Timor mortis conturbat me.

One to the ded gois all estatis,   *On: death: estates*
Princis, prelotis and potestatis,   *Princis, prelates and lords*
Baith riche and pur of al degre: *Both: poor*
   Timor mortis conturbat me.

He takis the knychtis in to feild
Anarmyt undir helme and scheild,   *Armed with: helmet*
Victour he is at all melle: *every battle*
   Timor mortis conturbat me.

That strang unmercifull tyrand   *strong*
Takis one the moderis breist sowkand   *on: sucking*
The bab full of benignite: *baby: grace*
   Timor mortis conturbat me.

He takis the campion in the stour,   *champion: combat*
The capitane closit in the tour,   *enclosed: tower*
The lady in bour full of bewte: *bower: beauty*
   Timor mortis conturbat me.

He sparis no lord for his piscence,   *puissance*
Na clerk for his intelligence;   *scholar*
His awfull strak may no man fle: *stroke: flee*
   Timor mortis conturbat me.

Art magicianis and astrologgis   *Masters of magic: astrologers*
Rethoris, logicianis and theologgis
     Rhetoricians, logicians and theologians
Thame helpis no conclusionis sle   *They help us to*
   Timor mortis conturbat me.

In medicyne the most practicianis,   *practical men*
Lechis, surrigianis and phisicianis,   *Leeches, surgeons and physicians*
Thame self fra ded may not supple: *from: deliver*
  Timor mortis conturbat me.

I se that makaris among the laif   *makers, i.e. poets: rest*
Playis heir ther pageant, syne gois to graif;   *Play: then go to the grave*
Sparit is nocht ther faculte: *Spared: not: profession*
  Timor mortis conturbat me.

He hes done petuously devour   *lamentably*
The noble Chaucer, of makaris flour,   *flower*
The Monk of Bery, and Gower, all thre:
  Timor mortis conturbat me.

The gude Syr Hew of Eglintoun
And eik Heryot and Wyntoun   *also*
He hes tane out of this cuntre:
  Timor mortis conturbat me.

That scorpion fell hes done infek   *corrupted*
Maister Johne Clerk and James Afflek
Fra balat making and trigidie: *From: ballad: tragedy*
  Timor mortis conturbat me.

Holland and Barbour he hes berevit;   *borne off*
Allace that he nocht with us levit   *Alas: left*
Schir Mungo Lokert of the Le:
  Timor mortis conturbat me.

Clerk of Tranent eik he hes tane
That maid the anteris of Gawane;   *adventures*
Schir Gilbert Hay endit hes he: *ended*
  Timor mortis conturbat me.

He hes Blind Hary and Sandy Traill
Slaine with his schour of mortall haill   *shower*
Quhilk Patrik Johnestoun myght nocht fle;   *Which*
  Timor mortis conturbat me.

He hes reft Merseir his endite,   *taken away: writing*
That did in luf so lifly write,   *love: vigorously*
So schort, so quyk, of sentence hie: *lofty theme*
 Timor mortis conturbat me.

He hes tane Roull of Aberdene,
And gentill Roull of Corstorphin;
Two bettir fallowis did no man se:
 Timor mortis conturbat me.

In Dumferemlyne he hes done roune *spoken*
With Maister Robert Henrisoun;
Schir Johne the Ros enbrast hes he:
 Timor mortis conturbat me.

And he hes now tane, last of aw,
Gud gentill Stobo and Quintyne Schaw,
Of quham all wichtis hes pete: *whom: men: pity*
 Timor mortis conturbat me.

Gud Maister Walter Kennedy
In poynt of dede lyis veraly,   *At point of death*
Gret reuth it wer that so suld be: *pity*
 Timor mortis conturbat me.

Sen he hes all my brether tane,   *Since*
He will nocht lat me lif alane;
On forse I man his nyxt pray be: *Inevitably: must: prey*
 Timor mortis conturbat me.

Sen for the ded remeid is none,
Best is that we for dede dispone   *make ready*
Eftir our deid that lif may we: *death: live*
 Timor mortis conturbat me.

JOHN SKELTON

WOFFULLY araid, *treated*
  My blode, man,
    For the ran, *thee*
It may not be naid; *denied*
  My body bloo and wan,
  Woffully araid.

Beholde me, I pray the, with all thi hole reson,
And be not so hard hartid, and ffor this encheson, *cause*
Sith I for thi sowle sake was slayne in good seson,
Begylde and betraide by Judas fals treson;
    Unkyndly entretid, *treated*
    With sharpe corde sore fretid, *chafed*
    The Jewis me thretid *threatened*
   They mowid, they grynnèd, they scornyd me,
   Condempynyd to deth, as thou maist se,
    Woffully araid.

Thus nakyd am I nailid, O man, for thy sake!
I love the, then love me; why slepist thou? awake!
Remembir my tendir hart-rote for the brake, *heart's root*
With panys my vaynys constreyned to crake;
    Thus toggid to and fro, *tugged*
    Thus wrappid all in woo *woe*
    Whereas never man was so,
   Entretid thus in most cruel wyse,
   Was like a lombe offerd in sacrifice,
    Woffully araid.

Off sharpe thorne I have worne a crowne on my hede,
So paynyd, so straynyd, so rufull, so red;
Thus bobbid, thus robbid, thus for thy love ded, *cheated*
Onfaynyd not deynyd my blod for to shed; *disdained*
    My fete and handes sore
    The sturdy nailis bore;
    What myght I suffir more
   Than I have don, O man, for the?
   Cum when thou list, wellcum to me,
    Woffully araid.

Off record thy good Lord I have beyn and schal bee;
I am thyn, thou artt myne, my brother I call thee;
The love I enterly; see whatt ys befall me!
Sore bettyng, sore thretyng, to make thee, man, all fre

beating: threatening

> Why art thou unkynde?
> Why hast nott mee yn mynde?
> Cum yitt, and thou schalt fynde
> Myne endlys mercy and grace;
> See how a spere my hert dyd race,   *spear: cut*
> Woffully arayd.

Deyr brother, noo other thyng I off thee desyre
Butt gyve me thyne hert fre to rewarde myn hyre:
I wrought the, I bowght the frome eternal fyre;
I pray the aray the tooward my hyght empyre,   *high*

> Above the oryent,
> Wheroff I am regent,
> Lord God omnypotent,
> Wyth me to reyn yn endlys welthe;
> Remember, man, thy sawlys helthe.

> Woffully arayd,
> My blode, man,
> For the ran,
> Hytt may nott be nayd;
> My body blow and wan,   *blue*
> Woffully arayde.

From THE GARLANDE OF LAURELL

TO MASTRES MARGERY WENTWORTHE

WITH margerain jentyll,   *marjoram*
The flowre of goodlyhede,
Enbrowdred the mantill
Is of your maydenhede.

Plainly, I can not glose,   *flatter*
Ye be, as I devyne,
The praty primrose,
The goodly columbyne.
   With margerain jantill,
The flowre of goodlyhede,
Enbrawderyd the mantyll
Is of yowre maydenhede.

Benynge, corteise and meke,
With wordes well devysid,
In you, who list to seke,
Be vertus well comprysid.
   With margerain jantill,
The flowre of goodlyhede,
Enbrawderid the mantill
Is of yowr maydenhede.

TO MAYSTRES MARGARET HUSSEY

   MIRRY Margaret,
As mydsomer flowre,
Jentill as fawcoun
Or hawke of the towre;   *soaring*
   With solace and gladnes,
Moche mirthe and no madnes,
All good and no badnes;
So joyously,
So maydenly,
So womanly
Her demenyng;
In every thynge
Far, far passynge
That I can endyght,
Or suffyce to wryght
Of mirry Margarete,
As mydsomer flowre,
Jentyll as fawcoun
Or hawke of the towre.

As pacient and as styll
And as full of good wyll
As fayre Isaphill;   *Hypsipyle*
Colyaunder,   *Coriander*
Swete pomaunder,
Good Cassaunder;   *Cassandra*
Stedfast of thought,
Wele-made, wele-wrought;
Far may be sought
Erst that ye can fynde
So corteise, so kynde
As mirry Margarete,
This midsomer flowre,
Jentyll as fawcoun
Or hawke of the towre.

GAVIN DOUGLAS

From THE AENEID

[THE TROJAN HORSE]

THE Grekis chiftanys, irkit of the weir   *weary: war*
Bypast or than samony langsum yeir,
            That had lasted so many tedious years
And oft rebutyt by fatale destany,   *repulsed*
Ane huge hors, lyke ane gret hil, in hy   *haste*
Craftely thai wrocht in wirschip of Pallas
(Of sawyn beche the ribbis forgyt was)   *forged*
Fenyeand ane oblacioune, as it had be   *Feigned: sacrifice*

For prosper returnyng hame in thar cuntre –
The voce this wys throu owt the cite woyk.   *spread*
Of choys men syne, walit by cut, thai tuke

        selected: then: chosen by lot
A gret numbyr, and hyd in bylgis dern   *the depths: secretly*
Within that best, in mony huge cavern;
Schortly, the belly was stuffit every deill   *part*
Ful of knychtis armyt in plait of steill.

Thair standis into the sycht of Troy ane ile   *sight: isle*
Weil knawin by name, hecht Tenedos, umquhile   *called: once*
Myghty of gudis quhil Priamus ryng sa stude;

       Rich: Priam's kingdom stood

Now it is bot a fyrth in the sey flude,   *bay*
A raid onsikkyr for schip or ballyngare.   *road unsafe: ships*
In desert costis of this iland thar
The Grekis thame ful secretly withdrew,
We wenyng thame hame passit and adew,   *believing*
And, with gude wynd, of Myce the realm had socht. *Greece*
Quharfor al thai of Troy, blyth as thai mocht,   *might*
Thair langsum duyl and murnyng dyd away,   *lamentation*
Kest up the portis and yschit furth to play, *Cast: gates: issued*
The Grekis tentis desyrus forto se
And voyd placis quhar thai war wont to be,
The cost and strandis left desert al cleyn.
'Heir stude the army of Dolopeis,' sum wald meyn,
'Cruel Achil heir stentit his pailyeon;   *pitched his tent*
Quhar stude the navy, lo the place yonder down;
Heir the ostis war wont to joyn in feild.'   *armies were*
And sum wondring the scaithfull gyft beheld   *harmful*
Suldbe offerit to the onweddit Pallas;   *chaste*
Thai mervellit fast the hors samekill was.   *huge*
Bot Tymetes exortis first of all
It forto leid and draw within the wall
And forto set it in the cheif palyce –
Quhidder for dissait I not, or for malyce, *Whether: deceit: know not*
Or destany of Troy wald sa suldbe.
Bot Capis than, with ane othir menye   *group*
Quhilk bettir avys thar myndis set apon,   *Who*
Bad cast or drown into the sey onone   *anon*
That suspek presand of the Grekis dissait, *present: deceitful*
Or kyndill tharundir flambe of fyris hait,   *hot*
Or forto rype that holkit hug belly, *open up: hollowed: huge*
And the hyd hyrnys to sers and weil espy. *hidden chambers: search*
Quhat nedis mair? The onstabill common voce
Dixidit was in mony seir purpos,
Quhen thidder come before thame al onone,
Followand a gret rowt, the prest Laocon *Followed by: crowd: excited*

From the cheif tempil rynnand in ful gret hy.   *running*
On far, 'O wrachit pepil,' gan he cry,   *Asar off*
'Quhou gret wodnes is this at ye now meyn,   *What: madness: that*
Your ennymyis away salit gif ye weyn,   *sailed: if you believe*
Or gif ye traist ony Grekis gyftis be   *trust: to be*
Withowt dissait, falshed and subtelte.
Knaw ye na bettir the quent Ulixes slycht?   *cunning: tricks*
Owder in this tre ar Grekis closit ful rycht,   *Either: timber*
Or this engyne is byggit to our skaith,   *built: harm*
To wach our wallis and our byggyngys bath,

                              watch: batter down our buildings

Or to confound and ourquhelm our cite.
Thar lurkis sum falshed tharin, trastis me.   *trust*
Lippyn nocht, Trojanys, I pray you, in this hors: *Trust*
Quhow ever it be, I dreid the Grekis fors,   *Greeks' force*
And thame that sendis this gyft always I feir.'
Thus sayand, with al his strenth a gret speir   *saying*
At the syde of that bysnyng best threw he,   *monstrous beast*
And in jonyngis of the thrawyn wame of tre   *joints: crooked womb*
Festynnyt the lance, that trymlyng gan to schaik; *Fastened: trembling*
The braid belly schudderit, and with the straik

                                   broad: shuddered: blow

The boys cavys sowndit and maid a dyn.   *hollow caves*
And had nocht beyn that owder his wit was thyn,   *had it not been*
Or that the fatis of goddis war contrary,
He had assayt, but ony langar tary,   *attempted: without: delay*
Hyd Grekis covert with irne to have rent owt;

                        Secretly hidden: spears: root out

Than suld thou, Troy, have standyn yit, but dowt,
                                   stood: without doubt

And the prowd palyce of Kyng Priamus
Suld have remanyt yit ful gloryus.   *remained*

SIR THOMAS WYATT

THEY flee from me that sometime did me seek
With naked foot stalking in my chamber.
I have seen them gentle, tame, and meek
That now are wild and do not remember
That sometime they put themselves in danger
To take bread at my hand; and now they range
Busily seeking with a continual change.

Thankèd be Fortune, it hath been otherwise
Twenty times better; but once in special,
In thin array after a pleasant guise,
When her loose gown from her shoulders did fall,
And she me caught in her arms long and small;
Therewith all sweetly did me kiss,
And softly said, 'Dear heart, how like you this?'

It was no dream: I lay broad waking.
But all is turnèd, thorough my gentleness,
Into a strange fashion of forsaking;
And I have leave to go of her goodness,
And she also to use newfangleness.
But since that I so kindly am servèd,
I would fain know what she hath deservèd.

MY LUTE, awake! Perform the last
Labour that thou and I shall waste,
And end that I have now begun;
For when this song is sung and past,
My lute, be still, for I have done.

As to be heard where ear is none,
As lead to grave in marble stone,
My song may pierce her heart as soon.
Should we then sigh, or sing, or moan?
No, no, my lute, for I have done.

The rocks do not so cruelly
Repulse the waves continually
As she my suit and affection,
So that I am past remedy,
Whereby my lute and I have done.

Proud of the spoil that thou hast got
Of simple hearts thorough Love's shot,
By whom, unkind, thou hast them won,
Think not he hath his bow forgot,
Although my lute and I have done.

Vengeance shall fall on thy disdain
That makest but game on earnest pain.
Think not alone under the sun
Unquit to cause thy lover's plain,   *complaint*
Although my lute and I have done.

Perchance thee lie withered and old,
The winter nights that are so cold,
Plaining in vain unto the moon;
Thy wishes then dare not be told.
Care then who list, for I have done.

And then may chance thee to repent
The time that thou hast lost and spent,
To cause thy lover's sigh and swoon;
Then shalt thou know beauty but lent
And wish and want as I have done.

Now cease, my lute! This is the last
Labour that thou and I shall waste,
And ended is that we begun;
Now is this song both sung and past.
My lute, be still, for I have done.

MINE own John Poyntz, since ye delight to know
   The cause why that homeward I me draw,
   And flee the press of courts whereso they go
Rather than to live thrall under the awe
   Of lordly looks, wrapped within my cloak,
   To will and lust learning to set a law,
It is not for because I scorn or mock
   The power of them to whom Fortune hath lent
   Charge over us, of right to strike the stroke;
But true it is that I have always meant
   Less to esteem them than the common sort,
   Of outward things that judge in their intent
Without regard what doth inward resort.
   I grant sometime that of glory the fire
   Doth touch my heart: me list not to report
Blame by honour and honour to desire.
   But how may I this honour now attain
   That cannot dye the colour black a liar?
My Poyntz, I cannot frame my tongue to feign,
   To cloak the truth for praise, without desert,
   Of them that list all vice for to retain.
I cannot honour them that sets their part
   With Venus and with Bacchus all their life long,
   Nor hold my peace of them although I smart.
I cannot crouch nor kneel, nor do so great a wrong
   To worship them like God on earth alone,
   That are as wolves these silly lambs among.
I cannot with my words complain and moan
   And suffer naught; nor smart without complaint,
   Nor turn the word that from my mouth is gone.
I cannot speak and look like a saint,
   Use wiles for wit and make deceit a pleasure,
   And call craft counsel, for profit still to paint.
I cannot wrest the law to fill the coffer,
   With innocent blood to feed myself fat,
   And do most hurt where most help I offer.
I am not he that can allow the state
   Of high Caesar and damn Cato to die,
   That with his death did 'scape out of the gate

From Caesar's hands, if Livy do not lie,
    And would not live where liberty was lost:
    So did his heart the common weal apply.
I am not he such eloquence to boast,
    To make the crow singing as the swan,
    Nor call the lion of coward beasts the most,
That cannot take a mouse as the cat can:
    And he that dieth for hunger of the gold
    Call him Alexander, and say that Pan
Passeth Apollo in music many fold;
    Praise Sir Thopas for a noble tale,
    And scorn the story that the Knight told;
Praise him for counsel that is drunk of ale;
    Grin when he laugheth, that beareth all the sway,
    Frown when he frowneth and groan when he is pale;
On others' lust to hang both night and day:
    None of these points would ever frame in me.
    My wit is naught, I cannot learn the way;
And much the less of things that greater be,
    That asken help of colours of device
    To join the mean with each extremity,
With the nearest virtue to cloak always the vice;
    And, as to purpose likewise it shall fall,
    To press the virtue that it may not rise;
As drunkenness good fellowship to call;
    The friendly foe with his double face
    Say he is gentle and courteous therewithal;
And say that Favel hath a goodly grace
    In eloquence; and cruelty to name
    Zeal of justice and change in time and place;
And he that suffereth offence without blame
    Call him pitiful, and him true and plain
    That raileth wreckless to every man's shame;
Say he is rude that cannot lie and feign,
    The lecher a lover, and tyranny
    To be the right of a prince's reign.
I cannot, I! No, no, it will not be!
    This is the cause that I could never yet
    Hang on their sleeves that way, as thou mayest see,

A chip of chance more than a pound of wit.
  This maketh me at home to hunt and hawk
  And in foul weather at my book to sit;
In frost and snow then with my bow to stalk.
  No man doth mark whereso I ride or go;
  In lusty leas at liberty I walk,
And of these news I feel nor weal nor woe,
  Save that a clog doth hang yet at my heel:
  No force for that for it is ordered so,
That I may leap both hedge and dyke full well.
  I am not now in France to judge the wine,
  With saffron sauce the delicates to feel;   *taste*
Nor yet in Spain where one must him incline,
  Rather than to be, outwardly to seem.
  I meddle not with wits that be so fine,
Nor Flanders cheer letteth not my sight to deem
                                 preventeth: judge
  Of black and white, nor taketh my wit away
  With beastliness they, beasts, do so esteem;
Nor I am not where Christ is given in prey
  For money, poison, and treason at Rome,
  A common practice usèd night and day.
But here I am in Kent and Christendom
  Among the Muses where I read and rhyme;
  Where if thou list, my Poyntz, for to come,
Thou shalt be judge how I do spend my time.

    Is IT possible
    That so high debate,
    So sharp, so sore, and of such rate,
    Should end so soon and was begun so late?
    Is it possible?

    Is it possible
    So cruel intent,
    So hasty heat and so soon spent,
    From love to hate, and thence for to relent?
    Is it possible?

Is it possible
That any may find
Within one heart so diverse mind,
To change or turn as weather and wind?
Is it possible?

Is it possible
To spy it in an eye
That turns as oft as chance on die?
The truth whereof any can try?
Is it possible?

It is possible
For to turn so oft,
To bring that lowest that was most aloft,
And to fall highest yet to light soft.
It is possible.

All is possible,
Whoso list believe.
Trust therefore first and after preve,   *prove*
As men wed ladies by licence and leave,
All is possible.

AND wilt thou leave me thus?
Say nay, say nay, for shame,
To save me from the blame
Of all my grief and grame.   *sorrow*
And wilt thou leave me thus?
    Say nay, say nay!

And wilt thou leave me thus,
That hath lovèd thee so long,
In wealth and woe among?
And is thy heart so strong
As for to leave me thus?
    Say nay, say nay!

And wilt thou leave me thus,
That hath given thee my heart,
Never for to depart,
Neither for pain nor smart?
And wilt thou leave me thus?
  Say nay, say nay!

And wilt thou leave me thus
And have no more pity
Of him that loveth thee?
Alas, thy cruelty!
And wilt thou leave me thus?
  Say nay, say nay!

FORGET not yet the tried intent
Of such a truth as I have meant,
My great travail so gladly spent.
    Forget not yet.

Forget not yet when first began
The weary life ye know since when,
The suit, the service none tell can.
    Forget not yet.

Forget not yet the great assays,   *attempts*
The cruel wrong, the scornful ways,
The painful patience in denays.   *denials*
    Forget not yet.

Forget not yet, forget not this,
How long ago hath been and is
The mind that never meant amiss.
    Forget not yet.

Forget not then thine own approved
The which so long hath thee so loved,
Whose steadfast faith yet never moved.
    Forget not this.

WHAT should I say
Since faith is dead
And truth away
From you is fled?
Should I be led
With doubleness?
Nay, nay, mistress!

I promised you
And you promised me
To be as true
As I would be,
But since I see
Your double heart
Farewell, my part!   *share*

Though for to take
It is not my mind
But for to forsake
One so unkind
And as I find
So will I trust,
Farewell, unjust!

Can ye say nay   *deny*
But you said
That I alway
Should be obeyed?
And thus betrayed
Ere that I wist,   *knew*
Farewell, unkissed!

HENRY HOWARD, EARL OF SURREY

THE sootë season, that bud and bloom forth brings,   *sweet*
With green hath clad the hill and eke the vale;   *also*
The nightingale with feathers new she sings;
The turtle to her make hath told her tale.   *turtledove: mate*

Summer is come, for every spray now springs;
The hart hath hung his old head on the pale;
The buck in brake his winter coat he flings;
The fishes float with new-repairèd scale;
The adder all her slough away she slings;
The swift swallow pursueth the flies small;
The busy bee her honey now she mings;   *remembers*
Winter is worn that was the flowers' bale.   *enemy*
  And thus I see among these pleasant things
  Each care decays, and yet my sorrow springs.

ALAS, so all things now do hold their peace,
Heaven and earth disturbed in nothing;
The beasts, the air, the birds their song do cease;
The night's chare the stars about doth bring.   *chariot*
Calm is the sea, the waves work less and less;
So am not I, whom love, alas, doth wring,
Bringing before my face the great increase
Of my desires, whereat I weep and sing
In joy and woe as in a doubtful ease.
For my sweet thoughts sometime do pleasure bring,
But by and by the cause of my disease
Gives me a pang that inwardly doth sting,
  When that I think what grief it is again
  To live and lack the thing should rid my pain.

NORFOLK sprang thee, Lambeth holds thee dead,
Clere of the County of Cleremont though hight;   *called*
Within the womb of Ormond's race thou bred,
And saw'st thy cousin crownèd in thy sight.
Shelton for love, Surrey for lord thou chase: *chose*
Ay me, while life did last that league wast tender;
Tracing whose steps thou sawest Kelsall blaze,
Laundersey burnt, and battered Bullen render.
At Muttrell gates, hopeless of all recure,   *recovery*
Thine Earl half dead gave in thy hand his Will;
Which cause did thee this pining death procure,
Ere summers four times seven thou could'st fulfil.

Ah, Clere, if love had booted, care, or cost,   *served*
Heaven had not won, nor Earth so timely lost.

So CRUEL PRISON how could betide, alas,
As proud Windsor, where I in lust and joy
With a king's son my childish years did pass,
In greater feast than Priam's sons of Troy;

Where each sweet place returns a taste full sour:
The large green courts, where we were wont to hove, *linger*
With eyes cast up unto the maidens' tower,
And easy sighs, such as folk draw in love;

The stately sales; the ladies bright of hue;   *halls*
The dances short, long tales of great delight,
With words and looks that tigers could but rue,
Where each of us did plead the other's right;

The palm-play, where, despoilèd for the game,
With dazèd eyes oft we by gleams of love
Have missed the ball and got sight of our dame
To bait her eyes which kept the leads above;   *windows*

The gravelled ground, with sleeves tied on the helm,
                    tiltyard: helmet
On foaming horse, with swords and friendly hearts,
With cheer as though the one should overwhelm,
Where we have fought and chasèd oft with darts;   *spears*

With silver drops the meads yet spread for ruth,   *pity*
In active games of nimbleness and strength
Where we did strain, trailèd by swarms of youth,
Our tender limbs, that yet shot up in length;

The secret groves, which oft we made resound
Of pleasant plaint and of our ladies' praise,   *complaint*
Recording soft what grace each one had found,
What hope of speed, what dread of long delays;

The wild forest, the clothèd holts with green,   *copses*
With reins availed and swift y-breathèd horse,
With cry of hounds and merry blasts between,
Where we did chase the fearful hart a-force;

The void walls eke, that harboured us each night;   *also*
Wherewith, alas, revive within my breast
The sweet accord, such sleeps as yet delight,
The pleasant dreams, the quiet bed of rest,

The secret thoughts imparted with such trust,
The wanton talk, the divers change of play,
The friendship sworn, each promise kept so just,
Wherewith we passed the winter nights away.

And with this thought the blood forsakes my face,
The tears berain my cheek of deadly hue;
The which, as soon as sobbing sighs, alas,
Upsuppèd have, thus I my plaint renew: *consumed*

'O place of bliss, renewer of my woes,
Give me account where is my noble fere,   *friend*
Whom in thy walls thou did'st each night enclose,
To other lief, but unto me most dear.'   *beloved*

Each stone, alas, that doth my sorrow rue,
Returns thereto a hollow sound of plaint.
Thus I alone, where all my freedom grew,
In prison pine with bondage and restraint,

And with remembrance of the greater grief,
To banish the less I find my chief relief.

From THE AENEID

[THE TROJAN HORSE]

THE GREEKS' chieftains, all irkèd with the war
Wherein they wasted had so many years
And oft repulsed by fatal destiny,
A huge horse made, high-raisèd like a hill,
By the divine science of Minerva;
Of cloven fir compacted were his ribs;
For their return a feignèd sacrifice,
The fame whereof so wandered it at point.
In the dark bulk they closed bodies of men   *enclosed*
Chosen by lot, and did enstuff by stealth
The hollow womb with armèd soldiers.

   There stands in sight an isle hight Tenedon,   *called*
Rich and of fame while Priam's kingdom stood:
Now but a bay, and road unsure for ship.
Hither them secretly the Greeks withdrew,
Shrouding themselves under the desert shore.
And, weening we they had been fled and gone,   *believing*
And with that wind had fet the land of Greece,   *reached*
Troy discharged her long continued dole.
The gates cast up, we issued out to play,
The Greekish camp desirous to behold,
The places void and the forsaken coasts.
Here Pyrrhus' band, there fierce Achilles pight, *pitched camp*
Here rode their ships, there did their battles join.
Astonied some the scatheful gift beheld,   *harmful*
Behight by vow unto the chaste Minerve,
All wond'ring at the hugeness of the horse.
   And first Timoetes 'gan advise
Within the walls to lead and draw the same,
And place it eke amid the palace court:
Whether of guile, or Troy's fate it would.
Capys, with some of judgement more discreet,
Willed it to drown, or underset with flame
The suspect present of the Greeks' deceit,
Or bore and gouge the hollow caves uncouth.

So diverse ran the giddy people's mind.
  Lo! foremost of a rout that followed him,
Kindled Laöcoon hasted from the tower,   *Excited*
Crying far off, 'O wretched citizens,
What so great kind of frenzy fretteth you?
Deem ye the Greeks our enemies to be gone?
Or any Greekish gifts can you suppose
Devoid of guile? Is so Ulysses known?
Either the Greeks are in this timber hid,
Or this an engine is t' annoy our walls,
To view our towers, and overwhelm our town.
Here lurks some craft. Good Troyans, give no trust
Unto this horse, for what so ever it be,
I dread the Greeks, yea, when they offer gifts.'
And with that word, with all his force a dart   *spear*
He launchèd then into that crooked womb:
Which trembling stack, and shook within the side,   *stuck*
Wherewith the caves 'gan hollowly resound.
And but for fates and for our blind forecast,
The Greeks' device and guile had he descried,
Troy yet had stand, and Priam's towers so high.

GEORGE GASCOIGNE

'AND if I did, what then?
  Are you aggrieved therefore?
The sea hath fish for every man,
  And what would you have more?'

Thus did my mistress once
  Amaze my mind with doubt;
And popped a question for the nonce,
  To beat my brains about.

Whereto I thus replied:
  'Each fisherman can wish
That all the seas at every tide
  Were his alone to fish.

'And so did I, in vain;
   But since it may not be,
Let such fish there as find the gain,
   And leave the loss for me.

'And with such luck and loss
   I will content myself,
Till tides of turning time may toss
   Such fishers on the shelf.

'And when they stick on sands,
   That every man may see,
Then will I laugh and clap my hands,
   As they do now at me.'

SIR EDWARD DYER

THE lowest trees have tops, the ant her gall,
The fly her spleen, the little spark his heat;
The slender hairs cast shadows, though but small,
And bees have stings, although they be not great;
   Seas have their source, and so have shallow springs;
   And love is love, in beggars and in kings.

Where waters smoothest run, there deepest are the fords,
The dial stirs, yet none perceives it move;
The firmest faith is found in fewest words,
The turtles do not sing, and yet they love;
   True hearts have ears and eyes, no tongues to speak;
   They hear and see, and sigh, and then they break.

NICHOLAS BRETON

IN THE merry month of May,
In a morn by break of day,
Forth I walked by the wood side,
Whereas May was in his pride.

There I spièd all alone
Phyllida and Corydon.
Much ado there was, God wot,
He would love and she would not.
She said, never man was true;
He said, none was false to you.
He said, he had loved her long;
She said, love should have no wrong.
Corydon would kiss her then;
She said, maids must kiss no men,
Till they did for good and all.
Then she made the shepherd call
All the heavens to witness truth,
Never loved a truer youth.
Thus with many a pretty oath,
Yea and nay, and faith and troth,
Such as silly shepherds use,
When they will not love abuse,
Love which had been long deluded,
Was with kisses sweet concluded:
And Phyllida with garlands gay
Was made the Lady of the May.

EDMUND SPENSER

EPITHALAMIUM

YE LEARNÈD SISTERS which have oftentimes
Been to me aiding, others to adorn,
Whom ye thought worthy of your graceful rhymes,
That even the greatest did not greatly scorn
To hear their names sung in your simple lays,
But joyèd in their praise;
And when ye list your own mishaps to mourn,
Which death, or love, or Fortune's wreck did raise,
Your string could soon to sadder tenor turn,
And teach the woods and waters to lament
Your doleful dreariment;

Now lay those sorrowful complaints aside,
And having all your heads with garland crowned,
Help me mine own love's praises to resound,
Ne let the name of any be envied: *Nor*
So Orpheus did for his own bride,
So I unto myself alone will sing,
The woods shall to me answer and my echo ring.

Early before the world's light-giving lamp
His golden beam upon the hills doth spread,
Having dispersed the night's uncheerful damp,
Do ye awake, and with fresh lustihead
Go to the bower of my belovèd love,
My truest turtledove;
Bid her awake; for Hymen is awake,
And long since ready forth his masque to move,
With his bright tead that flames with many a flake,   *torch*
And many a bachelor to wait on him,
In their fresh garments trim.
Bid her awake therefore and soon her dight,   *dress*
For lo! the wishèd day is come at last,
That shall for all the pains and sorrows past
Pay to her usury of long delight;
And whilest she doth her dight,
Do ye to her of joy and solace sing,
That all the woods may answer and your echo ring.

Bring with you all the nymphs that you can hear
Both of the rivers and the forests green,
And of the sea that neighbours to her near,
All with gay garlands goodly well beseen.
And let them also with them bring in hand
Another gay garland
For my fair love of lilies and of roses,
Bound truelove-wise with a blue silk riband.
And let them make great store of bridal posies,
And let them eke bring store of other flowers   *also*
To deck the bridal bowers.
And let the ground whereas her foot shall tread,

For fear the stones her tender foot should wrong,
Be strewed with fragrant flowers all along,
And diapered like the discoloured mead.   *variegated*
Which done, do at her chamber door await,
For she will waken straight,
The whiles do ye this song unto her sing,
The woods shall to you answer and your echo ring.

Ye nymphs of Mulla, which with careful heed
The silver scaly trouts do tend full well,
And greedy pikes which use therein to feed
(Those trouts and pikes all others do excel)
And ye likewise which keep the rushy lake,
Where none do fishes take,
Bind up the locks the which hang scattered light,
And in his waters, which your mirror make,
Behold your faces as the crystal bright,
That when you come whereas my love doth lie,
No blemish she may spy.
And eke ye lightfoot maids which keep the deer,
That on the hoary mountain use to tower,
And the wild wolves which seek them to devour,
With your steel darts do chase from coming near,
Be also present here,
To help to deck her and to help to sing,
That all the woods may answer and your echo ring.

Wake now, my love, awake; for it is time;
The rosy morn long since left Tithon's bed,
All ready to her silver coach to climb,
And Phoebus 'gins to show his glorious head.
Hark how the cheerful birds do chant their lays
And carol of love's praise.
The merry lark her matins sings aloft,
The thrush replies, the mavis descant plays,   *thrush*
The ousel shrills, the ruddock warbles soft,
So goodly all agree with sweet consent,
To this day's merriment.
Ah, my dear love, why do ye sleep thus long,

When meeter were that ye should now awake,
T' await the coming of your joyous make, *mate*
And harken to the birds' love-learnèd song,
The dewy leaves among?
For they of joy and pleasance to you sing,
That all the woods them answer and their echo ring.

My love is now awake out of her dream,
And her fair eyes, like stars that dimmèd were
With darksome cloud, now show their goodly beams
More bright than Hesperus his head doth rear.
Come now, ye damsels, daughters of delight,
Help quickly her to dight,
But first come ye, fair hours, which were begot
In Jove's sweet paradise, of day and night,
Which do the seasons of the year allot,
And all that ever in this world is fair
Do make and still repair.
And ye three handmaids of the Cyprian queen,
The which do still adorn her beauty's pride,
Help to adorn my beautifullest bride;
And as ye her array, still throw between
Some graces to be seen,
And as ye use to Venus, to her sing,
The whiles the woods shall answer and your echo ring.

Now is my love all ready forth to come;
Let all the virgins therefore well await,
And ye fresh boys that tend upon her groom
Prepare yourselves; for he is coming straight.
Set all your things in seemly good array
Fit for so joyful day,
The joyfull'st day that ever sun did see.
Fair sun, show forth thy favourable ray,
And let thy lifefull heat not fervent be
For fear of burning her sunshiny face,
Her beauty to disgrace.
O fairest Phoebus, father of the Muse,
If ever I did honour thee aright,

Or sing the thing that mote thy mind delight,   *may*
Do not thy servant's simple boon refuse,
But let this day, let this one day, be mine,
Let all the rest be thine.
Then I thy sovereign praises loud will sing,
That all the woods shall answer and their echo ring.

Hark how the minstrels 'gin to shrill aloud
Their merry music that resounds from far,
The pipe, the tabor, and the trembling crowd,
That well agree withouten breach or jar,
But most of all the damsels do delight,
When they their timbrels smite,
And thereunto do dance and carol sweet,
That all the senses they do ravish quite,
The whiles the boys run up and down the street,
Crying aloud with strong confusèd noise,
As if it were one voice.
'Hymen iö Hymen, Hymen,' they do shout,
That even to the heavens their shouting shrill
Doth reach, and all the firmament doth fill,
To which the people standing all about,
As in approvance do thereto applaud
And loud advance her laud,
And evermore they 'Hymen, Hymen,' sing,
That all the woods them answer and their echo ring.

Lo! where she comes along with portly pace   *stately*
Like Phoebe from her chamber of the east,
Arising forth to run her mighty race,
Clad all in white, that seems a virgin best.   *becomes*
So well it her beseems that ye would ween   *think*
Some angel she had been.
Her long loose yellow locks like golden wire,
Sprinkled with pearl, and pearling flowers atween,   *between*
Do like a golden mantle her attire,
And being crownèd with a garland green,
Seem like some maiden queen.
Her modest eyes abashèd to behold

So many gazers, as on her do stare,
Upon the holy ground affixèd are.
Ne dare lift up her countenance too bold,
But blush to hear her praises sung so loud,
So far from being proud.
Nathless do ye still loud her praises sing.   *Nevertheless*
That all the woods may answer and your echo ring.

Tell me, ye merchants' daughters, did ye see
So fair a creature in your town before,
So sweet, so lovely, and so mild as she,
Adorned with beauty's grace and virtue's store,
Her goodly eyes like sapphires shining bright,
Her forehead ivory white,
Her cheeks like apples which the sun hath ruddied,
Her lips like cherries charming men to bite,
Her breast like to a bowl of cream uncrudded,
Her paps like lilies budded,
Her snowy neck like to a marble tower,
And all her body like a palace fair,
Ascending up with many a stately stair,
To honour's seat and chastity's sweet bower?
Why stand ye still, ye virgins, in amaze,
Upon her so to gaze,
Whiles ye forget your former lay to sing,
To which the woods did answer and your echo ring?

But if you saw that which no eyes can see,
The inward beauty of her lively sprite,   *spirit*
Garnished with heavenly gifts of high degree,
Much more then would ye wonder at that sight,
And stand astonished like to those which read
Medusa's mazeful head.
There dwells sweet love and constant chastity,
Unspotted faith and comely womanhood,
Regard of honour and mild modesty;
There virtue reigns as queen in royal throne,
And giveth laws alone,
The which the base affections do obey,

And yield their services unto her will;
Ne thought of thing uncomely ever may
Thereto approach to tempt her mind to ill.
Had ye once seen these her celestial treasures,
And unrevealèd pleasures,
Then would ye wonder and her praises sing,
That all the woods should answer and your echo ring.

Open the temple gates unto my love,
Open them wide that she may enter in,
And all the posts adorn as doth behove,
And all the pillars deck with garlands trim,
For to receive this saint with honour due,
That cometh in to you.
With trembling steps and humble reverence,
She cometh in, before th' Almighty's view.
Of her, ye virgins, learn obedience,
When so ye come into those holy places,
To humble your proud faces:
Bring her up to th' high altar, that she may
The sacred ceremonies there partake,
The which do endless matrimony make,
And let the roaring organs loudly play
The praises of the Lord in lively notes,
The whiles with hollow throats
The choristers the joyous anthem sing,
That all the woods may answer and their echo ring.

Behold whiles she before the altar stands
Hearing the holy priest that to her speaks
And blesseth her with his two happy hands,
How the red roses flush up in her cheeks,
And the pure snow with goodly vermeil stain,   *vermilion*
Like crimson dyed in grain,
That even th' angels which continually
About the sacred altar do remain,
Forget their service and about her fly,
Oft peeping in her face that seems more fair,
The more they on it stare.

But her sad eyes, still fastened on the ground,
Are governèd with goodly modesty,
That suffers not one look to glance awry,
Which may let in a little thought unsound.
Why blush ye, love, to give to me your hand,
The pledge of all our band?
Sing ye, sweet angels, alleluya sing,
That all the woods may answer and your echo ring.

Now all is done; bring home the bride again,
Bring home the triumph of our victory,
Bring home with you the glory of her gain,
With joyance bring her and with jollity.
Never had man more joyful day than this,
Whom heaven would heap with bliss.
Make feast therefore now all this livelong day,
This day for ever to me holy is;
Pour out the wine without restraint or stay,
Pour not by cups, but by the bellyful,
Pour out to all that wull,   *will*
And sprinkle all the posts and walls with wine,
That they may sweat, and drunken be withal.
Crown ye God Bacchus with a coronal,
And Hymen also crown with wreaths of vine,
And let the Graces dance unto the rest;
For they can do it best:
The whiles the maidens do their carol sing,
To which the woods shall answer and their echo ring.

Ring ye the bells, ye young men of the town,
And leave your wonted labours for this day:
This day is holy; do ye write it down,
That ye for ever it remember may.
This day the sun is in his chiefest height,
With Barnaby the bright,
From whence declining daily by degrees,
He somewhat loseth of his heat and light,
When once the Crab behind his back he sees.
But for this time it ill-ordainèd was,

To choose the longest day in all the year,
And shortest night, when longest fitter were:
Yet never day so long, but late would pass.
Ring ye the bells, to make it wear away,
And bonfires make all day,
And dance about them, and about them sing,
That all the woods may answer and your echo ring.

Ah, when will this long weary day have end,
And lend me leave to come unto my love?
How slowly do their hours their numbers spend!
How slowly does sad Time his feathers move!
Haste thee, O fairest planet, to thy home
Within the western foam;
Thy tirèd steeds long since have need of rest.
Long though it be, at last we see it gloom,
And the bright evening star with golden crest
Appear out of the east.
Fair child of beauty, glorious lamp of love
That all the host of heaven in ranks dost lead,
And guidest lovers through the nightës dread,
How cheerfully thou lookest from above,
And seem'st to laugh atween thy twinkling light
As joying in the sight
Of these glad many which for joy do sing,
That all the woods them answer and their echo ring.

Now cease, ye damsels, your delights forepast;
Enough is it, that all the day was yours;
Now day is done, and night is nighing fast;
Now bring the bride into the bridal bowers.
Now night is come, now soon her disarray,
And in her bed her lay;
Lay her in lilies and in violets,
And silken curtains over her display,
And odoured sheets, and Arras coverlets.
Behold how goodly my fair love does lie
In proud humility;
Like unto Maia, when as Jove her took,

In Tempe, lying on the flowery grass,
'Twixt sleep and wake, after she weary was,
With bathing in the Acidalian brook.
Now it is night, ye damsels may be gone,
And leave my love alone,
And leave likewise your former lay to sing;
The woods no more shall answer, nor your echo ring.

Now welcome, night, thou night so long expected,
That long day's labour does at last defray,
And all my cares, which cruel love collected,
Hast summed in one, and cancellèd for ay:
Spread thy broad wing over my love and me,
That no man may us see,
And in thy sable mantle us enwrap,
From fear of peril and foul horror free.
Let no false treason seek us to entrap,
Nor any dread disquiet once annoy
The safety of our joy:
But let the night be calm and quietsome,
Without tempestuous storms or sad affray;
Like as when Jove with fair Alcmena lay,
When he begot the great Tirynthian groom;
Or like as when he with thyself did lie,
And begot majesty.
And let the maids and young men cease to sing;
Ne let the woods them answer, nor their echo ring.

Let no lamenting cries, nor doleful tears,
Be heard all night within nor yet without;
Ne let false whispers, breeding hidden fears,
Break gentle sleep with misconceivèd doubt.
Let no deluding dreams nor dreadful sights
Make sudden sad affrights;
Ne let house-fires, nor lightning's helpless harms,
Ne let the Puck, nor other evil sprites,
Ne let mischievous witches with their charms,
Ne let hobgoblins, names whose sense we see not,
Fray us with things that be not.   *Frighten*

Let not the screech owl nor the stork be heard;
Nor the night raven that still deadly yells,
Nor damnèd ghosts called up with mighty spells,
Nor grisly vultures make us once affeared:
Ne let th' unpleasant quire of frogs still croaking
Make us to wish their choking.
Let none of these their dreary accents sing;
Ne let the woods them answer, nor their echo ring.

But let still silence true night-watches keep,
That sacred peace may in assurance reign,
And timely sleep, when it is time to sleep,
May pour his limbs forth on your pleasant plain,
The whiles an hundred little winged loves,
Like divers feathered doves,
Shall fly and flutter round about your bed,
And in the secret dark, that none reproves,
Their pretty stealths shall work, and snares shall spread
To filch away sweet snatches of delight,
Concealed through covert night.
Ye sons of Venus, play your sports at will,
For greedy pleasure, careless of your toys,
Thinks more upon her paradise of joys,
Than what ye do, albeit good or ill,
All night therefore attend your merry play,
For it will soon be day:
Now none doth hinder you, that say or sing;
Ne will the woods now answer, nor your echo ring.

Who is the same, which at my window peeps?
Or whose is that fair face, that shines so bright?
Is it not Cynthia, she that never sleeps,
But walks about high heaven all the night?
O fairest Goddess, do thou not envy
My love with me to spy;
For thou likewise did'st love, though now unthought,
And for a fleece of wool, which privily
The Latmian shepherd once unto thee brought,
His pleasures with thee wrought.

Therefore to us be favourable now;
And sith of women's labours thou hast charge,
And generation goodly dost enlarge,
Incline thy will t' effect our wishful vow,
And the chaste womb inform with timely seed,
That may our comfort breed:
Till which we cease our hopeful hap to sing;
Ne let the woods us answer, nor our echo ring.

And thou, great Juno, which with awful might
The laws of wedlock still dost patronise,
And the religion of the faith first plight
With sacred rites hast taught to solemnise:
And eke for comfort often callèd art
Of women in their smart,
Eternally bind thou this lovely band,
And all thy blessings unto us impart.
And thou glad Genius, in whose gentle hand
The bridal bower and genial bed remain,
Without blemish or stain,
And the sweet pleasures of their love's delight
With secret aid dost succour and supply,
Till they bring forth the fruitful progeny,
Send us the timely fruit of this same night.
And thou, fair Hebe, and thou, Hymen free,
Grant that it may so be.
Till which we cease your further praise to sing,
Ne any woods shall answer, nor your echo ring.

And ye high heavens, the temple of the Gods,
In which a thousand torches flaming bright
Do burn, that to us wretched earthly clods
In dreadful darkness lend desirèd light;
And all ye powers which in the same remain,
More than we men can feign,
Pour out your blessings on us plenteously,
And happy influence upon us rain,
That we may raise a large posterity,
Which from the earth, which they may long possess,

With lasting happiness,
Up to your haughty palaces may mount,
And for the guerdon of their glorious merit
May heavenly tabernacles there inherit,
Of blessèd saints for to increase the count.
So let us rest, sweet love, in hope of this,
And cease till then our timely joys to sing;
The woods no more us answer, nor our echo ring.

Song made in lieu of many ornaments,
With which my love should duly have been decked,
Which cutting off through hasty accidents,
Ye would not stay your due time to expect,
But promised both to recompense,
Be unto her a goodly ornament,
And for short time an endless monument.

From AMORETTI

MOST glorious Lord of Life, that on this day
  Did'st make thy triumph over death and sin:
  And having harrowed hell, did'st bring away
  Captivity thence captive us to win:
This joyous day, dear Lord, with joy begin,
  And grant that we for whom Thou diddest die
  Being with Thy dear blood clean washed from sin,
  May live for ever in felicity.
And that Thy love we weighing worthily,
  May likewise love Thee for the same again:
  And for Thy sake that all like dear did'st buy,
  With love may one another entertain.
So let us love, dear love, like as we ought,
  Love is the lesson which the Lord us taught.

ONE DAY I wrote her name upon the strand,
    But came the waves and washèd it away:
    Again I wrote it with a second hand,
    But came the tide, and made my pains his prey.
'Vain man,' said she, 'that dost in vain assay,   *attempt*
    A mortal thing so to immortalise,
    For I myself shall like to this decay,
    And eke my name be wipèd out likewise.'   *also*
'Not so,' quod I, 'let baser things devise
    To die in dust, but you shall live by fame:
    My verse your virtues rare shall eternise,
    And in the heavens write your glorious name.
Where whenas Death shall all the world subdue,
    Our love shall live, and later life renew.'

From THE FAERIE QUEENE

[THE CAVE OF DESPAIR]

ERE LONG they come, where that same wicked wight   *creature*
    His dwelling has, low in an hollow cave,
    Far underneath a craggy cliff ypight,   *placed*
    Dark, doleful, dreary, like a greedy grave,
    That still for carrion carcasses doth crave:
    On top whereof aye dwelt the ghastly owl,
    Shrieking his baleful note, which ever drave   *drove*
    Far from that haunt all other cheerful fowl;
And all about it wandering ghosts did wail and howl.

And all about old stocks and stubs of trees,
    Whereon nor fruit nor leaf was ever seen,
    Did hang upon the ragged rocky knees;
    On which had many wretches hangèd been,
    Whose carcasses were scattered on the green,
    And thrown about the cliffs. Arrivèd there,
    That bare-head knight, for dread and doleful teen,   *affliction*
    Would fain have fled, ne durst approachen near,   *nor*
But th' other forced him stay, and comforted in fear.

That darksome cave they enter, where they find
    That cursèd man, low sitting on the ground,
    Musing full sadly in his sullen mind;
    His griesy locks, long growen and unbound,   *grey*
    Disordered hung about his shoulders round,
    And hid his face; through which his hollow eyne
    Looked deadly dull, and starèd as astound;
    His rawbone cheeks, through penury and pine,
Were shrunk into his jaws, as he did never dine.

His garment nought but many ragged clouts,
    With thorns together pinned and patchèd was,
    The which his naked sides he wrapped abouts;
    And him beside there lay upon the grass
    A dreary corse, whose life away did pass,
    All wallowed in his own yet lukewarm blood,
    That from his wound yet wellèd fresh, alas;
    In which a rusty knife fast fixèd stood,
And made an open passage for the gushing flood.

Which piteous spectacle, approving true
    The woeful tale that Trevisan had told,
    Whenas the gentle Red Cross Knight did view,
    With fiery zeal he burnt in courage bold,
    Him to avenge, before his blood were cold,
    And to the villain said, 'Thou damnèd wight,
    The author of this fact we here behold,
    What justice can but judge against thee right,
With thine own blood to price his blood, here shed in sight?'
      pay for

'What frantic fit', quoth he, 'hath thus distraught
    Thee, foolish man, so rash a doom to give?
    What justice ever other judgement taught,
    But he should die, who merits not to live?
    None else to death this man despairing drive,
    But his own guilty mind deserving death.
    Is then unjust to each his due to give?
    Or let him die, that loatheth living breath?
Or let him die at ease, that liveth here uneath?   *uneasily*

'Who travels by the weary wand'ring way,
  To come unto his wishèd home in haste,
  And meets a flood, that doth his passage stay,
  Is not great grace to help him over past,
  Or free his feet, that in the mire stick fast?
  Most envious man, that grieves at neighbour's good,
  And fond, that joyest in the woe thou hast,
  Why wilt not let him pass, that long hath stood
Upon the bank, yet wilt thyself not pass the flood?

'He there does now enjoy eternal rest
  And happy ease, which thou dost want and crave,
  And further from it daily wanderest.
  What if some little pain the passage have,
  That makes frail flesh to fear the bitter wave?
  Is not short pain well borne, that brings long ease,
  And lays the soul to sleep in quiet grave?
  Sleep after toil, port after stormy seas,
Ease after war, death after life does greatly please.'

The knight much wondered at his sudden wit,
  And said, 'The term of life is limited,
  Ne may a man prolong, nor shorten it;
  The soldier may not move from watchful stead,
  Nor leave his stand, until his captain bed.'   *bid*
  'Who life did limit by almighty doom,'
  Quoth he, 'knows best the terms establishèd;
  And he, that points the sentinel his room,   *post*
Doth license him depart at sound of morning drum.

'Is not his deed, whatever thing is done,
  In heaven and earth? Did not he all create
  To die again? All ends that was begun.
  Their times in his eternal book of fate
  Are written sure, and have their certain date.
  Who then can strive with strong necessity,
  That holds the world in his still changing state,
  Or shun the death ordained by destiny?
When hour of death is come, let none ask whence, nor why.

'The longer life, I wot the greater sin,   *know*
  The greater sin, the greater punishment:
  All those great battles, which thou boasts to win,
  Through strife, and bloodshed, and avengëment,
  Now praised, hereafter dear thou shalt repent;
  For life must life, and blood must blood repay.
  Is not enough thy evil life forespent?
  For he, that once hath missèd the right way,
The further he doth go, the further he doth stray.

'Then do no further go, no further stray,
  But here lie down, and to thy rest betake,
  Th' ill to prevent, that life ensuen may.
  For what hath life, that may it lovèd make,
  And gives not rather cause it to forsake?
  Fear, sickness, age, loss, labour, sorrow, strife,
  Pain, hunger, cold, that makes the heart to quake;
  And ever fickle Fortune rageth rife,
All which, and thousands mo do make a loathsome life.' *more*

[THE BOWER OF BLISS]

EFTSOONS they heard a most melodious sound, *Forthwith*
  Of all that mote delight a dainty ear, *may*
  Such as at once might not on living ground,
  Save in this Paradise, be heard elsewhere.
  Right hard it was, for wight, which did it hear, *person*
  To read, what manner music that mote be;
  For all that pleasing is to living ear
  Was there consorted in one harmony,
Birds, voices, instruments, winds, waters, all agree.

The joyous birds shrouded in cheerful shade
  Their notes unto the voice attempered sweet;
  Th' angelical soft trembling voices made
  To th' instruments divine respondence meet; *fitting*
  The silver-sounding instruments did meet
  With the base murmur of the water's fall;
  The water's fall with difference discreet,

Now soft, now loud, unto the wind did call;
The gentle warbling wind low answerèd to all.

There, whence that music seemèd heard to be,
  Was the fair witch herself now solacing,
  With a new lover, whom through sorcery
  And witchcraft she from far did thither bring;
  There she had him now laid a-slumbering,
  In secret shade, after long wanton joys;
  Whilst round them pleasantly did sing
  Many fair ladies, and lascivious boys,
That ever mixed their song with light licentious toys.

And all that while, right over him she hung,
  With her false eyes fast fixèd in his sight,
  As seeking medicine, whence she was stung,
  Or greedily depasturing delight;   *feeding on*
  And oft inclining down with kisses light,
  For fear of waking him, his lips bedewed,
  And through his humid eyes did suck his sprite,   *spirit*
  Quite molten into lust and pleasure lewd;
Wherewith she sighèd soft, as if his case she rued.

The whiles some one did chant this lovely lay:
  'Ah, see, who so fair thing dost fain to see,
  In springing flower the image of the day.
  Ah, see the Virgin Rose, how sweetly she
  Dost first peep forth with bashful modesty,
  That fairer seems, the less ye see her may.
  Lo, see soon after, how more bold and free
  Her barèd bosom she doth broad display.
Lo, see soon after, how she fades, and falls away.

'So passeth, in the passing of a day,
  Of mortal life the leaf, the bud, the flower,
  Ne more doth flourish after first decay,   *Nor*
  That erst was sought to deck both bed and bower,
  Of many a lady, and many a paramour.
  Gather therefore the rose, whilst yet is prime,

For soon comes age, that will her pride deflower.
Gather the rose of love, whilst yet is time,
Whilst loving thou may'st lovèd be with equal crime.'

[MUTABILITY]

FOR all that from her springs, and is y-bred,
    However fair it flourish for a time,
    Yet see we soon decay; and, being dead,
    To turn again unto their earthly slime.
    Yet, out of their decay and mortal crime,
    We daily see new creatures to arise;
    And of their winter spring another prime,
    Unlike in form, and changed by strange disguise:
So turn they still about, and change in restless wise.

As for her tenants; that is, man and beasts,
    The beasts we daily see massacrèd die,
    As thralls and vassals unto men's behests:
    And men themselves do change continually,
    From youth to eld, from wealth to poverty,   *age*
    From good to bad, from bad to worst of all.
    Ne do their bodies only flit and fly;
    But eke their minds (which they immortal call)   *also*
Still change and vary thoughts, as new occasions fall.

Ne is the water in more constant case;   *Nor*
    Whether those same on high, or these below.
    For, th' Ocean moveth still, from place to place;
    And every river still doth ebb and flow;
    Ne any lake, that seems most still and slow,
    Ne pool so small, that can his smoothness hold,
    When any wind doth under heaven blow;
    With which the clouds are also tossed and rolled;
Now like great hills; and, straight, like sluices, them unfold.

So likewise are all wat'ry living wights
    Still tossed, and turnèd, with continual change,
    Never abiding in their steadfast plights.

The fish, still floating, do at random range,
And never rest; but evermore exchange
Their dwelling-places, as the streams them carry;
Ne have the wat'ry fowls a certain grange,
Wherein to rest, ne in one stead do tarry;   *place*
But flitting still do fly, and still their places vary.

Next is the air; which who feels not by sense
  (For of all sense it is the middle mean)
  To flit still? and, with subtle influence
  Of his thin spirit, all creatures to maintain,
  In state of life? O weak life! that does lean
  On thing so tickle as th' unsteady air;   *uncertain*
  Which every hour is changed, and altered clean
  With every blast that bloweth foul or fair:
The fair doth it prolong; the foul doth it impair.

Therein the changes infinite behold,
  Which to her creatures every minute chance:
  Now, boiling hot; straight, freezing deadly cold;
  Now, fair sun-shine, that makes all skip and dance;
  Straight, bitter storms and baleful countenance,
  That makes them all to shiver and to shake:
  Rain, hail, and snow do pay them sad penance,
  And dreadful thunderclaps (that make them quake)
With flames and flashing lights that thousand changes make.

Last is the fire; which, though it live for ever,
  Ne can be quenchèd quite; yet, every day,
  We see his parts, so soon as they do sever,
  To lose their heat, and shortly to decay;
  So makes herself his own consuming prey,
  Ne any living creature doth he breed:
  But all, that are of others bred, doth slay;
  And, with their death, his cruel life doth feed;
Nought leaving but their barren ashes, without seed.

Thus, all these four (the which the groundwork be
  Of all the world, and of all living wights)

To thousand sorts of Change we subject see.
Yet are they changed (by other wondrous sleights)
Into themselves, and lose their native mights:
The fire to air, and th' air to water sheer,
And water into earth; yet water fights
With fire, and air with earth approaching near;
Yet all are in one body, and as one appear.

SIR PHILIP SIDNEY

MY TRUE LOVE hath my heart and I have his,
   By just exchange one for another given.
I hold his dear, and mine he cannot miss;
   There never was a better bargain driven.
     My true love hath my heart and I have his.

His heart in me keeps him and me in one,
   My heart in him his thoughts and senses guides;
He loves my heart, for once it was his own;
   I cherish his, because in me it bides.
     My true love hath my heart and I have his.

WITH how sad steps, O Moon, thou climb'st the skies!
How silently, and with how wan a face!
What! may it be that even in heavenly place
That busy archer his sharp arrows tries?
Sure, if that long-with-love-acquainted eyes
Can judge of love, thou feel'st a lover's case;
I read it in thy looks; thy languished grace
To me, that feel the like, thy state descries.
Then, even of fellowship, O Moon, tell me,
Is constant love deemed there but want of wit?
Are beauties there as proud as here they be?
Do they above love to be loved, and yet
   Those lovers scorn whom that love doth possess?
   Do they call virtue there ungratefulness?

Loving in truth, and fain in verse my love to show,
That she, dear she, might take some pleasure of my pain,
Pleasure might cause her read, reading might make her know,
Knowledge might pity win, and pity grace obtain,
I sought fit words to paint the blackest face of woe,
Studying inventions fine, her wits to entertain:
Oft turning others' leaves, to see if thence would flow
Some fresh and fruitful showers upon my sunburned brain.
But words came halting forth, wanting Invention's stay,
Invention, Nature's child, fled stepdame Study's blows,
And others' feet still seemed but strangers in my way.
Thus, great with child to speak, and helpless in my throes,
  Biting my truant pen, beating myself for spite,
  'Fool,' said my Muse to me, 'look in thy heart and write.'

Leave me, O Love, which reachest but to dust,
And thou, my mind, aspire to higher things.
Grow rich in that which never taketh rust:
Whatever fades but fading pleasure brings.
Draw in thy beams, and humble all thy might,
To that sweet yoke, where lasting freedoms be:
Which breaks the clouds and opens forth the light
That doth both shine and give us sight to see.
Oh, take fast hold, let that light be thy guide,
In this small course which birth draws out to death,
And think how evil becometh him to slide,
Who seeketh heaven, and comes of heavenly breath.
  Then farewell, world! Thy uttermost I see.
  Eternal Love, maintain thy life in me!

JOHN LYLY

Cupid and my Campaspe played
At cards for kisses; Cupid paid.
He stakes his quiver, bow and arrows,
His mother's doves and team of sparrows,
Loses them too; then down he throws

The coral of his lip, the rose
Growing on 's cheek (but none knows how),
With these the crystal of his brow,
And then the dimple of his chin:
All these did my Campaspe win.
At last he set her both his eyes;
She won, and Cupid blind did rise.
O Love! has she done this to thee?
What shall, alas, become of me?

SIR FULKE GREVILLE

I, WITH whose colours Myra dressed her head,
I, that wore posies of her own hand-making,
I, that mine own name in the chimneys read
By Myra finely wrought ere I was waking:
　　Must I look on, in hope time coming may
　　With change bring back my turn again to play?

I, that on Sunday at the church-stile found,
A garland sweet, with true-love knots in flowers,
Which I to wear about mine arms was bound,
That each of us might know that all was ours:
　　Must I now lead an idle life in wishes,
　　And follow Cupid for his loaves and fishes?

I, that did wear the ring her mother left,
I, for whose love she gloried to be blamed,
I, with whose eyes her eyes committed theft,
I, who did make her blush when I was named:
　　Must I lose ring, flowers, blush, theft, and go naked,
　　Watching with sighs, till dead love be awakèd?

I, that, when drowsy Argus fell asleep,
Like jealousy o'erwatchèd his desire,
Was even warnèd modesty to keep,
While her breath, speaking, kindled Nature's fire:
　　Must I look on a-cold, while others warm them?
　　Do Vulcan's brothers in such fine nets arm them?

Was it for this that I might Myra see
Washing the water with her beauties white?
Yet would she never write her love to me.
Thinks wit of change, while thoughts are in delight?
  Mad girls must safely love, as they may leave;
  No man can print a kiss; lines may deceive.

GEORGE PEELE

His golden locks time hath to silver turned.
  Oh, time too swift! Oh, swiftness never ceasing!
His youth 'gainst time and age hath ever spurned,
  But spurned in vain; youth waneth by increasing:
Beauty, strength, youth, are flowers but fading seen;
Duty, faith, love, are roots, and ever green.

His helmet now shall make a hive for bees;
  And, lovers' sonnets turned to holy psalms,
A man-at-arms must now serve on his knees,
  And feed on prayers, which are age's alms:
But though from court to cottage he depart,
His saint is sure of his unspotted heart.

And when he saddest sits in homely cell,
  He'll teach his swains this carol for a song:
'Blest be the hearts that wish my sovereign well,
  Curst be the souls that think her any wrong.'
Goddess, allow this agèd man his right,
To be your beadsman now, that was your knight.

THOMAS LODGE

LOVE in my bosom like a bee
  Doth suck his sweet;
Now with his wings he plays with me,
  Now with his feet.
With mine eyes he makes his nest,
His bed amidst my tender breast;
My kisses are his daily feast;
And yet he robs me of my rest.
  Ah, wanton, will ye?

And if I sleep, then percheth he
  With pretty flight,
And makes his pillow of my knee
  The livelong night.
Strike I my lute, he tunes the string;
He music plays if so I sing;
He lends me every lovely thing;
Yet cruel he my heart doth sting.
  Whist, wanton, still ye!

Else I with roses every day
  Will whip you hence;
And bind you, when you long to play,
  For your offence.
I'll shut mine eyes to keep you in.
I'll make you fast it for your sin,
I'll count your power not worth a pin.
Alas! what hereby shall I win
  If he gainsay me?

What if I beat the wanton boy
  With many a rod?
He will repay me with annoy,
  Because a god.
Then sit thou safely on my knee,
And let thy bower my bosom be;
Lurk in mine eyes, I like of thee.
O Cupid, so thou pity me,
  Spare not, but play thee!

CHIDIOCK TICHBORNE

[ON THE EVE OF HIS EXECUTION]

MY PRIME of youth is but a frost of cares,
  My feast of joy is but a dish of pain,
My crop of corn is but a field of tares,
  And all my good is but vain hope of gain;
    The day is past, and yet I saw no sun,
    And now I live, and now my life is done.

My tale was heard and yet it was not told,
  My fruit is fallen and yet my leaves are green,
My youth is spent and yet I am not old,
  I saw the world and yet I was not seen;
    My thread is cut, and yet it is not spun,
    And now I live, and now my life is done.

I sought my death and found it in my womb,
  I looked for life and saw it was a shade,
I trod the earth and knew it was my tomb,
  And now I die, and now I was but made;
    My glass is full, and now my glass is run,
    And now I live, and now my life is done.

ROBERT SOUTHWELL

THE BURNING BABE

As I IN hoary winter's night stood shivering in the snow,
Surprised I was with sudden heat which made my heart to glow;
And lifting up a fearful eye to view what fire was near,
A pretty Babe all burning bright did in the air appear;
Who, scorchèd with excessive heat, such floods of tears did shed,
As though his floods should quench his flames which with his tears
  were fed.
'Alas!' quoth he, 'but newly born in fiery heats I fry,
Yet none approach to warm their hearts or feel my fire but I.
My faultless breast the furnace is, the fuel wounding thorns;
Love is the fire, and sighs the smoke, the ashes shame and scorns;

The fuel justice layeth on, and mercy blows the coals;
The metal in this furnace wrought are men's defilèd souls:
For which, as now on fire I am to work them to their good,
So will I melt into a bath to wash them in my blood.'
With this he vanished out of sight and swiftly sunk away,
And straight I callèd unto mind that it was Christmas Day.

SAMUEL DANIEL

CARE-CHARMER Sleep, son of the sable Night,
Brother to Death, in silent darkness born,
Relieve my languish, and restore the light,
With dark forgetting of my care's return.
And let the day be time enough to mourn
The shipwreck of my ill-adventured youth;
Let waking eyes suffice to wail their scorn,
Without the torment of the night's untruth.
Cease, dreams, the images of day-desires,
To model forth the passion of the morrow;
Never let rising sun approve you liars,
To add more grief to aggravate my sorrow.
  Still let me sleep, embracing clouds in vain;
  And never wake to feel the day's disdain.

LET others sing of knights and paladins
In agèd accents and untimely words;
Paint shadows in imaginary lines,
Which well the reach of their high wits records:
But I must sing of thee, and those fair eyes
Authentic shall my verse in time to come;
When yet th' unborn shall say, 'Lo, where she lies,
Whose beauty made him speak that else was dumb.'
These are the arks, the trophies I erect,
That fortify thy name against old age;
And these thy sacred virtues must protect
Against the dark, and Time's consuming rage.
  Though th' error of my youth in them appear,
  Suffice they show I lived and loved thee dear.

HENRY CONSTABLE

DIAPHENIA like the daffodowndilly,
White as the sun, fair as the lily,
    Heigh ho, how I do love thee!
I do love thee as my lambs
Are belovèd of their dams.
    How blest were I if thou would'st prove me!

Diaphenia like the spreading roses,
That in thy sweets all sweets encloses,
    Fair sweet, how I do love thee!
I do love thee as each flower
Loves the sun's life-giving power.
    For, dead, thy breath to life might move me.

Diaphenia like to all things blessèd,
When all thy praises are expressèd,
    Dear joy, how I do love thee!
As the birds do love the spring,
Or the bees their careful king.
    Then in requite, sweet virgin, love me!

Also attributed to Henry Chettle

MICHAEL DRAYTON

SINCE there's no help, come, let us kiss and part.
Nay, I have done; you get no more of me;
And I am glad, yea, glad with all my heart,
That thus so cleanly I myself can free.
Shake hands for ever; cancel all our vows;
And when we meet at any time again,
Be it not seen in either of our brows
That we one jot of former love retain.
Now at the last gasp of Love's latest breath,
When, his pulse failing, Passion speechless lies,
When Faith is kneeling by his bed of death,
And Innocence is closing up his eyes;

Now, if thou would'st, when all have given him over,
From death to life thou might'st him yet recover.

SOME atheist or vile infidel in love,
When I do speak of thy divinity,
May blaspheme thus, and say I flatter thee,
And only write my skill in verse to prove.
See miracles, ye unbelieving! See
A dumb-born Muse, made to express the mind,
A cripple hand to write, yet lame by kind,
One by thy name, the other touching thee.
Blind were mine eyes, till they were seen of thine,
And mine ears deaf by thy fame healèd be;
My vices cured by virtues sprung from thee,
My hopes revived, which long in grave had lain:
    All unclean thoughts, foul sprites, cast out in me
    By thy great power, and by strong faith in thee.

So WELL I love thee as without thee I
Love nothing; if I might choose, I'd rather die
Than be one day debarred thy company.

Since beasts and plants do grow and live and move,
Beasts are those men that such a life approve:
He only lives that deadly is in love.

The corn, that in the ground is sown, first dies,
And of one seed do many ears arise;
Love, this world's corn, by dying multiplies.

The seeds of love first by thy eyes were thrown
Into a ground untilled, a heart unknown
To bear such fruit, till by thy hands 'twas sown.

Look as your looking-glass by chance may fall,
Divide, and break in many pieces small,
And yet shows forth the self-same face in all,

Proportions, features, graces, just the same,
And in the smallest piece as well the name
Of fairest one deserves as in the richest frame;

So all my thoughts are pieces but of you,
Which put together make a glass so true
As I therein no other's face but yours can view.

CHRISTOPHER MARLOWE

THE PASSIONATE SHEPHERD TO HIS LOVE

COME live with me, and be my love,
And we will all the pleasures prove,
That valleys, groves, hills, and fields,
Woods, or steepy mountain yields.

And we will sit upon the rocks,
Seeing the shepherds feed their flocks,
By shallow rivers to whose falls
Melodious birds sing madrigals.

And I will make thee beds of roses,
And a thousand fragrant posies,
A cap of flowers, and a kirtle,
Embroidered all with leaves of myrtle;

A gown made of the finest wool,
Which from our pretty lambs we pull;
Fair linèd slippers for the cold,
With buckles of the purest gold;

A belt of straw and ivy buds,
With coral clasps and amber studs:
And if these pleasures may thee move,
Come live with me, and be my love.

The shepherds' swains shall dance and sing
For thy delight each May morning.
If these delights thy mind may move,
Then live with me, and be my love.

From OVID'S ELEGIES

IN SUMMER'S HEAT and mid-time of the day
To rest my limbs upon a bed I lay;
One window shut, the other open stood,
Which gave such light as twinkles in a wood,
Like twilight glimpse at setting of the sun,
Or night being past and yet not day begun.
Such light to shamefast maidens must be shown,
Where they may sport, and seem to be unknown.
Then came Corinna in a long loose gown,
Her white neck hid with tresses hanging down:
Resembling fair Semiramis going to bed
Or Laïs of a thousand wooers sped.
I snatched her gown; being thin, the harm was small,
Yet strived she to be coverèd therewithal.
And striving thus as one that would be cast,
Betrayed herself, and yielded at the last.
Stark naked as she stood before mine eye,
Not one wen in her body could I spy.
What arms and shoulders did I touch and see,
How apt her breasts were to be touched by me!
How smooth a belly under her waist saw I!
How large a leg, and what a lusty thigh!
To leave the rest, all liked me passing well;
I clinged her naked body, down she fell.
Judge you the rest; being tired she bade me kiss.
Jove send me more such afternoons as this.

From HERO AND LEANDER

AT SESTOS Hero dwelt; Hero the fair,
Whom young Apollo courted for her hair,
And offered as a dower his burning throne,
Where she should sit for men to gaze upon.
The outside of her garments were of lawn,
The lining purple silk, with gilt stars drawn;
Her wide sleeves green, and bordered with a grove,
Where Venus in her naked glory strove
To please the careless and disdainful eyes
Of proud Adonis, that before her lies;
Her kirtle blue, whereon was many a stain,
Made with the blood of wretched lovers slain.
Upon her head she wear a myrtle wreath,
From whence her veil reached to the ground beneath.
Her veil was artificial flowers and leaves,
Whose workmanship both man and beast deceives.
Many would praise the sweet smell as she passed,
When 'twas the odour which her breath forth cast;
And there for honey bees have sought in vain,
And, beat from thence, have lighted there again.
About her neck hung chains of pebble stone,
Which, lightened by her neck, like diamonds shone.
She wear no gloves, for neither sun nor wind
Would burn or parch her hands, but to her mind,
Or warm or cool them, for they took delight
To play upon those hands, they were so white.
Buskins of shells all silvered usèd she,
And branched with blushing coral to the knee,
Where sparrows perched, of hollow pearl and gold,
Such as the world would wonder to behold;
Those with sweet water oft her handmaid fills,
Which, as she went, would chirrup through the bills.
Some say, for her the fairest Cupid pined,
And, looking in her face, was strooken blind.
But this is true: so like was one the other,
As he imagined Hero was his mother;
And oftentimes into her bosom flew,

About her naked neck his bare arms threw,
And laid his childish head upon her breast,
And, with still panting rocked, there took his rest.
So lovely fair was Hero, Venus' nun,
As Nature wept, thinking she was undone,
Because she took more from her than she left,
And of such wondrous beauty her bereft;
Therefore, in sign her treasure suffered wrack,
Since Hero's time hath half the world been black.

    Amorous Leander, beautiful and young
(Whose tragedy divine Musaeus sung),
Dwelt at Abydos; since him dwelt there none
For whom succeeding times make greater moan.
His dangling tresses that were never shorn,
Had they been cut and unto Colchos borne,
Would have allured the vent'rous youth of Grèece
To hazard more than for the Golden Fleece.
Fair Cynthia wished his arms might be her sphere;
Grief makes her pale, because she moves not there.
His body was as straight as Circe's wand;
Jove might have sipped out nectar from his hand.
Even as delicious meat is to the taste,
So was his neck in touching, and surpassed
The white of Pelops' shoulder. I could tell ye
How smooth his breast was, and how white his belly,
And whose immortal fingers did imprint
That heavenly path, with many a curious dint,
That runs along his back; but my rude pen
Can hardly blazon forth the loves of men,
Much less of powerful gods: let it suffice,
That my slack Muse sings of Leander's eyes,
Those orient cheeks and lips, exceeding his
That leapt into the water for a kiss
Of his own shadow, and despising many,
Died ere he could enjoy the love of any.
Had wild Hippolytus Leander seen,
Enamoured of his beauty had he been;
His presence made the rudest peasant melt,
That in the vast uplandish country dwelt,

The barbarous Thracian soldier, moved with nought,
Was moved with him, and for his favour sought.
Some swore he was a maid in man's attire,
For in his looks were all that men desire,
A pleasant smiling cheek, a speaking eye,
A brow for love to banquet royally;
And such as knew he was a man would say,
'Leander, thou art made for amorous play.
Why art thou not in love, and loved of all?
Though thou be fair, yet be not thine own thrall.'

   The men of wealthy Sestos, every year,
For his sake whom their goddess held so dear,
Rose-cheeked Adonis, kept a solemn feast.
Thither resorted many a wandering guest
To meet their loves; such as had none at all
Came lovers home from this great festival;
For every street, like to a firmament,
Glistered with breathing stars, who, where they went,
Frighted the melancholy earth, which deemed
Eternal heaven to burn, for so it seemed,
As if another Phaëton had got
The guidance of the sun's rich chariot.
But far above the loveliest Hero shined,
And stole away th' enchanted gazer's mind;
For like sea-nymphs inveigling harmony,
So was her beauty to the standers-by.
Nor that night-wandering pale and wat'ry star
(When yawning dragons draw her thirling car
From Latmus' mount up to the gloomy sky,
Where, crowned with blazing light and majesty,
She proudly sits) more over-rules the flood
Than she the hearts of those that near her stood.
Even as when gaudy nymphs pursue the chase,
Wretched Ixion's shaggy-footed race,
Incensed with savage heat, gallop amain
From steep pine-bearing mountains to the plain,
So ran the people forth to gaze upon her,
And all that viewed her were enamoured on her.
And as in fury of a dreadful fight,

Their fellows being slain or put to flight,
Poor soldiers stand with fear of death dead strooken,
So at her presence all surprised and tooken,
Await the sentence of her scornful eyes:
He whom she favours lives, the other dies.
There might you see one sigh, another rage,
And some (their violent passions to assuage)
Compile sharp satires; but, alas, too late,
For faithful love will never turn to hate.
And many, seeing great princes were denied,
Pined as they went, and thinking on her died.
On this feast day, oh, cursèd day and hour!
Went Hèro thorough Sestos, from her tower
To Venus' temple, where unhappily,
As after chanced, they did each other spy.
So fair a church as this, had Venus none;
The walls were of discoloured jasper stone,
Wherein was Proteus carvèd, and o'erhead,
A lively vine of green sea-agate spread,
Where, by one hand, light-headed Bacchus hung,
And with the other, wine from grapes out-wrung.
Of crystal shining fair the pavement was;
The town of Sestos called it Venus' glass;
There might you see the Gods in sundry shapes,
Committing heady riots, incest, rapes;
For know that underneath this radiant floor
Was Danae's statue in a brazen tower;
Jove slyly stealing from his sister's bed,
To dally with Idalian Ganimed,
And for his love Europa bellowing loud,
And tumbling with the rainbow in a cloud;
Blood-quaffing Mars heaving the iron net,
Which limping Vulcan and his Cyclops set;
Love kindling fire to burn such towns as Troy;
Sylvanus weeping for the lovely boy
That now is turned into a cypress-tree,
Under whose shade the wood-gods love to be.
And in the midst a silver altar stood;
There Hero sacrificing turtles' blood,

Veiled to the ground, veiling her eyelids close,
And modestly they opened as she rose;
Thence flew Love's arrow with the golden head,
And thus Leander was enamourèd.
Stone still he stood, and evermore he gazed,
Till with the fire that from his count'nance blazed,
Relenting Hero's gentle heart was strook,
Such force and virtue hath an amorous look.

    It lies not in our power to love or hate,
For will in us is overruled by Fate.
When two are stripped, long ere the course begin
We wish that one should lose, the other win;
And one especially do we affect
Of two gold ingots, like in each respect.
The reason no man knows; let it suffice,
What we behold is censured by our eyes.
Where both deliberate, the love is slight;
Who ever loved, that loved not at first sight?

SIR WALTER RALEGH

THE PASSIONATE MAN'S PILGRIMAGE

SUPPOSED TO BE WRITTEN BY
ONE AT THE POINT OF DEATH

GIVE me my scallop shell of quiet,
My staff of faith to walk upon,
My scrip of joy, immortal diet,
My bottle of salvation,
My gown of glory, hope's true gage,
And thus I'll take my pilgrimage.

Blood must be my body's balmer,
No other balm will there be given,
Whilst my soul like a white palmer
Travels to the land of heaven,
Over the silver mountains,
Where spring the nectar fountains;

And there I'll kiss
The bowl of bliss,
And drink my eternal fill
On every milken hill.
My soul will be a-dry before,
But after it will ne'er thirst more.

And by the happy blissful way
More peaceful pilgrims I shall see,
That have shook off their gowns of clay
And go apparelled fresh like me.
I'll bring them first
To slake their thirst,
And then to taste those nectar suckets
At the clear wells
Where sweetness dwells,
Drawn up by saints in crystal buckets.

And when our bottles and all we
Are filled with immortality,
Then the holy paths we'll travel
Strewed with rubies thick as gravel,
Ceilings of diamonds, sapphire floors,
High walls of coral and pearl bowers.

From thence to heaven's bribeless hall
Where no corrupted voices brawl,
No conscience molten into gold,
Nor forged accusers bought and sold,
No cause deferred, nor vain-spent journey,
For there Christ is the King's Attorney,
Who pleads for all without degrees,
And he hath angels, but no fees.

When the grand twelve million jury,
Of our sins with sinful fury,
'Gainst our souls black verdicts give,
Christ pleads his death, and then we live.
Be thou my speaker, taintless pleader,
Unblotted lawyer, true proceeder;

Thou movest salvation even for alms:
Not with a bribèd lawyer's palms.

And this is my eternal plea
To Him that made heaven, earth and sea:
Seeing my flesh must die so soon,
And want a head to dine next noon,
Just at the stroke when my veins start and spread
Set on my soul an everlasting head.
Then am I ready like a palmer fit,
To tread those blest paths which before I writ.

THE AUTHOR'S EPITAPH, MADE BY HIMSELF

EVEN such is Time, which takes in trust
Our youth, our joys, and all we have,
And pays us but with age and dust;
Who in the dark and silent grave,
When we have wandered all our ways,
Shuts up the story of our days:
And from which earth, and grave, and dust,
The Lord shall raise me up, I trust.

As YOU came from the holy land
   Of Walsingham
Met you not with my true love
   By the way as you came?

'How shall I know your true love
   That have met many one
As I went to the holy land
   That have come, that have gone?'

She is neither white nor brown
   But as the heavens fair;
There is none hath a form so divine
   In the earth or the air.

'Such an one did I meet, good sir,
  Such an angelic face
Who like a queen, like a nymph did appear
  By her gait, by her grace.'

She hath left me here all alone
  All alone as unknown
Who sometimes did me lead with herself
  And me loved as her own.

'What's the cause that she leaves you alone
  And a new way doth take,
Who loved you once as her own
  And her joy did you make?'

I have loved her all my youth
  But now old as you see
Love likes not the falling fruit
  From the withered tree.

Know that Love is a careless child
  And forgets promise past;
He is blind, he is deaf when he list
  And in faith never fast.

His desire is a dureless content
  And a trustless joy;
He is won with a world of despair
  And is lost with a toy.

Of womenkind such indeed is the love
  Or the word 'love' abused
Under which many childish desires
  And conceits are excused.

But Love is a durable fire
  In the mind ever burning:
Never sick, never old, never dead,
  From itself never turning.

WILLIAM SHAKESPEARE

SONGS FROM THE PLAYS

WHEN daisies pied and violets blue
　　And lady-smocks all silver-white
And cuckoo-buds of yellow hue
　　Do paint the meadows with delight,
The cuckoo then, on every tree,
Mocks married men; for thus sings he,
　　　　Cuckoo!
Cuckoo, cuckoo! Oh, word of fear,
Unpleasing to a married ear!

When shepherds pipe on oaten straws
　　And merry larks are ploughmen's clocks,
When turtles tread, and rooks, and daws,
　　And maidens bleach their summer smocks,
The cuckoo then, on every tree,
Mocks married men; for thus sings he,
　　　　Cuckoo!
Cuckoo, cuckoo! Oh, word of fear,
Unpleasing to a married ear!

WHEN icicles hang by the wall,
　　And Dick the shepherd blows his nail,
And Tom bears logs into the hall,
　　And milk comes frozen home in pail,
When blood is nipped and ways be foul,
Then nightly sings the staring owl,
　　　　Tu-whit,
Tu-who! a merry note,
While greasy Joan doth keel the pot.

When all aloud the wind doth blow,
　　And coughing drowns the parson's saw,
And bird sits brooding in the snow,
　　And Marian's nose looks red and raw,

When roasted crabs hiss in the bowl,
Then nightly sings the staring owl,
      Tu-whit,
Tu-who! a merry note,
While greasy Joan doth keel the pot.

O MISTRESS MINE, where are you roaming?
Oh, stay and hear; your true love's coming,
   That can sing both high and low.
Trip no further, pretty sweeting;
Journeys end in lovers meeting,
   Every wise man's son doth know.

What is love? 'Tis not hereafter;
Present mirth hath present laughter;
   What's to come is still unsure.
In delay there lies no plenty;
Then come kiss me, sweet and twenty,
   Youth's a stuff will not endure.

   SIGH no more, ladies, sigh no more;
     Men were deceivers ever,
   One foot in sea and one on shore,
     To one thing constant never.
   Then sigh not so, but let them go,
     And be you blithe and bonny,
   Converting all your sounds of woe
     Into Hey nonny, nonny.

   Sing no more ditties, sing no moe,
     Of dumps so dull and heavy;
   The fraud of men was ever so,
     Since summer first was leavy.
   Then sigh not so, but let them go,
     And be you blithe and bonny,
   Converting all your sounds of woe
     Into Hey nonny, nonny.

FEAR no more the heat o' the sun,
  Nor the furious winter's rages;
Thou thy worldly task hast done,
  Home art gone, and ta'en thy wages.
Golden lads and girls all must,
As chimney-sweepers, come to dust.

Fear no more the frown o' the great,
  Thou art past the tyrant's stroke;
Care no more to clothe and eat,
  To thee the reed is as the oak.
The sceptre, learning, physic, must
All follow this, and come to dust.

Fear no more the lightning-flash,
  Nor the all-dreaded thunder-stone;
Fear not slander, censure rash;
  Thou hast finished joy and moan.
All lovers young, all lovers must
Consign to thee, and come to dust.

No exorciser harm thee!
Nor no witchcraft charm thee!
Ghost unlaid forbear thee!
Nothing ill come near thee!
Quiet consummation have;
And renownèd be thy grave!

FULL fathom five thy father lies;
  Of his bones are coral made;
Those are pearls that were his eyes:
  Nothing of him that doth fade,
But doth suffer a sea-change
Into something rich and strange.
Sea-nymphs hourly ring his knell:
                    Ding-dong.
  Hark! now I hear them:
                    Ding-dong bell.

SONNETS

SHALL I compare thee to a summer's day?
Thou art more lovely and more temperate;
Rough winds do shake the darling buds of May,
And summer's lease hath all too short a date;
Sometime too hot the eye of heaven shines,
And often is his gold complexion dimmed,
And every fair from fair sometime declines,
By chance, or nature's changing course, untrimmed;
But thy eternal summer shall not fade,
Nor lose possession of that fair thou ow'st,
Nor shall Death brag thou wand'rest in his shade,
When in eternal lines to time thou grow'st:
    So long as men can breathe, or eyes can see,
    So long lives this, and this gives life to thee.

WHEN, in disgrace with Fortune and men's eyes,
I all alone beweep my outcast state,
And trouble deaf heaven with my bootless cries,
And look upon myself and curse my fate,
Wishing me like to one more rich in hope,
Featured like him, like him with friends possessed,
Desiring this man's art, and that man's scope,
With what I most enjoy contented least,
Yet in these thoughts myself almost despising,
Haply I think on thee, and then my state,
Like to the lark at break of day arising
From sullen earth, sings hymns at heaven's gate,
    For thy sweet love remembered such wealth brings,
    That then I scorn to change my state with kings.

WHEN to the sessions of sweet silent thought
I summon up remembrance of things past,
I sigh the lack of many a thing I sought,
And with old woes new wail my dear time's waste;
Then can I drown an eye, unused to flow,

For precious friends hid in death's dateless night,
And weep afresh love's long-since-cancelled woe,
And moan th' expense of many a vanished sight;
Then can I grieve at grievances foregone,
And heavily from woe to woe tell o'er
The sad account of fore-bemoanèd moan,
Which I new pay as if not paid before.
  But if the while I think on thee, dear friend,
  All losses are restored and sorrows end.

FULL many a glorious morning have I seen
Flatter the mountain tops with sovereign eye,
Kissing with golden face the meadows green,
Gilding pale streams with heavenly alchemy;
Anon permit the basest clouds to ride
With ugly rack on his celestial face,
And from the forlorn world his visage hide,
Stealing unseen to west with this disgrace:
Even so my sun one early morn did shine
With all-triumphant splendour on my brow;
But, out alack, he was but one hour mine,
The region cloud hath masked him from me now.
  Yet him for this my love no whit disdaineth;
  Suns of the world may stain, when heaven's sun staineth.

NOT marble nor the gilded monuments
Of princes shall outlive this powerful rhyme,
But you shall shine more bright in these contents
Than unswept stone, besmeared with sluttish time.
When wasteful war shall statues overturn,
And broils root out the work of masonry,
Nor Mars his sword nor war's quick fire shall burn
The living record of your memory.
'Gainst death and all-oblivious enmity
Shall you pace forth; your praise shall still find room,
Even in the eyes of all posterity
That wears this world out to the ending doom.
  So, till the judgement that yourself arise,
  You live in this, and dwell in lovers' eyes.

TIRED with all these, for restful death I cry:
As to behold desert a beggar born,
And needy nothing trimmed in jollity,
And purest faith unhappily forsworn,
And gilded honour shamefully misplaced,
And maiden virtue rudely strumpeted,
And right perfection wrongfully disgraced,
And strength by limping sway disablèd,
And art made tongue-tied by authority,
And folly, doctor-like, controlling skill,
And simple truth miscalled simplicity,
And captive good attending captain ill.
    Tired with all these, from these would I be gone,
    Save that to die I leave my love alone.

NO LONGER mourn for me when I am dead
Than you shall hear the surly sullen bell
Give warning to the world that I am fled
From this vile world with vilest worms to dwell:
Nay, if you read this line, remember not
The hand that writ it, for I love you so,
That I in your sweet thoughts would be forgot,
If thinking on me then should make you woe.
Oh, if, I say, you look upon this verse,
When I perhaps compounded am with clay,
Do not so much as my poor name rehearse;
But let your love even with my life decay.
    Lest the wise world should look into your moan,
    And mock you with me after I am gone.

THEY that have power to hurt, and will do none,
That do not do the thing they most do show,
Who, moving others, are themselves as stone,
Unmovèd, cold, and to temptation slow:
They rightly do inherit heaven's graces,
And husband nature's riches from expense;
They are the lords and owners of their faces,
Others but stewards of their excellence.
The summer's flower is to the summer sweet,

Though to itself it only live and die,
But if that flower with base infection meet,
The basest weed outbraves his dignity:
    For sweetest things turn sourest by their deeds;
    Lilies that fester smell far worse than weeds.

WHEN in the chronicle of wasted time
I see descriptions of the fairest wights,
And beauty making beautiful old rhyme,
In praise of ladies dead and lovely knights,
Then, in the blazon of sweet beauty's best,
Of hand, of foot, of lip, of eye, of brow,
I see their antique pen would have expressed
Even such a beauty as you master now.
So all their praises are but prophecies
Of this our time, all you prefiguring;
And, for they looked but with divining eyes,
They had not skill enough your worth to sing:
    For we, which now behold these present days,
    Have eyes to wonder, but lack tongues to praise.

LET me not to the marriage of true minds
Admit impediments; love is not love
Which alters when it alteration finds,
Or bends with the remover to remove.
Oh no, it is an ever-fixèd mark,
That looks on tempests, and is never shaken;
It is the star to every wandering bark,
Whose worth's unknown, although his height be taken.
Love's not Time's fool, though rosy lips and cheeks
Within his bending sickle's compass come;
Love alters not with his brief hours and weeks,
But bears it out even to the edge of doom.
    If this be error, and upon me proved,
    I never writ, nor no man ever loved.

TH' EXPENSE of spirit in a waste of shame
Is lust in action; and till action, lust
Is perjured, murd'rous, bloody, full of blame,
Savage, extreme, rude, cruel, not to trust,
Enjoyed no sooner but despisèd straight,
Past reason hunted, and no sooner had,
Past reason hated, as a swallowed bait,
On purpose laid to make the taker mad.
Mad in pursuit and in possession so,
Had, having, and in quest to have, extreme,
A bliss in proof and, proved, a very woe,
Before a joy proposed, behind a dream.
   All this the world well knows, yet none knows well,
   To shun the heaven that leads men to this hell.

MY MISTRESS' eyes are nothing like the sun,
Coral is far more red than her lips red,
If snow be white, why then her breasts are dun,
If hairs be wires, black wires grow on her head.
I have seen roses damasked, red and white,
But no such roses see I in her cheeks,
And in some perfumes is there more delight
Than in the breath that from my mistress reeks.
I love to hear her speak, yet well I know
That music hath a far more pleasing sound,
I grant I never saw a goddess go,
My mistress when she walks treads on the ground.
   And yet, by heaven, I think my love as rare
   As any she belied with false compare.

POOR soul, the centre of my sinful earth,
My sinful earth these rebel powers array,
Why dost thou pine within and suffer dearth,
Painting thy outward walls so costly gay?
Why so large cost, having so short a lease,
Dost thou upon thy fading mansion spend?
Shall worms, inheritors of this excess,

Eat up thy charge? Is this the body's end?
Then, soul, live thou upon thy servant's loss,
And let that pine to aggravate thy store;
Buy terms divine in selling hours of dross;
Within be fed, without be rich no more:
　So shalt thou feed on death, that feeds on men,
　And death once dead, there's no more dying then.

THE PHOENIX AND THE TURTLE

LET the bird of loudest lay,
On the sole Arabian tree,
Herald sad and trumpet be,
To whose sound chaste wings obey.

But thou shrieking harbinger,
Foul precurrer of the fiend,
Augur of the fever's end,
To this troop come thou not near!

From this session interdict
Every fowl of tyrant wing,
Save the eagle, feathered king:
Keep the obsequy so strict.

Let the priest in surplice white,
That defunctive music can,
Be the death-divining swan,
Lest the requiem lack his right.

And thou treble-dated crow,
That thy sable gender makest
With the breath thou givest and takest,
'Mongst our mourners shalt thou go.

Here the anthem doth commence:
Love and constancy is dead;
Phoenix and the turtle fled
In a mutual flame from hence.

So they loved, as love in twain
Had the essence but in one;
Two distincts, division none;
Number there in love was slain.

Hearts remote, yet not asunder;
Distance, and no space was seen
'Twixt the turtle and his queen;
But in them it were a wonder.

So between them love did shine,
That the turtle saw his right
Flaming in the phoenix' sight;
Either was the other's mine.

Property was thus appalled,
That the self was not the same;
Single nature's double name
Neither two nor one was called.

Reason, in itself confounded,
Saw division grow together,
To themselves yet either neither,
Simple were so well compounded,

That it cried, 'How true a twain
Seemeth this concordant one!
Love hath reason, reason none,
If what parts can so remain.'

Whereupon it made this threne
To the phoenix and the dove,
Co-supremes and stars of love,
As chorus to their tragic scene.

Threnos

Beauty, truth, and rarity,
Grace in all simplicity,
Here enclosed in cinders lie.

Death is now the phoenix' nest;
And the turtle's loyal breast
To eternity doth rest,

Leaving no posterity:
'Twas not their infirmity,
It was married chastity.

Truth may seem, but cannot be;
Beauty brag, but 'tis not she;
Truth and beauty buried be.

To this urn let those repair
That are either true or fair;
For these dead birds sigh a prayer.

GEORGE CHAPMAN

From THE ILIAD

[THE DEATH OF HECTOR]

THUS forth his sword flew, sharp and broad, and bore a deadly
    weight,
With which he rushed in. And look how an eagle from her
    height
Stoops to the rapture of a lamb, or cuffs a timorous hare:
So fell in Hector, and at him Achilles; his mind's fare
Was fierce and mighty; his shield cast a sun-like radiance,
Helm nodded, and his four plumes shook; and, when he raised his
    lance,
Up Hesperus rose 'mongst the evening stars. His bright and
    sparkling eyes
Looked through the body of his foe, and sought through all that
    prize
The next way to his thirsted life. Of all ways only one
Appeared to him; and that was where the unequal winding bone
That joins the shoulders and the neck had place, and where there lay
The speeding way to death; and there his quick eye could display

The place it sought, even through those arms his friend Patroclus
  wore,
When Hector slew him. There he aimed, and there his javelin tore
Stern passage quite through Hector's neck, yet missed it so his
  throat,
It gave him power to change some words; but down to earth it got
His fainting body. Then triumphed divine Aeacides:
'Hector,' he said, 'thy heart supposed that in my friend's decease
Thy life was safe, my absent arm not cared for. Fool! He left
One at the fleet that bettered him, and he it is that reft
Thy strong knees thus. And now the dogs and fowls in foulest use
Shall tear thee up, thy corse exposed to all the Greeks' abuse.'

  He, fainting, said: 'Let me implore, even by thy knees and soul
And thy great parents; do not see a cruelty so foul
Inflicted on me. Brass and gold receive at any rate
And quit my person, that the peers and ladies of our state
May tomb it, and to sacred fire turn thy prophane decrees.'

  'Dog,' he replied, 'urge not my ruth by parents, soul, nor knees.
I would to God that any rage would let me eat thee raw,
Sliced into pieces, so beyond the right of any law
I taste thy merits. And believe it flies the force of man
To rescue thy head from the dogs. Give all the gold they can,
If ten or twenty times so much as friends would rate thy price
Were tendered here, with vows of more, to buy the cruelties
I here have vowed, and, after that, thy father with his gold
Would free thyself – all that should fail to let thy mother hold
Solemnities of death with thee and do thee such a grace
To mourn thy whole corse on a bed – which piecemeal I'll deface
With fowls and dogs.' He, dying, said: 'I, knowing thee well,
  foresaw
Thy now tried tyranny, nor hoped for any other law,
Of nature, or of nations: and that fear forced much more
Than death my flight, which never touched at Hector's foot before.
A soul of iron informs me. Mark, what vengeance the equal fates
Will give me of thee for this rage, when in the Scaean gates
Phoebus and Paris meet with thee.' Thus Death's hand closed his
  eyes,
His soul flying his fair limbs to hell, mourning his destinies
To part so with his youth and strength. Thus dead, thus Thetis' son

His prophecy answered: 'Die thou now; when my short thread is
    spun,
I'll bear it as the will of Jove.' This said, his brazen spear
He drew and stuck by; then his arms, that all embrewèd were,
He spoiled his shoulders off. Then all the Greeks ran in to him
To see his person, and admired his terror-stirring limb.
Yet none stood by that gave no wound to his so goodly form,
When each to other said: 'O Jove, he is not in the storm
He came to fleet in with his fire; he handles now more soft.'

THOMAS NASHE

ADIEU, farewell, earth's bliss,
This world uncertain is;
Fond are life's lustful joys,
Death proves them all but toys,
None from his darts can fly.
I am sick, I must die.
          Lord have mercy on us!

Rich men, trust not in wealth,
Gold cannot buy you health;
Physic himself must fade,
All things to end are made.
The plague full swift goes by;
I am sick, I must die.
          Lord have mercy on us!

Beauty is but a flower
Which wrinkles will devour;
Brightness falls from the air,
Queens have died young and fair,
Dust hath closed Helen's eye.
I am sick, I must die.
          Lord have mercy on us!

Strength stoops unto the grave,
Worms feed on Hector brave,
Swords may not fight with fate,
Earth still holds ope her gate.
'Come! come!' the bells do cry.
I am sick, I must die.
       Lord have mercy on us!

Wit with his wantonness
Tasteth death's bitterness;
Hell's executioner
Hath no ears for to hear
What vain art can reply.
I am sick, I must die.
       Lord have mercy on us!

Haste, therefore, each degree,
To welcome destiny.
Heaven is our heritage,
Earth but a player's stage;
Mount we unto the sky.
I am sick, I must die.
       Lord have mercy on us!

THOMAS CAMPION

WHEN thou must home to shades of underground,
   And there arrived, a new admirèd guest,
The beauteous spirits do engirt thee round,
   White Iope, blithe Helen and the rest,
To hear the stories of thy finished love
From that smooth tongue, whose music hell can move:

Then wilt thou speak of banqueting delights,
   Of masques and revels which sweet youth did make,
Of tourneys and great challenges of knights,
   And all these triumphs for thy beauty's sake.
When thou hast told these honours done to thee,
Then tell, oh, tell, how thou did'st murder me.

FOLLOW your saint, follow with accents sweet;
Haste you, sad notes, fall at her flying feet.
There, wrapped in cloud of sorrow, pity move,
And tell the ravisher of my soul I perish for her love.
But if she scorns my never-ceasing pain,
Then burst with sighing in her sight, and ne'er return again.

All that I sung still to her praise did tend.
Still she was first, still she my songs did end.
Yet she my love and music both doth fly,
The music that her echo is, and beauty's sympathy.
Then let my notes pursue her scornful flight;
It shall suffice that they were breathed, and died for her delight.

ROSE-CHEEKED Laura, come;
Sing thou smoothly with thy beauty's
Silent music, either other
    Sweetly gracing.

Lovely forms do flow
From concent divinely framèd;
Heaven is music, and thy beauty's
    Birth is heavenly.

These dull notes we sing
Discords need for helps to grace them;
Only beauty purely loving
    Knows no discord;

But still moves delight,
Like clear springs renewed by flowing,
Ever perfect, ever in them-
    selves eternal.

THERE IS a garden in her face,
    Where roses and white lilies grow;
A heavenly paradise is that place,

Wherein all pleasant fruits do flow.
There cherries grow which none may buy,
Till 'Cherry-ripe' themselves do cry.

Those cherries fairly do enclose
   Of orient pearl a double row,
Which when her lovely laughter shows,
   They look like rosebuds filled with snow.
Yet them nor peer nor prince can buy,
Till 'Cherry-ripe' themselves do cry.

Her eyes like angels watch them still;
   Her brows like bended bows do stand,
Threatening with piercing frowns to kill
   All that attempt with eye or hand
Those sacred cherries to come nigh,
Till 'Cherry-ripe' themselves do cry.

THOU ART NOT fair, for all thy red and white,
For all those rosy ornaments in thee;
Thou art not sweet, though made of mere delight,
Not fair nor sweet, unless thou pity me.
I will not soothe thy fancies: thou shalt prove
That beauty is no beauty without love.

Yet love not me, nor seek thou to allure
My thoughts with beauty, were it more divine:
Thy smiles and kisses I cannot endure,
I'll not be wrapped up in those arms of thine:
Now show it, if thou be a woman right –
Embrace, and kiss, and love me, in despite!

ANONYMOUS

WEEP you no more, sad fountains;
   What need you flow so fast?
Look how the snowy mountains

Heaven's sun doth gently waste.
But my sun's heavenly eyes
    View not your weeping,
    That now lies sleeping
Softly, now softly lies
      Sleeping.

Sleep is a reconciling,
    A rest that peace begets.
Doth not the sun rise smiling
    When fair at even he sets?
Rest you then, rest, sad eyes,
    Melt not in weeping,
    While she lies sleeping
Softly, now softly lies
      Sleeping.

I SAW my lady weep,
    And Sorrow proud to be advancèd so
In those fair eyes where all perfections keep.
    Her face was full of woe;
But such a woe, believe me, as wins more hearts,
Than Mirth can do with her enticing parts.

Sorrow was there made fair,
    And Passion wise, tears a delightful thing;
Silence beyond all speech a wisdom rare.
    She made her sighs to sing,
And all things with so sweet a sadness move,
As made my heart at once both grieve and love.

O fairer than aught else
    The world can show, leave off in time to grieve.
Enough, enough your joyful looks excels;
    Tears kills the heart, believe.
Oh, strive not to be excellent in woe,
Which only breeds your beauty's overthrow.

MY LOVE in her attire doth show her wit,
    It doth so well become her:
For every season she hath dressings fit,
    For winter, spring, and summer.
No beauty she doth miss,
    When all her robes are on;
But Beauty's self she is,
    When all her robes are gone.

THULE, the period of cosmography,
    Doth vaunt of Hecla, whose sulphureous fire
Doth melt the frozen clime and thaw the sky;
    Trinacrian Etna's flames ascend not higher:
These things seem wondrous, yet more wondrous I,
Whose heart with fear doth freeze, with love doth fry.

The Andalusian merchant that returns
    Laden with cochineal and china dishes,
Reports in Spain how strangely Fogo burns
    Amidst an ocean full of flying fishes:
These things seem wondrous, yet more wondrous I,
Whose heart with fear doth freeze, with love doth fry.

SIR HENRY WOTTON

ON HIS MISTRESS, THE QUEEN OF BOHEMIA

YOU meaner beauties of the night,
    Which poorly satisfy our eyes
More by your number than your light,
    You common people of the skies,
What are you, when the moon shall rise?

Ye violets that first appear,
    By your pure purple mantles known
Like the proud virgins of the year
    As if the spring were all your own,
What are you, when the rose is blown?

Ye curious chanters of the wood
   That warble forth Dame Nature's lays,
Thinking your passions understood
   By your weak accents; what's your praise
When Philomel her voice doth raise?

So when my mistress shall be seen
   In sweetness of her looks and mind,
By virtue first, then choice, a queen,
   Tell me, if she were not designed
Th' eclipse and glory of her kind?

JOHN DONNE

THE GOOD-MORROW

I WONDER, by my troth, what thou and I
Did till we loved? Were we not weaned till then?
But sucked on country pleasures childishly?
Or snorted we in the Seven Sleepers' den?
'Twas so; but this, all pleasures fancies be.
If ever any beauty I did see,
Which I desired, and got, 'twas but a dream of thee.

And now good morrow to our waking souls,
Which watch not one another out of fear;
For love all love of other sights controls,
And makes one little room an everywhere.
Let sea-discoverers to new worlds have gone,
Let maps to other, worlds on worlds have shown;
Let us possess one world, each hath one, and is one.

My face in thine eye, thine in mine appears,
And true plain hearts do in the faces rest,
Where can we find two better hemispheres
Without sharp north, without declining west?
Whatever dies was not mixed equally;
If our two loves be one, or thou and I
Love so alike that none do slacken, none can die.

SONG

Go and catch a falling star,
   Get with child a mandrake root,
Tell me where all past years are,
   Or who cleft the Devil's foot;
Teach me to hear mermaids singing,
Or to keep off envy's stinging,
       And find
       What wind
Serves to advance an honest mind.

If thou be'st born to strange sights,
   Things invisible to see,
Ride ten thousand days and nights
   Till Age snow white hairs on thee;
Thou, when thou return'st, wilt tell me
All strange wonders that befell thee,
       And swear
       Nowhere
Lives a woman true, and fair.

If thou find'st one, let me know,
   Such a pilgrimage were sweet.
Yet do not; I would not go,
   Though at next door we might meet.
Though she were true when you met her,
And last till you write your letter,
       Yet she
       Will be
False, ere I come, to two or three.

A NOCTURNAL UPON ST LUCY'S DAY
BEING THE SHORTEST DAY

'TIS the year's midnight, and it is the day's,
Lucy's, who scarce seven hours herself unmasks;
   The sun is spent, and now his flasks

Send forth light squibs, no constant rays;
   The world's whole sap is sunk;
The general balm th' hydroptic earth hath drunk,
Whither, as to the bed's feet, life is shrunk,
Dead and interred; yet all these seem to laugh,
Compared with me, who am their epitaph.

Study me then, you who shall lovers be
At the next world, that is, at the next spring:
   For I am every dead thing,
   In whom love wrought new alchemy.
     For his art did express
A quintessence even from nothingness,
From dull privations, and lean emptiness:
He ruined me, and I am rebegot
Of absence, darkness, death: things which are not.

All others, from all things, draw all that's good,
Life, soul, form, spirit, whence they being have;
   I, by Love's limbeck, am the grave
   Of all, that's nothing. Oft a flood
     Have we two wept, and so
Drowned the whole world, us two; oft did we grow
To be two Chaoses, when we did show
Care to ought else; and often absences
Withdrew our souls, and made us carcasses.

But I am by her death (which word wrongs her)
Of the first nothing the elixir grown;
   Were I a man, that I were one,
   I needs must know; I should prefer,
     If I were any beast,
Some ends, some means; yea plants, yea stones detest,
And love; all, all some properties invest;
If I an ordinary nothing were,
As shadow, a light, and body must be here.

But I am None; nor will my sun renew.
You lovers, for whose sake the lesser sun

At this time to the Goat is run
 To fetch new lust, and give it you,
  Enjoy your summer all;
Since she enjoys her long night's festival,
Let me prepare towards her, and let me call
This hour her vigil, and her eve, since this
Both the year's and the day's deep midnight is.

THE ECSTASY

WHERE, like a pillow on a bed,
 A pregnant bank swelled up, to rest
The violet's reclining head,
 Sat we two, one another's best.

Our hands were firmly cemented
 With a fast balm, which thence did spring;
Our eye-beams twisted, and did thread
 Our eyes upon one double string;

So to intergraft our hands, as yet
 Was all the means to make us one,
And pictures in our eyes to get
 Was all our propagation.

As 'twixt two equal armies Fate
 Suspends uncertain victory,
Our souls (which to advance their state
 Were gone out) hung 'twixt her and me.

And whilst our souls negotiate there,
 We like sepulchral statues lay;
All day the same our postures were,
 And we said nothing, all the day.

If any, so by love refined
 That he soul's language understood,
And by good love were grown all mind,
 Within convenient distance stood,

He (though he knew not which soul spake,
  Because both meant, both spake the same)
Might thence a new concoction take,
  And part far purer than he came.

This ecstasy doth unperplex
  (We said) and tell us what we love;
We see by this, it was not sex,
  We see, we saw not what did move:

But as all several souls contain
  Mixture of things, they know not what,
Love these mixed souls doth mix again,
  And makes both one, each this and that.

A single violet transplant,
  The strength, the colour, and the size
(All which before was poor, and scant),
  Redoubles still, and multiplies.

When love with one another so
  Interinanimates two souls,
That abler soul, which thence doth flow,
  Defects of loneliness controls.

We then, who are this new soul, know
  Of what we are composed, and made,
For th' atomies of which we grow
  Are souls, whom no change can invade.

But, oh alas! so long, so far
  Our bodies why do we forbear?
They are ours, though they are not we; we are
  The intelligences, they the sphere.

We owe them thanks, because they thus
  Did us, to us, at first convey,
Yielded their forces, sense, to us,
  Nor are dross to us, but allay.

On man heaven's influence works not so,
  But that it first imprints the air;
So soul into the soul may flow,
  Though it to body first repair.

As our blood labours to beget
  Spirits as like souls as it can;
Because such fingers need to knit
  That subtle knot which makes us man;

So must pure lovers' souls descend
  T' affections, and to faculties,
Which sense may reach and apprehend,
  Else a great prince in prison lies.

To our bodies turn we then, that so
  Weak men on love revealed may look;
Love's mysteries in souls do grow,
  But yet the body is his book.

And if some lover, such as we,
  Have heard this dialogue of one,
Let him still mark us, he shall see
  Small change, when we're to bodies gone.

THE FUNERAL

WHOEVER comes to shroud me, do not harm
    Nor question much
The subtle wreath of hair, which crowns my arm;
The mystery, the sign you must not touch,
    For 'tis my outward soul,
Viceroy to that, which then to heaven being gone,
    Will leave this to control,
And keep these limbs, her provinces, from dissolution.

For if the sinewy thread my brain lets fall
    Through every part,
Can tie those parts, and make me one of all;

These hairs which upwards grew, and strength and art
     Have from a better brain,
Can better do it; except she meant that I
     By this should know my pain,
As prisoners then are manacled, when they're condemned to die.

Whate'er she meant by it, bury it with me,
     For since I am
Love's martyr, it might breed idolatry,
If into others' hands these relics came;
     As 'twas humility
To afford to it all that a soul can do,
     So 'tis some bravery,
That since you would save none of me, I bury some of you.

From HOLY SONNETS

AT THE round earth's imagined corners blow
Your trumpets, angels, and arise, arise
From death, you numberless infinities
Of souls, and to your scattered bodies go:
All whom the flood did, and fire shall o'erthrow,
All whom war, dearth, age, agues, tyrannies,
Despair, law, chance, hath slain, and you whose eyes
Shall behold God, and never taste death's woe.
But let them sleep, Lord, and me mourn a space,
For if above all these my sins abound,
'Tis late to ask abundance of thy grace
When we are there. Here on this lowly ground
   Teach me how to repent; for that's as good
   As if thou had'st sealed my pardon, with thy blood.

DEATH, be not proud, though some have callèd thee
Mighty and dreadful, for thou art not so;
For those whom thou think'st thou dost overthrow
Die not, poor Death, nor yet can'st thou kill me.

From rest and sleep, which but thy pictures be,
Much pleasure; then from thee much more must flow;
And soonest our best men with thee do go,
Rest of their bones, and soul's delivery.
Thou'rt slave to Fate, chance, kings, and desperate men,
And dost with poison, war, and sickness dwell;
And poppy or charms can make us sleep as well,
And better than thy stroke. Why swell'st thou then?
　One short sleep past, we wake eternally,
　And death shall be no more. Death, thou shalt die.

BEN JONSON

SONG. TO CELIA

DRINK to me only with thine eyes,
　And I will pledge with mine;
Or leave a kiss but in the cup,
　And I'll not look for wine.
The thirst that from thy soul doth rise
　Doth ask a drink divine:
But might I of Jove's nectar sup,
　I would not change for thine.

I sent thee late a rosy wreath,
　Not so much honouring thee
As giving it a hope that there
　It could not withered be.
But thou thereon did'st only breathe,
　And send'st it back to me:
Since when it grows, and smells, I swear,
　Not of itself, but thee.

STILL to be neat, still to be dressed,
As you were going to a feast;
Still to be powdered, still perfumed:
Lady, it is to be presumed,
Though art's hid causes are not found,
All is not sweet, all is not sound.

Give me a look, give me a face,
That makes simplicity a grace;
Robes loosely flowing, hair as free:
Such sweet neglect more taketh me,
Than all th' adulteries of art;
They strike mine eyes, but not my heart.

TO PENSHURST

Thou art not, Penshurst, built to envious show,
Of touch, or marble; nor can'st boast a row
Of polished pillars, or a roof of gold;
Thou hast no lantern, whereof tales are told;
Or stair, or courts; but stand'st an ancient pile,
And, these grudged at, art reverenced the while.
Thou joy'st in better marks, of soil, of air,
Of wood, of water: therein thou art fair.
Thou hast thy walks for health, as well as sport:
Thy Mount, to which the Dryads do resort,
Where Pan and Bacchus their high feasts have made,
Beneath the broad beech, and the chestnut shade;
That taller tree, which of a nut was set,
At his great birth, where all the Muses met.
There, in the writhèd bark, are cut the names
Of many a Sylvan, taken with his flames,
And thence the ruddy satyrs oft provoke
The lighter fauns to reach thy lady's oak.
Thy copse, too, named of Gamage, thou hast there,
That never fails to serve thee seasoned deer,
When thou would'st feast, or exercise thy friends.
The lower land, that to the river bends,
Thy sheep, thy bullocks, kine, and calves do feed;
The middle grounds thy mares and horses breed.
Each bank doth yield thee conies; and the tops
Fertile of wood, Ashore and Sidney's copse,
To crown thy open table, doth provide
The purpled pheasant with the speckled side.
The painted partridge lies in every field,

And, for thy mess, is willing to be killed.
And if the high-swoll'n Medway fail thy dish,
Thou hast thy ponds, that pay thee tribute fish:
Fat, agèd carps, that run into thy net;
And pikes, now weary their own kind to eat,
As loth, the second draught, or cast to stay,
Officiously, at first, themselves betray;
Bright eels, that emulate them, and leap on land,
Before the fisher, or into his hand.
Then hath thy orchard fruit, thy garden flowers,
Fresh as the air, and new as are the hours.
The early cherry, with the later plum,
Fig, grape, and quince, each in his time doth come;
The blushing apricot and woolly peach
Hang on thy walls, that every child may reach.
And though thy walls be of the country stone,
They're reared with no man's ruin, no man's groan,
There's none, that dwell about them, wish them down;
But all come in, the farmer, and the clown:
And no one empty-handed, to salute
Thy lord, and lady, though they have no suit.
Some bring a capon, some a rural cake,
Some nuts, some apples; some that think they make
The better cheeses, bring them; or else send
By their ripe daughters, whom they would commend
This way to husbands; and whose baskets bear
An emblem of themselves, in plum, or pear.
But what can this (more than express their love)
Add to thy free provisions, far above
The need of such? whose liberal board doth flow,
With all that hospitality doth know!
Where comes no guest, but is allowed to eat,
Without his fear, and of the lord's own meat;
Where the same beer, and bread, and self-same wine,
That is his lordship's, shall be also mine.
And I not fain to sit (as some, this day,
At great men's tables) and yet dine away.
Here no man tells my cups; nor, standing by,
A waiter, doth my gluttony envy;

But gives me what I call, and lets me eat;
He knows, below, he shall find plenty of meat,
Thy tables hoard not up for the next day.
Nor, when I take my lodging, need I pray
For fire, or lights, or livery: all is there;
As if thou, then, wert mine, or I reigned here:
There's nothing I can wish, for which I stay.
That found King James, when hunting late this way,
With his brave son, the Prince, they saw thy fires
Shine bright on every hearth as the desires
Of thy Penates had been set on flame,
To entertain them; or the country came,
With all their zeal, to warm their welcome here.
What (great, I will not say, but) sudden cheer
Did'st thou, then, make them! and what praise was heaped
On thy good lady, then! who, therein, reaped
The just reward of her high housewifery;
To have her linen, plate, and all things nigh,
When she was far: and not a room, but dressed,
As if it had expected such a guest!
These, Penshurst, are thy praise, and yet not all.
Thy lady's noble, fruitful, chaste withal.
His children thy great lord may call his own:
A fortune in this age but rarely known.
They are, and have been taught religion: thence
Their gentler spirits have sucked innocence.
Each morn, and even, they are taught to pray,
With the whole household, and may, every day,
Read, in their virtuous parents' noble parts,
The mysteries of manners, arms, and arts.
Now, Penshurst, they that will proportion thee
With other edifices, when they see
Those proud, ambitious heaps, and nothing else,
May say, their lords have built, but thy lord dwells.

JOHN WEBSTER

CALL for the robin redbreast and the wren,
Since o'er shady groves they hover,
And with leaves and flowers do cover
The friendless bodies of unburied men.
Call unto his funeral dole
The ant, the fieldmouse, and the mole,
To rear him hillocks that shall keep him warm,
And, when gay tombs are robbed, sustain no harm;
But keep the wolf far thence, that's foe to men,
For with his nails he'll dig them up again.

RICHARD CORBET

THE FAERIES' FAREWELL

FAREWELL, rewards and faeries,
   Good housewives now may say;
For now foul sluts in dairies
   Do fare as well as they;
And though they sweep their hearths no less
   Than maids were wont to do,
Yet who of late for cleanliness
   Finds sixpence in her shoe?

Lament, lament, old abbeys,
   The faeries lost command:
They did but change priests' babies,
   But some have changed your land;
And all your children sprung from thence
   Are now grown Puritans;
Who live as changelings ever since
   For love of your domains.

At morning and at evening both
   You merry were and glad,
So little care of sleep or sloth
   These pretty ladies had.

When Tom came home from labour,
　Or Cis to milking rose,
Then merrily, merrily went their tabor,
　And nimbly went their toes.

Witness those rings and roundelays
　Of theirs, which yet remain,
Were footed in Queen Mary's days
　On many a grassy plain;
But, since of late Elizabeth,
　And later James, came in,
They never danced on any heath
　As when the time hath been.

By which we note the faeries
　Were of the old profession;
Their songs were Ave Marys,
　Their dances were procession.
But now, alas, they all are dead,
　Or gone beyond the seas,
Or farther for religion fled,
　Or else they take their ease.

A tell-tale in their company
　They never could endure,
And whoso kept not secretly
　Their mirth was punished sure.
It was a just and Christian deed
　To pinch such black and blue.
Oh, how the Commonwealth doth need
　Such justices as you!

Now they have left our quarters
　A register they have,
Who looketh to their charters,
　A man both wise and grave;
An hundred of their merry pranks
　By one that I could name
Are kept in store, con twenty thanks
　To William for the same.

I marvel who his cloak would turn
   When Puck had led him round,
Or where those walking fires would burn,
   Where Cureton would be found;
How Broker would appear to be,
   For whom this age doth mourn;
But that their spirits live in thee,
   In thee, old William Chourne.

To William Chourne of Staffordshire
   Give laud and praises due,
Who every meal can mend your cheer
   With tales both old and true.
To William all give audience,
   And pray ye for his noddle,
For all the faeries' evidence
   Were lost, if that were addle.

EDWARD, LORD HERBERT OF CHERBURY

ELEGY OVER A TOMB

MUST I then see, alas, eternal night
   Sitting upon those fairest eyes,
And closing all those beams, which once did rise
   So radiant and bright,
That light and heat in them to us did prove
     Knowledge and love?

Oh, if you did delight no more to stay
   Upon this low and earthly stage,
But rather chose an endless heritage,
   Tell us at least, we pray,
Where all the beauties that those ashes owed
     Are now bestowed?

Doth the sun now his light with yours renew?
   Have waves the curling of your hair?

Did you restore unto the sky and air
    The red, and white, and blue?
Have you vouchsafed to flowers since your death
      That sweetest breath?

Had not heaven's lights else in their houses slept,
    Or to some private life retired?
Must not the sky and air have else conspired,
     And in their regions wept?
Must not each flower else the earth could breed
      Have been a weed?

But thus enriched may we not yield some cause
    Why they themselves lament no more?
That must have changed the course they held before,
     And broke their proper laws,
Had not your beauties given this second birth
      To heaven and earth?

Tell us – for oracles must still ascend,
    For those that crave them at your tomb –
Tell us, where are those beauties now become,
     And what they now intend:
Tell us, alas, that cannot tell our grief,
      Or hope relief.

ROBERT HERRICK

DELIGHT IN DISORDER

A SWEET disorder in the dress
Kindles in clothes a wantonness:
A lawn about the shoulders thrown
Into a fine distraction,
An erring lace, which here and there
Enthrals the crimson stomacher,
A cuff neglectful and thereby
Ribbands to flow confusedly,

A winning wave, deserving note,
In the tempestuous petticoat,
A careless shoestring, in whose tie
I see a wild civility,
Do more bewitch me, than when art
Is too precise in every part.

TO THE VIRGINS,
TO MAKE MUCH OF TIME

GATHER ye rosebuds while ye may,
    Old Time is still a-flying;
And this same flower that smiles today,
    Tomorrow will be dying.

The glorious lamp of heaven, the sun
    The higher he's a-getting,
The sooner will his race be run,
    And nearer he's to setting.

That age is best which is the first,
    When youth and blood are warmer;
But being spent, the worse, and worst
    Times still succeed the former.

Then be not coy, but use your time,
    And while ye may, go marry;
For having lost but once your prime,
    You may for ever tarry. ·

TO ANTHEA,
WHO MAY COMMAND HIM ANYTHING

BID me to live, and I will live
    Thy Protestant to be;
Or bid me love, and I will give
    A loving heart to thee.

A heart as soft, a heart as kind,
 A heart as sound and free,
As in the whole world thou can'st find,
 That heart I'll give to thee.

Bid that heart stay, and it will stay,
 To honour thy decree;
Or bid it languish quite away,
 And 't shall do so for thee.

Bid me to weep, and I will weep,
 While I have eyes to see;
And having none, yet I will keep
 A heart to weep for thee.

Bid me despair, and I'll despair,
 Under that cypress-tree;
Or bid me die, and I will dare
 E'en death, to die for thee.

Thou art my life, my love, my heart,
 The very eyes of me;
And hast command of every part,
 To live and die for thee.

TO DAFFODILS

FAIR Daffodils, we weep to see
 You haste away so soon:
As yet the early-rising sun
 Has not attained his noon.
  Stay, stay,
  Until the hasting day
   Has run
  But to the Evensong;
And, having prayed together, we
 Will go with you along.

We have short time to stay as you,
　　We have as short a spring;
As quick a growth to meet decay,
　　As you, or anything.
　　　　We die,
　　　As your hours do, and dry
　　　　Away
　　　Like to the summer's rain;
Or as the pearls of morning's dew,
　　Ne'er to be found again.

THE NIGHT-PIECE, TO JULIA

Her eyes the glow-worm lend thee,
The shooting stars attend thee;
　　And the elves also,
　　Whose little eyes glow
Like the sparks of fire, befriend thee.

No will-o'-the-wisp mislight thee;
Nor snake or slow-worm bite thee;
　　But on, on thy way
　　Not making a stay,
Since ghost there's none to affright thee.

Let not the dark thee cumber.
What though the moon does slumber?
　　The stars of the night
　　Will lend thee their light,
Like tapers clear without number.

Then, Julia, let me woo thee,
Thus, thus to come unto me;
　　And when I shall meet
　　Thy silvery feet,
My soul I'll pour into thee.

TO ELECTRA

I DARE NOT ask a kiss;
   I dare not beg a smile;
Lest having that, or this,
   I might grow proud the while.

No, no, the utmost share
   Of my desire shall be
Only to kiss that air
   That lately kissèd thee.

UPON JULIA'S CLOTHES

WHENAS in silks my Julia goes,
Then, then, methinks, how sweetly flows
That liquefaction of her clothes!

Next, when I cast mine eyes and see
That brave vibration each way free,
Oh, how that glittering taketh me!

HENRY KING

AN EXEQUY

TO HIS MATCHLESS NEVER-TO-BE-FORGOTTEN FRIEND

ACCEPT, thou shrine of my dead saint,
Instead of dirges this complaint;
And, for sweet flowers to crown thy hearse,
Receive a strew of weeping verse
From thy grieved friend; whom thou might'st see
Quite melted into tears for thee.
   Dear loss! since thy untimely fate
My task hath been to meditate
On thee, on thee: thou art the book,
The library whereon I look

Though almost blind. For thee, loved clay!
I languish out, not live, the day,
Using no other exercise
But what I practise with mine eyes.
By which wet glasses I find out
How lazily time creeps about
To one that mourns: this, only this,
My exercise and business is;
So I compute the weary hours
With sighs dissolvèd into showers.

  Nor wonder if my time go thus
Backward and most preposterous:
Thou hast benighted me. Thy set
This eve of blackness did beget,
Who wast my day, though overcast
Before thou had'st thy noontide past,
And I remember must in tears
Thou scarce had'st seen so many years
As day tells hours. By thy clear sun
My love and fortune first did run;
But thou wilt never more appear
Folded within my hemisphere,
Since both thy light and motion,
Like a fled star, is fallen and gone;
And 'twixt me and my soul's dear wish
The earth now interposèd is,
Which such a strange eclipse doth make
As ne'er was read in almanac.

  I could allow thee for a time
To darken me and my sad clime;
Were it a month, a year, or ten,
I would thy exile live till then;
And all that space my mirth adjourn,
So thou would'st promise to return
And, putting off thy ashy shroud,
At length disperse this sorrow's cloud.

  But woe is me! The longest date
Too narrow is to calculate
These empty hopes. Never shall I

Be so much blest as to descry
A glimpse of thee, till that day come
Which shall the earth to cinders doom,
And a fierce fever must calcine
The body of this world, like thine,
My little world! That fit of fire
Once off, our bodies shall aspire
To our souls' bliss; then we shall rise,
And view ourselves with clearer eyes
In that calm region where no night
Can hide us from each other's sight.

  Meantime, thou hast her, Earth; much good
May my harm do thee. Since it stood
With heaven's will I might not call
Her longer mine, I give thee all
My short-lived right and interest
In her, whom living I loved best:
With a most free and bounteous grief,
I give thee what I could not keep.
Be kind to her; and prithee look
Thou write into thy Doomsday book
Each parcel of this rarity,
Which in thy casket shrined doth lie.
See that thou make thy reck'ning straight,
And yield her back again by weight;
For thou must audit on thy trust
Each grain and atom of this dust,
As thou wilt answer Him that lent,
Not gave thee, my dear monument.

  So close the ground, and 'bout her shade
Black curtains draw: my bride is laid.

  Sleep on, my love, in thy cold bed
Never to be disquieted.
My last goodnight! Thou wilt not wake
Till I thy fate shall overtake:
Till age, or grief, or sickness must
Marry my body to that dust
It so much loves; and fill the room
My heart keeps empty in thy tomb.

Stay for me there: I will not fail
To meet thee in that hollow vale.
And think not much of my delay;
I am already on the way,
And follow thee with all the speed
Desire can make, or sorrows breed.
Each minute is a short degree
And ev'ry hour a step towards thee.
At night when I betake to rest,
Next morn I rise nearer my west
Of life, almost by eight hours' sail,
Than when Sleep breathed his drowsy gale.

   Thus from the sun my bottom steers,
And my day's compass downward bears.
Nor labour I to stem the tide
Through which to thee I swiftly glide.

   'Tis true; with shame and grief I yield:
Thou, like the van, first took'st the field,
And gotten hast the victory
In thus adventuring to die
Before me, whose more years might crave
A just precedence in the grave.
But hark! my pulse, like a soft drum,
Beats my approach, tells thee I come;
And, slow howe'er my marches be,
I shall at last sit down by thee.

   The thought of this bids me go on,
And wait my dissolution
With hope and comfort. Dear! (forgive
The crime) I am content to live
Divided, with but half a heart,
Till we shall meet and never part.

GEORGE HERBERT

EASTER

I GOT ME flowers to strew thy way;
I got me boughs off many a tree;
But thou wast up by break of day,
And brought'st thy sweets along with thee.

The sun arising in the east,
Though he give light, and the east perfume,
If they should offer to contest
With thy arising, they presume.

Can there be any day but this,
Though many suns to shine endeavour?
We count three hundred, but we miss:
There is but one, and that one ever.

VIRTUE

SWEET DAY, so cool, so calm, so bright,
The bridal of the earth and sky:
The dew shall weep thy fall tonight,
        For thou must die.

Sweet rose, whose hue angry and brave
Bids the rash gazer wipe his eye:
Thy root is ever in its grave,
        And thou must die.

Sweet spring, full of sweet days and roses,
A box where sweets compacted lie:
My music shows ye have your closes,
        And all must die.

Only a sweet and virtuous soul,
Like seasoned timber, never gives;
But though the whole world turn to coal,
        Then chiefly lives.

THE COLLAR

I STRUCK the board, and cried, 'No more!
      I will abroad.
    What? shall I ever sigh and pine?
My lines and life are free; free as the road,
    Loose as the wind, as large as store.
      Shall I be still in suit?
    Have I no harvest but a thorn
    To let me blood, and not restore
    What I have lost with cordial fruit?
      Sure there was wine
Before my sighs did dry it; there was corn
    Before my tears did drown it.
  Is the year only lost to me?
    Have I no bays to crown it?
No flowers, no garlands gay? All blasted?
      All wasted?
    Not so, my heart; but there is fruit,
      And thou hast hands.
  Recover all thy sigh-blown age
On double pleasures; leave thy cold dispute
Of what is fit, and not. Forsake thy cage,
      Thy rope of sands,
Which petty thoughts have made, and made to thee
    Good cable, to enforce and draw,
      And be thy law,
  While thou did'st wink and would'st not see.
      Away; take heed:
      I will abroad.
Call in thy death's head there; tie up thy fears.
      He that forbears
    To suit and serve his need,
      Deserves his load.'
But as I raved and grew more fierce and wild
      At every word,
Methoughts I heard one calling, 'Child!'
    And I replied, 'My Lord.'

THE PULLEY

WHEN God at first made Man,
Having a glass of blessings standing by,
'Let us', said He, 'pour on him all we can:
Let the world's riches, which dispersèd lie,
     Contract into a span.'

So strength first made a way;
Then beauty flowed, then wisdom, honour, pleasure;
When almost all was out, God made a stay,
Perceiving that, alone of all His treasure,
     Rest in the bottom lay.

'For if I should', said He,
'Bestow this jewel also on my creature,
He would adore my gifts instead of me,
And rest in Nature, not the God of Nature:
     So both should losers be.

'Yet let him keep the rest,
But keep them with repining restlessness;
Let him be rich and weary, that at least,
If goodness lead him not, yet weariness
     May toss him to my breast.'

THE FLOWER

HOW FRESH, O Lord, how sweet and clean
Are thy returns! Ev'n as the flowers in spring,
    To which, besides their own demesne,
The late-passed frosts tributes of pleasure bring,
       Grief melts away
       Like snow in May,
    As if there were no such cold thing.

Who would have thought my shrivelled heart
Could have recovered greenness? It was gone
    Quite underground; as flowers depart
To see their mother-root, when they have blown;
       Where they together
       All the hard weather,
    Dead to the world, keep house unknown.

These are Thy wonders, Lord of power,
Killing and quick'ning, bringing down to hell
    And up to heaven in an hour;
Making a chiming of a passing-bell.
        We say amiss,
        This or that is.
    Thy word is all, if we could spell.

    Oh, that I once past changing were,
Fast in thy Paradise, where no flower can wither!
    Many a spring I shoot up fair,
Off'ring at heaven, growing and groaning thither:
        Nor doth my flower
        Want a spring shower,
    My sins and I joining together.

    But while I grow in a straight line,
Still upwards bent, as if heaven were mine own,
    Thy anger comes, and I decline:
What frost to that? What pole is not the zone,
        Where all things burn,
        When thou dost turn,
    And the least frown of thine is shown?

    And now in age I bud again,
After so many deaths I live and write;
    I once more smell the dew and rain,
And relish versing: O my only light,
        It cannot be
        That I am he
    On whom thy tempests fell all night.

    These are thy wonders, Lord of Love,
To make us see we are but flowers that glide;
    Which when we once can find and prove,
Thou hast a garden for us, where to bide.
        Who would be more,
        Swelling through store,
    Forfeit their Paradise by their pride.

LOVE

Love bade me welcome; yet my soul drew back,
    Guilty of dust and sin.
But quick-eyed Love, observing me grow slack
    From my first entrance in,
Drew nearer to me, sweetly questioning,
    If I lacked anything.

'A guest', I answered, 'worthy to be here.'
    Love said, 'You shall be he.'
'I, the unkind, ungrateful? Ah, my dear,
    I cannot look on thee.'
Love took my hand, and smiling did reply,
    'Who made the eyes but I?'

'Truth, Lord, but I have marred them; let my shame
    Go where it doth deserve.'
'And know you not', says Love, 'who bore the blame?'
    'My dear, then I will serve.'
'You must sit down,' says Love, 'and taste my meat.'
    So I did sit and eat.

THOMAS CAREW

Ask me no more where Jove bestows,
When June is past, the fading rose;
For in your beauty's orient deep
These flowers, as in their causes, sleep.

Ask me no more whither doth stray
The golden atoms of the day;
For in pure love heaven did prepare
Those powders to enrich your hair.

Ask me no more whither doth haste
The nightingale when May is past;
For in your sweet dividing throat
She winters and keeps warm her note.

Ask me no more where those stars light
That downwards fall in dead of night;
For in your eyes they sit, and there
Fixèd become as in their sphere.

Ask me no more if east or west
The phoenix builds her spicy nest;
For unto you at last she flies,
And in your fragrant bosom dies.

SIR WILLIAM D'AVENANT

THE LARK now leaves his wat'ry nest,
  And climbing shakes his dewy wings.
He takes this window for the east,
  And to implore your light he sings:
Awake, awake! The morn will never rise
Till she can dress her beauty at your eyes.

The merchant bows unto the seaman's star,
  The ploughman from the sun his season takes;
But still the lover wonders what they are
  Who look for day before his mistress wakes.
Awake, awake! Break through your veils of lawn!
Then draw your curtains, and begin the dawn!

EDMUND WALLER

  Go, lovely Rose,
Tell her that wastes her time and me
  That now she knows,
When I resemble her to thee,
How sweet and fair she seems to be.

  Tell her that's young
And shuns to have her graces spied,
  That had'st thou sprung
In deserts, where no men abide,
Thou must have uncommended died.

> Small is the worth
> Of beauty from the light retired;
> Bid her come forth,
> Suffer herself to be desired,
> And not blush so to be admired.
>
> Then die! that she
> The common fate of all things rare
> May read in thee:
> How small a part of time they share
> That are so wondrous sweet and fair!

JOHN MILTON

L'ALLEGRO

Hence, loathèd Melancholy,
  Of Cerberus and blackest Midnight born
In Stygian cave forlorn
  'Mongst horrid shapes, and shrieks, and sights unholy!
Find out some uncouth cell,
  Where brooding Darkness spreads his jealous wings,
And the night-raven sings:
  There, under ebon shades and low-browed rocks,
As ragged as thy locks,
  In dark Cimmerian desert ever dwell.
But come, thou Goddess fair and free,
In heaven y-clept Euphrosyne,
And by men heart-easing Mirth,
Whom lovely Venus, at a birth,
With two sister Graces more,
To ivy-crownèd Bacchus bore;
Or whether (as some sager sing)
The frolic wind that breathes the spring,
Zephyr, with Aurora playing,
As he met her once a-Maying,
There, on beds of violets blue,
And fresh-blown roses washed in dew,

Filled her with thee, a daughter fair,
So buxom, blithe, and debonair.
Haste thee, Nymph, and bring with thee
Jest, and youthful jollity,
Quips and cranks and wanton wiles,
Nods and becks and wreathèd smiles,
Such as hang on Hebe's cheek,
And love to live in dimple sleek;
Sport that wrinkled Care derides,
And Laughter holding both his sides.
Come, and trip it as you go
On the light fantastic toe;
And in thy right hand lead with thee
The mountain-nymph, sweet Liberty;
And, if I give thee honour due,
Mirth, admit me of thy crew,
To live with her, and live with thee,
In unreprovèd pleasures free;
To hear the lark begin his flight,
And, singing, startle the dull night,
From his watch-tower in the skies,
Till the dappled dawn doth rise;
Then to come, in spite of sorrow,
And at my window bid good-morrow,
Through the sweet-briar, or the vine,
Or the twisted eglantine;
While the cock, with lively din,
Scatters the rear of darkness thin,
And to the stack, or the barn-door,
Stoutly struts his dames before:
Oft listening how the hounds and horn
Cheerly rouse the slumbering morn,
From the side of some hoar hill,
Through the high wood echoing shrill;
Sometime walking, not unseen,
By hedgerow elms, on hillocks green,
Right against the eastern gate
Where the great Sun begins his state,
Robed in flames and amber light,

The clouds in thousand liveries dight;
While the ploughman, near at hand,
Whistles o'er the furrowed land,
And the milkmaid singeth blithe,
And the mower whets his scythe,
And every shepherd tells his tale
Under the hawthorn in the dale.
Straight mine eye hath caught new pleasures,
Whilst the landskip round it measures;
Russet lawns, and fallows grey,
Where the nibbling flocks do stray;
Mountains on whose barren breast
The labouring clouds do often rest;
Meadows trim with daisies pied;
Shallow brooks, and rivers wide;
Towers and battlements it sees
Bosomed high in tufted trees,
Where perhaps some beauty lies,
The cynosure of neighbouring eyes.
Hard by a cottage chimney smokes
From betwixt two agèd oaks,
Where Corydon and Thyrsis met
Are at their savoury dinner set
Of herbs and other country messes,
Which the neat-handed Phillis dresses;
And then in haste her bower she leaves
With Thestylis to bind the sheaves;
Or, if the earlier season lead,
To the tanned haycock in the mead.
Sometimes, with secure delight,
The upland hamlets will invite,
When the merry bells ring round,
And the jocund rebecks sound
To many a youth and many a maid,
Dancing in the chequered shade;
And young and old come forth to play
On a sunshine holiday,
Till the livelong daylight fail:
Then to the spicy nut-brown ale,

With stories told of many a feat,
How Faery Mab the junkets eat;
She was pinched and pulled, she said;
And he, by Friar's lantern led,
Tells how the drudging Goblin sweat
To earn his cream-bowl duly set,
When in one night, ere glimpse of morn,
His shadowy flail hath threshed the corn
That ten day-labourers could not end;
Then lies him down, the lubber fiend,
And, stretched out all the chimney's length,
Basks at the fire his hairy strength;
And crop-full out of doors he flings,
Ere the first cock his matin rings.
Thus done the tales, to bed they creep,
By whispering winds soon lulled asleep.
Towered cities please us then,
And the busy hum of men,
Where throngs of knights and barons bold,
In weeds of peace, high triumphs hold,
With store of ladies, whose bright eyes
Rain influence, and judge the prize
Of wit or arms, while both contend
To win her grace whom all commend.
There let Hymen oft appear
In saffron robe, with taper clear,
And pomp, and feast, and revelry,
With masques and antique pageantry;
Such sights as youthful poets dream
On summer eves by haunted stream.
Then to the well-trod stage anon,
If Jonson's learnèd sock be on,
Or sweetest Shakespeare, Fancy's child,
Warble his native woodnotes wild,
And ever, against eating cares,
Lap me in soft Lydian airs,
Married to immortal verse,
Such as the meeting soul may pierce,
In notes with many a winding bout

Of linkèd sweetness long drawn out,
With wanton heed and giddy cunning,
The melting voice through mazes running,
Untwisting all the chains that tie
The hidden soul of harmony;
That Orpheus' self may heave his head
From golden slumber on a bed
Of heaped Elysian flowers, and hear
Such strains as would have won the ear
Of Pluto, to have quite set free
His half-regained Eurydice.
These delights if thou can'st give,
Mirth, with thee I mean to live.

IL PENSEROSO

HENCE, vain deluding Joys,
    The brood of Folly without father bred!
How little you bested,
    Or fill the fixèd mind with all your toys!
Dwell in some idle brain,
    And fancies fond with gaudy shapes possess,
As thick and numberless
    As the gay motes that people the sunbeams,
Or likest hovering dreams,
    The fickle pensioners of Morpheus' train.
But, hail! thou Goddess sage and holy!
Hail, divinest Melancholy!
Whose saintly visage is too bright
To hit the sense of human sight;
And therefore to our weaker view
O'erlaid with black staid Wisdom's hue;
Black, but such as in esteem
Prince Memnon's sister might beseem,
Or that starred Ethiop queen that strove
To set her beauty's praise above
The sea-nymphs, and their powers offended.

Yet thou art higher far descended:
Thee bright-haired Vesta, long of yore,
To solitary Saturn bore;
His daughter she; in Saturn's reign
Such mixture was not held a stain:
Oft in glimmering bowers and glades
He met her, and in secret shades
Of woody Ida's inmost grove,
Whilst yet there was no fear of Jove.
Come, pensive Nun, devout and pure,
Sober, steadfast, and demure,
All in a robe of darkest grain,
Flowing with majestic train,
And sable stole of cypress lawn
Over thy decent shoulders drawn.
Come; but keep thy wonted state,
With even step, and musing gait,
And looks commercing with the skies,
Thy rapt soul sitting in thine eyes:
There, held in holy passion still,
Forget thyself to marble, till
With a sad leaden downward cast
Thou fix them on the earth as fast;
And join with thee calm Peace and Quiet,
Spare Fast, that oft with gods doth diet,
And hears the Muses in a ring
Aye round about Jove's altar sing;
And add to these retirèd Leisure,
That in trim gardens takes his pleasure;
But, first and chiefest, with thee bring
Him that yon soars on golden wing,
Guiding the fiery-wheelèd throne,
The Cherub Contemplation;
And the mute Silence hist along,
'Less Philomel will deign a song,
In her sweetest saddest plight,
Smoothing the rugged brow of Night,
While Cynthia checks her dragon yoke
Gently o'er th' accustomed oak.

Sweet bird, that shunn'st the noise of folly,
Most musical, most melancholy!
Thee, chauntress, oft the woods among
I woo, to hear thy evensong;
And, missing thee, I walk unseen
On the dry smooth-shaven green,
To behold the wandering moon,
Riding near her highest noon,
Like one that had been led astray
Through the heavens' wide pathless way,
And oft, as if her head she bowed,
Stooping through a fleecy cloud.
Oft, on plat of rising ground,
I hear the far-off curfew sound,
Over some wide-watered shore,
Swinging slow with sullen roar;
Or, if the air will not permit,
Some still removèd place will fit,
Where glowing embers through the room
Teach light to counterfeit a gloom,
Far from all resort of mirth,
Save the cricket on the hearth,
Or the bellman's drowsy charm
To bless the doors from nightly harm.
Or let my lamp, at midnight hour,
Be seen in some high lonely tower,
Where I may oft outwatch the Bear
With thrice-great Hermes, or unsphere
The spirit of Plato, to unfold
What worlds or what vast regions hold
The immortal mind that hath forsook
Her mansion in this fleshly nook;
And of those demons that are found
In fire, air, flood, or underground,
Whose power hath a true consent
With planet or with element.
Sometime let gorgeous Tragedy
In sceptred pall come sweeping by,
Presenting Thebes, or Pelops' line,

Or the tale of Troy divine,
Or what (though rare) of later age
Ennobled hath the buskined stage.
But, O sad Virgin! that thy power
Might raise Musaeus from his bower;
Or bid the soul of Orpheus sing
Such notes as, warbled to the string,
Drew iron tears down Pluto's cheek,
And made Hell grant what Love did seek;
Or call up him that left half-told
The story of Cambuscan bold,
Of Camball, and of Algarsife,
And who had Canace to wife,
That owned the virtuous ring and glass,
And of the wondrous horse of brass
On which the Tartar king did ride;
And if aught else great bards beside
In sage and solemn tunes have sung,
Of tourneys, and of trophies hung,
Of forests, and enchantments drear,
Where more is meant than meets the ear.
Thus, Night, oft see me in thy pale career,
Till civil-suited Morn appear,
Not tricked and frounced as she was wont
With the Attic boy to hunt,
But kerchiefed in a comely cloud,
While rocking winds are piping loud,
Or ushered with a shower still,
When the gust hath blown his fill,
Ending on the rustling leaves,
With minute drops from off the eaves.
And, when the sun begins to fling
His flaring beams, me, Goddess, bring
To archèd walks of twilight groves,
And shadows brown, that Sylvan loves,
Of pine, or monumental oak,
Where the rude axe with heavèd stroke
Was never heard the nymphs to daunt,
Or fright them from their hallowed haunt.

There, in close covert, by some brook,
Where no profaner eye may look,
Hide me from day's garish eye,
While the bee with honeyed thigh,
That her flowery work doth sing,
And the waters murmuring,
With such consort as they keep,
Entice the dewy-feathered Sleep;
And let some strange mysterious dream
Wave at his wings in airy stream
Of lively portraiture displayed,
Softly on my eyelids laid;
And, as I wake, sweet music breathe
Above, about, or underneath,
Sent by some Spirit to mortals good,
Or the unseen Genius of the wood.
But let my due feet never fail
To walk the studious cloister's pale,
And love the high embowèd roof,
With antique pillars massy-proof,
And storeyed windows richly dight,
Casting a dim religious light.
There let the pealing organ blow,
To the full-voiced quire below,
In service high and anthems clear,
As may with sweetness, through mine ear,
Dissolve me into ecstasies,
And bring all Heaven before mine eyes.
And may at last my weary age
Find out the peaceful hermitage,
The hairy gown and mossy cell,
Where I may sit and rightly spell
Of every star that heaven doth show,
And every herb that sips the dew,
Till old experience do attain
To something like prophetic strain.
These pleasures, Melancholy, give;
And I with thee will choose to live.

LYCIDAS

In this monody the author bewails a learned friend, unfortunately drowned in his passage from Chester on the Irish Seas, 1637; and, by occasion, foretells the ruin of our corrupted clergy, then in their height.

YET once more, O ye laurels, and once more,
Ye myrtles brown, with ivy never sere,
I come to pluck your berries harsh and crude,
And with forced fingers rude
Shatter your leaves before the mellowing year.
Bitter constraint and sad occasion dear
Compels me to disturb your season due;
For Lycidas is dead, dead ere his prime,
Young Lycidas, and hath not left his peer.
Who would not sing for Lycidas? He knew
Himself to sing, and build the lofty rhyme.
He must not float upon his watery bier
Unwept, and welter to the parching wind,
Without the meed of some melodious tear.
  Begin, then, Sisters of the sacred well
That from beneath the seat of Jove doth spring;
Begin, and somewhat loudly sweep the string.
Hence with denial vain and coy excuse;
So may some gentle Muse
With lucky words favour my destined urn,
And as he passes turn,
And bid fair peace be to my sable shroud.
For we were nursed upon the self-same hill,
Fed the same flock, by fountain, shade, and rill.
  Together both, ere the high lawns appeared
Under the opening eyelids of the morn,
We drove afield, and both together heard
What time the grey-fly winds her sultry horn,
Battening our flocks with the fresh dews of night,
Oft till the star that rose, at evening, bright
Toward heaven's descent had sloped his westering wheel.
Meanwhile the rural ditties were not mute,
Tempered to the oaten flute;
Rough Satyrs danced, and Fauns with cloven heel

From the glad sound would not be absent long,
And old Damoetas loved to hear our song.

But, oh! the heavy change, now thou art gone,
Now thou art gone and never must return!
Thee, Shepherd, thee the woods and desert caves,
With wild thyme and the gadding vine o'ergrown,
And all their echoes mourn.
The willows and the hazel copses green
Shall now no more be seen
Fanning their joyous leaves to thy soft lays.
As killing as the canker to the rose,
Or taint-worm to the weanling herds that graze,
Or frost to flowers, that their gay wardrobe wear,
When first the whitethorn blows;
Such, Lycidas, thy loss to shepherd's ear.

Where were ye, Nymphs, when the remorseless deep
Closed o'er the head of your loved Lycidas?
For neither were ye playing on the steep,
Where your old bards, the famous Druids, lie,
Nor on the shaggy top of Mona high,
Nor yet where Deva spreads her wizard stream.
Ay me! I fondly dream,
Had ye been there! . . . for what could that have done?
What could the Muse herself that Orpheus bore,
The Muse herself, for her enchanting son,
Whom universal nature did lament,
When, by the rout that made the hideous roar,
His gory visage down the stream was sent,
Down the swift Hebrus to the Lesbian shore?

Alas! what boots it with uncessant care
To tend the homely, slighted, shepherd's trade,
And strictly meditate the thankless Muse?
Were it not better done, as others use,
To sport with Amaryllis in the shade,
Or with the tangles of Neaera's hair?
Fame is the spur that the clear spirit doth raise
(That last infirmity of noble mind)
To scorn delights and live laborious days;
But the fair guerdon when we hope to find,

And think to burst out into sudden blaze,
Comes the blind Fury with th' abhorrèd shears,
And slits the thin-spun life. 'But not the praise,'
Phoebus replied, and touched my trembling ears:
'Fame is no plant that grows on mortal soil,
Nor in the glistering foil
Set off to the world, nor in broad rumour lies,
But lives and spreads aloft by those pure eyes
And perfect witness of all-judging Jove;
As he pronounces lastly on each deed,
Of so much fame in heaven expect thy meed.'

   O fountain Arethuse, and thou honoured flood,
Smooth-sliding Mincius, crowned with vocal reeds,
That strain I heard was of a higher mood.
But now my oat proceeds,
And listens to the herald of the sea,
That came in Neptune's plea.
He asked the waves, and asked the felon winds,
What hard mishap hath doomed this gentle swain?
And questioned every gust of rugged wings
That blows from off each beakèd promontory.
They knew not of his story;
And sage Hippotades their answer brings,
That not a blast was from his dungeon strayed;
The air was calm, and on the level brine
Sleek Panope with all her sisters played.
It was that fatal and perfidious bark,
Built in the eclipse, and rigged with curses dark,
That sunk so low that sacred head of thine.

   Next, Camus, reverend sire, went footing slow,
His mantle hairy, and his bonnet sedge,
Inwrought with figures dim, and on the edge
Like to that sanguine flower inscribed with woe.
'Ah! who hath reft', quoth he, 'my dearest pledge?'
Last came, and last did go,
The Pilot of the Galilean lake;
Two massy keys he bore of metals twain
(The golden opes, the iron shuts amain).
He shook his mitred locks, and stern bespake:

'How well could I have spared for thee, young swain,
Enow of such as for their bellies' sake
Creep, and intrude, and climb into the fold!
Of other care they little reck'ning make
Than how to scramble at the shearers' feast,
And shove away the worthy bidden guest.
Blind mouths! that scarce themselves know how to hold
A sheep-hook, or have learnt aught else the least
That to the faithful herdman's art belongs!
What recks it them? What need they? They are sped;
And, when they list, their lean and flashy songs
Grate on their scrannel pipes of wretched straw;
The hungry sheep look up, and are not fed,
But, swoll'n with wind, and the rank mist they draw,
Rot inwardly, and foul contagion spread;
Besides what the grim wolf with privy paw
Daily devours apace, and nothing said;
But that two-handed engine at the door
Stands ready to smite once, and smite no more.'
  Return, Alpheus; the dread voice is past
That shrunk thy streams; return, Sicilian Muse,
And call the vales, and bid them hither cast
Their bells and flowerets of a thousand hues.
Ye valleys low, where the mild whispers use
Of shades, and wanton winds, and gushing brooks,
On whose fresh lap the swart star sparely looks,
Throw hither all your quaint enamelled eyes,
That on the green turf suck the honeyed showers,
And purple all the ground with vernal flowers.
Bring the rathe primrose that forsaken dies,
The tufted crow-toe, and pale jessamine,
The white pink, and the pansy freaked with jet,
The glowing violet,
The musk-rose, and the well-attired woodbine,
With cowslips wan that hang the pensive head,
And every flower that sad embroidery wears;
Bid amaranthus all his beauty shed,
And daffodillies fill their cups with tears,
To strew the laureate hearse where Lycid lies.

For so, to interpose a little ease,
Let our frail thoughts dally with false surmise.
Ay me! whilst thee the shores and sounding seas
Wash far away, where'er thy bones are hurled;
Whether beyond the stormy Hebrides,
Where thou perhaps under the whelming tide
Visit'st the bottom of the monstrous world;
Or whether thou, to our moist vows denied,
Sleep'st by the fable of Bellerus old,
Where the great vision of the guarded mount
Looks towards Namancos and Bayona's hold.
Look homeward, Angel, now, and melt with ruth:
And, O ye dolphins, waft the hapless youth.

Weep no more, woeful shepherds, weep no more,
For Lycidas, your sorrow, is not dead,
Sunk though he be beneath the wat'ry floor.
So sinks the day-star in the ocean bed,
And yet anon repairs his drooping head,
And tricks his beams, and with new-spangled ore
Flames in the forehead of the morning sky:
So Lycidas sunk low, but mounted high,
Through the dear might of Him that walked the waves,
Where, other groves and other streams along,
With nectar pure his oozy locks he laves,
And hears the unexpressive nuptial song,
In the blest kingdoms meek of joy and love.
There entertain him all the saints above,
In solemn troops, and sweet societies,
That sing, and singing in their glory move,
And wipe the tears for ever from his eyes.
Now, Lycidas, the shepherds weep no more;
Henceforth thou art the Genius of the shore,
In thy large recompense, and shalt be good
To all that wander in that perilous flood.

Thus sang the uncouth swain to the oaks and rills,
While the still morn went out with sandals grey;
He touched the tender stops of various quills,
With eager thought warbling his Doric lay.

And now the sun had stretched out all the hills,
And now was dropped into the western bay.
At last he rose, and twitched his mantle blue:
Tomorrow to fresh woods, and pastures new.

[ON HIS BLINDNESS]

WHEN I consider how my light is spent
　Ere half my days in this dark world and wide,
　And that one talent which is death to hide
Lodged with me useless, though my soul more bent
To serve therewith my Maker, and present
　My true account, lest He returning chide,
　'Doth God exact day-labour, light denied?'
I fondly ask. But Patience, to prevent
That murmur, soon replies, 'God doth not need
　Either man's work or his own gifts. Who best
　Bear His mild yoke, they serve Him best. His state
Is kingly: thousands at His bidding speed,
　And post o'er land and ocean without rest;
　They also serve who only stand and wait.'

[ON HIS LATE WIFE]

METHOUGHT I saw my late espousèd saint
　Brought to me like Alcestis from the grave,
　Whom Jove's great son to her glad husband gave,
Rescued from Death by force, though pale and faint.
Mine, as whom washed from spot of child-bed taint
　Purification in the Old Law did save,
　And such as yet once more I trust to have
Full sight of her in Heaven without restraint,
Came vested all in white, pure as her mind.
　Her face was veiled; yet to my fancied sight
　Love, sweetness, goodness, in her person shined
So clear as in no face with more delight.
　But, oh! as to embrace me she inclined,
　I waked, she fled, and day brought back my night.

From COMUS

THE STAR that bids the shepherd fold
Now the top of heaven doth hold;
And the gilded car of day
His glowing axle doth allay
In the steep Atlantic stream;
And the slope sun his upward beam
Shoots against the dusky pole,
Pacing toward the other goal
Of his chamber in the east.
Meanwhile, welcome joy and feast,
Midnight shout and revelry,
Tipsy dance and jollity.
Braid your locks with rosy twine,
Dropping odours, dropping wine.
Rigour now is gone to bed;
And Advice with scrupulous head,
Strict Age, and sour Severity,
With their grave saws, in slumber lie.
We, that are of purer fire,
Imitate the starry quire,
Who, in their nightly watchful spheres,
Lead in swift round the months and years.
The sounds and seas, with all their finny drove,
Now to the moon in wavering morris move;
And on the tawny sands and shelves
Trip the pert fairies and the dapper elves.
By dimpled brook and fountain-brim,
The wood-nymphs, decked with daisies trim,
Their merry wakes and pastimes keep:
What hath night to do with sleep?
Night hath better sweets to prove;
Venus now wakes, and wakens Love.
Come, let us our rites begin;
'Tis only daylight that makes sin,
Which these dun shades will ne'er report.
Hail, goddess of nocturnal sport,
Dark-veiled Cotytto, to whom the secret flame

Of midnight torches burns! mysterious dame,
That ne'er art called but when the dragon womb
Of Stygian darkness spets her thickest gloom,
And makes one blot of all the air!
Stay thy cloudy ebon chair,
Wherein thou rid'st with Hecat, and befriend
Us thy vowed priests, till utmost end
Of all thy dues be done, and none left out,
Ere the blabbing eastern scout,
The nice Morn on th' Indian steep,
From her cabined loophole peep,
And to the telltale Sun descry
Our concealed solemnity.
Come, knit hands, and beat the ground
In a light fantastic round.

From PARADISE LOST

[THE ARGUMENT]

OF MAN'S first disobedience, and the fruit
Of that forbidden tree whose mortal taste
Brought death into the world, and all our woe,
With loss of Eden, till one greater Man
Restore us, and regain the blissful seat,
Sing, Heavenly Muse, that on the secret top
Of Oreb, or of Sinai, did'st inspire
That shepherd who first taught the chosen seed
In the beginning how the heavens and earth
Rose out of chaos; or, if Sion hill
Delight thee more, and Siloa's brook that flowed
Fast by the oracle of God, I thence
Invoke thy aid to my advent'rous song
That with no middle flight intends to soar
Above th' Aonian mount, while it pursues
Things unattempted yet in prose or rhyme.
And chiefly Thou, O Spirit, that dost prefer
Before all temples the upright heart and pure,
Instruct me, for Thou know'st; Thou from the first

Wast present, and, with mighty wings outspread,
Dove-like sat'st brooding on the vast abyss,
And mad'st it pregnant: what in me is dark
Illumine, what is low raise and support;
That to the height of this great argument
I may assert eternal Providence,
And justify the ways of God to men.

   Say first – for Heaven hides nothing from thy view,
Nor the deep tract of Hell – say first what cause
Moved our grand Parents, in that happy state,
Favoured of Heaven so highly, to fall off
From their Creator, and transgress His will
For one restraint, lords of the world besides.
Who first seduced them to that foul revolt?

   The infernal Serpent; he it was whose guile,
Stirred up with envy and revenge, deceived
The mother of mankind; what time his pride
Had cast him out from Heaven, with all his host
Of rebel Angels; by whose aid, aspiring
To set himself in glory above his peers,
He trusted to have equalled the Most High,
If he opposed; and, with ambitious aim
Against the throne and monarchy of God,
Raised impious war in Heaven and battle proud,
With vain attempt. Him the Almighty Power
Hurled headlong flaming from th' ethereal sky,
With hideous ruin and combustion, down
To bottomless perdition, there to dwell
In adamantine chains and penal fire,
Who durst defy the Omnipotent to arms.

   Nine times the space that measures day and night
To mortal men, he, with his horrid crew,
Lay vanquished, rolling in the fiery gulf,
Confounded, though immortal. But his doom
Reserved him to more wrath; for now the thought
Both of lost happiness and lasting pain
Torments him: round he throws his baleful eyes,
That witnessed huge affliction and dismay,
Mixed with obdurate pride and steadfast hate.

At once, as far as angels' ken, he views
The dismal situation waste and wild.
A dungeon horrible, on all sides round,
As one great furnace flamed; yet from those flames
No light; but rather darkness visible
Served only to discover sights of woe,
Regions of sorrow, doleful shades, where peace
And rest can never dwell; hope never comes
That comes to all; but torture without end
Still urges, and a fiery deluge, fed
With ever-burning sulphur unconsumed.
　　Such place eternal justice had prepared
For those rebellious; here their prison ordained
In utter darkness, and their portion set,
As far removed from God and light of Heaven
As from the centre thrice to th' utmost pole.
Oh, how unlike the place from whence they fell!

[A HYMN TO LIGHT]

HAIL, holy Light, offspring of Heaven first-born!
Or of th' Eternal coeternal beam
May I express thee unblamed? since God is light,
And never but in unapproachèd light
Dwelt from eternity – dwelt then in thee,
Bright effluence of bright essence increate!
Or hear'st thou rather pure ethereal stream,
Whose fountain who shall tell? Before the Sun,
Before the Heavens, thou wert, and at the voice
Of God, as with a mantle, did'st invest
The rising world of waters dark and deep,
Won from the void and formless Infinite!
Thee I revisit now with bolder wing,
Escaped the Stygian Pool, though long detained
In that obscure sojourn, while in my flight,
Through utter and through middle darkness borne,
With other notes than to th' Orphean lyre
I sung of Chaos and eternal Night,

Taught by the Heavenly Muse to venture down
The dark descent, and up to re-ascend,
Though hard and rare. Thee I revisit safe,
And feel thy sovran vital lamp; but thou
Revisit'st not these eyes, that roll in vain
To find thy piercing ray, and find no dawn;
So thick a drop serene hath quenched their orbs,
Or dim suffusion veiled. Yet not the more
Cease I to wander where the Muses haunt
Clear spring, or shady grove, or sunny hill,
Smit with the love of sacred song; but chief
Thee, Sion, and the flowery brooks beneath,
That wash thy hallowed feet, and warbling flow,
Nightly I visit; nor sometimes forget
Those other two equalled with me in fate,
So were I equalled with them in renown,
Blind Thamyris and blind Maeonides,
And Tiresias and Phineas, prophets old.
Then feed on thoughts that voluntary move
Harmonious numbers; as the wakeful bird
Sings darkling, and, in shadiest covert hid,
Tunes her nocturnal note. Thus with the year
Seasons return; but not to me returns
Day, or the sweet approach of even or morn
Or sight of vernal bloom, or summer's rose,
Or flocks, or herds, or human face divine;
But cloud instead and ever-during dark
Surrounds me, from the cheerful ways of men
Cut off, and, for the book of knowledge fair,
Presented with a universal blank
Of Nature's works, to me expunged and rased,
And wisdom at one entrance quite shut out.
So much the rather thou, Celestial Light,
Shine inward, and the mind through all her powers
Irradiate; there plant eyes; all mist from thence
Purge and disperse, that I may see and tell
Of things invisible to mortal sight.

[EDEN]

EDEN stretched her line
From Auran eastward to the royal towers
Of great Seleucia, built by the Grecian kings,
Or where the sons of Eden long before
Dwelt in Telassar. In this pleasant soil
His far more pleasant garden God ordained.
Out of the fertile ground he caused to grow
All trees of noblest kind for sight, smell, taste;
And all amid them stood the Tree of Life,
High eminent, blooming ambrosial fruit
Of vegetable gold; and next to life,
Our death, the Tree of Knowledge, grew fast by –
Knowledge of good, bought dear by knowing ill.
Southward through Eden went a river large,
Nor changed his course, but through the shaggy hill
Passed underneath ingulfed; for God had thrown
That mountain, as his garden-mould, high raised
Upon the rapid current, which, through veins
Of porous earth with kindly thirst up-drawn,
Rose a fresh fountain, and with many a rill
Watered the garden; thence united fell
Down the steep glade, and met the nether flood,
Which from his darksome passage now appears,
And now, divided into four main streams,
Runs diverse, wandering many a famous realm
And country whereof here needs no account;
But rather to tell how, if Art could tell
How, from that sapphire fount the crispèd brooks,
Rolling on orient pearl and sands of gold,
With mazy error under pendent shades,
Ran nectar, visiting each plant, and fed
Flowers worthy of Paradise, which not nice Art
In beds and curious knots, but Nature boon
Poured forth profuse on hill, and dale, and plain,
Both where the morning sun first warmly smote
The open field, and where th' unpiercèd shade
Imbrowned the noontide bowers. Thus was this place,

A happy rural seat of various view:
Groves whose rich trees wept odorous gums and balm;
Others whose fruit, burnished with golden rind,
Hung amiable – Hesperian fables true,
If true, here only – and of delicious taste.
Betwixt them lawns, or level downs, and flocks
Grazing the tender herb, were interposed,
Or palmy hillock; or the flowery lap
Of some irriguous valley spread her store,
Flowers of all hue, and without thorn the rose.
Another side, umbrageous grots and caves
Of cool recess, o'er which the mantling vine
Lays forth her purple grape, and gently creeps
Luxuriant; meanwhile murmuring waters fall
Down the slope hills dispersed, or in a lake,
That to the fringèd bank with myrtle crowned
Her crystal mirror holds, unite their streams.
The birds their quire apply; airs, vernal airs,
Breathing the smell of field and grove, attune
The trembling leaves, while universal Pan,
Knit with the Graces and the Hours in dance,
Led on th' eternal Spring. Not that fair field
Of Enna, where Proserpin gathering flowers,
Herself a fairer flower, by gloomy Dis
Was gathered – which cost Ceres all that pain
To seek her through the world – nor that sweet grove
Of Daphne, by Orontes and th' inspired
Castalian spring, might with this Paradise
Of Eden strive; nor that Nyseian isle,
Girt with the river Triton, where old Cham,
Whom Gentiles Ammon call and Libyan Jove,
Hid Amalthea, and her florid son,
Young Bacchus, from his stepdame Rhea's eye;
Nor, where Abassin kings their issue guard,
Mount Amara (though this by some supposed
True Paradise) under th' Ethiop line
By Nilus' head, enclosed with shining rock,
A whole day's journey high, but wide remote
From this Assyrian garden, where the Fiend

Saw undelighted all delight, all kind
Of living creatures, new to sight and strange.
Two of far nobler shape, erect and tall,
God-like erect, with native honour clad
In naked majesty, seemed lords of all,
And worthy seemed; for in their looks divine
The image of their glorious Maker shone,
Truth, wisdom, sanctitude severe and pure –
Severe, but in true filial freedom placed,
Whence true authority in men: though both
Not equal, as their sex not equal seemed;
For contemplation he and valour formed,
For softness she and sweet attractive grace:
He for God only, she for God in him.
His fair large front and eye sublime declared
Absolute rule; and hyacinthine locks
Round from his parted forelock manly hung
Clustering, but not beneath his shoulders broad:
She, as a veil down to the slender waist,
Her unadornèd golden tresses wore
Dishevelled, but in wanton ringlets waved
As the vine curls her tendrils – which implied
Subjection, but required with gentle sway,
And by her yielded, by him best received
Yielded, with coy submission, modest pride,
And sweet, reluctant, amorous delay.
Nor those mysterious parts were then concealed;
Then was not guilty shame. Dishonest shame
Of Nature's works, honour dishonourable,
Sin-bred, how have ye troubled all mankind
With shows instead, mere shows of seeming pure,
And banished from man's life his happiest life,
Simplicity and spotless innocence!
So passed they naked on, nor shunned the sight
Of God or Angel; for they thought no ill:
So hand in hand they passed, the loveliest pair
That ever since in love's embraces met –
Adam the goodliest man of men since born
His sons; the fairest of her daughters Eve.

Under a tuft of shade that on a green
Stood whispering soft, by a fresh fountain-side,
They sat them down; and, after no more toil
Of their sweet gardening labour than sufficed
To recommend cool Zephyr, and made ease
More easy, wholesome thirst and appetite
More grateful, to their supper-fruits they fell –
Nectarine fruits, which the compliant boughs
Yielded them, sidelong as they sat recline
On the soft downy bank damasked with flowers.
The savoury pulp they chew, and in the rind,
Still as they thirsted, scoop the brimming stream;
Nor gentle purpose, nor endearing smiles
Wanted, nor youthful dalliance, as beseems
Fair couple linked in happy nuptial league,
Alone as they. About them frisking played
All beasts of th' earth, since wild, and of all chase
In wood or wilderness, forest or den.
Sporting the lion ramped, and in his paw
Dandled the kid; bears, tigers, ounces, pards,
Gambolled before them; th' unwieldy elephant,
To make them mirth, used all his might, and wreathed
His lithe proboscis; close the serpent sly,
Insinuating, wove with Gordian twine
His braided train, and of his fatal guile
Gave proof unheeded. Others on the grass
Couched, and, now filled with pasture, gazing sat,
Or bedward ruminating; for the sun,
Declined, was hasting now with prone career
To th' Ocean Isles, and in th' ascending scale
Of Heaven the stars that usher evening rose. . . .

From SAMSON AGONISTES

Oh, how comely it is, and how reviving
To the spirits of just men long oppressed,
When God into the hands of their deliverer
Puts invincible might,

To quell the mighty of the earth, the oppressor,
The brute and boisterous force of violent men,
Hardy and industrious to support
Tyrannic power, but raging to pursue
The righteous, and all such as honour truth!
He all their ammunition
And feats of war defeats,
With plain heroic magnitude of mind
And celestial vigour armed;
Their armouries and magazines contemns,
Renders them useless, while
With wingèd expedition
Swift as the lightning glance he executes
His errand on the wicked, who, surprised,
Lose their defence, distracted and amazed.

ALL is best, though oft we doubt
What the unsearchable dispose
Of Highest Wisdom brings about,
And ever best found in the close.
Oft He seems to hide His face,
But unexpectedly returns,
And to His faithful champion hath in place
Bore witness gloriously; whence Gaza mourns,
And all that band them to resist
His uncontrollable intent.
His servants He, with new acquist
Of true experience from this great event,
With peace and consolation hath dismissed,
And calm of mind, all passion spent.

SIR JOHN SUCKLING

OUT upon it, I have loved
  Three whole days together!
And am like to love three more,
  If it hold fair weather.

Time shall moult away his wings
 Ere he shall discover
In the whole wide world again
 Such a constant lover.

But a pox upon 't, no praise
 There is due at all to me:
Love with me had made no stay,
 Had it any been but she.

Had it any been but she,
 And that very very face,
There had been at least ere this
 A dozen dozen in her place.

Why so pale and wan, fond lover?
 Prithee, why so pale?
Will, when looking well can't move her,
 Looking ill prevail?
 Prithee, why so pale?

Why so dull and mute, young sinner?
 Prithee, why so mute?
Will, when speaking well can't win her,
 Saying nothing do 't?
 Prithee, why so mute?

Quit, quit for shame! This will not move;
 This cannot take her.
If of herself she will not love,
 Nothing can make her:
 The devil take her!

SAMUEL BUTLER

From HUDIBRAS

FOR his religion it was fit
To match his learning and his wit:
'Twas Presbyterian true blue,
For he was of that stubborn crew
Of errant Saints, whom all men grant
To be the true Church Militant:
Such as do build their faith upon
The holy text of pike and gun;
Decide all controversies by
Infallible artillery;
And prove their doctrine orthodox
By Apostolic blows and knocks;
Call fire and sword and desolation
A godly-thorough-Reformation,
Which always must be carried on,
And still be doing, never done:
As if religion were intended
For nothing else but to be mended.
A sect whose chief devotion lies
In odd perverse antipathies;
In falling out with that or this,
And finding somewhat still amiss:
More peevish, cross, and splenetic
Than dog distract, or monkey sick;
That with more care keep holiday
The wrong, than others the right way;
Compound for sins they are inclined to,
By damning those they have no mind to;
Still so perverse and opposite,
As if they worshipped God for spite.
The self-same thing they will abhor
One way, and long another for.
Free Will they one way disavow,
Another, nothing else allow.
All piety consists therein

In them, in other men all sin.
Rather than fail, they will defy
That which they love most tenderly,
Quarrel with minced pies, and disparage
Their best and dearest friend, plum porridge;
Fat pig and goose itself oppose,
And blaspheme custard through the nose.
Th' Apostles of this fierce religion,
Like Mahomet's, were ass and widgeon,
To whom our Knight, by fast instinct
Of wit and temper was so linked
As if hypocrisy and nonsense
Had got th' advowson of his conscience.

RICHARD CRASHAW

A HYMN TO THE NAME AND HONOUR
OF THE ADMIRABLE ST TERESA

LOVE, thou art absolute sole lord
Of life and death. To prove the word,
We'll now appeal to none of all
Those thy old soldiers, great and tall,
Ripe men of martyrdom, that could reach down
With strong arms their triumphant crown;
Such as could with lusty breath
Speak loud into the face of death
Their great Lord's glorious name; to none
Of those whose spacious bosoms spread a throne
For love at large to fill. Spare blood and sweat,
And see him take a private seat,
Making his mansion in the mild
And milky soul of a soft child.
   Scarce has she learnt to lisp the name
Of martyr; yet she thinks it shame
Life should so long play with that breath
Which spent can buy so brave a death.

She never undertook to know
What death with love should have to do;
Nor has she e'er yet understood
Why to show love she should shed blood.
Yet though she cannot tell you why,
She can love, and she can die.

Scarce has she blood enough to make
A guilty sword blush for her sake;
Yet has she a heart dares hope to prove
How much less strong is death than love.

Be love but there, let poor six years
Be posed with the maturest fears
Man trembles at, you straight shall find
Love knows no nonage, nor the mind.
'Tis love, not years or limbs, that can
Make the martyr, or the man.

Love touched her heart, and lo! it beats
High, and burns with such brave heats;
Such thirsts to die, as dares drink up,
A thousand cold deaths in one cup.
Good reason. For she breathes all fire.
Her weak breast heaves with strong desire
Of what she may with fruitless wishes
Seek for amongst her mother's kisses.

Since 'tis not to be had at home
She'll travel to a martyrdom.
No home for hers confesses she
But where she may a martyr be.

She'll to the Moors and trade with them
For this unvalued diadem;
She'll offer them her dearest breath,
With Christ's name in 't, in change for death.
She'll bargain with them, and will give
Them God, and teach them how to live
In Him; or, if they this deny,
For Him she'll teach them how to die.
So shall she leave amongst them sown
Her Lord's blood; or at least her own.

Farewell then, all the world! Adieu!

Teresa is no more for you.
Farewell, all pleasures, sports, and joys
(Never till now esteemèd toys);
Farewell, whatever dear may be,
Mother's arms or father's knee!
Farewell, house, and farewell, home!
She's for the Moors, and martyrdom.

   Sweet, not so fast! Lo! thy fair Spouse
Whom thou seek'st with so swift vows,
Calls thee back, and bids thee come
T' embrace a milder martyrdom.

   Blest powers forbid thy tender life
Should bleed upon a barbarous knife;
Or some base hand have power to rase
Thy breast's chaste cabinet, and uncase
A soul kept there so sweet. Oh no;
Wise heav'n will never have it so.
Thou art love's victim; and must die
A death more mystical and high.
Into love's arms thou shalt let fall
A still-surviving funeral.
His is the dart must make the death
Whose stroke shall taste thy hallowed breath;
A dart thrice dipped in that rich flame
Which writes thy Spouse's radiant Name
Upon the roof of heav'n; where ay
It shines, and with a sovereign ray
Beats bright upon the burning faces
Of souls which in that name's sweet graces
Find everlasting smiles. So rare,
So spiritual, pure, and fair
Must be th' immortal instrument
Upon whose choice point shall be sent
A life so loved; and that there be
Fit executioners for thee,
The fair'st and first-born sons of fire,
Blest Seraphim, shall leave their quire
And turn love's soldiers, upon thee
To exercise their archery.

Oh, how oft shalt thou complain
Of a sweet and subtle pain!
Of intolerable joys!
Of a death, in which who dies
Loves his death, and dies again.
And would for ever so be slain;
And lives, and dies, and knows not why
To live, but that he thus may never leave to die!
How kindly will thy gentle heart
Kiss the sweetly killing dart!
And close in his embraces keep
Those delicious wounds that weep
Balsam to heal themselves with! Thus,
When these thy deaths, so numerous,
Shall all at last die into one,
And melt thy soul's sweet mansion;
Like a soft lump of incense, hasted
By too hot a fire, and wasted
Into perfuming clouds, so fast
Shalt thou exhale to Heav'n at last
In a resolving sigh, and then –
Oh, what? Ask not the tongues of men,
Angels cannot tell. Suffice,
Thyself shall feel thine own full joys
And hold them fast for ever. There
So soon as thou shalt first appear,
The moon of maiden stars, thy white
Mistress, attended by such bright
Souls as thy shining self, shall come
And in her first ranks make thee room;
Where 'mongst her snowy family
Immortal welcomes wait for thee.

Oh, what delight, when revealed life shall stand
And teach thy lips heav'n with his hand;
On which thou now may'st to thy wishes
Heap up thy consecrated kisses.
What joys shall seize thy soul, when she
Bending her blessèd eyes on thee
(Those second smiles of heav'n) shall dart

Her mild rays through thy melting heart!
  Angels, thy old friends, there shall greet thee,
Glad at their own home now to meet thee.
  All thy good works which went before
And waited for thee at the door,
Shall own thee there, and all in one
Weave a constellation
Of crowns, with which the King, thy Spouse,
Shall build up thy triumphant brows.
  All thy old woes shall now smile on thee,
And thy pains sit bright upon thee;
All thy sorrows here shall shine,
All thy suff'rings be divine.
Tears shall take comfort, and turn gems,
And wrongs repent to diadems.
Ev'n thy deaths shall live, and new
Dress the soul that erst they slew.
Thy wounds shall blush to such bright scars
As keep account of the Lamb's wars.
  Those rare works where thou shalt leave writ
Love's noble history, with wit
Taught thee by none but Him, while here
They feed our souls, shall clothe thine there.
Each heav'nly word, by whose hid flame
Our hard hearts shall strike fire, the same
Shall flourish on thy brows, and be
Both fire to us and flame to thee;
Whose light shall live bright in thy face
By glory, in our hearts by grace.
  Thou shalt look round about, and see
Thousands of crowned souls throng to be
Themselves thy crown; sons of thy vows,
The virgin births, with which thy sovereign Spouse
Made fruitful thy fair soul. Go now,
And with them all about thee bow
To Him. 'Put on,' He'll say, 'put on
My rosy Love, that thy rich zone,
Sparkling with the sacred flames
Of thousand souls, whose happy names

Heav'n keeps upon thy score (thy bright
Life brought them first to kiss the light
That kindled them to stars), and so
Thou with the Lamb, thy Lord, shalt go;
And wheresoe'er he sets his white
Steps, walk with Him those ways of light
Which who in death would live to see
Must learn in life to die like thee.'

AN EPITAPH

UPON A YOUNG MARRIED COUPLE
DEAD AND BURIED TOGETHER

TO THESE, whom death again did wed,
This grave's their second marriage-bed.
For though the hand of Fate could force
'Twixt soul and body a divorce,
It could not sunder man and wife,
'Cause they both livèd but one life.
Peace, good reader. Do not weep.
Peace, the lovers are asleep.
They, sweet turtles, folded lie
In the last knot love could tie.
And though they lie as they were dead,
Their pillow stone, their sheets of lead
(Pillow hard, and sheets not warm),
Love made the bed; they'll take no harm.
Let them sleep, let them sleep on,
Till this stormy night be gone,
Till th' eternal morrow dawn;
Then the curtains will be drawn
And they wake into a light
Whose day shall never die in night.

SIR JOHN DENHAM

From COOPER'S HILL

THAMES! the most loved of all the Ocean's sons
By his old sire, to his embraces runs,
Hasting to pay his tribute to the sea,
Like mortal life to meet eternity.
Though with those streams he no resemblance hold,
Whose foam is amber, and their gravel gold;
His genuine and less guilty wealth t' explore,
Search not his bottom, but survey his shore,
O'er which he kindly spreads his spacious wing,
And hatches plenty for th' ensuing spring;
Nor then destroys it with too fond a stay,
Like mothers which their infants overlay;
Nor with a sudden and impetuous wave,
Like profuse kings, resumes the wealth he gave.
No unexpected inundations spoil
The mower's hopes, nor mock the ploughman's toil,
But godlike his unwearied bounty flows;
First loves to do, then loves the good he does.
Nor are his blessings to his banks confined,
But free and common as the sea or wind;
When he, to boast or to disperse his stores,
Full of the tributes of his grateful shores,
Visits the world, and in his flying towers
Brings home to us, and makes both Indies ours;
Finds wealth where 'tis, bestows it where it wants,
Cities in deserts, woods in cities plants.
So that to us no thing, no place is strange,
While his fair bosom is the world's exchange.
Oh, could I flow like thee; and make thy stream
My great example, as it is my theme!
Though deep, yet clear; though gentle, yet not dull;
Strong without rage, without o'erflowing full. . . .

ABRAHAM COWLEY

THE WISH

WELL then! I now do plainly see
This busy world and I shall ne'er agree.
The very honey of all earthly joy
Does of all meats the soonest cloy;
    And they, methinks, deserve my pity
Who for it can endure the stings,
The crowd, and buzz, and murmurings,
    Of this great hive, the city.

Ah, yet, ere I descend to the grave,
May I a small house and large garden have;
And a few friends, and many books, both true,
Both wise, and both delightful too!
    And since Love ne'er will from me flee,
A mistress moderately fair,
And good as guardian angels are,
    Only beloved and loving me.

O fountains! when in you shall I
Myself, eased of unpeaceful thoughts, espy?
O fields! O woods! when, when shall I be made
The happy tenant of your shade?
    Here's the spring-head of Pleasure's flood:
Here's wealthy Nature's treasury,
Where all the riches lie that she
    Has coined and stamped for good.

Pride and ambition here
Only in far-fetched metaphors appear;
Here nought but winds can hurtful murmurs scatter,
And nought but Echo flatter.
    The gods, when they descended, hither
From heaven did always choose their way;
And therefore we may boldly say
    That 'tis the way too thither.

How happy here should I
And one dear She live, and embracing die!
She who is all the world, and can exclude,
In deserts, solitude.
    I should have then this only fear:
Lest men, when they my pleasures see,
Should hither throng to live like me,
    And so make a city here.

RICHARD LOVELACE

TO ALTHEA, FROM PRISON

WHEN Love with unconfinèd wings
    Hovers within my gates,
And my divine Althea brings
    To whisper at the grates;
When I lie tangled in her hair
    And fettered to her eye,
The birds that wanton in the air
    Know no such liberty.

When flowing cups run swiftly round
    With no allaying Thames,
Our careless heads with roses crowned,
    Our hearts with loyal flames;
When thirsty grief in wine we steep,
    When healths and draughts go free,
Fishes that tipple in the deep
    Know no such liberty.

When, linnet-like confinèd, I
    With shriller throat shall sing
The sweetness, mercy, majesty
    And glories of my King;
When I shall voice aloud how good
    He is, how great should be,
Enlargèd winds that curl the flood
    Know no such liberty.

Stone walls do not a prison make,
　　Nor iron bars a cage;
Minds innocent and quiet take
　　That for an hermitage:
If I have freedom in my love
　　And in my soul am free,
Angels alone that soar above
　　Enjoy such liberty.

TO LUCASTA, GOING BEYOND THE SEAS

IF TO BE absent were to be
　　Away from thee;
Or that when I am gone
　　You or I were alone;
Then, my Lucasta, might I crave
Pity from the blustering wind, or swallowing wave.

But I'll not sigh one blast or gale
　　To swell my sail,
Or pay a tear to 'suage
　　The foaming blue-god's rage;
For whether he will let me pass
Or no, I'm still as happy as I was.

Though seas and land betwixt us both,
　　Our faith and troth,
Like separated souls,
　　All time and space controls:
Above the highest sphere we meet
Unseen, unknown, and greet as Angels greet.

So then we do anticipate
　　Our after-fate,
And are alive i' the skies,
　　If thus our lips and eyes
Can speak like spirits unconfined
In Heaven, their earthy bodies left behind.

TO LUCASTA, GOING TO THE WARS

TELL me not, sweet, I am unkind,
    That from the nunnery
Of thy chaste breast and quiet mind
    To war and arms I fly.

True, a new mistress now I chase,
    The first foe in the field;
And with a stronger faith embrace
    A sword, a horse, a shield.

Yet this inconstancy is such
    As you too shall adore;
I could not love thee, dear, so much,
    Loved I not honour more.

ANDREW MARVELL

TO HIS COY MISTRESS

HAD we but world enough, and time,
This coyness, Lady, were no crime.
We would sit down, and think which way
To walk, and pass our long love's day.
Thou by the Indian Ganges' side
Should'st rubies find: I by the tide
Of Humber would complain. I would
Love you ten years before the Flood;
And you should, if you please, refuse
Till the conversion of the Jews.
My vegetable love should grow
Vaster than empires, and more slow;
An hundred years should go to praise
Thine eyes, and on thy forehead gaze;
Two hundred to adore each breast;
But thirty thousand to the rest;
An age at least to every part,
And the last age should show your heart;

For, Lady, you deserve this state,
Nor would I love at lower rate.
   But at my back I always hear
Time's wingèd chariot hurrying near:
And yonder all before us lie
Deserts of vast Eternity.
Thy beauty shall no more be found;
Nor, in thy marble vault, shall sound
My echoing song: then worms shall try
That long-preserved virginity;
And your quaint honour turn to dust,
And into ashes all my lust.
The grave's a fine and private place,
But none, I think, do there embrace.
   Now therefore, while the youthful hue
Sits on thy skin like morning dew,
And while thy willing soul transpires
At every pore with instant fires,
Now let us sport us while we may;
And now, like amorous birds of prey,
Rather at once our time devour,
Than languish in his slow-chapped power.
Let us roll all our strength, and all
Our sweetness, up into one ball;
And tear our pleasures with rough strife
Thorough the iron gates of life.
Thus, though we cannot make our sun
Stand still, yet we will make him run.

THE GARDEN

How vainly men themselves amaze
To win the palm, the oak, or bays;
And their uncessant labours see
Crowned from some single herb or tree,
Whose short and narrow-vergèd shade
Does prudently their toils upbraid;
While all flowers and all trees do close
To weave the garlands of repose.

Fair Quiet, have I found thee here,
And Innocence, thy sister dear?
Mistaken long, I sought you then
In busy companies of men.
Your sacred plants, if here below,
Only among the plants will grow.
Society is all but rude,
To this delicious solitude.

No white nor red was ever seen
So amorous as this lovely green.
Fond lovers, cruel as their flame,
Cut in these trees their mistress' name.
Little, alas, they know, or heed,
How far these beauties hers exceed!
Fair trees! wheresoe'er your barks I wound,
No name shall but your own be found.

When we have run our passion's heat,
Love hither makes his best retreat.
The gods, that mortal beauty chase,
Still in a tree did end their race:
Apollo hunted Daphne so,
Only that she might laurel grow;
And Pan did after Syrinx speed,
Not as a nymph, but for a reed.

What wondrous life is this I lead!
Ripe apples drop about my head;
The luscious clusters of the vine
Upon my mouth do crush their wine;
The nectarine and curious peach
Into my hands themselves do reach;
Stumbling on melons, as I pass,
Ensnared with flowers, I fall on grass.

Meanwhile the mind, from pleasure less,
Withdraws into its happiness:
The mind, that ocean where each kind
Does straight its own resemblance find;

Yet it creates, transcending these,
Far other worlds, and other seas;
Annihilating all that's made
To a green thought in a green shade.

Here at the fountain's sliding foot,
Or at some fruit-tree's mossy root,
Casting the body's vest aside,
My soul into the boughs does glide;
There, like a bird, it sits and sings,
Then whets and combs its silver wings;
And, till prepared for longer flight,
Waves in its plumes the various light.

Such was the happy Garden-state,
While Man there walked without a mate:
After a place so pure and sweet,
What other help could yet be meet!
But 'twas beyond a mortal's share
To wander solitary there:
Two paradises 'twere in one
To live in Paradise alone.

How well the skilful gardener drew
Of flowers and herbs this dial new!
Where, from above, the milder sun
Does through a fragrant zodiac run;
And, as it works, the industrious bee
Computes its time as well as we.
How could such sweet and wholesome hours
Be reckoned, but with herbs and flowers!

AN HORATIAN ODE UPON
CROMWELL'S RETURN FROM IRELAND

THE forward youth that would appear
Must now forsake his Muses dear,
    Nor in the shadows sing
    His numbers languishing.

'Tis time to leave the books in dust,
And oil th' unusèd armour's rust,
  Removing from the wall
  The corselet of the hall.

So restless Cromwell could not cease
In th' inglorious arts of peace,
  But through advent'rous war
  Urged his active star;

And, like the three-forked lightning, first
Breaking the clouds where it was nursed,
  Did thorough his own side
  His fiery way divide;

For 'tis all one to courage high,
The emulous or enemy;
  And, with such, to enclose
  Is more than to oppose.

Then burning through the air he went,
And palaces and temples rent;
  And Caesar's head at last
  Did through his laurels blast.

'Tis madness to resist or blame
The force of angry heaven's flame;
  And, if we would speak true,
  Much to the man is due,

Who, from his private gardens, where
He lived reservèd and austere,
  As if his highest plot
  To plant the bergamot,

Could by industrious valour climb
To ruin the great work of Time,
  And cast the kingdom old
  Into another mould.

Though Justice against Fate complain,
And plead the ancient rights in vain
 (But those do hold or break
 As men are strong or weak),

Nature, that hateth emptiness,
Allows of penetration less,
 And therefore must make room
 Where greater spirits come.

What field of all the Civil Wars,
Where his were not the deepest scars?
 And Hampton shows what part
 He had of wiser art;

Where, twining subtle fears with hope,
He wove a net of such a scope
 That Charles himself might chase
 To Carisbrooke's narrow case;

That thence the royal actor borne
The tragic scaffold might adorn,
 While round the armèd bands
 Did clap their bloody hands.

He nothing common did or mean
Upon that memorable scene,
 But with his keener eye
 The axe's edge did try;

Nor called the Gods, with vulgar spite,
To vindicate his helpless right,
 But bowed his comely head
 Down, as upon a bed.

This was that memorable hour
Which first assured the forcèd power:
 So when they did design
 The Capitol's first line,

A bleeding head, where they begun,
Did fright the architects to run;
   And yet in that the State
   Foresaw its happy fate.

And now the Irish are ashamed
To see themselves in one year tamed:
   So much one man can do,
   That does both act and know.

They can affirm his praises best,
And have, though overcome, confessed
   How good he is, how just,
   And fit for highest trust;

Nor yet grown stiffer with command,
But still in the Republic's hand:
   How fit he is to sway
   That can so well obey!

He to the Commons' feet presents
A kingdom for his first year's rents;
   And, what he may, forbears
   His fame to make it theirs;

And has his sword and spoils ungirt,
To lay them at the public's skirt.
   So when the falcon high
   Falls heavy from the sky,

She, having killed, no more does search,
But on the next green bough to perch;
   Where, when he first does lure,
   The falconer has her sure.

What may not then our Isle presume
While victory his crest does plume!
   What may not others fear,
   If thus he crowns each year!

A Caesar he, ere long, to Gaul,
To Italy an Hannibal,
    And to all states not free
    Shall climacteric be.

The Pict no shelter now shall find
Within his particoloured mind,
    But from this valour sad
    Shrink underneath the plaid;

Happy if in the tufted brake
The English hunter him mistake,
    Nor lay his hounds in near
    The Caledonian deer.

But thou, the War's and Fortune's son,
March indefatigably on;
    And for the last effect
    Still keep the sword erect:

Besides the force it has to fright
The spirits of the shady night,
    The same arts that did gain
    A power must it maintain.

HENRY VAUGHAN

THE RETREAT

HAPPY those early days, when I
Shined in my angel-infancy!
Before I understood this place
Appointed for my second race,
Or taught my soul to fancy aught
But a white celestial thought;
When yet I had not walked above
A mile or two from my first love,
And looking back, at that short space,
Could see a glimpse of his bright face;

When on some gilded cloud, or flower,
My gazing soul would dwell an hour,
And in those weaker glories spy
Some shadows of eternity;
Before I taught my tongue to wound
My conscience with a sinful sound,
Or had the black art to dispense
A several sin to every sense,
But felt through all this fleshly dress
Bright shoots of everlastingness.

Oh, how I long to travel back,
And tread again that ancient track!
That I might once more reach that plain
Where first I left my glorious train;
From whence the enlightened spirit sees
That shady City of Palm-trees.
But ah! my soul with too much stay
Is drunk, and staggers in the way.
Some men a forward motion love,
But I by backward steps would move,
And when this dust falls to the urn
In that state I came, return.

THEY are all gone into the world of light!
    And I alone sit lingering here;
Their very memory is fair and bright,
    And my sad thoughts doth clear.

It glows and glitters in my cloudy breast
    Like stars upon some gloomy grove,
Or those faint beams in which this hill is dressed,
    After the sun's remove.

I see them walking in an air of glory,
    Whose light doth trample on my days:
My days, which are at best but dull and hoary,
    Mere glimmering and decays.

O holy Hope! and high Humility,
　　High as the heavens above!
These are your walks, and you have showed them me,
　　To kindle my cold love.

Dear beauteous Death! the jewel of the Just,
　　Shining nowhere but in the dark;
What mysteries do lie beyond thy dust,
　　Could man outlook that mark!

He that hath found some fledged bird's nest may know,
　　At first sight, if the bird be flown;
But what fair well or grove he sings in now,
　　That is to him unknown.

And yet, as angels in some brighter dreams
　　Call to the soul, when man doth sleep;
So some strange thoughts transcend our wonted themes,
　　And into glory peep.

If a star were confined into a tomb,
　　Her captive flames must needs burn there;
But when the hand that locked her up gives room,
　　She'll shine through all the sphere.

O Father of eternal life, and all
　　Created glories under thee!
Resume thy spirit from this world of thrall
　　Into true liberty.

Either disperse these mists, which blot and fill
　　My perspective still as they pass,
Or else remove Thee hence unto that hill,
　　Where I shall need no glass.

THE WORLD

I SAW Eternity the other night
Like a great Ring of pure and endless light,
 All calm as it was bright;
And round beneath it, Time, in hours, days, years,
 Driven by the spheres,
Like a vast shadow moved, in which the world
 And all her train were hurled.
The doting Lover in his quaintest strain
 Did there complain;
Near him, his lute, his fancy, and his flights,
 Wit's sour delights;
With gloves and knots, the silly snares of pleasure;
 Yet his dear treasure
All scattered lay, while he his eyes did pour
 Upon a flower.

The darksome Statesman hung with weights and woe,
Like a thick midnight fog, moved there so slow
 He did nor stay nor go;
Condemning thoughts, like sad eclipses, scowl
 Upon his soul,
And clouds of crying witnesses without
 Pursued him with one shout.
Yet digged the mole, and, lest his ways be found,
 Worked under ground,
Where he did clutch his prey; but One did see
 That policy.
Churches and altars fed him, perjuries
 Were gnats and flies;
It rained about him blood and tears, but he
 Drank them as free.

The fearful Miser on a heap of rust
Sat pining all his life there, did scarce trust
 His own hands with the dust;
Yet would not place one piece above, but lives
 In fear of thieves.

Thousands there were as frantic as himself,
And hugged each one his pelf.
The downright Epicure placed heaven in sense
And scorned pretence;
While others, slipped into a wide excess,
Said little less;
The weaker sort, slight, trivial wares enslave,
Who think them brave;
And poor despisèd Truth sat counting by
Their victory.

Yet some, who all this while did weep and sing,
And sing and weep, soared up into the Ring;
But most would use no wing.
'Oh, fools,' said I, 'thus to prefer dark night
Before true light,
To live in grots, and caves, and hate the day
Because it shows the way,
The way which from this dead and dark abode
Leaps up to God,
A way where you might tread the sun, and be
More bright than he.'
But as I did their madness so discuss,
One whispered thus,
This Ring the Bridegroom did for none provide
But for his Bride.

CHILDHOOD

I CANNOT reach it; and my striving eye
Dazzles at it, as at eternity.

Were now that chronicle alive,
Those white designs which children drive,
And the thoughts of each harmless hour,
With their content too in my pow'r,
Quickly would I make my path even,
And by mere playing go to heaven.

Why should men love
A wolf, more than a lamb or dove?
Or choose hell-fire and brimstone streams
Before bright stars and God's own beams?
Who kisseth thorns will hurt his face,
But flowers do both refresh and grace;
And sweetly living – fie on men! –
Are, when dead, medicinal then;
If seeing much should make staid eyes,
And long experience should make wise;
Since all that age doth teach is ill,
Why should I not love childhood still?
Why, if I see a rock or shelf,
Shall I from thence cast down myself?
Or by complying with the world,
From the same precipice be hurled?
Those observations are but foul,
Which make me wise to lose my soul.

And yet the practice worldlings call
Business, and weighty action all,
Checking the poor child for his play,
But gravely cast themselves away.
Dear, harmless age! the short, swift span
Where weeping Virtue parts with man;
Where love without lust dwells, and bends
What way we please without self-ends.

An age of mysteries! which he
Must live that would God's face see
Which angels guard, and with it play,
Angels! which foul men drive away.

How do I study now, and scan
Thee more than e'er I studied man,
And only see through a long night
Thy edges and thy bordering light!
Oh, for thy centre and midday!
For sure that is the narrow way!

SIR CHARLES SEDLEY

LOVE still has something of the sea,
  From whence his mother rose;
No time his slaves from Doubt can free,
  Nor give their thoughts repose:

They are becalmed in clearest days,
  And in rough weather tossed;
They wither under cold delays,
  Or are in tempests lost.

One while they seem to touch the port,
  Then straight into the main,
Some angry wind in cruel sport
  The vessel drives again.

At first Disdain and Pride they fear,
  Which if they chance to 'scape,
Rivals and Falsehood soon appear
  In a more dreadful shape.

By such degrees to Joy they come,
  And are so long withstood,
So slowly they receive the sum,
  It hardly does them good.

'Tis cruel to prolong a pain,
  And to defer a joy,
Believe me, gentle Celemene,
  Offends the wingèd Boy.

An hundred thousand oaths your fears
  Perhaps would not remove;
And if I gazed a thousand years
  I could no deeper love.

JOHN WILMOT, EARL OF ROCHESTER

A SONG

ABSENT from thee, I languish still;
   Then ask me not, when I return?
The straying fool 'twill plainly kill
   To wish all day, all night to mourn.

Dear! from thine arms then let me fly,
   That my fantastic mind may prove
The torments it deserves to try
   That tears my fixed heart from my love.

When, wearied with a world of woe,
   To thy safe bosom I retire
Where love and peace and truth does flow,
   May I contented there expire,

Lest, once more wandering from that Heaven,
   I fall on some base heart unblest,
Faithless to thee, false, unforgiven,
   And lose my everlasting rest.

LOVE AND LIFE

ALL my past life is mine no more;
   The flying hours are gone,
Like transitory dreams given o'er
Whose images are kept in store
   By memory alone.

Whatever is to come is not:
   How can it then be mine?
The present moment's all my lot,
And that, as fast as it is got,
   Phyllis, is wholly thine.

Then talk not of inconstancy,
　False hearts, and broken vows;
If I, by miracle, can be
This livelong minute true to thee,
　'Tis all that heaven allows.

ANONYMOUS

SIR PATRICK SPENS

THE King sits in Dunfermline town,
　Drinking the blude-red wine;
'O whare will I get a skeely skipper,　　　　　*skilful*
　To sail this new ship of mine?'

O up and spake an eldern knight,　　　　　*old*
　Sat at the King's right knee:
'Sir Patrick Spens is the best sailor,
　That ever sail'd the sea.'

Our King has written a braid letter,
　And seal'd it with his hand,
And sent it to Sir Patrick Spens,
　Was walking on the strand.

'To Noroway, to Noroway,　　　　　*Norway*
　To Noroway o'er the faem;　　　　　*foam*
The King's daughter o' Noroway,
　'Tis thou maun bring her hame.'　　　　　*must: home*

The first word that Sir Patrick read,
　Sae loud loud laugh'd he;　　　　　*So*
The neist word that Sir Patrick read　　　　　*next*
　The tear blinded his e'e.　　　　　*eye*

'O wha is this has done this deed,　　　　　*who*
　And tauld the King o' me,
To send us out, at this time o' year,
　To sail upon the sea?

'Be it wind, be it weet, be it hail, be it sleet,   *wet*
  Our ship must sail the faem;
The King's daughter o' Noroway,
  'Tis we must fetch her hame.'

They hoysed their sails on Monenday morn,
  Wi' a' the speed they may;   *all*
They hae landed in Noroway,
  Upon a Wodensday.

They hadna been a week, a week,
  In Noroway, but twae,   *two*
When that the lords o' Noroway
  Began aloud to say,

'Ye Scottishmen spend a' our King's goud,   *gold*
  And a' our Queenis fee.'   *money*
'Ye lie, ye lie, ye liars loud!
  Fu' loud I hear ye lie.   *Full*

'For I brought as much white monie,   *silver*
  As gane my men and me,
And I brought a half-fou o' gude red goud,
  Out o'er the sea wi' me.

'Make ready, make ready, my merrymen a'!
  Our gude ship sails the morn.'
'Now, ever alake, my master dear,   *alack*
  I fear a deadly storm!

'I saw the new moon, late yestreen,   *yesterday evening*
  Wi' the auld moon in her arm;
And, if we gang to sea, master,   *go*
  I fear we'll come to harm.'

They hadna sail'd a league, a league,
   A league but barely three,
When the lift grew dark, and the wind blew   *sky*
    loud,
    And gurly grew the sea.   *stormy*

The ankers brak, and the topmasts lap,
                   anchors break: leap
   It was sic a deadly storm;   *such*
And the waves cam o'er the broken ship,
   Till a' her sides were torn.

'O where will I get a gude sailor,
   To take my helm in hand,
Till I get up to the tall top-mast,
   To see if I can spy land?'

'O here am I, a sailor gude,
   To take the helm in hand,
Till you go up to the tall top-mast;
   But I fear you'll ne'er spy land.'

He hadna gane a step, a step,
   A step but barely ane,   *one*
When a bout flew out of our goodly ship,   *bolt*
   And the salt sea it came in.

'Gae, fetch a web o' the silken claith,   *cloth*
   Another o' the twine,   *coarse linen*
And wap them into our ship's side,   *bind*
   And let na the sea come in.'   *not*

They fetched a web o' the silken claith,
   Another o' the twine,
And they wapped them round that gude ship's
    side,
   But still the sea came in.

O laith, laith, were our gude Scots lords   *loath*
  To weet their cork-heel'd shoon!
But lang or a' the play was play'd,
  They wat their hats aboon.   *above their hats*

And mony was the feather-bed,   *many*
  That flatter'd on the faem;
And mony was the gude lord's son,
  That never mair cam hame.

The ladyes wrang their fingers white,   *wrung*
  The maidens tore their hair,
A' for the sake of their true loves;
  For them they'll see nae mair.

O lang, lang, may the ladyes sit,
  Wi' their fans into their hand,
Before they see Sir Patrick Spens
  Come sailing to the strand!

And lang, lang, may the maidens sit,
  Wi' their goud kaims in their hair,   *gold combs*
A' waiting for their ain dear loves!   *own*
  For them they'll see nae mair.

Half owre, half owre to Aberdour,   *over: Aberdeen*
  'Tis fifty fathoms deep,
And there lies gude Sir Patrick Spens,
  Wi' the Scots lords at his feet.

FAIR HELEN

I wish I were where Helen lies,
Night and day on me she cries;
O that I were where Helen lies,
  On fair Kirconnell Lea!

Curst be the heart that thought the thought,
And curst the hand that fired the shot,
When in my arms burd Helen dropt,   *buried*
  And died to succour me!

O think na ye my heart was sair,   *not: sore*
When my love dropt down and spak nae mair!
There did she swoon wi' meikle care,   *great*
  On fair Kirconnell Lea.

As I went down the water side,
None but my foe to be my guide,
None but my foe to be my guide,
  On fair Kirconnell Lea;

I lighted down, my sword to draw,
I hackèd him in pieces sma',   *small*
I hackèd him in pieces sma',
  For her sake that died for me.

O Helen fair, beyond compare!
I'll make a garland o' thy hair,
Shall bind my heart for evermair,
  Until the day I die.

O that I were where Helen lies!
Night and day on me she cries;
Out of my bed she bids me rise,
  Says, 'Haste and come to me!'

O Helen fair! O Helen chaste!
If I were with thee, I were blest,
Where thou lies low, and takes thy rest,
  On fair Kirconnell Lea.

I wish my grave were growing green,
A winding sheet drawn owre my een,   *over: eyes*
And I in Helen's arms lying,
  On fair Kirconnell Lea.

I wish I were where Helen lies!
Night and day on me she cries;
And I am weary of the skies,
 For her sake that died for me.

A LYKE-WAKE DIRGE

THIS ae nighte, this ae nighte,
 Every nighte and alle;
Fire and fleet and candle lighte,   *floor*
 And Christe receive thy saule.   *soul*

When thou from hence away are past,
 Every nighte and alle;
To Whinny-muir thou com'st at last;
 And Christe receive thy saule.

If ever thou gavest hosen and shoon,
 Every nighte and alle;
Sit thee down and put them on;
 And Christe receive thy saule.

If hosen and shoon thou ne'er gav'st nane   *none*
 Every nighte and alle;
The whinnes sall prick thee to the bare bane;   *bone*
 And Christe receive thy saule.

From Whinny-muir when thou may'st pass,
 Every nighte and alle;
To Brigg o' Dread thou com'st at last;
 And Christe receive thy saule.

From Brigg o' Dread when thou may'st pass,
 Every nighte and alle;
To Purgatory fire thou com'st at last;
 And Christe receive thy saule.

If ever thou gavest meat or drink,
 Every nighte and alle;
The fire shall never make thee shrink;
 And Christe receive thy saule.

If meat or drink thou ne'er gav'st nane,
 Every nighte and alle;
The fire will burn thee to the bare bane;
 And Christe receive thy saule.

This ae nighte, this ae nighte,
 Every nighte and alle;
Fire and fleet and candle lighte,
 And Christe receive thy saule.

MARIE HAMILTON

WORD's gane to the kitchen,   *gone*
 And word's gane to the ha',   *hall*
That Marie Hamilton gangs wi' bairn, *goes*
 To the hichest Stewart of a'.   *highest*

He's courted her in the kitchen,
 He's courted her in the ha',
He's courted her in the laigh cellar, *low*
 And that was warst of a'!

She's tyed it in her apron,
 And she's thrown it in the sea,
Says, 'Sink ye, swim ye, bonny wee babe,
 You'll ne'er get mair o' me.'

Down then cam the auld Queen,   *old*
 Goud tassels tying her hair –   *Gold*
'O, Marie, where's the bonny wee babe,
 That I heard greet sae sair?'   *weep so sore*

'There was never a babe intill my room,   *in*
  As little designs to be;
It was but a touch o' my sair side,
  Come o'er my fair bodie.'

'O, Marie, put on your robes o' black,
  Or else your robes o' brown,
For ye maun gang wi' me the night,   *must*
  To see fair Edinbro' town.'

'I winna put on my robes o' black,   *will not*
  Nor yet my robes o' brown,
But I'll put on my robes o' white,
  To shine through Edinbro' town.'

When she gaed up the Cannogate,   *went*
  She laugh'd loud laughters three;
But whan she cam down the Cannogate,
  The tear blinded her e'e.   *eye*

When she gaed up the Parliament stair,
  The heel cam aff her shee,   *off: shoe*
And lang or she cam down again,   *long ere*
  She was condemn'd to dee.   *die*

When she cam down the Cannogate,
  The Cannogate sae free,
Mony a ladie look'd o'er her window,   *Many: out of*
  Weeping for this ladie.

'Ye need nae weep for me,' she says,   *not*
  'Ye need nae weep for me,
For had I not slain mine own sweet babe,
  This death I wadna dee.   *would not*

'Bring me a bottle of wine,' she says,
  'The best that e'er ye hae,
That I may drink to my weil wishers,
  And they may drink to me.

'Here's a health to the jolly sailors,
　　That sail upon the main,
Let them never let on to my father and mother,
　　But what I'm coming hame.

'Here's a health to the jolly sailors,
　　That sail upon the sea;
Let them never let on to my father and mother,
　　That I cam here to dee.

'Oh, little did my mother think,
　　The day she cradled me,
What lands I was to travel through,
　　What death I was to dee.

'Oh, little did my father think,
　　The day he held up me,
What lands I was to travel through,
　　What death I was to dee.

'Last night I wash'd the Queen's feet,
　　And gently laid her down;
And a' the thanks I've gotten the nicht,　　　*tonight*
　　To be hang'd in Edinbro' town.

'Last nicht there was four Maries,
　　The nicht there'l be but three;
There was Marie Seton, and Marie Beton,
　　And Marie Carmichael, and me.'

EDWARD, EDWARD

'WHY dois your brand sae drap wi' bluid,　　*sword*
　　　　Edward, Edward?
Why dois your brand sae drap wi' bluid?
　　　And why sae sad gang yee, O?'　　　　*go*
'O, I hae killed my hauke sae guid,
　　　　Mither, mither:
O, I hae killed my hauke sae guid;
　　　And I had nae mair bot hee, O.'

'Your haukis bluid was nevir sae reid;   *red*
    Edward, Edward.
Your haukis bluid was nevir sae reid;
    My deir son I tell thee, O.'
'O, I hae killed my reid-roan steid,   *steed*
    Mither, mither:
O, I hae killed my reid-roan steid,
    That erst was sae fair and frie, O.'   *free*

'Your steid was auld, and ye hae gat mair,
    Edward, Edward:
Your steid was auld, and ye hae gat mair,
    Sum other dule ye drie, O.'   *grief you suffer*
'O, I hae killed my fadir deir,   *father dear*
    Mither, mither:
O, I hae killed my fadir deir
    Alas! and wae is mee, O!'

'And whatten penance wul ye drie for that?
    Edward, Edward.
And whatten penance will ye drie for that?
    My deir son, now tell me, O.'
'Ile set my feit in yonder boat,   *feet*
    Mither, mither:
Ile set my feit in yonder boat,
    And Ile fare ovir the sea, O.'

'And what wul ye doe wi' your towirs and your ha',   *hall*
    Edward, Edward?
And what wul ye doe wi' your towirs and your ha',
    That were sae fair to see, O?'
'Ile let thame stand tul they doun fa',   *them: till: fall*
    Mither, mither:
Ile let thame stand tul they doun fa',
    For here nevir mair maun I bee, O.'   *must*

'And what wul ye leive to your bairns and your wife,
    Edward, Edward?
And what wul ye lieve to your bairns and your wife,
    Whan ye gang ovir the sea, O?'

'The warldis room, late them beg thrae life,   *world's space*
    Mither, mither:
The warldis room, let them beg thrae life,
    For thame nevir mair wul I see, O.'

'And what wul ye leive to your ain mither deir,   *own*
    Edward, Edward:
And what wul ye leive to your ain mither deir,
    My deir son, now tell mee, O.'
'The curse of hell frae me sall ye beir,   *shall ye bear*
    Mither, mither:
The curse of hell frae me sall ye beir,
    Sic counseils ye gave to me, O.'   *Such*

JOHN DRYDEN

From ABSALOM AND ACHITOPHEL

IN PIOUS TIMES, ere priestcraft did begin
Before polygamy was made a sin,
When man on many multiplied his kind,
Ere one to one was cursèdly confined,
When Nature prompted and no law denied
Promiscuous use of concubine and bride,
Then Israel's monarch after Heav'n's own heart
His vig'rous warmth did variously impart
To wives and slaves, and, wide as his command,
Scattered his Maker's image through the land.
Michal, of royal blood, the crown did wear,
A soil ungrateful to the tiller's care:
Not so the rest; for several mothers bore
To god-like David several sons before.
But since like slaves his bed they did ascend,
No true succession could their seed attend.
Of all this num'rous progeny was none
So beautiful, so brave, as Absalon:
Whether, inspired by some diviner lust,
His father got him with a greater gust,

Or that his conscious destiny made way
By manly beauty to imperial sway.
Early in foreign fields he won renown
With kings and states allied to Israel's crown;
In peace the thoughts of war he could remove
And seemed as he were only born for love.
Whate'er he did was done with so much ease,
In him alone 'twas natural to please;
His motions all accompanied with grace,
And Paradise was opened in his face.
With secret joy indulgent David viewed
His youthful image in his son renewed;
To all his wishes nothing he denied
And made the charming Annabel his bride.
What faults he had (for who from faults is free?)
His father could not or he would not see.
Some warm excesses, which the law forbore,
Were construed youth that purged by boiling o'er;
And Amnon's murder by a specious name
Was called a just revenge for injured fame.
Thus praised and loved, the noble youth remained,
While David undisturbed in Sion reigned.
But life can never be sincerely blest;
Heaven punishes the bad, and proves the best.
The Jews, a headstrong, moody, murm'ring race
As ever tried th' extent and stretch of grace;
God's pampered people, whom, debauched with ease,
No king could govern nor no God could please;
Gods they had tried of every shape and size
That godsmiths could produce or priests devise;
These Adam-wits, too fortunately free,
Began to dream they wanted liberty;
And when no rule, no precedent was found
Of men by laws less circumscribed and bound,
They led their wild desires to woods and caves
And thought that all but savages were slaves.
They who, when Saul was dead, without a blow
Made foolish Ishbosheth the crown forgo;
Who banished David did from Hebron bring,

And with a general shout proclaimed him King;
Those very Jews who at their very best
Their humour more than loyalty expressed,
Now wondered why so long they had obeyed
An idol monarch which their hands had made;
Thought they might ruin him they could create
Or melt him to that golden calf, a state.
But these were random bolts; no formed design
Nor int'rest made the factious crowd to join:
The sober part of Israel, free from stain,
Well knew the value of a peaceful reign;
And looking backward with a wise affright
Saw seams of wounds dishonest to the sight,
In contemplation of whose ugly scars
They cursed the memory of civil wars.
The mod'rate sort of men, thus qualified,
Inclined the balance to the better side;
And David's mildness managed it so well,
The bad found no occasion to rebel.
But when to sin our biased nature leans,
The careful Devil is still at hand with means
And providently pimps for ill desires:
The good old cause, revived, a plot requires,
Plots true or false are necessary things,
To raise up commonwealths and ruin kings.

MACFLECKNOE

ALL human things are subject to decay
And, when Fate summons, monarchs must obey.
This Flecknoe found, who, like Augustus, young
Was called to empire and had governed long,
In prose and verse was owned without dispute
Through all the realms of Nonsense absolute.
This agèd prince, now flourishing in peace
And blest with issue of a large increase,
Worn out with business, did at length debate
To settle the succession of the State;

And pond'ring which of all his sons was fit
To reign and wage immortal war with wit,
Cried, ' 'Tis resolved, for Nature pleads that he
Should only rule who most resembles me.
Shadwell alone my perfect image bears,
Mature in dullness from his tender years;
Shadwell alone of all my sons is he
Who stands confirmed in full stupidity.
The rest to some faint meaning make pretence,
But Shadwell never deviates into sense.
Some beams of wit on other souls may fall,
Strike through and make a lucid interval;
But Shadwell's genuine night admits no ray,
His rising fogs prevail upon the day.
Besides, his goodly fabric fills the eye
And seems designed for thoughtless majesty,
Thoughtless as monarch oaks that shade the plain
And, spread in solemn state, supinely reign.
Heywood and Shirley were but types of thee,
Thou last great prophet of tautology.
Even I, a dunce of more renown than they,
Was sent before but to prepare thy way,
And coarsely clad in Norwich drugget came
To teach the nations in thy greater name.
My warbling lute, the lute I whilom strung,
When to King John of Portugal I sung,
Was but the prelude to that glorious day,
When thou on silver Thames did'st cut thy way,
With well-timed oars before the royal barge,
Swelled with the pride of thy celestial charge,
And, big with hymn, commander of an host;
The like was ne'er in Epsom blankets tossed.
Methinks I see the new Arion sail,
The lute still trembling underneath thy nail.
At thy well-sharpened thumb from shore to shore
The treble squeaks for fear, the basses roar;
Echoes from Pissing Alley "Shadwell" call,
And "Shadwell" they resound from Aston Hall.
About thy boat the little fishes throng,

As at the morning toast that floats along.
Sometimes, as prince of thy harmonious band,
Thou wield'st thy papers in thy threshing hand.
St André's feet ne'er kept more equal time,
Not ev'n the feet of thy own *Psyche*'s rhyme:
Though they in number as in sense excel,
So just, so like tautology, they fell
That, pale with envy, Singleton forswore
The lute and sword which he in triumph bore,
And vowed he ne'er would act Villerius more.'
Here stopped the good old sire and wept for joy,
In silent raptures of the hopeful boy.
All arguments, but most his plays, persuade
That for anointed dullness he was made.

Close to the walls which fair Augusta bind
(The fair Augusta much to fears inclined),
An ancient fabric raised t' inform the sight
There stood of yore, and Barbican it hight;
A watch-tower once, but now, so fate ordains,
Of all the pile an empty name remains;
From its old ruins brothel-houses rise,
Scenes of lewd loves and of polluted joys,
Where their vast courts the mother-strumpets keep,
And, undisturbed by watch, in silence sleep.
Near there a Nursery erects its head,
Where queens are formed and future heroes bred
Where unfledged actors learn to laugh and cry,
Where infant punks their tender voices try,
And little Maximins the gods defy.
Great Fletcher never treads in buskins here,
Nor greater Jonson dares in socks appear;
But gentle Simkin just reception finds
Amidst this monument of vanished minds;
Pure clinches the suburbian muse affords
And Panton waging harmless war with words.
Here Flecknoe, as a place to fame well known,
Ambitiously designed his Shadwell's throne.
For ancient Dekker prophesied long since
That in this pile should reign a mighty prince,

Born for a scourge of wit and flail of sense,
To whom true dullness should some *Psyches* owe,
But worlds of *Misers* from his pen should flow;
Humorists and hypocrites it should produce,
Whole Raymond families and tribes of Bruce.
   Now empress Fame had published the renown
Of Shadwell's coronation through the town.
Roused by report of fame, the nations meet
From near Bunhill and distant Watling Street.
No Persian carpets spread th' imperial way,
But scattered limbs of mangled poets lay;
From dusty shops neglected authors come,
Martyrs of pies and relics of the bum.
Much Heywood, Shirley, Ogleby there lay,
But loads of Shadwell almost choked the way.
Bilked stationers for yeomen stood prepared
And Herringman was captain of the guard.
The hoary prince in majesty appeared,
High on a throne of his own labours reared.
At his right hand our young Ascanius sat,
Rome's other hope and pillar of the State.
His brows thick fogs instead of glories grace,
And lambent dullness played around his face.
As Hannibal did to the altars come,
Sworn by his sire a mortal foe to Rome;
So Shadwell swore, nor should his vow be vain,
That he till death true dullness would maintain;
And, in his father's right and realm's defence,
Ne'er to have peace with wit nor truce with sense.
The king himself the sacred unction made,
As king by office and as priest by trade.
In his sinister hand, instead of ball,
He placed a mighty mug of potent ale;
Love's Kingdom to his right he did convey,
At once his sceptre and his rule of sway;
Whose righteous lore the prince had practised young
And from whose loins recorded *Psyche* sprung.
His temples, last, with poppies were o'erspread,
That nodding seemed to consecrate his head.

Just at that point of time, if fame not lie,
On his left hand twelve reverend owls did fly.
So Romulus, 'tis sung, by Tiber's brook,
Presage of sway from twice six vultures took.
Th' admiring throng loud acclamations make
And omens of his future empire take.
The sire then shook the honours of his head,
And from his brows damps of oblivion shed
Full on the filial dullness: long he stood,
Repelling from his breast the raging God;
At length burst out in this prophetic mood:
  'Heavens bless my son! From Ireland let him reign
To far Barbados on the western main;
Of his dominion may no end be known
And greater than his father's be his throne;
Beyond *Love's Kingdom* let him stretch his pen!'
He paused, and all the people cried 'Amen.'
Then thus continued he: 'My son, advance
Still in new impudence, new ignorance.
Success let others teach, learn thou from me
Pangs without birth and fruitless industry.
Let *Virtuosos* in five years be writ,
Yet not one thought accuse thy toil of wit.
Let gentle George in triumph tread the stage,
Make Dorimant betray and Loveit rage;
Let Cully, Cockwood, Fopling charm the pit,
And in their folly show the writer's wit.
Yet still thy fools shall stand in thy defence
And justify their author's want of sense.
Let them be all by thy own model made
Of dullness, and desire no foreign aid,
That they to future ages may be known,
Not copies drawn, but issue of thy own.
Nay, let thy men of wit too be the same,
All full of thee and differing but in name.
But let no alien Sedley interpose
To lard with wit thy hungry Epsom prose.
And when false flow'rs of rhet'ric thou would'st cull,
Trust Nature, do not labour to be dull;

But write thy best and top; and in each line
Sir Formal's oratory will be thine.
Sir Formal, though unsought, attends thy quill
And does thy northern dedications fill.
Nor let false friends seduce thy mind to fame
By arrogating Jonson's hostile name;
Let father Flecknoe fire thy mind with praise
And uncle Ogleby thy envy raise.
Thou art my blood, where Jonson has no part;
What share have we in nature or in art?
Where did his wit on learning fix a brand
And rail at arts he did not understand?
Where made he love in Prince Nicander's vein
Or swept the dust in Psyche's humble strain?
Where sold he bargains, "whipstitch, kiss my arse",
Promised a play and dwindled to a farce?
When did his Muse from Fletcher scenes purloin
As thou whole Eth'rege dost transfuse to thine?
But so transfused as oil on waters flow,
His always floats above, thine sinks below.
This is thy province, this thy wondrous way,
New humours to invent for each new play:
This is that boasted bias of thy mind,
By which one way to dullness 'tis inclined,
Which makes thy writings lean on one side still,
And, in all changes, that way bends thy will.
Nor let thy mountain belly make pretence
Of likeness; thine's a tympany of sense.
A tun of man in thy large bulk is writ,
But sure thou'rt but a kilderkin of wit.
Like mine, thy gentle numbers feebly creep;
Thy tragic Muse gives smiles, thy comic sleep.
With whate'er gall thou set'st thyself to write,
Thy inoffensive satires never bite;
In thy felonious heart though venom lies,
It does but touch thy Irish pen, and dies.
Thy genius calls thee not to purchase fame
In keen iambics, but mild anagram.
Leave writing plays, and choose for thy command

Some peaceful province in Acrostic-land.
There thou may'st wings display and altars raise,
And torture one poor word ten thousand ways;
Or, if thou would'st thy different talents suit,
Set thy own songs, and sing them to thy lute.'
He said, but his last words were scarcely heard,
For Bruce and Longville had a trap prepared,
And down they sent the yet declaiming bard.
Sinking he left his drugget robe behind,
Borne upwards by a subterranean wind.
The mantle fell to the young prophet's part
With double portion of his father's art.

From THE HIND AND THE PANTHER

A MILK-WHITE HIND, immortal and unchanged,
Fed on the lawns and in the forest ranged;
Without unspotted, innocent within,
She feared no danger, for she knew no sin.
Yet had she oft been chased with horns and hounds
And Scythian shafts; and many wingèd wounds
Aimed at her heart; was often forced to fly,
And doomed to death, though fated not to die.
    Not so her young; for their unequal line
Was hero's make, half human, half divine.
Their earthly mould obnoxious was to fate,
Th' immortal part assumed immortal state.
Of these a slaughtered army lay in blood,
Extended o'er the Caledonian wood,
Their native walk; whose vocal blood arose
And cried for pardon on their perjured foes.
Their fate was fruitful, and the sanguine seed,
Endued with souls, increased the sacred breed.
So captive Israel multiplied in chains,
A num'rous exile, and enjoyed her pains.
With grief and gladness mixed, their mother viewed
Her martyred offspring and their race renewed;

Their corps to perish, but their kind to last,
So much the deathless plant the dying fruit surpassed.
   Panting and pensive now she ranged alone,
And wandered in the kingdoms once her own.
The common hunt, though from their range restrained
By sov'reign power, her company disdained,
Grinned as they passed, and with a glaring eye
Gave gloomy signs of secret enmity.
'Tis true she bounded by and tripped so light,
They had not time to take a steady sight;
For truth has such a face and such a mien
As to be loved needs only to be seen.

A SONG FOR ST CECILIA'S DAY

NOVEMBER 22, 1687

FROM harmony, from heavenly harmony
      This universal frame began;
   When Nature underneath a heap
      Of jarring atoms lay,
   And could not heave her head,
The tuneful voice was heard from high,
      'Arise, ye more than dead.'
Then cold and hot and moist and dry
   In order to their stations leap,
      And Music's power obey.
From harmony, from heavenly harmony
      This universal frame began:
      From harmony to harmony
Through all the compass of the notes it ran,
The diapason closing full in Man.

What passion cannot Music raise and quell?
      When Jubal struck the chorded shell,
   His listening brethren stood around,
      And, wondering, on their faces fell
   To worship that celestial sound:

Less than a god they thought there could not dwell
 Within the hollow of that shell,
 That spoke so sweetly, and so well.
What passion cannot Music raise and quell?

  The trumpet's loud clangour
   Excites us to arms
  With shrill notes of anger
   And mortal alarms.
  The double double double beat
   Of the thundering drum
   Cries, 'Hark! The foes come;
Charge, charge, 'tis too late to retreat.'

  The soft complaining flute
  In dying notes discovers
  The woes of hopeless lovers,
Whose dirge is whispered by the warbling lute.

  Sharp violins proclaim
  Their jealous pangs and desperation,
  Fury, frantic indignation,
  Depth of pains and height of passion,
   For the fair, disdainful dame.

  But oh! what art can teach,
  What human voice can reach
   The sacred organ's praise?
   Notes inspiring holy love,
  Notes that wing their heavenly ways
   To mend the choirs above.

Orpheus could lead the savage race,
And trees unrooted left their place,
  Sequacious of the lyre;
But bright Cecilia raised the wonder higher:
When to her organ vocal breath was given,
An angel heard, and straight appeared
  Mistaking earth for heaven.

Grand Chorus

As from the power of sacred lays
   The spheres began to move,
And sung the great Creator's praise
   To all the blest above;
So when the last and dreadful hour
This crumbling pageant shall devour,
The trumpet shall be heard on high,
The dead shall live, the living die,
And Music shall untune the sky.

From THE AENEID

[THE TROJAN HORSE]

BY DESTINY compelled, and in despair,
The Greeks grew weary of the tedious war,
And by Minerva's aid a fabric reared,
Which like a steed of monstrous height appeared:
The sides were planked with pine; they feigned it made
For their return, and this the vow they paid.
Thus they pretend, but in the hollow side
Selected numbers of their soldiers hide:
With inward arms the dire machine they load,
And iron bowels stuff the dark abode.
In sight of Troy lies Tenedos, an isle
(While Fortune did on Priam's empire smile)
Renowned for wealth; but, since, a faithless bay,
Where ships exposed to wind and weather lay.
There was their fleet concealed. We thought, for Greece
Their sails were hoisted, and our fears release.
The Trojans, cooped within their walls so long,
Unbar their gates, and issue in a throng,
Like swarming bees, and with delight survey
The camp deserted, where the Grecians lay:
The quarters of the sev'ral chiefs they showed;
Here Phoenix, here Achilles, made abode;
Here joined the battles; there the navy rode.

Part on the pile their wond'ring eyes employ:
The pile by Pallas raised to ruin Troy.
Thymoetes first ('tis doubtful whether hired,
Or so the Trojan destiny required)
Moved that the ramparts might be broken down,
To lodge the monster fabric in the town.
But Capys, and the rest of sounder mind,
The fatal present to the flames designed,
Or to the wat'ry deep; at least to bore
The hollow sides, and hidden frauds explore.
The giddy vulgar, as their fancies guide,
With noise say nothing, and in parts divide.
Laöcoon, followed by a num'rous crowd,
Ran from the fort, and cried, from far, aloud:
'O wretched countrymen! what fury reigns?
What more than madness has possessed your brains?
Think you the Grecians from your coasts are gone?
And are Ulysses' arts no better known?
This hollow fabric either must enclose,
Within its blind recess, our secret foes;
Or 'tis an engine raised above the town,
T' o'erlook the walls, and then to batter down.
Somewhat is sure designed, by fraud or force:
Trust not their presents, nor admit the horse.'
Thus having said, against the steed he threw
His forceful spear, which, hissing as it flew,
Pierced through the yielding planks of jointed wood,
And trembling in the hollow belly stood.
The sides, transpierced, return a rattling sound,
And groans of Greeks enclosed come issuing through the
    wound.
And, had not Heav'n the fall of Troy designed,
Or had not men been fated to be blind,
Enough was said and done t' inspire a better mind.
Then had our lances pierced the treach'rous wood,
And Ilian tow'rs and Priam's empire stood.

MATTHEW PRIOR

TO A CHILD OF QUALITY

Five years old, 1704. The Author then forty

LORDS, knights, and squires, the num'rous band
  That wear the fair Miss Mary's fetters,
Were summoned by her high command
  To show their passion by their letters.

My pen among the rest I took,
  Lest those bright eyes that cannot read
Should dart their kindling fires, and look
  The pow'r they have to be obeyed.

Nor quality, nor reputation,
  Forbid me yet my flame to tell;
Dear Five-years-old befriends my passion,
  And I may write till she can spell.

For, while she makes her silkworms beds
  With all the tender things I swear;
Whilst all the house my passion reads,
  In papers round her baby's hair;

She may receive and own my flame,
  For, though the strictest prudes should know it,
She'll pass for a most virtuous dame,
  And I for an unhappy poet.

Then too, alas! when she shall tear
  The lines some younger rival sends,
She'll give me leave to write, I fear,
  And we shall still continue friends.

For, as our diff'rent ages move,
  'Tis so ordained (would Fate but mend it!)
That I shall be past making love
  When she begins to comprehend it.

JONATHAN SWIFT

VERSES ON THE DEATH OF DR SWIFT, D.S.P.D.

Written by himself, November 1731

As ROCHEFOUCAULD his Maxims drew
From Nature, I believe 'em true:
They argue no corrupted mind
In him; the fault is in mankind.

This Maxim more than all the rest
Is thought too base for human breast:
'In all distresses of our friends
We first consult our private ends,
While Nature, kindly bent to ease us,
Points out some circumstance to please us.'

If this, perhaps, your patience move,
Let reason and experience prove.

We all behold with envious eyes
Our equal raised above our size;
Who would not at a crowded show
Stand high himself, keep others low?
I love my friend as well as you,
But would not have him stop my view;
Then let me have the higher post:
I ask but for an inch at most.

If, in a battle, you should find
One, whom you love of all mankind,
Had some heroic action done,
A champion killed, or trophy won;
Rather than thus be overtopped,
Would you not wish his laurels cropped?

Dear honest Ned is in the gout,
Lies racked with pain, and you without:
How patiently you hear him groan!
How glad the case is not your own!

What poet would not grieve to see
His brethren write as well as he?
But rather than they should excel,
He'd wish his rivals all in hell.

Her end when Emulation misses,
She turns to envy, stings, and hisses:
The strongest friendship yields to pride,
Unless the odds be on our side.

Vain humankind! fantastic race!
Thy various follies who can trace?
Self-love, ambition, envy, pride,
Their empires in our hearts divide:
Give others riches, pow't, and station,
'Tis all on me an usurpation.
I have no title to aspire;
Yet, when you sink, I seem the higher;
In Pope I cannot read a line,
But with a sigh I wish it mine:
When he can in one couplet fix
More sense than I can do in six,
It gives me such a jealous fit,
I cry, 'Pox take him, and his wit!'

Why must I be outdone by Gay,
In my own hum'rous biting way?

Arbuthnot is no more my friend,
Who dares to irony pretend;
Which I was born to introduce,
Refined it first, and showed its use.

St John as well as Pult'ney knows
That I had some repute for prose;
And, till they drove me out of date,
Could maul a Minister of State.
If they have mortified my pride,
And made me throw my pen aside;
If with such talents heav'n hath blessed 'em,
Have I not reason to detest 'em?

To all my foes, dear Fortune, send
Thy gifts, but never to my friend:
I tamely can endure the first,
But this with envy makes me burst.

Thus much may serve by way of proem;
Proceed we therefore to our poem.

The time is not remote, when I
Must by the course of Nature die:
When, I foresee, my special friends
Will try to find their private ends:
Though it is hardly understood
Which way my death can do them good,
Yet thus, methinks, I hear 'em speak:
'See, how the Dean begins to break!
Poor gentleman, he droops apace!
You plainly find it in his face.
That old vertigo in his head
Will never leave him, till he's dead.
Besides, his memory decays:
He recollects not what he says;
He cannot call his friends to mind;
Forgets the place where last he dined;
Plies you with stories o'er and o'er,
He told them fifty times before.
How does he fancy we can sit,
To hear his out-of-fashioned wit?
But he takes up with younger folks,
Who for his wine will bear his jokes.
Faith, he must make his stories shorter,
Or change his comrades once a quarter:
In half the time he talks them round,
There must another set be found.

'For poetry, he's past his prime:
He takes an hour to find a rhyme;
His fire is out, his wit decayed,
His fancy sunk, his Muse a jade.
I'd have him throw away his pen;
But there's no talking to some men!'

And then their tenderness appears,
By adding largely to my years:
'He's older than he would be reckoned,
And well remembers Charles the Second.

'He hardly drinks a pint of wine;
And that, I doubt, is no good sign.
His stomach too begins to fail:

Last year we thought him strong and hale;
But now he's quite another thing;
I wish he may hold out till spring!'

Then hug themselves, and reason thus:
'It is not yet so bad with us.'

In such a case they talk in tropes,
And by their fears express their hopes:
Some great misfortune to portend,
No enemy can match a friend;
With all the kindness they profess,
The merit of a lucky guess
(When daily how-d'-ye's come of course,
And servants answer: 'Worse and worse')
Would please 'em better than to tell
That 'God be praised, the Dean is well.'
Then he who prophesied the best
Approves his foresight to the rest:
'You know, I always feared the worst,
And often told you so at first.'
He'd rather choose that I should die
Than his prediction prove a lie.
Not one foretells I shall recover;
But all agree to give me over.

Yet should some neighbour feel a pain,
Just in the parts where I complain,
How many a message would he send?
What hearty prayers that I should mend?
Enquire what regimen I kept?
What gave me ease, and how I slept?
And more lament, when I was dead,
Than all the sniv'llers round my bed.

My good companions, never fear;
For though you may mistake a year,
Though your prognostics run too fast,
They must be verified at last.

Behold the fatal day arrive!
'How is the Dean? He's just alive.
Now the departing prayer is read;
He hardly breathes. The Dean is dead.'

Before the passing-bell begun,
The news through half the town has run.
'Oh, may we all for death prepare!
What has he left? And who's his heir?
I know no more than what the news is;
'Tis all bequeathed to public uses.
To public use! A perfect whim!
What had the public done for him!
Mere envy, avarice, and pride!
He gave it all – but, first, he died.
And had the Dean, in all the nation,
No worthy friend, no poor relation?
So ready to do strangers good,
Forgetting his own flesh and blood!'

   Now Grub Street wits are all employed;
With elegies the town is cloyed:
Some paragraph in ev'ry paper,
To curse the Dean, or bless the Drapier

   The doctors, tender of their fame,
Wisely on me lay all the blame:
'We must confess his case was nice;
But he would never take advice;
Had he been ruled, for aught appears,
He might have lived these twenty years:
For when we opened him, we found
That all his vital parts were sound.'

   From Dublin soon to London spread,
'Tis told at Court, 'The Dean is dead.'
   Kind Lady Suffolk in the spleen
Runs laughing up to tell the Queen.
The Queen, so gracious, mild, and good,
Cries, 'Is he gone? 'Tis time he should.
He's dead, you say; then let him rot;
I'm glad the medals were forgot.
I promised him, I own; but when?
I only was the Princess then;
But now, as consort of a king,
You know 'tis quite a diff'rent thing.'
   Now Chartres at Sir Robert's levee,

Tells, with a sneer, the tidings heavy:
'Why, is he dead without his shoes?'
Cries Bob. 'I'm sorry for the news.
Oh, were the wretch but living still,
And in his place my good friend Will;
Or had a mitre on his head
Provided Bolingbroke were dead.'

Now Curll his shop from rubbish drains;
Three genuine tomes of Swift's remains.
And then, to make them pass the glibber,
Revised by Tibbalds, Moore and Cibber.
He'll treat me as he does my betters,
Publish my Will, my Life, my Letters.
Revive the libels born to die;
Which Pope must bear as well as I.

Here shift the scene, to represent
How those I love my death lament.
Poor Pope will grieve a month; and Gay
A week; and Arbuthnot a day.

St John himself will scarce forbear
To bite his pen, and drop a tear.
The rest will give a shrug, and cry,
'I'm sorry; but we all must die.'
Indiff'rence clad in Wisdom's guise
All fortitude of mind supplies;
For how can stony bowels melt
In those who never pity felt;
When we are lashed, they kiss the rod;
Resigning to the will of God.

The fools, my juniors by a year,
Are tortured with suspense and fear;
Who wisely thought my age a screen,
When Death approached, to stand between:
The screen removed, their hearts are trembling;
They mourn for me without dissembling.

My female friends, whose tender hearts
Have better learned to act their parts,
Receive the news in doleful dumps:
'The Dean is dead (and what is trumps?)

Then Lord have mercy on his soul.
(Ladies, I'll venture for the vole.)
Six deans they say must bear the pall.
(I wish I knew what king to call.)
Madam, your husband will attend
The funeral of so good a friend.
No, Madam, 'tis a shocking sight;
And he's engaged tomorrow night!
My Lady Club would take it ill
If he should fail at her quadrille.
He loved the Dean. (I led a heart.)
But, dearest friends, they say, must part.
His time was come; he ran his race;
We hope he's in a better place.'

Why do we grieve that friends should die?
No loss more easy to supply.
One year is past: a diff'rent scene;
No further mention of the Dean;
Who now, alas, no more is missed
Than if he never did exist.
Where's now this fav'rite of Apollo?
Departed; and his works must follow:
Must undergo the common fate;
His kind of wit is out of date.
Some country squire to Lintot goes,
Enquires for Swift in verse and prose.
Says Lintot, 'I have heard the name;
He died a year ago.' 'The same.'
He searcheth all his shop in vain.
'Sir, you may find them in Duck Lane:
I sent them, with a load of books,
Last Monday to the pastry cook's.
To fancy they could live a year!
I find you're but a stranger here.
The Dean was famous in his time;
And had a kind of knack at rhyme:
His way of writing now is past;
The town hath got a better taste:
I keep no antiquated stuff;

But, spick and span, I have enough.
Pray, do but give me leave to show 'em:
Here's Colley Cibber's Birthday Poem.
This Ode you never yet have seen,
By Stephen Duck, upon the Queen.
Then, here's a Letter finely penned
Against the Craftsman and his friend;
It clearly shows that all reflection
On Ministers is disaffection.
Next, here's Sir Robert's Vindication,
And Mr Henley's last Oration:
The hawkers have not got 'em yet,
Your honour please to buy a set?

    'Here's Wolston's Tracts, the twelfth edition;
'Tis read by ev'ry politician;
The country Members, when in town,
To all their boroughs send them down:
You never met a thing so smart;
The courtiers have them all by heart;
Those maids of honour who can read
Are taught to use them for their Creed.
The rev'rend author's good intention
Hath been rewarded with a pension;
He doth an honour to his gown,
By bravely running priestcraft down;
He shows, as sure as God's in Gloucester,
That Jesus was a grand imposter,
That all his miracles were cheats,
Performed as jugglers do their feats;
The Church had never such a writer;
A shame he hath not got a mitre!'

    Suppose me dead; and then suppose
A club assembled at the Rose;
Where, from discourse of this and that,
I grow the subject of their chat;
And, while they toss my name about,
With favour some, and some without,
One quite indiff'rent in the cause,
My character impartial draws:

'The Dean, if we believe report,
Was never ill received at Court.
As for his works in verse and prose,
I own myself no judge of those;
Nor can I tell what critics thought 'em;
But this I know, all people bought 'em;
As with a moral view designed
To cure the vices of mankind:
His vein, ironically grave,
Exposed the fool, and lashed the knave;
To steal a hint was never known,
But what he writ was all his own.

'He never thought an honour done him
Because a duke was proud to own him;
Would rather slip aside and choose
To talk with wits in dirty shoes;
Despised the fools with stars and garters,
So often seen caressing Chartres:
He never courted men in station,
Nor persons had in admiration;
Of no man's greatness was afraid,
Because he sought for no man's aid.
Though trusted long in great affairs,
He gave himself no haughty airs;
Without regarding private ends,
Spent all his credit for his friends;
And only chose the wise and good;
No flatt'rers, no allies in blood;
But succoured virtue in distress,
And seldom failed of good success;
As numbers in their hearts must own,
Who, but for him, had been unknown.

'With princes kept a due decorum,
But never stood in awe before 'em:
He followed David's lesson just,
"In princes never put thy trust."
And, would you make him truly sour,
Provoke him with a slave in pow'r.
The Irish Senate, if you named,

With what impatience he declaimed!
Fair LIBERTY was all his cry;
For her he stood prepared to die;
For her he boldly stood alone;
For her he oft exposed his own.
Two kingdoms, just as faction led,
Had set a price upon his head;
But not a traitor could be found
To sell him for six hundred pound.

'Had he but spared his tongue and pen,
He might have rose like other men;
But, pow'r was never in his thought,
And wealth he valued not a groat;
Ingratitude he often found,
And pitied those who meant the wound;
But kept the tenor of his mind
To merit well of humankind;
Nor made a sacrifice of those
Who still were true, to please his foes.
He laboured many a fruitless hour
To reconcile his friends in pow'r;
Saw mischief by a faction brewing,
While they pursued each other's ruin.
But, finding vain was all his care,
He left the Court in mere despair.

'And, oh! how short are human schemes!
Here ended all our golden dreams.
What St John's skill in state affairs,
What Ormond's valour, Oxford's cares,
To save their sinking country lent,
Was all destroyed by one event.
Too soon that previous life was ended,
On which alone our weal depended.
When up a dang'rous faction starts,
With wrath and vengeance in their hearts:
By solemn league and cov'nant bound,
To ruin, slaughter, and confound;
To turn religion to a fable,
And make the Government a Babel:

Pervert the laws, disgrace the gown,
Corrupt the Senate, rob the Crown;
To sacrifice old England's glory,
And make her infamous in story.
When such a tempest shook the land,
How could unguarded virtue stand?

'With horror, grief, despair, the Dean
Beheld their dire destructive scene:
His friends in exile, or the Tow'r,
Himself within the frown of pow'r;
Pursued by base envenomed pens,
Far to the land of slaves and fens;
A servile race in folly nursed,
Who truckle most when treated worst.

'By innocence and resolution,
He bore continual persecution;
While numbers to preferment rose,
Whose merits were, to be his foes.
When, ev'n his own familiar friends,
Intent upon their private ends,
Like renegadoes now he feels,
Against him lifting up their heels.

'The Dean did by his pen defeat
An infamous destructive cheat;
Taught fools their int'rest how to know,
And gave them arms to ward the blow.
Envy hath owned it was his doing
To save that helpless land from ruin;
While they who at the steerage stood,
And reaped the profit, sought his blood.

'To save them from their evil fate,
In him was held a crime of state.
A wicked monster on the Bench,
Whose fury blood could never quench;
As vile and profligate a villain,
As modern Scroggs, or old Tressilian;
Who long all justice had discarded,
Nor feared he God, nor Man regarded;
Vowed on the Dean his rage to vent,

And make him of his zeal repent;
But heav'n his innocence defends,
The grateful people stands his friends:
Not strains of law, nor judge's frown,
Nor topics brought to please the Crown,
Nor witness hired, nor jury picked,
Prevail to bring him in convict.

    'In exile with a steady heart,
He spent his life's declining part;
Where folly, pride, and faction sway,
Remote from St John, Pope, and Gay.

    'His friendship there to few confined,
Were always of the middling kind:
No fools of rank, a mongrel breed,
Who fain would pass for lords indeed:
Where titles give no right, or pow'r,
And peerage is a withered flow'r,
He would have held it a disgrace,
If such a wretch had known his face.
On rural squires, that kingdom's bane,
He vented oft his wrath in vain:
Biennial squires to market brought;
Who sell their souls and votes for naught;
The country stripped go joyful back,
To rob the church, their tenants rack,
Go snacks with thieves and reparees
And keep the peace to pick up fees:
In every job to have a share,
A jail or barrack to repair;
And turn the tax for public roads
Commodious for their own abodes.

    'Perhaps I may allow the Dean
Had too much satire in his vein;
And seemed determined not to starve it,
Because no age could more deserve it.
Yet malice never was his aim;
He lashed the vice, but spared the name.
No individual could resent,
Where thousands equally were meant.

His satire points at no defect,
But what all mortals may correct;
For he abhorred that senseless tribe
Who call it humour when they jibe:
He spared a hump or crooked nose,
Whose owners set not up for beaux.
True genuine dullness moved his pity,
Unless it offered to be witty.
Those who their ignorance confessed
He ne'er offended with a jest;
But laughed to hear an idiot quote
A verse from Horace learned by rote.

  'He knew an hundred pleasant stories,
With all the turns of Whigs and Tories;
Was cheerful to his dying day,
And friends would let him have his way.

  'He gave the little wealth he had
To build a house for fools and mad;
And showed, by one satiric touch,
No nation wanted it so much.
That kingdom he hath left his debtor,
I wish it soon may have a better.'

AMBROSE PHILIPS

TO MISS CHARLOTTE PULTENEY

In her Mother's arms

TIMELY blossom, infant fair,
Fondling of a happy pair,
Every morn, and every night,
Their solicitous delight,
Sleeping, waking, still at ease,
Pleasing, without skill to please,
Little gossip, blithe and hale,
Tattling many a broken tale,
Singing many a tuneless song,
Lavish of a heedless tongue,

Simple maiden, void of art,
Babbling out the very heart,
Yet abandoned to thy will,
Yet imagining no ill,
Yet too innocent to blush,
Like the linlet in the bush,
To the mother-linnet's note
Moduling her slender throat,
Chirping forth thy petty joys,
Wanton in the change of toys,
Like the linnet green, in May,
Flitting to each bloomy spray,
Wearied then, and glad of rest,
Like the linlet in the nest.
This thy present happy lot,
This, in time, will be forgot:
Other pleasures, other cares,
Ever-busy Time prepares;
And thou shalt in thy daughter see,
This picture, once, resembled thee.

JOHN GAY

From FABLES

THE LION, THE FOX, AND THE GEESE

A LION, tired with State affairs,
Quite sick of pomp, and worn with cares,
Resolved remote from noise and strife
In peace to pass his latter life.
    It was proclaimed; the day was set;
Behold the gen'ral council met.
The Fox was Viceroy named. The crowd
To the new Regent humbly bowed:
Wolves, bears and mighty tigers bend,
And strive who most shall condescend.
He straight assumes a solemn grace,
Collects his wisdom in his face,

The crowd admire his wit, his sense:
Each word hath weight and consequence;
The flatt'rer all his art displays:
He who hath power is sure of praise.
A fox stepped forth before the rest,
And thus the servile throng addressed.

'How vast his talents, born to rule,
And trained in virtue's honest school!
What clemency his temper sways!
How uncorrupt are all his ways!
Beneath his conduct and command
Rapine shall cease to waste the land;
His brain hath stratagem and art,
Prudence and mercy rule his heart.
What blessings must attend the nation
Under this good administration!'

He said. A Goose, who distant stood,
Harangued apart the cackling brood.

'Whene'er I hear a knave commend,
He bids me shun his worthy friend.
What praise! What mighty commendation!
But 'twas a fox that spoke th' oration.
Foxes this government may prize
As gentle, plentiful and wise;
If they enjoy these sweets, 'tis plain,
We geese must feel a tyrant reign.
What havock now shall thin our race!
When every petty clerk in place,
To prove his taste, and seem polite,
Will feed on geese both noon and night.'

ALEXANDER POPE

From WINDSOR FOREST

SEE! from the brake the whirring pheasant springs,
And mounts exulting on triumphant wings:
Short is his joy; he feels the fiery wound,
Flutters in blood, and panting beats the ground.

Ah! what avail his glossy, varying dyes,
His purple crest, and scarlet-circled eyes,
The vivid green his shining plumes unfold,
His painted wings, and breast that flames with gold?
  Nor yet, when moist Arcturus clouds the sky,
The woods and fields their pleasing toils deny.
To plains with well-breathed beagles we repair,
And trace the mazes of the circling hare
(Beasts, urged by us, their fellow-beasts pursue,
And learn of man each other to undo).
With slaught'ring guns th' unwearied fowler roves,
When frosts have whitened all the naked groves;
Where doves in flocks the leafless trees o'ershade,
And lonely woodcocks haunt the wat'ry glade.
He lifts the tube, and levels with his eye;
Straight a short thunder breaks the frozen sky:
Oft, as in airy rings they skim the heath,
The clam'rous lapwings feel the leaden death:
Oft, as the mounting larks their notes prepare,
They fall, and leave their little lives in air.
  In genial spring, beneath the quiv'ring shade,
Where cooling vapours breathe along the mead,
The patient fisher takes his silent stand,
Intent, his angle trembling in his hand:
With looks unmoved, he hopes the scaly breed,
And eyes the dancing cork, and bending reed.
Our plenteous streams a various race supply,
The bright-eyed perch with fins of Tyrian dye,
The silver eel, in shining volumes rolled,
The yellow carp, in scales bedropped with gold,
Swift trouts, diversified with crimson stains,
And pikes, the tyrants of the wat'ry plains.

From AN ESSAY ON CRITICISM

A LITTLE LEARNING is a dang'rous thing;
Drink deep, or taste not the Pierian spring:
There shallow draughts intoxicate the brain,
And drinking largely sobers us again.

Fired at first sight with what the Muse imparts,
In fearless youth we tempt the heights of arts,
While from the bounded level of our mind
Short views we take, nor see the lengths behind;
But more advanced, behold with strange surprise
New distant scenes of endless science rise!
So pleased at first the tow'ring Alps we try,
Mount o'er the vales, and seem to tread the sky,
Th' eternal snows appear already past,
And the first clouds and mountains seem the last;
But, those attained, we tremble to survey
The growing labours of the lengthened way,
Th' increasing prospects tire our wand'ring eyes,
Hills peep o'er hills, and Alps on Alps arise!
    A perfect judge will read each work of wit
With the same spirit that its author writ:
Survey the whole, nor seek slight faults to find
Where nature moves, and rapture warms the mind;
Nor lose, for that malignant dull delight,
The gen'rous pleasure to be charmed with wit.
But in such lays as neither ebb, nor flow,
Correctly cold, and regularly low,
That shunning faults, one quiet tenor keep;
We cannot blame indeed – but we may sleep.
In wit, as nature, what affects our hearts
Is not th' exactness of peculiar parts;
'Tis not a lip, or eye, we beauty call,
But the joint force and full result of all.
Thus when we view some well-proportioned dome
(The world's just wonder, and ev'n thine, O Rome!)
No single parts unequally surprise,
All comes united to th' admiring eyes;
No monstrous height, or breadth, or length appear;
The whole at once is bold, and regular.

From THE RAPE OF THE LOCK

CLOSE by those meads, for ever crowned with flow'rs,
Where Thames with pride surveys his rising tow'rs,
There stands a structure of majestic frame,
Which from the neighb'ring Hampton takes its name.
Here Britain's statesmen oft the fall foredoom
Of foreign tyrants and of nymphs at home;
Here thou, great Anna! whom three realms obey,
Dost sometimes counsel take – and sometimes tea.
 Hither the heroes and the nymphs resort,
To taste awhile the pleasures of a Court;
In various talk th' instructive hours they passed,
Who gave the ball, or paid the visit last;
One speaks the glory of the British Queen,
And one describes a charming Indian screen;
A third interprets motions, looks, and eyes;
At ev'ry word a reputation dies.
Snuff, or the fan, supply each pause of chat,
With singing, laughing, ogling, *and all that.*

From THE DUNCIAD

SHE COMES! She comes! The sable throne behold
Of Night primeval and of Chaos old!
Before her, Fancy's gilded clouds decay,
And all its varying rainbows die away.
Wit shoots in vain its momentary fires,
The meteor drops, and in a flash expires,
As one by one, at dread Medea's strain,
The sick'ning stars fade off th' ethereal plain;
As Argus' eyes by Hermes' wand oppressed,
Closed one by one to everlasting rest;
Thus at her felt approach, and secret might,
Art after Art goes out, and all is Night.
See skulking Truth to her old cavern fled,
Mountains of Casuistry heaped o'er her head!
Philosophy, that leaned on Heav'n before,
Shrinks to her second cause, and is no more.

Physic of Metaphysic begs defence,
And Metaphysic calls for aid on Sense!
See Mystery to Mathematics fly!
In vain! They gaze, turn giddy, rave, and die.
Religion blushing veils her sacred fires,
And unawares Morality expires.
For public Flame, nor private, dares to shine;
Nor human Spark is left, nor Glimpse divine!
Lo! thy dread Empire, Chaos! is restored;
Light dies before thy uncreating word;
Thy hand, great Anarch! lets the curtain fall,
And universal Darkness buries all.

From AN ESSAY ON MAN

KNOW then thyself, presume not God to scan;
The proper study of mankind is Man.
Placed on this isthmus of a middle state,
A being darkly wise, and rudely great:
With too much knowledge for the Sceptic side,
With too much weakness for the Stoic's pride,
He hangs between; in doubt to act, or rest;
In doubt to deem himself a god, or beast;
In doubt his mind or body to prefer;
Born but to die, and reas'ning but to err;
Alike in ignorance, his reason such,
Whether he thinks too little, or too much:
Chaos of thought and passion, all confused;
Still by himself abused, or disabused;
Created half to rise, and half to fall;
Great lord of all things, yet a prey to all;
Sole judge of truth, in endless error hurled:
The glory, jest, and riddle of the world!

Go, wondrous creature! mount where science guides,
Go, measure earth, weigh air, and state the tides;
Instruct the planets in what orbs to run,
Correct old Time, and regulate the sun;
Go, soar with Plato to th' empyreal sphere,
To the first good, first perfect, and first fair;

Or tread the mazy round his follow'rs trod,
And quitting sense call imitating God;
As Eastern priests in giddy circles run,
And turn their heads to imitate the sun.
Go, teach Eternal Wisdom how to rule –
Then drop into thyself, and be a fool!

EPISTLE TO ARBUTHNOT

Being the Prologue to the Satires

P. SHUT, shut the door, good John! fatigued, I said,
Tie up the knocker, say I'm sick, I'm dead.
The Dog Star rages! Nay, 'tis past a doubt,
All Bedlam, or Parnassus, is let out:
Fire in each eye, and papers in each hand,
They rave, recite, and madden round the land.

    What walls can guard me, or what shades can hide?
They pierce my thickets, through my grot they glide;
By land, by water, they renew the charge;
They stop the chariot, and they board the barge.
No place is sacred, not the church is free;
Ev'n Sunday shines no Sabbath Day to me;
Then from the Mint walks forth the man of rhyme,
Happy to catch me just at dinner-time.

    Is there a parson, much bemused in beer,
A maudlin poetess, a rhyming peer,
A clerk, foredoomed his father's soul to cross,
Who pens a stanza, when he should engross?
Is there, who, locked from ink and paper, scrawls
With desp'rate charcoal round his darkened walls?
All fly to Twitnam, and in humble strain
Apply to me, to keep them mad or vain.
Arthur, whose giddy son neglects the laws,
Imputes to me and my damned works the cause:
Poor Cornus sees his frantic wife elope,
And curses wit, and poetry, and Pope.

    Friend to my life! (which did you not prolong,
The world had wanted many an idle song)
What drop or nostrum can this plague remove?

Or which must end me, a fool's wrath or love?
A dire dilemma! Either way I'm sped:
If foes, they write, if friends, they read me dead.
Seized and tied down to judge, how wretched I!
Who can't be silent, and who will not lie.
To laugh were want of goodness and of grace,
And to be grave exceeds all pow'r of face.
I sit with sad civility, I read
With honest anguish, and an aching head;
And drop at last, but in unwilling ears,
This saving counsel, 'Keep your piece nine years.'

'Nine years!' cries he, who high in Drury Lane,
Lulled by soft zephyrs through the broken pane,
Rhymes ere he wakes, and prints before term ends,
Obliged by hunger, and request of friends.
'The piece, you think, is incorrect? Why, take it,
I'm all submission, what you'd have it, make it.'

Three things another's modest wishes bound,
My friendship, and a prologue, and ten pound.

Pitholeon sends to me: 'You know his Grace,
I want a patron; ask him for a place.'
Pitholeon libelled me – 'but here's a letter
Informs you, sir, 'twas when he knew no better.
Dare you refuse him? Curll invites to dine,
He'll write a *Journal*, or he'll turn divine.'

Bless me! a packet – ' 'Tis a stranger sues,
A Virgin Tragedy, an Orphan Muse.'
If I dislike it, 'Furies, death and rage!'
If I approve, 'Commend it to the stage.'
There (thank my stars) my whole commission ends,
The play'rs and I are, luckily, no friends.
Fired that the house reject him, ' 'Sdeath, I'll print it,
And shame the fools— Your int'rest, sir, with Lintot!'
'Lintot, dull rogue! will think your price too much.'
'Not, sir, if you revise it, and retouch.'
All my demurs but double his attacks;
At last he whispers, 'Do; and we go snacks.'
Glad of a quarrel, straight I clap the door.
Sir, let me see your works and you no more.

'Tis sung, when Midas' ears began to spring
(Midas, a sacred person and a king)
His very minister who spied them first
(Some say his queen) was forced to speak, or burst.
And is not mine, my friend, a sorer case,
When ev'ry coxcomb perks them in my face?
A. Good friend, forbear! you deal in dang'rous things.
I'd never name queens, ministers, or kings;
Keep close to ears, and those let asses prick;
'Tis nothing— *P.* Nothing? if they bite and kick?
Out with it, Dunciad! let the secret pass,
That secret to each fool, that he's an ass:
The truth once told (and wherefore should we lie?)
The queen of Midas slept, and so may I.
   You think this cruel? Take it for a rule,
No creature smarts so little as a fool.
Let peals of laughter, Codrus! round thee break,
Thou unconcerned can'st hear the mighty crack:
Pit, box, and gall'ry in convulsions hurled,
Thou stand'st unshook amidst a bursting world.
Who shames a scribbler? Break one cobweb through,
He spins the slight, self-pleasing thread anew:
Destroy his fib or sophistry, in vain,
The creature's at his dirty work again,
Throned in the centre of his thin designs,
Proud of a vast extent of flimsy lines!
Whom have I hurt? Has poet yet, or peer,
Lost the arched eyebrow, or Parnassian sneer?
And has not Colley still his lord, and whore?
His butchers Henley, his Freemasons Moore?
Does not one table Bavius still admit?
Still to one bishop Philips seem a wit?
Still Sappho— *A.* Hold! for God's sake – you'll offend!
No names! – be calm! – learn prudence of a friend!
I too could write, and I am twice as tall;
But foes like these— *P.* One flatt'rer's worse than all.
Of all mad creatures, if the learn'd are right,
It is the slaver kills, and not the bite.
A fool quite angry is quite innocent:

Alas! 'tis ten times worse when they *repent*.
    One dedicates in high heroic prose,
And ridicules beyond a hundred foes;
One from all Grub Street will my fame defend,
And, more abusive, calls himself my friend.
This prints my letters, that expects a bribe,
And others roar aloud, 'Subscribe, subscribe.'
    There are, who to my person pay their court:
I cough like Horace, and, though lean, am short,
Ammon's great son one shoulder had too high,
Such Ovid's nose, and 'Sir! you have an eye' –
Go on, obliging creatures, make me see
All that disgraced my betters met in me.
Say for my comfort, languishing in bed,
'Just so immortal Maro held his head';
And when I die, be sure you let me know
Great Homer died three thousand years ago.
    Why did I write? What sin to me unknown
Dipped me in ink, my parents', or my own?
As yet a child, nor yet a fool to fame,
I lisped in numbers, for the numbers came.
I left no calling for this idle trade,
No duty broke, no father disobeyed.
The Muse but served to ease some friend, not wife,
To help me through this long disease, my life,
To second, Arbuthnot! thy art and care,
And teach the being you preserved, to bear.
    But why then publish? Granville the polite,
And knowing Walsh, would tell me I could write;
Well-natured Garth enflamed with early praise;
And Congreve loved, and Swift endured my lays;
The courtly Talbot, Somers, Sheffield read;
Ev'n mitred Rochester would nod the head,
And St John's self (great Dryden's friend before)
With open arms received one poet more.
Happy my studies, when by these approved!
Happier their author, when by these beloved!
From these the world will judge of men and books,
Not from the Burnets, Oldmixons, and Cookes.

Soft were my numbers! Who could take offence,
While pure description held the place of sense?
Like gentle Fanny's was my flow'ry theme,
A painted mistress, or a purling stream.
Yet then did Gildon draw his venal quill –
I wished the man a dinner, and sat still.
Yet then did Dennis rave in furious fret;
I never answered – I was not in debt.
If want provoked, or madness made them print,
I waged no war with Bedlam or the Mint.

Did some more sober critic come abroad;
If wrong, I smiled; if right, I kissed the rod.
Pains, reading, study, are their just pretence,
And all they want is spirit, taste, and sense.
Commas and points they set exactly right,
And 'twere a sin to rob them of their mite.
Yet ne'er one sprig of laurel graced these ribalds,
From slashing Bentley down to piddling Tibbalds:
Each wight, who reads not, and but scans and spells,
Each word-catcher, that lives on syllables,
Ev'n such small critics some regard may claim,
Preserved in Milton's or in Shakespeare's name.
Pretty! in amber to observe the forms
Of hairs, or straws, or dirt, or grubs, or worms!
The things, we know, are neither rich nor rare,
But wonder how the devil they got there.

Were others angry: I excused them too;
Well might they rage, I gave them but their due.
A man's true merit 'tis not hard to find;
But each man's secret standard in his mind,
That casting-weight pride adds to emptiness,
This, who can gratify? for who can guess?
The bard whom pilfered Pastorals renown,
Who turns a Persian tale for half a crown,
Just writes to make his barrenness appear,
And strains, from hard-bound brains, eight lines a year;
He, who still wanting, though he lives on theft,
Steals much, spends little, yet has nothing left;
And he, who now to sense, now nonsense leaning,

Means not, but blunders round about a meaning;
And he, whose fustian's so sublimely bad,
It is not poetry, but prose run mad:
All these, my modest satire bade translate,
And owned that nine such poets made a Tate.
How did they fume, and stamp, and roar, and chafe!
And swear, not Addison himself was safe.

    Peace to all such! but were there one whose fires
True Genius kindles, and fair Fame inspires;
Blest with each talent and each art to please,
And born to write, converse, and live with ease:
Should such a man, too fond to rule alone,
Bear, like the Turk, no brother near the throne.
View him with scornful, yet with jealous eyes,
And hate for arts that caused himself to rise;
Damn with faint praise, assent with civil leer,
And without sneering, teach the rest to sneer;
Willing to wound, and yet afraid to strike,
Just hint a fault, and hesitate dislike;
Alike reserved to blame, or to commend,
A tim'rous foe, and a suspicious friend;
Dreading ev'n fools, by flatterers besieged,
And so obliging, that he ne'er obliged;
Like Cato, give his little Senate laws,
And sit attentive to his own applause;
While wits and Templars ev'ry sentence raise,
And wonder with a foolish face of praise:
Who but must laugh, if such a man there be?
Who would not weep, if Atticus were he?

    What though my name stood rubric on the walls,
Or plastered posts, with claps, in capitals?
Or smoking forth, a hundred hawkers' load,
On wings of winds came flying all abroad?
I sought no homage from the race that write;
I kept, like Asian monarchs, from their sight:
Poems I heeded (now be-rhymed so long)
No more than thou, great George! a birthday song.
I ne'er with wits or witlings passed my days,
To spread about the itch of verse and praise;

Nor like a puppy, daggled through the town,
To fetch and carry sing-song up and down;
Nor at rehearsals sweat, and mouthed and cried,
With handkerchief and orange at my side;
But sick of fops, and poetry, and prate,
To Bufo left the whole Castalian state.
  Proud as Apollo on his forkèd hill,
Sat full-blown Bufo, puffed by ev'ry quill;
Fed with soft dedication all day long,
Horace and he went hand in hand in song.
His library (where busts of poets dead
And a true Pindar stood without a head)
Received of wits an undistinguished race,
Who first his judgement asked, and then a place:
Much they extolled his pictures, much his seat,
And flattered ev'ry day, and some days eat;
Till grown more frugal in his riper days,
He paid some bards with port, and some with praise;
To some a dry rehearsal was assigned,
And others (harder still) he paid in kind.
Dryden alone (what wonder?) came not nigh,
Dryden alone escaped this judging eye;
But still the great have kindness in reserve,
He helped to bury whom he helped to starve.
  May some choice patron bless each grey goose quill!
May ev'ry Bavius have his Bufo still!
So, when a statesman wants a day's defence,
Or Envy holds a whole week's war with Sense,
Or simple pride for flatt'ry makes demands,
May dunce by dunce be whistled off my hands!
Blest be the great! for those they take away,
And those they left me; for they left me Gay;
Left me to see neglected genius bloom,
Neglected die, and tell it on his tomb:
Of all thy blameless life the sole return
My verse, and Queensb'ry weeping o'er thy urn!
  Oh, let me live my own, and die so too!
(To live and die is all I have to do):
Maintain a poet's dignity and ease,

And see what friends, and read what books I please;
Above a patron, though I condescend
Sometimes to call a minister my friend.
I was not born for Courts or great affairs;
I pay my debts, believe, and say my prayers;
Can sleep without a poem in my head;
Nor know if Dennis be alive or dead.

    Why am I asked what next shall see the light?
Heav'ns! was I born for nothing but to write?
Has life no joys for me? or (to be grave)
Have I no friend to serve, no soul to save?
'I found him close with Swift' – 'Indeed? No doubt',
Cries prating Balbus, 'something will come out.'
'Tis all in vain, deny it as I will.
'No, such a genius never can lie still';
And then for mine obligingly mistakes
The first lampoon Sir Will or Bubo makes.
Poor guiltless I! and can I choose but smile,
When ev'ry coxcomb knows me by my style?

    Curst be the verse, how well soe'er it flow,
That tends to make one worthy man my foe,
Give virtue scandal, innocence a fear,
Or from the soft-eyed virgin steal a tear!
But he who hurts a harmless neighbour's peace,
Insults fall'n worth, or beauty in distress,
Who loves a lie, lame slander helps about,
Who writes a libel, or who copies out:
That fop, whose pride affects a patron's name,
Yet absent, wounds an author's honest fame;
Who can your merit selfishly approve,
And show the sense of it without the love;
Who has the vanity to call you friend,
Yet wants the honour, injured, to defend;
Who tells whate'er you think, whate'er you say,
And if he lie not, must at least betray;
Who to the Dean, and silver bell can swear,
And sees at Canons what was never there;
Who reads, but with a lust to misapply,
Make satire a lampoon, and fiction lie.

A lash like mine no honest man shall dread,
But all such babbling blockheads in his stead.

    Let Sporus tremble— *A.* What? that thing of silk,
Sporus, that mere white curd of ass's milk?
Satire or sense, alas! can Sporus feel?
Who breaks a butterfly upon a wheel?
P. Yet let me flap this bug with gilded wings,
This painted child of dirt, that stinks and stings;
Whose buzz the witty and the fair annoys,
Yet wit ne'er tastes, and beauty ne'er enjoys:
So well-bred spaniels civilly delight
In mumbling of the game they dare not bite.
Eternal smiles his emptiness betray,
As shallow streams run dimpling all the way.
Whether in florid impotence he speaks,
And, as the prompter breathes, the puppet squeaks;
Or at the ear of Eve, familiar toad,
Half froth, half venom, spits himself abroad,
In puns, or politics, or tales, or lies,
Or spite, or smut, or rhymes, or blasphemies.
His wit all see-saw, between that and this,
Now high, now low, now master up, now miss,
And he himself one vile antithesis.
Amphibious thing! that acting either part,
The trifling head or the corrupted heart,
Fop at the toilet, flatt'rer at the board,
Now trips a lady, and now struts a lord.
Eve's tempter thus the rabbins have expressed,
A cherub's face, a reptile all the rest;
Beauty that shocks you, parts that none will trust;
Wit that can creep, and pride that licks the dust.

    Not Fortune's worshipper, nor fashion's fool,
Not lucre's madman, nor ambition's tool,
Not proud, nor servile – be one poet's praise,
That, if he pleased, he pleased by manly ways:
That flatt'ry, ev'n to kings, he held a shame,
And thought a lie in verse or prose the same.
That not in fancy's maze he wandered long,
But stooped to truth, and moralised his song:

That not for fame, but virtue's better end,
He stood the furious foe, the timid friend,
The damning critic, half-approving wit,
The coxcomb hit, or fearing to be hit;
Laughed at the loss of friends he never had,
The dull, the proud, the wicked, and the mad;
The distant threats of vengeance on his head,
The blow unfelt, the tear he never shed;
The tale revived, the lie so oft o'erthrown,
Th' imputed trash, and dullness not his own;
The morals blackened when the writings 'scape,
The libelled person, and the pictured shape;
Abuse, on all he loved, or loved him, spread,
A friend in exile, or a father dead;
The whisper, that to greatness still too near,
Perhaps, yet vibrates on his sov'reign's ear –
Welcome for thee, fair Virtue! all the past;
For thee, fair Virtue! welcome ev'n the last!
    A. But why insult the poor, affront the great?
P. A knave's a knave, to me, in ev'ry state:
Alike my scorn, if he succeed or fail,
Sporus at court, or Japhet in a jail,
A hireling scribbler, or a hireling peer,
Knight of the post corrupt, or of the shire;
If on a pillory, or near a throne,
He gain his prince's ear, or lose his own.
    Yet soft by nature, more a dupe than wit,
Sappho can tell you how this man was bit;
This dreaded sat'rist Dennis will confess
Foe to his pride, but friend to his distress:
So humble, he has knocked at Tibbald's door,
Has drunk with Cibber – nay, has rhymed for Moore.
Full ten years slandered, did he once reply?
Three thousand suns went down on Welsted's lie.
To please a mistress one aspersed his life;
He lashed him not, but let her be his wife.
Let Budgel charge low Grub Street on his quill,
And write whate'er he pleased, except his Will;
Let the two Curlls of town and Court abuse

His father, mother, body, soul, and Muse.
Yet why? That Father held it for a rule,
It was a sin to call our neighbour fool:
That harmless Mother thought no wife a whore:
Hear this, and spare his family, James Moore!
Unspotted names, and memorable long!
If there be force in virtue, or in song.

Of gentle blood (part shed in honour's cause,
While yet in Britain honour had applause)
Each parent sprung— *A.* What fortune, pray? – *P.* Their own.
And better got than Bestia's from the throne.
Born to no pride, inheriting no strife,
Nor marrying discord in a noble wife,
Stranger to civil and religious rage,
The good man walked innoxious through his age.
Nor Courts he saw, no suits would ever try,
Nor dared an oath, nor hazarded a lie.
Unlearn'd, he knew no schoolman's subtle art,
No language, but the language of the heart.
By nature honest, by experience wise,
Healthy by temp'rance, and by exercise;
His life, though long, to sickness past unknown,
His death was instant, and without a groan.
Oh, grant me thus to live, and thus to die!
Who sprung from kings shall know less joy than I.

O Friend! may each domestic bliss be thine!
Be no unpleasing melancholy mine:
Me, let the tender office long engage,
To rock the cradle of reposing age,
With lenient arts extend a mother's breath,
Make Languor smile, and smooth the bed of Death,
Explore the thought, explain the asking eye,
And keep a while one parent from the sky!
On cares like these if length of days attend,
May heav'n, to bless those days, preserve my friend,
Preserve him social, cheerful, and serene,
And just as rich as when he served a queen.
A. Whether that blessing be denied or giv'n,
Thus far was right, the rest belongs to heav'n.

JOHN DYER

From GRONGAR HILL

GRONGAR HILL invites my song,
Draw the landskip bright and strong;
Grongar, in whose mossy cells
Sweetly musing Quiet dwells;
Grongar, in whose silent shade,
For the modest Muses made,
So oft I have, the evening still,
At the fountain of a rill,
Sate upon a flow'ry bed,
With my hand beneath my head;
And strayed my eyes o'er Towy's flood,
Over mead and over wood,
From house to house, from hill to hill,
Till Contemplation had her fill.
About his chequered sides I wind,
And leave his brooks and meads behind,
And groves and grottoes where I lay,
And vistas shooting beams of day;
Wide and wider spreads the vale,
As circles on a smooth canal:
The mountains round, unhappy fate,
Sooner or later, of all height,
Withdraw their summits from the skies,
And lessen as the others rise;
Still the prospect wider spreads,
Adds a thousand woods and meads,
Still it widens, widens still,
And sinks the newly risen hill.

JAMES THOMSON

From THE SEASONS

[WINTER]

BUT HARK! the nightly winds, with hollow voice,
Blow, blust'ring, from the south – the frost subdued,
Gradual, resolves into a weeping thaw.
Spotted, the mountains shine; loose sleet descends,
And floods the country round; the rivers swell,
Impatient for the day. – Those sullen seas,
That wash th' ungenial Pole, will rest no more,
Beneath the shackles of the mighty north;
But, rousing all their waves, resistless heave –
And hark! – the length'ning roar, continuous, runs
Athwart the rifted main; at once, it bursts,
And piles a thousand mountains to the clouds!
Ill fares the bark, the wretches' last resort,
That, lost amid the floating fragments, moors
Beneath the shelter of an icy isle;
While night o'erwhelms the sea, and horror looks
More horrible. Can human hearts endure
Th' assembled mischiefs, that besiege them round:
Unlist'ning hunger, fainting weariness,
The roar of winds, and waves, the crush of ice,
Now ceasing, now renewed, with louder rage,
And bellowing round the main? Nations remote,
Shook from their midnight slumbers, deem they hear
Portentous thunder in the troubled sky.
More to embroil the deep, Leviathan,
And his unwieldy train, in horrid sport,
Tempest the loosened brine; while, through the gloom,
Far from the dire, unhospitable shore,
The lion's rage, the wolf's sad howl is heard,
And all the fell society of night.

SAMUEL JOHNSON

THE VANITY OF HUMAN WISHES

The tenth satire of Juvenal imitated

LET Observation with extensive view
Survey mankind from China to Peru;
Remark each anxious toil, each eager strife,
And watch the busy scenes of crowded life;
Then say how hope and fear, desire and hate,
O'erspread with snares the clouded maze of fate,
Where wav'ring Man, betrayed by vent'rous pride,
To tread the dreary paths without a guide,
As treach'rous phantoms in the mist delude,
Shuns fancied ills, or chases airy good;
How rarely Reason guides the stubborn choice,
Rules the bold hand, or prompts the suppliant voice;
How nations sink, by darling schemes oppressed,
When Vengeance listens to the fool's request.
Fate wings with ev'ry wish th' afflictive dart,
Each gift of Nature, and each grace of Art;
With fatal heat impetuous courage glows,
With fatal sweetness elocution flows,
Impeachment stops the speaker's pow'rful breath,
And restless fire precipitates on death.
    But, scarce observed, the knowing and the bold
Fall in the gen'ral massacre of gold;
Wide-wasting pest! that rages unconfined,
And crowds with crimes the records of mankind:
For gold his sword the hireling ruffian draws,
For gold the hireling judge distorts the laws;
Wealth heaped on wealth, nor truth nor safety buys,
The dangers gather as the treasures rise.
    Let Hist'ry tell where rival kings command,
And dubious title shakes the madded land,
When statutes glean the refuse of the sword,
How much more safe the vassal than the lord,
Low skulks the hind beneath the rage of pow'r,
And leaves the wealthy traitor in the Tow'r,

Untouched his cottage, and his slumbers sound,
Though Confiscation's vultures hover round.
　The needy traveller, serene and gay,
Walks the wild heath, and sings his toil away.
Does envy seize thee? crush th' upbraiding joy,
Increase his riches and his peace destroy;
Now fears in dire vicissitude invade,
The rustling brake alarms, and quiv'ring shade,
Nor light nor darkness bring his pain relief,
One shows the plunder, and one hides the thief.
　Yet still one gen'ral cry the skies assails,
And gain and grandeur load the tainted gales;
Few know the toiling statesman's fear or care,
Th' insidious rival and the gaping heir.
　Once more, Democritus, arise on earth,
With cheerful wisdom and instructive mirth,
See motley life in modern trappings dressed,
And feed with varied fools th' eternal jest:
Thou who could'st laugh where Want enchained Caprice,
Toil crushed Conceit, and Man was of a piece;
Where Wealth unloved without a mourner died;
And scarce a sycophant was fed by Pride;
Where ne'er was known the form of mock debate,
Or seen a new-made mayor's unwieldy state;
Where change of fav'rites made no change of laws,
And senates heard before they judged a cause;
How would'st thou shake at Britain's modish tribe,
Dart the quick taunt, and edge the piercing gibe?
Attentive truth and nature to descry,
And pierce each scene with philosophic eye,
To thee were solemn toys or empty show,
The robes of pleasure and the veils of woe:
All aid the farce, and all thy mirth maintain,
Whose joys are causeless, or whose griefs are vain.
　Such was the scorn that filled the sage's mind,
Renewed at ev'ry glance on humankind;
How just that scorn ere yet thy voice declare,
Search ev'ry state, and canvass ev'ry prayer.
　Unnumbered suppliants crowd Preferment's gate,

Athirst for wealth, and burning to be great;
Delusive Fortune hears th' incessant call,
They mount, they shine, evaporate, and fall.
On ev'ry stage the foes of peace attend,
Hate dogs their flight, and Insult mocks their end.
Love ends with hope, the sinking statesman's door
Pours in the morning worshipper no more;
For growing names the weekly scribbler lies,
To growing wealth the dedicator flies;
From ev'ry room descends the painted face,
That hung the bright Palladium of the place;
And smoked in kitchens, or in auctions sold,
To better features yields the frame of gold;
For now no more we trace in ev'ry line
Heroic worth, benevolence divine:
The form distorted justifies the fall,
And Detestation rids th' indignant wall.

But will not Britain hear the last appeal,
Sign her foes' doom, or guard her fav'rites' zeal?
Through Freedom's sons no more remonstrance rings,
Degrading nobles and controlling kings;
Our supple tribes repress their patriot throats,
Ask no questions but the price of votes;
With weekly libels and septennial ale,
Their wish is full to riot and to rail.

In full-blown dignity, see Wolsey stand,
Law in his voice, and fortune in his hand:
To him the Church, the realm, their pow'rs consign,
Through him the rays of regal bounty shine;
Turned by his nod the stream of honour flows,
His smile alone security bestows:
Still to new heights his restless wishes tow'r,
Claim leads to claim, and pow'r advances pow'r;
Till conquest unresisted ceased to please,
And rights submitted, left him none to seize.
At length his sov'reign frowns – the train of state
Mark the keen glance, and watch the sign to hate.
Where'er he turns he meets a stranger's eye,
His suppliants scorn him, and his foll'wers fly;

At once is lost the pride of awful state,
The golden canopy, the glitt'ring plate,
The regal palace, the luxurious board,
The liv'ried army, and the menial lord.
With age, with cares, with maladies oppressed,
He seeks the refuge of monastic rest.
Grief aids disease, remembered folly stings,
And his last sighs reproach the faith of kings.

Speak thou, whose thoughts at humble peace repine,
Shall Wolsey's wealth, with Wolsey's end, be thine?
Or liv'st thou now, with safer pride content,
The wisest justice on the banks of Trent?
For why did Wolsey, near the steeps of fate,
On weak foundations raise th' enormous weight?
Why but to sink beneath misfortune's blow,
With louder ruin to the gulfs below?

What gave great Villiers to th' assassin's knife,
And fixed disease on Harley's closing life?
What murdered Wentworth, and what exiled Hyde,
By kings protected, and to kings allied?
What but their wish indulged in courts to shine,
And pow'r too great to keep or to resign?

When first the college rolls receive his name,
The young enthusiast quits his ease for fame;
Through all his veins the fever of renown
Burns from the strong contagion of the gown;
O'er Bodley's dome his future labours spread,
And Bacon's mansion trembles o'er his head.
Are these thy views? Proceed, illustrious youth,
And Virtue guard thee to the throne of Truth!
Yet should thy soul indulge the gen'rous heat,
Till captive Science yields her last retreat;
Should Reason guide thee with her brightest ray,
And pour on misty Doubt resistless day;
Should no false kindness lure to loose delight,
Nor praise relax, nor difficulty fright;
Should tempting Novelty thy cell refrain,
And Sloth effuse her opiate fumes in vain;
Should Beauty blunt on fops her fatal dart,

Nor claim the triumph of a lettered heart;
Should no disease thy torpid veins invade,
Nor Melancholy's phantoms haunt thy shade;
Yet hope not life from grief or danger free,
Nor think the doom of Man reversed for thee:
Deign on the passing world to turn thine eyes,
And pause awhile from letters to be wise;
There mark what ills the scholar's life assail,
Toil, envy, want, the patron, and the jail.
See nations slowly wise, and meanly just,
To buried merit raise the tardy bust.
If dreams yet flatter, once again attend,
Hear Lydiat's life and Galileo's end.

Nor deem, when Learning her last prize bestows,
The glitt'ring eminence exempt from foes;
See when the vulgar 'scapes, despised or awed,
Rebellion's vengeful talons seize on Laud,
From meaner minds, though smaller fines content,
The plundered palace or sequestered rent;
Marked out by dang'rous parts he meets the shock,
And fatal Learning leads him to the block:
Around his tomb let Art and Genius weep,
But hear his death, ye blockheads, hear and sleep.

The festal blazes, the triumphal show,
The ravished standard, and the captive foe,
The senate's thanks, the gazette's pompous tale,
With force resistless o'er the brave prevail.
Such bribes the rapid Greek o'er Asia whirled,
For such the steady Romans shook the world;
For such in distant lands the Britons shine,
And stain with blood the Danube or the Rhine;
This pow'r has praise, that virtue scarce can warm,
Till fame supplies the universal charm.
Yet Reason frowns on War's unequal game,
Where wasted nations raise a single name,
And mortgaged states their grandsires' wreaths regret
From age to age in everlasting debt;
Wreaths which at last the dear-bought right convey
To rust on medals, or on stones decay.

On what foundation stands the warrior's pride?
How just his hopes let Swedish Charles decide;
A frame of adamant, a soul of fire,
No dangers fright him, and no labours tire;
O'er love, o'er fear, extends his wide domain,
Unconquered lord of pleasure and of pain;
No joys to him pacific sceptres yield,
War sounds the trump, he rushes to the field;
Behold surrounding kings their pow'rs combine,
And one capitulate, and one resign;
Peace courts his hand, but spreads her charms in vain;
'Think nothing gained', he cries, 'till nought remain,
On Moscow's walls till Gothic standards fly,
And all be mine beneath the polar sky.'
The march begins in military state,
And nations on his eye suspended wait;
Stern Famine guards the solitary coast,
And Winter barricades the realms of Frost;
He comes, nor want nor cold his course delay;
Hide, blushing Glory, hide Pultowa's day:
The vanquished hero leaves his broken bands,
And shows his miseries in distant lands;
Condemned a needy suppliant to wait,
While ladies interpose, and slaves debate.
But did not Chance at length her error mend?
Did no subverted empire mark his end?
Did rival monarchs give the fatal wound?
Or hostile millions press him to the ground?
His fall was destined to a barren strand,
A petty fortress, and a dubious hand;
He left the name, at which the world grew pale,
To point a moral, or adorn a tale.

All times their scenes of pompous woes afford,
From Persia's tyrant to Bavaria's lord.
In gay hostility, and barb'rous pride,
With half mankind embattled at his side,
Great Xerxes comes to seize the certain prey,
And starves exhausted regions in his way;
Attendant Flatt'ry counts his myriads o'er,

Till counted myriads sooth his pride no more;
Fresh praise is tried till madness fires his mind,
The waves he lashes, and enchains the wind;
New pow'rs are claimed, new pow'rs are still bestowed,
Till rude resistance lops the spreading god;
The daring Greeks deride the martial show,
And heap their valleys with the gaudy foe;
Th' insulted sea with humbler thoughts he gains,
A single skiff to speed his flight remains;
Th' encumbered oar scarce leaves the dreaded coast
Through purple billows and a floating host.

   The bold Bavarian, in a luckless hour,
Tries the dread summits of Caesarean pow'r,
With unexpected legions bursts away,
And sees defenceless realms receive his sway.
Short sway! Fair Austria spreads her mournful charms,
The Queen, the beauty, sets the world in arms;
From hill to hill the beacons' rousing blaze
Spreads wide the hope of plunder and of praise;
The fierce Croatian, and the wild Hussar,
With all the sons of Ravage crowd the war;
The baffled prince in honour's flatt'ring bloom
Of hasty greatness finds the fatal doom,
His foes' derision, and his subjects' blame,
And steals to death from anguish and from shame.

   Enlarge my life with multitude of days!
In health, in sickness, thus the suppliant prays;
Hides from himself his state, and shuns to know,
That life protracted is protracted woe.
Time hovers o'er, impatient to destroy,
And shuts up all the passages of joy;
In vain their gifts the bounteous seasons pour,
The fruit autumnal, and the vernal flow'r,
With listless eyes the dotard views the store,
He views, and wonders that they please no more;
Now pall the tasteless meats, and joyless wines,
And Luxury with sighs her slave resigns.
Approach, ye minstrels, try the soothing strain,
Diffuse the tuneful lenitives of pain:

No sounds, alas! would touch th' impervious ear,
Though dancing mountains witnessed Orpheus near;
Nor lute nor lyre his feeble pow'rs attend,
Nor sweeter music of a virtuous friend,
But everlasting dictates crowd his tongue,
Perversely grave, or positively wrong.
The still returning tale, and ling'ring jest,
Perplex the fawning niece and pampered guest,
While growing hopes scarce awe the gath'ring sneer,
And scarce a legacy can bribe to hear;
The watchful guests still hint the last offence;
The daughter's petulance, the son's expense,
Improve his heady rage with treach'rous skill,
And mould his passions till they make his will.

Unnumbered maladies his joints invade,
Lay siege to life and press the dire blockade;
But unextinguished av'rice still remains,
And dreaded losses aggravate his pains;
He turns, with anxious heart and crippled hands,
His bonds of debt, and mortgages of lands;
Or views his coffers with suspicious eyes,
Unlocks his gold, and counts it till he dies.

But grant, the virtues of a temp'rate prime
Bless with an age exempt from scorn or crime;
An age that melts with unperceived decay,
And glides in modest innocence away;
Whose peaceful day Benevolence endears,
Whose night congratulating Conscience cheers;
The gen'ral fav'rite as the gen'ral friend:
Such age there is, and who shall wish its end?

Yet ev'n on this her load Misfortune flings,
To press the weary minutes' flagging wings:
New sorrow rises as the day returns,
A sister sickens, or a daughter mourns.
Now kindred Merit fills the sable bier,
Now lacerated Friendship claims a tear;
Year chases year, decay pursues decay,
Still drops some joy from with'ring life away;
New forms arise, and diff'rent views engage,

Superfluous lags the vet'ran on the stage,
Till pitying Nature signs the last release,
And bids afflicted Worth retire to peace.
  But few there are whom hours like these await,
Who set unclouded in the gulfs of Fate.
From Lydia's monarch should the search descend,
By Solon cautioned to regard his end,
In life's last scene what prodigies surprise,
Fears of the brave, and follies of the wise!
From Marlb'rough's eyes the streams of dotage flow,
And Swift expires a driv'ller and a show.
  The teeming mother, anxious for her race,
Begs for each birth the fortune of a face:
Yet Vane could tell what ills from beauty spring;
And Sedley cursed the form that pleased a king.
Ye nymphs of rosy lips and radiant eyes,
Whom Pleasure keeps too busy to be wise,
Whom Joys with soft varieties invite
By day the frolic, and the dance by night;
Who frown with vanity, who smile with art,
And ask the latest fashion of the heart;
What care, what rules your heedless charms shall save,
Each nymph your rival, and each youth your slave?
Against your fame with Fondness Hate combines,
The rival batters, and the lover mines.
With distant voice neglected Virtue calls,
Less heard and less, the faint remonstrance falls;
Tired with contempt, she quits the slipp'ry reign,
And Pride and Prudence take her seat in vain.
In crowd at once, where none the pass defend,
The harmless freedom, and the private friend.
The guardians yield, by force superior plied;
To Int'rest, Prudence; and to Flatt'ry, Pride.
Here Beauty falls betrayed, despised, distressed,
And hissing Infamy proclaims the rest.
  Where then shall Hope and Fear their objects find?
Must dull Suspense corrupt the stagnant mind?
Must helpless Man, in ignorance sedate,
Roll darkling down the torrent of his fate?

Must no dislike alarm, no wishes rise,
No cries invoke the mercies of the skies?
Enquirer, cease; petitions yet remain,
Which Heav'n may hear, nor deem religion vain.
Still raise for good the supplicating voice,
But leave to Heav'n the measure and the choice.
Safe in His pow'r, whose eyes discern afar
The secret ambush of a specious prayer.
Implore His aid, in His decisions rest,
Secure, whate'er He gives, He gives the best.
Yet when the sense of sacred presence fires,
And strong devotion to the skies aspires,
Pour forth thy fervours for a healthful mind,
Obedient passions, and a will resigned;
For love, which scarce collective Man can fill;
For patience sov'reign o'er transmuted ill;
For faith, that panting for a happier seat,
Count death kind Nature's signal of retreat:
These goods for Man the laws of Heav'n ordain,
These goods He grants, who grants the pow'r to gain;
With these celestial Wisdom calms the mind,
And makes the happiness she does not find.

ON THE DEATH OF DR ROBERT LEVET

CONDEMNED to Hope's delusive mine,
   As on we toil from day to day,
By sudden blasts, or slow decline,
   Our social comforts drop away.

Well tried through many a varying year,
   See LEVET to the grave descend;
Officious, innocent, sincere,
   Of ev'ry friendless name the friend.

Yet still he fills Affection's eye,
   Obscurely wise, and coarsely kind;
Nor, lettered Arrogance, deny
   Thy praise to merit unrefined.

When fainting Nature called for aid,
    And hov'ring Death prepared the blow,
His vig'rous remedy displayed
    The power of art without the show.

In Misery's darkest caverns known,
    His useful care was ever nigh,
Where hopeless Anguish poured his groan,
    And lonely Want retired to die,

No summons mocked by chill delay,
    No petty gain disdained by pride,
The modest wants of ev'ry day
    The toil of ev'ry day supplied.

His virtues walked their narrow round,
    Nor made a pause, nor left a void;
And sure th' Eternal Master found
    The single talent well employed.

The busy day, the peaceful night,
    Unfelt, uncounted, glided by;
His frame was firm, his powers were bright,
    Though now his eightieth year was nigh.

Then with no throbbing fiery pain,
    No cold gradations of decay,
Death broke at once the vital chain,
    And freed his soul the nearest way.

WILLIAM SHENSTONE

WRITTEN AT AN INN AT HENLEY

To THEE, fair freedom! I retire
    From flattery, cards, and dice, and din;
Nor art thou found in mansions higher
    Than the low cot or humble inn.

'Tis here with boundless power I reign;
　　And every health which I begin,
Converts dull port to bright champagne;
　　Such freedom crowns it at an inn.

I fly from pomp, I fly from plate!
　　I fly from falsehood's specious grin!
Freedom I love, and form I hate,
　　And choose my lodgings at an inn.

Here, waiter! take my sordid ore,
　　Which lackeys else might hope to win;
It buys what courts have not in store;
　　It buys me freedom at an inn.

And now once more I shape my way
　　Through rain or shine, through thick or thin,
Secure to meet, at close of day,
　　With kind reception at an inn.

Whoe'er has travelled life's dull round,
　　Where'er his stages may have been,
May sigh to think he still has found
　　The warmest welcome at an inn.

THOMAS GRAY

ELEGY WRITTEN IN A COUNTRY CHURCHYARD

THE CURFEW tolls the knell of parting day,
The lowing herd winds slowly o'er the lea,
The ploughman homeward plods his weary way,
And leaves the world to darkness and to me.

Now fades the glimmering landscape on the sight,
And all the air a solemn stillness holds,
Save where the beetle wheels his droning flight,
And drowsy tinklings lull the distant folds;

Save that from yonder ivy-mantled tower
The moping owl does to the moon complain
Of such as, wandering near her secret bower,
Molest her ancient solitary reign.

Beneath those rugged elms, that yew-tree's shade,
Where heaves the turf in many a mouldering heap,
Each in his narrow cell for ever laid,
The rude forefathers of the hamlet sleep.

The breezy call of incense-breathing morn,
The swallow twittering from the straw-built shed,
The cock's shrill clarion, or the echoing horn,
No more shall rouse them from their lowly bed.

For them no more the blazing hearth shall burn,
Or busy housewife ply her evening care;
No children run to lisp their sire's return,
Or climb his knees the envied kiss to share.

Oft did the harvest to their sickle yield,
Their furrow oft the stubborn glebe has broke;
How jocund did they drive their team afield!
How bowed the woods beneath their sturdy stroke!

Let not Ambition mock their useful toil,
Their homely joys and destiny obscure;
Nor Grandeur hear, with a disdainful smile,
The short and simple annals of the poor.

The boast of heraldry, the pomp of power,
And all that beauty, all that wealth e'er gave,
Awaits alike the inevitable hour.
The paths of glory lead but to the grave.

Nor you, ye Proud, impute to these the fault,
If Memory o'er their tomb no trophies raise,
Where through the long-drawn aisle and fretted vault
The pealing anthem swells the note of praise.

Can storied urn or animated bust
Back to its mansion call the fleeting breath?
Can Honour's voice provoke the silent dust,
Or Flattery soothe the dull cold ear of Death?

Perhaps in this neglected spot is laid
Some heart once pregnant with celestial fire;
Hands that the rod of empire might have swayed,
Or waked to ecstasy the living lyre.

But Knowledge to their eyes her ample page
Rich with the spoils of time did ne'er unroll;
Chill Penury repressed their noble rage,
And froze the genial current of the soul.

Full many a gem of purest ray serene
The dark unfathomed caves of ocean bear:
Full many a flower is born to blush unseen
And waste its sweetness on the desert air.

Some village-Hampden that with dauntless breast
The little tyrant of his fields withstood;
Some mute inglorious Milton here may rest,
Some Cromwell guiltless of his country's blood.

The applause of listening senates to command,
The threats of pain and ruin to despise,
To scatter plenty o'er a smiling land,
And read their history in a nation's eyes,

Their lot forbade: nor circumscribed alone
Their growing virtues, but their crimes confined;
Forbade to wade through slaughter to a throne,
And shut the gates of mercy on mankind,

The struggling pangs of conscious truth to hide,
To quench the blushes of ingenuous shame,
Or heap the shrine of Luxury and Pride
With incense kindled at the Muse's flame.

Far from the madding crowd's ignoble strife
Their sober wishes never learned to stray;
Along the cool sequestered vale of life
They kept the noiseless tenor of their way.

Yet even these bones from insult to protect
Some frail memorial still erected nigh,
With uncouth rhymes and shapeless sculpture decked,
Implored the passing tribute of a sigh.

Their names, their years, spelt by the unlettered Muse,
The place of fame and elegy supply:
And many a holy text around she strews,
That teach the rustic moralist to die.

For who to dumb Forgetfulness a prey,
This pleasing anxious being e'er resigned,
Left the warm precincts of the cheerful day,
Nor cast one longing lingering look behind?

On some fond breast the parting soul relies,
Some pious drops the closing eye requires;
Even from the tomb the voice of Nature cries,
Even in our ashes live their wonted fires.

For thee who, mindful of the unhonoured dead,
Dost in these lines their artless tale relate;
If chance, by lonely Contemplation led,
Some kindred spirit shall inquire thy fate,

Haply some hoary-headed swain may say,
'Oft have we seen him at the peep of dawn
Brushing with hasty steps the dews away
To meet the sun upon the upland lawn.

'There at the foot of yonder nodding beech
That wreathes its old fantastic roots so high,
His listless length at noontide would he stretch,
And pore upon the brook that babbles by.

'Hard by yon wood, now smiling as in scorn,
Muttering his wayward fancies he would rove,
Now drooping, woeful wan, like one forlorn,
Or crazed with care, or crossed in hopeless love.

'One morn I missed him on the customed hill,
Along the heath and near his favourite tree;
Another came; nor yet beside the rill,
Nor up the lawn, nor at the wood was he;

'The next with dirges due in sad array
Slow through the church-way path we saw him borne.
Approach and read (for thou can'st read) the lay,
Graved on the stone beneath yon agèd thorn.'

THE EPITAPH

Here rests his head upon the lap of earth
A youth to Fortune and to Fame unknown.
Fair Science frowned not on his humble birth,
And Melancholy marked him for her own.

Large was his bounty and his soul sincere,
Heaven did a recompense as largely send:
He gave to Misery all he had, a tear,
He gained from Heaven ('twas all he wished) a friend.

No farther seek his merits to disclose,
Or draw his frailties from their dread abode
(There they alike in trembling hope repose),
The bosom of his Father and his God.

THE BARD

A Pindaric Ode

I.1

'RUIN seize thee, ruthless king!
Confusion on thy banners wait,
Though fanned by Conquest's crimson wing
They mock the air with idle state.
Helm nor hauberk's twisted mail,
Nor even thy virtues, tyrant, shall avail
To save thy secret soul from nightly fears,
From Cambria's curse, from Cambria's tears!'
Such were the sounds, that o'er the crested pride
Of the first Edward scattered wild dismay,
As down the steep of Snowdon's shaggy side
He wound with toilsome march his long array.
Stout Gloucester stood aghast in speechless trance:
'To arms!' cried Mortimer and couched his quivering lance.

I.2

On a rock, whose haughty brow
Frowns o'er old Conway's foaming flood,
Robed in the sable garb of woe,
With haggard eyes the poet stood
(Loose his beard and hoary hair
Streamed, like a meteor, to the troubled air);
And, with a master's hand and prophet's fire,
Struck the deep sorrows of his lyre.
'Hark, how each giant-oak and desert cave
Sighs to the torrent's awful voice beneath!
O'er thee, O King! their hundred arms they wave,
Revenge on thee in hoarser murmurs breathe;
Vocal no more, since Cambria's fatal day,
To high-born Hoel's harp or soft Llewellyn's lay.

I.3

'Cold is Cadwallo's tongue,
That hushed the stormy main:
Brave Urien sleeps upon his craggy bed:
Mountains, ye mourn in vain

Modred, whose magic song
Made huge Plinlimmon bow his cloud-topped head.
On dreary Arvon's shore they lie,
Smeared with gore and ghastly pale:
Far, far aloof the affrighted ravens sail;
The famished eagle screams and passes by.
Dear lost companions of my tuneful art,
Dear as the light that visits these sad eyes,
Dear as the ruddy drops that warm my heart,
Ye died amidst your dying country's cries –
No more I weep. They do not sleep.
On yonder cliffs, a grisly band,
I see them sit, they linger yet,
Avengers of their native land;
With me in dreadful harmony they join,
And weave with bloody hands the tissue of thy line.

2.1

'   "Weave the warp and weave the woof,
The winding-sheet of Edward's race.
Give ample room and verge enough
The characters of hell to trace.
Mark the year and mark the night,
When Severn shall re-echo with affright
The shrieks of death, through Berkeley's roofs that ring,
Shrieks of an agonising king!
She-wolf of France, with unrelenting fangs,
That tear'st the bowels of thy mangled mate,
From thee be born who o'er thy country hangs
The scourge of Heaven. What terrors round him wait!
Amazement in his van, with Flight combined,
And Sorrow's faded form, and Solitude behind.

2.2

'   "Mighty victor, mighty lord,
Low on his funeral couch he lies!
No pitying heart, no eye, afford
A tear to grace his obsequies.
Is the sable warrior fled?
Thy son is gone. He rests among the dead.

The swarm that in thy noon-tide beam were born?
Gone to salute the rising morn.
Fair laughs the morn and soft the zephyr blows,
While proudly riding o'er the azure realm
In gallant trim the gilded vessel goes;
Youth on the prow and Pleasure at the helm;
Regardless of the sweeping whirlwind's sway,
That, hushed in grim repose, expects his evening-prey.

2.3

' "Fill high the sparkling bowl,
The rich repast prepare,
Reft of a crown, he may yet share the feast:
Close by the regal chair
Fell Thirst and Famine scowl
A baleful smile upon their baffled guest.
Heard ye the din of battle bray,
Lance to lance and horse to horse?
Long years of havoc urge their destined course,
And through the kindred squadrons mow their way.
Ye towers of Julius, London's lasting shame,
With many a foul and midnight murder fed,
Revere his consort's faith, his father's fame,
And spare the meek usurper's holy head.
Above, below, the rose of snow,
Twined with her blushing foe, we spread:
The bristled Boar in infant-gore
Wallows beneath the thorny shade.
Now, brothers, bending o'er the accursèd loom,
Stamp we our vengeance deep and ratify his doom.

3.1

' "Edward, lo! to sudden fate
(Weave we the woof. The thread is spun.)
Half of thy heart we consecrate.
(The web is wove. The work is done.)"
Stay, oh, stay! nor thus forlorn
Leave me unblessed, unpitied, here to mourn:
In yon bright track, that fires the western skies,
They melt, they vanish from my eyes.

But oh! what solemn scenes on Snowdon's height
Descending slow their glittering skirts unroll?
Visions of glory, spare my aching sight,
Ye unborn ages, crowd not on my soul!
No more our long-lost Arthur we bewail.
All-hail, ye genuine kings, Britannia's issue, hail!

3.2

'Girt with many a baron bold
Sublime their starry fronts they rear;
And gorgeous dames, and statesmen old
In bearded majesty, appear.
In the midst a form divine!
Her eye proclaims her of the Briton-line;
Her lion-port, her awe-commanding face,
Attempered sweet to virgin-grace.
What strings symphonious tremble in the air,
What strains of vocal transport round her play!
Hear from the grave, great Taliessin, hear;
They breathe a soul to animate thy clay.
Bright Rapture calls and, soaring as she sings,
Waves in the eyes of Heaven her many-coloured wings.

3.3

'The verse adorn again
Fierce war and faithful love,
And truth severe, by fairy fiction dressed.
In buskined measures move
Pale Grief and pleasing Pain,
With Horror, tyrant of the throbbing breast.
A voice as of the cherub-choir
Gales from blooming Eden bear;
And distant warblings lessen on my ear,
That lost in long futurity expire.
Fond impious man, think'st thou yon sanguine cloud,
Raised by thy breath, has quenched the orb of day?
Tomorrow he repairs the golden flood,
And warms the nations with redoubled ray.
Enough for me: with joy I see
The different doom our fates assign.

Be thine despair and sceptred care;
To triumph, and to die, are mine.'
He spoke, and headlong from the mountain's height
Deep in the roaring tide he plunged to endless night.

WILLIAM COLLINS

ODE TO EVENING

IF AUGHT of oaten stop or pastoral song
May hope, chaste Eve, to soothe thy modest ear,
 Like thy own solemn springs,
 Thy springs and dying gales,

O nymph reserved, while now the bright-haired sun
Sits in yon western tent, whose cloudy skirts,
 With brede ethereal wove,
 O'erhang his wavy bed;

Now air is hushed, save where the weak-eyed bat
With short shrill shriek flits by on leathern wing,
 Or where the beetle winds
 His small but sullen horn,

As oft he rises, 'midst the twilight path,
Against the pilgrim borne in heedless hum:
 Now teach me, maid composed,
 To breathe some softened strain,

Whose numbers stealing through thy darkening vale
May not unseemly with its stillness suit;
 As musing slow, I hail
 Thy genial loved return!

For when thy folding star arising shows
His paly circlet, at his warning lamp
 The fragrant hours, and elves
 Who slept in flowers the day,

And many a nymph who wreathes her brows with sedge,
And sheds the freshening dew, and, lovelier still,
    The Pensive Pleasures sweet,
    Prepare thy shadowy car:

Then lead, calm votaress, where some sheety lake
Cheers the lone heath, or some time-hallowed pile,
    Or upland fallows grey
    Reflect its last cool gleam.

But when chill blustering winds or driving rain
Forbid my willing feet, be mine the hut
    That from the mountain's side
    Views wilds and swelling floods,

And hamlets brown, and dim-discovered spires,
And hears their simple bell, and marks o'er all
    Thy dewy fingers draw
    The gradual dusky veil.

While Spring shall pour his showers, as oft he wont,
And bathe thy breathing tresses, meekest Eve!
    While Summer loves to sport
    Beneath thy lingering light;

While sallow Autumn fills thy lap with leaves,
Or Winter, yelling through the troublous air,
    Affrights thy shrinking train,
    And rudely rends thy robes;

So long, sure-found beneath the sylvan shed,
Shall Fancy, Friendship, Science, rose-lipped Health,
    Thy gentlest influence own,
    And hymn thy favourite name!

ODE, WRITTEN IN THE
BEGINNING OF THE YEAR 1746

How sleep the brave, who sink to rest
By all their country's wishes blest!
When Spring, with dewy fingers cold,
Returns to deck their hallowed mould,
She there shall dress a sweeter sod
Than Fancy's feet have ever trod.

By fairy hands their knell is wrung,
By forms unseen their dirge is sung;
There Honour comes, a pilgrim grey,
To bless the turf that wraps their clay,
And Freedom shall awhile repair
To dwell a weeping hermit there!

CHRISTOPHER SMART

From JUBILATE AGNO

For I will consider my cat Jeffrey.

For he is the servant of the Living God, duly and daily serving Him.

For at the first glance of the glory of God in the east he worships in his way.

For this is done by wreathing his body seven times round with elegant quickness.

For then he leaps up to catch the musk, which is the blessing of God upon his prayer.

For he rolls upon prank to work it in.

For having done duty and received blessing he begins to consider himself.

For this he performs in ten degrees.

For first he looks upon his forepaws to see if they are clean.

For secondly he kicks up behind to clear away there.

For thirdly he works it upon stretch with the forepaws extended.

For fourthly he sharpens his paws by wood.

For fifthly he washes himself.

For sixthly he rolls upon wash.

For seventhly he fleas himself, that he may not be interrupted upon the beat.

For eighthly he rubs himself against a post.

For ninthly he looks up for his instructions.

For tenthly he goes in quest of food.

For having considered God and himself he will consider his neighbour.

For if he meets another cat he will kiss her in kindness.

For when he takes his prey he plays with it to give it chance.

For one mouse in seven escapes by his dallying.

For when his day's work is done his business more properly begins.

For he keeps the Lord's watch in the night against the adversary.

For he counteracts the powers of darkness by his electrical skin and glaring eyes.

For he counteracts the Devil, who is death, by brisking about the life.

For in his morning orisons he loves the sun and the sun loves him.

For he is of the tribe of tiger.

For the cherub cat is a term of the angel tiger.

For he has the subtlety and hissing of a serpent, which in goodness he suppresses.

For he will not do destruction, if he is well fed, neither will he spit without provocation.

For he purrs in thankfulness, when God tells him he's a good cat.

For he is an instrument for the children to learn benevolence upon.

For every house is incomplete without him and a blessing is lacking in the spirit.

For the Lord commanded Moses concerning the cats at the departure of the Children of Israel from Egypt.

For every family had one cat at least in the bag.

For the English cats are the best in Europe.

For he is the cleanest in the use of his forepaws of any quadruped.

For the dexterity of his defence is an instance of the love of God to him exceedingly.

For he is the quickest to his mark of any creature.

For he is tenacious of his point.

For he is a mixture of gravity and waggery.

For he knows that God is his Saviour.

For there is nothing sweeter than his peace when at rest.

For there is nothing brisker than his life when in motion.

For he is of the Lord's poor and so indeed is he called by
benevolence perpetually – Poor Jeffrey! Poor Jeffrey! The rat has
bit thy throat.

For I bless the name of the Lord Jesus that Jeffrey is better.

For the divine spirit comes about his body to sustain it in complete
cat.

For his tongue is exceeding pure so that it has in purity what it
wants in music.

For he is docile and can learn certain things.

For he can set up with gravity, which is patience upon approbation.

For he can fetch and carry, which is patience in employment.

For he can jump over a stick, which is patience upon proof
positive.

For he can spraggle upon waggle at the word of command.

For he can jump from an eminence into his master's bosom.

For he can catch the cork and toss it again.

For he is hated by the hypocrite and miser.

For the former is afraid of detection.

For the latter refuses the charge.

For he camels his back to bear the first notion of business.

For he is good to think on, if a man would express himself neatly.

For he is made a great figure in Egypt for his signal service.

For he killed the Icneumon rat very pernicious by land.

For his ears are so acute that they sting again.

For from this proceeds the passing quickness of his attention.

For by stroking of him I have found out electricity.

For I perceived God's light about him both wax and fire.

For the electrical fire is the spiritual substance, which God sends
from heaven to sustain the bodies both of man and beast.

For God has blessed him in the variety of his movements.

For, though he cannot fly, he is an excellent clamberer.

For his motions upon the face of the earth are more than any other
quadruped.

For he can tread to all the measures upon the music.

For he can swim for life.

For he can creep.

From A SONG TO DAVID

GREAT, valiant, pious, good, and clean,
Sublime, contemplative, serene,
 Strong, constant, pleasant, wise!
Bright effluence of exceeding grace:
Best man! – the swiftness and the race,
 The peril, and the prize!

Great – from the lustre of his crown,
From Samuel's horn and God's renown,
 Which is the people's voice;
For all the host, from rear to van,
Applauded and embraced the man –
 The man of God's own choice.

Valiant – the word and up he rose –
The fight – he triumphed o'er the foes,
 Whom God's just laws abhor;
And, armed in gallant faith, he took
Against the boaster, from the brook,
 The weapons of the war.

Pious – magnificent and grand;
'Twas he the famous temple planned
 (The seraph in his soul):
Foremost to give the Lord his dues,
Foremost to bless the welcome news,
 And foremost to condole.

Good – from Jehudah's genuine vein,
From God's best nature good in grain,
 His aspect and his heart;
To pity, to forgive, to save,
Witness En-gedi's conscious cave,
 And Shimei's blunted dart.

Clean – if perpetual prayer be pure,
And love, which could itself innure
　　To fasting and to fear –
Clean in his gestures, hands, and feet,
To smite the lyre, the dance complete,
　　To play the sword and spear.

Sublime – invention ever young,
Of vast conception, towering tongue,
　　To God the eternal theme;
Notes from yon exaltations caught,
Unrivalled royalty of thought,
　　O'er meaner strains supreme.

Contemplative – on God to fix
His musings, and above the six
　　The Sabbath day he blessed;
'Twas then his thoughts self-conquest pruned,
And heavenly melancholy tuned,
　　To bless and bear the rest.

Serene – to sow the seeds of peace,
Remembering, when he watched the fleece,
　　How sweetly Kidron purled –
To further knowledge, silence vice,
And plant perpetual paradise,
　　When God had calmed the world.

Strong – in the Lord, who could defy
Satan, and all his powers that lie
　　In sempiternal night;
And hell, and horror, and despair
Were as the lion and the bear
　　To his undaunted might.

Constant – in love to God, THE TRUTH,
Age, manhood, infancy, and youth –
　　To Jonathan his friend
Constant, beyond the verge of death;
And Ziba, and Mephibosheth,
　　His endless fame attend.

Pleasant – and various as the year;
Man, soul, and angel, without peer,
   Priest, champion, sage, and boy;
In armour, or in ephod clad,
His pomp, his piety was glad;
   Majestic was his joy.

Wise – in recovery from his fall,
Whence rose his eminence o'er all,
   Of all the most reviled;
The light of Israel in his ways,
Wise are his precepts, prayer and praise,
   And counsel to his child.

OLIVER GOLDSMITH

THE DESERTED VILLAGE

SWEET AUBURN! loveliest village of the plain,
Where health and plenty cheered the labouring swain,
Where smiling spring its earliest visit paid,
And parting summer's lingering blooms delayed:
Dear lovely bowers of innocence and ease,
Seats of my youth, when every sport could please,
How often have I loitered o'er thy green,
Where humble happiness endeared each scene;
How often have I paused on every charm,
The sheltered cot, the cultivated farm,
The never-failing brook, the busy mill,
The decent church that topped the neighbouring hill,
The hawthorn bush, with seats beneath the shade,
For talking age and whispering lovers made.
How often have I blessed the coming day,
When toil remitting lent its turn to play,
And all the village train, from labour free,
Led up their sports beneath the spreading tree,
While many a pastime circled in the shade,
The young contending as the old surveyed;

And many a gambol frolicked o'er the ground,
And sleights of art and feats of strength went round.
And still, as each repeated pleasure tired,
Succeeding sports the mirthful band inspired;
The dancing pair that simply sought renown,
By holding out to tire each other down;
The swain mistrustless of his smutted face,
While secret laughter tittered round the place;
The bashful virgin's sidelong looks of love,
The matron's glance that would those looks reprove.
These were thy charms, sweet village! sports like these,
With sweet succession, taught even toil to please;
These round thy bowers their cheerful influence shed;
These were thy charms – but all these charms are fled.

   Sweet smiling village, loveliest of the lawn,
Thy sports are fled and all thy charms withdrawn;
Amidst thy bowers the tyrant's hand is seen,
And desolation saddens all thy green;
One only master grasps the whole domain,
And half a tillage stints thy smiling plain;
No more thy glassy brook reflects the day,
But, choked with sedges, works its weedy way;
Along thy glades, a solitary guest,
The hollow-sounding bittern guards its nest;
Amidst thy desert walks the lapwing flies,
And tires their echoes with unvaried cries;
Sunk are thy bowers in shapeless ruin all,
And the long grass o'ertops the mouldering wall;
And trembling, shrinking from the spoiler's hand,
Far, far away, thy children leave the land.

   Ill fares the land, to hastening ills a prey,
Where wealth accumulates and men decay:
Princes and lords may flourish or may fade;
A breath can make them, as a breath has made;
But a bold peasantry, their country's pride,
When once destroyed, can never be supplied.

   A time there was, ere England's griefs began,
When every rood of ground maintained its man;
For him light labour spread her wholesome store,

Just gave what life required, but gave no more:
His best companions, innocence and health;
And his best riches, ignorance of wealth.

But times are altered; trade's unfeeling train
Usurp the land and dispossess the swain;
Along the lawn, where scattered hamlets rose,
Unwieldy wealth and cumbrous pomp repose;
And every want to opulence allied,
And every pang that folly pays to pride.
Those gentle hours that plenty bade to bloom,
Those calm desires that asked but little room,
Those healthful sports that graced the peaceful scene,
Lived in each look and brightened all the green;
These, far departing, seek a kinder shore,
And rural mirth and manners are no more.

Sweet Auburn! parent of the blissful hour,
Thy glades forlorn confess the tyrant's power.
Here as I take my solitary rounds,
Amidst thy tangling walks and ruined grounds,
And, many a year elapsed, return to view
Where once the cottage stood, the hawthorn grew,
Remembrance wakes with all her busy train,
Swells at my breast, and turns the past to pain.

In all my wanderings round this world of care,
In all my griefs – and God has given my share –
I still had hopes my latest hours to crown,
Amidst these humble bowers to lay me down;
To husband out life's taper at the close,
And keep the flame from wasting by repose.
I still had hopes, for pride attends us still,
Amidst the swains to show my book-learned skill,
Around my fire an evening group to draw,
And tell of all I felt and all I saw;
And, as a hare whom hounds and horns pursue
Pants to the place from whence at first she flew,
I still had hopes, my long vexations past,
Here to return – and die at home at last.

O blest retirement, friend to life's decline,
Retreats from care, that never must be mine,

How happy he who crowns in shades like these
A youth of labour with an age of ease;
Who quits a world where strong temptations try
And, since 'tis hard to combat, learns to fly!
For him no wretches, born to work and weep,
Explore the mine or tempt the dangerous deep;
No surly porter stands in guilty state
To spurn imploring famine from the gate;
But on he moves to meet his latter end,
Angels around befriending virtue's friend;
Bends to the grave with unperceived decay,
While resignation gently slopes the way;
And, all his prospects brightening to the last,
His heaven commences ere the world be past!

Sweet was the sound, when oft at evening's close
Up yonder hill the village murmur rose;
There, as I passed with careless steps and slow,
The mingling notes came softened from below;
The swain responsive as the milkmaid sung,
The sober herd that lowed to meet their young;
The noisy geese that gabbled o'er the pool,
The playful children just let loose from school;
The watchdog's voice that bayed the whispering wind,
And the loud laugh that spoke the vacant mind;
These all in sweet confusion sought the shade,
And filled each pause the nightingale had made.
But now the sounds of population fail,
No cheerful murmurs fluctuate in the gale,
No busy steps the grass-grown foot-way tread,
For all the bloomy flush of life is fled.
All but yon widowed, solitary thing
That feebly bends beside the plashy spring;
She, wretched matron, forced, in age, for bread,
To strip the brook with mantling cresses spread,
To pick her wintry faggot from the thorn,
To seek her nightly shed and weep till morn;
She only left of all the harmless train,
The sad historian of the pensive plain.

Near yonder copse, where once the garden smiled,

And still where many a garden flower grows wild;
There, where a few torn shrubs the place disclose,
The village preacher's modest mansion rose.
A man he was to all the country dear,
And passing rich with forty pounds a year;
Remote from towns he ran his godly race,
Nor e'er had changed, nor wished to change, his place;
Unpractised he to fawn, or seek for power,
By doctrines fashioned to the varying hour;
Far other aims his heart had learned to prize,
More skilled to raise the wretched than to rise.
His house was known to all the vagrant train,
He chid their wanderings, but relieved their pain;
The long-remembered beggar was his guest,
Whose beard descending swept his agèd breast;
The ruined spendthrift, now no longer proud,
Claimed kindred there and had his claims allowed;
The broken soldier, kindly bade to stay,
Sat by his fire and talked the night away;
Wept o'er his wounds, or tales of sorrow done,
Shouldered his crutch, and showed how fields were won.
Pleased with his guests, the good man learned to glow,
And quite forgot their vices in their woe;
Careless their merits or their faults to scan,
His pity gave ere charity began.
    Thus to relieve the wretched was his pride,
And even his failings leaned to virtue's side;
But in his duty prompt at every call,
He watched and wept, he prayed and felt, for all.
And, as a bird each fond endearment tries
To tempt its new-fledged offspring to the skies,
He tried each art, reproved each dull delay,
Allured to brighter worlds and led the way.
    Beside the bed where parting life was laid,
And sorrow, guilt, and pain by turns dismayed,
The reverend champion stood. At his control,
Despair and anguish fled the struggling soul;
Comfort came down the trembling wretch to raise,
And his last faltering accents whispered praise.

At church, with meek and unaffected grace,
His looks adorned the venerable place;
Truth from his lips prevailed with double sway,
And fools, who came to scoff, remained to pray.
The service past, around the pious man,
With steady zeal, each honest rustic ran;
Even children followed with endearing wile,
And plucked his gown, to share the good man's smile.
His ready smile a parent's warmth expressed,
Their welfare pleased him and their cares distressed;
To them his heart, his love, his griefs were given,
But all his serious thoughts had rest in Heaven.
As some tall cliff that lifts its awful form,
Swells from the vale, and midway leaves the storm,
Though round its breast the rolling clouds are spread,
Eternal sunshine settles on its head.

Beside yon straggling fence that skirts the way,
With blossomed furze unprofitably gay,
There, in his noisy mansion, skilled to rule,
The village master taught his little school;
A man severe he was, and stern to view;
I knew him well, and every truant knew;
Well had the boding tremblers learned to trace
The day's disasters in his morning face;
Full well they laughed, with counterfeited glee,
At all his jokes, for many a joke had he;
Full well the busy whisper, circling round,
Conveyed the dismal tidings when he frowned;
Yet he was kind, or, if severe in aught,
The love he bore to learning was in fault;
The village all declared how much he knew;
'Twas certain he could write and cipher too;
Lands he could measure, terms and tides presage,
And even the story ran that he could gauge.
In arguing too, the parson owned his skill,
For even though vanquished, he could argue still;
While words of learnèd length and thundering sound
Amazed the gazing rustics ranged around,
And still they gazed, and still the wonder grew,

That one small head could carry all he knew.
　But past is all his fame. The very spot
Where many a time he triumphed is forgot.
Near yonder thorn, that lifts its head on high,
Where once the signpost caught the passing eye,
Low lies that house where nutbrown draughts inspired,
Where greybeard mirth and smiling toil retired,
Where village statesmen talked with looks profound,
And news much older than their ale went round.
Imagination fondly stoops to trace
The parlour splendours of that festive place;
The white-washed wall, the nicely sanded floor,
The varnished clock that clicked behind the door;
The chest contrived a double debt to pay,
A bed by night, a chest of drawers by day;
The pictures placed for ornament and use,
The twelve good rules, the royal game of goose;
The hearth, except when winter chilled the day,
With aspen boughs and flowers and fennel gay;
While broken tea-cups, wisely kept for show,
Ranged o'er the chimney, glistened in a row.
　Vain, transitory splendours! Could not all
Reprieve the tottering mansion from its fall!
Obscure it sinks, nor shall it more impart
An hour's importance to the poor man's heart;
Thither no more the peasant shall repair
To sweet oblivion of his daily care;
No more the farmer's news, the barber's tale,
No more the woodman's ballad shall prevail;
No more the smith his dusky brow shall clear,
Relax his ponderous strength and lean to hear;
The host himself no longer shall be found
Careful to see the mantling bliss go round;
Nor the coy maid, half willing to be pressed,
Shall kiss the cup to pass it to the rest.
　Yes! let the rich deride, the proud disdain,
These simple blessings of the lowly train;
To me more dear, congenial to my heart,
One native charm than all the gloss of art;

Spontaneous joys, where Nature has its play,
The soul adopts and owns their first-born sway;
Lightly they frolic o'er the vacant mind,
Unenvied, unmolested, unconfined.
But the long pomp, the midnight masquerade,
With all the freaks of wanton wealth arrayed,
In these, ere triflers half their wish obtain,
The toiling pleasure sickens into pain;
And, e'en while fashion's brightest arts decoy,
The heart distrusting asks if this be joy.

 Ye friends to truth, ye statesmen, who survey
The rich man's joys increase, the poor's decay,
'Tis yours to judge how wide the limits stand
Between a splendid and a happy land.
Proud swells the tide with loads of freighted ore,
And shouting Folly hails them from her shore;
Hoards, even beyond the miser's wish abound,
And rich men flock from all the world around.
Yet count our gains! This wealth is but a name
That leaves our useful products still the same.
Not so the loss. The man of wealth and pride
Takes up a space that many poor supplied;
Space for his lake, his park's extended bounds,
Space for his horses, equipage and hounds;
The robe that wraps his limbs in silken sloth
Has robbed the neighbouring fields of half their growth;
His seat, where solitary sports are seen,
Indignant spurns the cottage from the green;
Around the world each needful product flies,
For all the luxuries the world supplies;
While thus the land, adorned for pleasure all,
In barren splendour feebly waits the fall.

 As some fair female unadorned and plain,
Secure to please while youth confirms her reign,
Slights every borrowed charm that dress supplies,
Nor shares with art the triumph of her eyes;
But when those charms are passed, for charms are frail,
When time advances and when lovers fail,
She then shines forth, solicitous to bless,

In all the glaring impotence of dress:
Thus fares the land, by luxury betrayed,
In Nature's simplest charms at first arrayed;
But verging to decline, its splendours rise,
Its vistas strike, its palaces surprise;
While, scourged by famine from the smiling land,
The mournful peasant leads his humble band;
And while he sinks, without one arm to save,
The country blooms – a garden and a grave.

   Where then, ah! where, shall poverty reside,
To 'scape the pressure of continuous pride?
If to some common's fenceless limits strayed,
He drives his flock to pick the scanty blade,
Those fenceless fields the sons of wealth divide,
And e'en the bare-worn common is denied.

   If to the city sped – what waits him there?
To see profusion that he must not share;
To see ten thousand baneful arts combined
To pamper luxury and thin mankind;
To see those joys the sons of pleasure know
Extorted from his fellow-creature's woe.
Here while the courtier glitters in brocade,
There the pale artist plies the sickly trade;
Here while the proud their long-drawn pomps display,
There the black gibbet glooms beside the way.
The dome where Pleasure holds her midnight reign
Here, richly decked, admits the gorgeous train;
Tumultuous grandeur crowds the blazing square,
The rattling chariots clash, the torches glare.
Sure, scenes like these no troubles e'er annoy!
Sure, these denote one universal joy!
Are these thy serious thoughts? Ah, turn thine eyes
Where the poor, houseless, shivering female lies.
She once, perhaps, in village plenty blest,
Has wept at tales of innocence distressed;
Her modest looks the cottage might adorn,
Sweet as the primrose peeps beneath the thorn;
Now lost to all; her friends, her virtue fled,
Near her betrayer's door she lays her head,

And pinched with cold and shrinking from the shower,
With heavy heart deplores that luckless hour,
When idly first, ambitious of the town,
She left her wheel and robes of country brown.

Do thine, sweet Auburn, thine, the loveliest train,
Do thy fair tribes participate her pain?
Even now, perhaps, by cold and hunger led,
At proud men's doors they ask a little bread!

Ah, no! To distant climes, a dreary scene,
Where half the convex world intrudes between,
Through torrid tracts with fainting steps they go,
Where wild Altama murmurs to their woe.
Far different there from all that charmed before
The various terrors of that horrid shore:
Those blazing suns that dart a downward ray,
And fiercely shed intolerable day;
Those matted woods where birds forget to sing,
But silent bats in drowsy clusters cling;
Those poisonous fields with rank luxuriance crowned,
Where the dark scorpion gathers death around;
Where at each step the stranger fears to wake
The rattling terrors of the vengeful snake;
Where crouching tigers wait their hapless prey,
And savage men more murderous still than they;
While oft in whirls the mad tornado flies,
Mingling the ravaged landscape with the skies.
Far different these from every former scene,
The cooling brook, the grassy-vested green,
The breezy covert of the warbling grove,
That only sheltered thefts of harmless love.

Good Heaven! what sorrows gloomed that parting day
That called them from their native walks away;
When the poor exiles, every pleasure past,
Hung round their bowers and fondly looked their last,
And took a long farewell, and wished in vain
For seats like these beyond the westering main;
And shuddering still to face the distant deep,
Returned and wept, and still returned to weep.
The good old sire the first prepared to go

To new-found worlds, and wept for others' woe;
But for himself, in conscious virtue brave,
He only wished for worlds beyond the grave.
His lovely daughter, lovelier in her tears,
The fond companion of his helpless years,
Silent went next, neglectful of her charms,
And left a lover's for a father's arms.
With louder plaints the mother spoke her woes,
And blessed the cot where every pleasure rose;
And kissed her thoughtless babes with many a tear,
And clasped them close, in sorrow doubly dear;
Whilst her fond husband strove to lend relief
In all the silent manliness of grief.

O Luxury! thou cursed by Heaven's decree,
How ill exchanged are things like these for thee!
How do thy potions with insidious joy
Diffuse their pleasure only to destroy!
Kingdoms, by thee to sickly greatness grown,
Boast of a florid vigour not their own.
At every draught more large and large they grow,
A bloated mass of rank unwieldy woe;
Till sapped their strength and every part unsound,
Down, down they sink and spread a ruin round.

Even now the devastation is begun,
And half the business of destruction done;
Even now, methinks, as pondering here I stand,
I see the rural virtues leave the land.
Down where yon anchoring vessel spreads the sail,
That idly waiting flaps with every gale,
Downward they move, a melancholy band,
Pass from the shore and darken all the strand.
Contented toil and hospitable care,
And kind connubial tenderness are there;
And piety, with wishes placed above,
And steady loyalty and faithful love.
And thou, sweet Poetry, thou loveliest maid,
Still first to fly where sensual joys invade;
Unfit, in these degenerate times of shame,
To catch the heart or strike for honest fame;

Dear charming nymph, neglected and decried,
My shame in crowds, my solitary pride;
Thou source of all my bliss and all my woe,
That found'st me poor at first and keep'st me so;
Thou guide by which the nobler arts excel,
Thou nurse of every virtue, fare thee well!
Farewell, and oh! where'er thy voice be tried,
On Torno's cliffs or Pambamarca's side,
Whether where equinoctial fervours glow,
Or winter wraps the polar world in snow,
Still let thy voice, prevailing over time,
Redress the rigours of the inclement clime;
Aid slighted truth; with thy persuasive strain
Teach erring man to spurn the rage of gain;
Teach him that states of native strength possessed,
Though very poor, may still be very blest;
That trade's proud empire hastes to swift decay,
As ocean sweeps the laboured mole away;
While self-dependent power can time defy,
As rocks resist the billows and the sky.

WILLIAM COWPER

From OLNEY HYMNS

LIGHT SHINING OUT OF DARKNESS

GOD moves in a mysterious way
   His wonders to perform;
He plants His footsteps in the sea,
   And rides upon the storm.

Deep in unfathomable mines
   Of never-failing skill
He treasures up His bright designs,
   And works His sovereign will.

Ye fearful saints, fresh courage take,
   The clouds ye so much dread
Are big with mercy, and shall break
   In blessings on your head.

Judge not the Lord by feeble sense,
   But trust Him for His grace;
Behind a frowning providence
   He hides a smiling face.

His purposes will ripen fast,
   Unfolding every hour;
The bud may have a bitter taste,
   But sweet will be the flower.

Blind unbelief is sure to err,
   And scan His work in vain:
God is His own interpreter,
   And He will make it plain.

VERSES

*Supposed to be written by Alexander Selkirk during his
solitary abode in the island of Juan Fernandez*

I AM monarch of all I survey;
   My right there is none to dispute;
From the centre all round to the sea,
   I am lord of the fowl and the brute.
O Solitude! where are the charms
   That sages have seen in thy face?
Better dwell in the midst of alarms
   Than reign in this horrible place.

I am out of humanity's reach,
   I must finish my journey alone,
Never hear the sweet music of speech;
   I start at the sound of my own.
The beasts that roam over the plain
   My form with indifference see;
They are so unacquainted with man,
   Their tameness is shocking to me.

Society, friendship, and love,
   Divinely bestowed upon man,
Oh, had I the wings of a dove,
   How soon would I taste you again!
My sorrows I then might assuage
   In the ways of religion and truth,
Might learn from the wisdom of age,
   And be cheered by the sallies of youth.

Religion! What treasure untold
   Resides in that heavenly word!
More precious than silver and gold,
   Or all that this earth can afford.
But the sound of the church-going bell
   These valleys and rocks never heard,
Never sighed at the sound of a knell,
   Or smiled when a sabbath appeared.

Ye winds, that have made me your sport,
   Convey to this desolate shore
Some cordial endearing report
   Of a land I shall visit no more.
My friends – do they now and then send
   A wish or a thought after me?
Oh, tell me I yet have a friend,
   Though a friend I am never to see.

How fleet is a glance of the mind!
   Compared with the speed of its flight,
The tempest itself lags behind,
   And the swift-wingèd arrows of light.
When I think of my own native land,
   In a moment I seem to be there;
But alas! recollection at hand
   Soon hurries me back to despair.

But the sea-fowl is gone to her nest,
   The beast is laid down in his lair,
Even here is a season of rest,
   And I to my cabin repair.

There's mercy in every place,
    And mercy, encouraging thought!
Gives even affliction a grace,
    And reconciles man to his lot.

THE POPLAR FIELD

THE poplars are felled; farewell to the shade
And the whispering sound of the cool colonnade;
The winds play no longer and sing in the leaves,
Nor Ouse on his bosom their image receives.

Twelve years have elapsed since I first took a view
Of my favourite field, and the bank where they grew;
And now in the grass behold they are laid
And the tree is my seat that once lent me a shade!

The blackbird has fled to another retreat
Where the hazels afford him a screen from the heat,
And the scene where his melody charmed me before
Resounds with his sweet-flowing ditty no more.

My fugitive years are all hasting away,
And I must ere long lie as lowly as they
With a turf on my breast and a stone at my head,
Ere another such grove shall arise in its stead.

'Tis a sight to engage me, if anything can,
To muse on the perishing pleasures of man;
Though his life be a dream, his enjoyments, I see,
Have a being less durable even than he.

THE CASTAWAY

OBSCUREST night involved the sky,
    The Atlantic billows roared,
When such a destined wretch as I,
    Washed headlong from on board,
Of friends, of hope, of all bereft,
His floating home for ever left.

No braver chief could Albion boast
   Than he with whom he went,
Nor ever ship left Albion's coast
   With warmer wishes sent.
He loved them both, but both in vain,
Nor him beheld, nor her again.

Not long beneath the whelming brine,
   Expert to swim, he lay;
Nor soon he felt his strength decline,
   Or courage die away;
But waged with death a lasting strife,
Supported by despair of life.

He shouted: nor his friends had failed
   To check the vessel's course,
But so the furious blast prevailed
   That, pitiless perforce,
They left their outcast mate behind,
And scudded still before the wind.

Some succour yet they could afford;
   And such as storms allow,
The cask, the coop, the floated cord,
   Delayed not to bestow.
But he (they knew) nor ship nor shore,
Whate'er they gave, should visit more.

Nor, cruel as it seemed, could he
   Their haste himself condemn,
Aware that flight, in such a sea,
   Alone could rescue them;
Yet bitter felt it still to die
Deserted, and his friends so nigh.

He long survives, who lives an hour
   In ocean, self-upheld;
And so long he, with unspent power,
   His destiny repelled;
And ever, as the minutes flew,
Entreated help, or cried 'Adieu!'

At length, his transient respite past,
  His comrades, who before
Had heard his voice in every blast,
  Could catch the sound no more:
For then, by toil subdued, he drank
  The stifling wave, and then he sank.

No poet wept him; but the page
  Of narrative sincere,
That tells his name, his worth, his age,
  Is wet with Anson's tear:
And tears by bards or heroes shed
Alike immortalise the dead.

I therefore purpose not, or dream,
  Descanting on his fate,
To give the melancholy theme
  A more enduring date:
But misery still delights to trace
Its semblance in another's case.

No voice divine the storm allayed,
  No light propitious shone,
When, snatched from all effectual aid,
  We perished, each alone:
But I beneath a rougher sea,
And whelmed in deeper gulfs than he.

GEORGE CRABBE

From THE VILLAGE

I GRANT indeed that fields and flocks have charms
For him that grazes or for him that farms;
But when amid such pleasing scenes I trace
The poor laborious natives of the place,
And see the midday sun, with fervid ray,
On their bare heads and dewy temples play;
While some, with feebler heads and fainter hearts,

Deplore their fortune, yet sustain their parts:
Then shall I dare these real ills to hide
In tinsel trappings of poetic pride?

   No; cast by Fortune on a frowning coast,
Which neither groves nor happy valleys boast;
Where other cares than those the Muse relates,
And other shepherds dwell with other mates;
By such examples taught, I paint the Cot,
As Truth will paint it, and as Bards will not:
Nor you, ye poor, of lettered scorn complain,
To you the smoothest song is smooth in vain;
O'ercome by labour, and bowed down by time,
Feel you the barren flattery of a rhyme?
Can poets soothe you, when you pine for bread,
By winding myrtles round your ruined shed?
Can their light tales your weighty griefs o'erpower,
Or glad with airy mirth the toilsome hour?

   Lo! where the heath, with withering brake grown o'er,
Lends the light turf that warms the neighbouring poor;
From thence a length of burning sand appears,
Where the thin harvest waves its withered ears;
Rank weeds, that every art and care defy,
Reign o'er the land, and rob the blighted rye:
There thistles stretch their prickly arms afar,
And to the ragged infant threaten war;
There poppies nodding, mock the hope of toil;
There the blue bugloss paints the sterile soil;
Hardy and high, above the slender sheaf,
The slimy mallow waves her silky leaf;
O'er the young shoot the charlock throws a shade,
And clasping tares cling round the sickly blade;
With mingled tints the rocky coasts abound,
And a sad splendour vainly shines around.

   So looks the nymph whom wretched arts adorn,
Betrayed by man, then left for man to scorn;
Whose cheek in vain assumes the mimic rose,
While her sad eyes the troubled breast disclose;
Whose outward splendour is but folly's dress,
Exposing most, when most it gilds distress.

From THE BOROUGH

[PETER GRIMES]

THUS by himself compelled to live each day,
To wait for certain hours the tide's delay;
At the same times the same dull views to see,
The bounding marsh-bank and the blighted tree;
The water only, when the tides were high,
When low, the mud half-covered and half-dry;
The sun-burnt tar that blisters on the planks,
And bank-side stakes in their uneven ranks;
Heaps of entangled weeds that slowly float,
As the tide rolls by the impeded boat.
　　When tides were neap, and, in the sultry day,
Through the tall bounding mud-banks made their way,
Which on each side rose swelling, and below
The dark warm flood ran silently and slow;
There anchoring, Peter chose from man to hide,
There hang his head, and view the lazy tide
In its hot slimy channel slowly glide;
Where the small eels that left the deeper way
For the warm shore, within the shallows play;
Where gaping mussels, left upon the mud,
Slope their short passage to the fallen flood –
Here dull and hopeless he'd lie down and trace
How sidelong crabs had scrawled their crooked race;
Or sadly listen to the tuneless cry
Of fishing gull or clanging golden-eye;
What time the sea-birds to the marsh would come,
And the loud bittern, from the bull-rush home,
Gave from the salt-ditch side the bellowing boom:
He nursed the feelings these dull scenes produce,
And loved to stop beside the opening sluice;
Where the small stream, confined in narrow bound,
Ran with a dull, unvaried, saddening sound;
Where all, presented to the eye or ear,
Oppressed the soul with misery, grief, and fear.

WILLIAM BLAKE

From SONGS OF INNOCENCE

THE LAMB

LITTLE LAMB, who made thee?
    Dost thou know who made thee?
Gave thee life, and bid thee feed
By the stream and o'er the mead;
Gave thee clothing of delight,
Softest clothing, woolly, bright;
Gave thee such a tender voice,
Making all the vales rejoice?
    Little Lamb, who made thee?
    Dost thou know who made thee?

Little Lamb, I'll tell thee,
    Little Lamb, I'll tell thee:
He is callèd by thy name,
For He calls himself a Lamb.
He is meek, and He is mild;
He became a little child.
I, a child, and thou a lamb,
We are callèd by His name.
    Little Lamb, God bless thee!
    Little Lamb, God bless thee!

HOLY THURSDAY

'TWAS on a Holy Thursday, their innocent faces clean,
The children walking two and two, in red and blue and green,
Grey-headed beadles walked before, with wands as white as snow,
Till into the high dome of Paul's they like Thames' waters flow.

Oh, what a multitude they seemed, these flowers of London town!
Seated in companies they sit with radiance all their own.
The hum of multitudes was there, but multitudes of lambs,
Thousands of little boys and girls raising their innocent hands.

Now like a mighty wind they raise to heaven the voice of song,
Or like harmonious thunderings the seats of heaven among.
Beneath them sit the agèd men, wise guardians of the poor;
Then cherish pity, lest you drive an angel from your door.

NURSE'S SONG

WHEN the voices of children are heard on the green
And laughing is heard on the hill,
My heart is at rest within my breast
And everything else is still.

'Then come home, my children, the sun is gone down
And the dews of night arise;
Come, come, leave off play, and let us away
Till the morning appears in the skies.'

'No, no, let us play, for it is yet day
And we cannot go to sleep;
Besides, in the sky the little birds fly
And the hills are all covered with sheep.'

'Well, well, go and play till the light fades away
And then go home to bed.'
The little ones leaped and shouted and laughed
And all the hills echoèd.

From SONGS OF EXPERIENCE

THE SICK ROSE

O ROSE, thou art sick!
The invisible worm
That flies in the night,
In the howling storm,

Has found out thy bed
Of crimson joy,
And his dark secret love
Does thy life destroy.

THE TIGER

TIGER! Tiger! burning bright
In the forests of the night,
What immortal hand or eye
Could frame thy fearful symmetry?

In what distant deeps or skies
Burnt the fire of thine eyes?
On what wings dare he aspire?
What the hand dare seize the fire?

And what shoulder, and what art,
Could twist the sinews of thy heart?
And when thy heart began to beat,
What dread hand? and what dread feet?

What the hammer? what the chain?
In what furnace was thy brain?
What the anvil? what dread grasp
Dare its deadly terrors clasp?

When the stars threw down their spears,
And watered heaven with their tears,
Did he smile his work to see?
Did he who made the Lamb make thee?

Tiger! Tiger! burning bright
In the forests of the night,
What immortal hand or eye,
Dare frame thy fearful symmetry?

LONDON

I WANDER through each chartered street,
Near where the chartered Thames does flow,
And mark in every face I meet
Marks of weakness, marks of woe.

In every cry of every man,
In every infant's cry of fear,
In every voice, in every ban,
The mind-forged manacles I hear.

How the chimney-sweeper's cry
Every blackening church appals;
And the hapless soldier's sigh
Runs in blood down palace walls.

But most through midnight streets I hear
How the youthful harlot's curse
Blasts the new-born infant's tear,
And blights with plagues the marriage hearse.

A POISON TREE

I WAS angry with my friend:
I told my wrath, my wrath did end.
I was angry with my foe:
I told it not, my wrath did grow.

And I watered it in fears,
Night and morning with my tears;
And I sunnèd it with smiles,
And with soft deceitful wiles.

And it grew both day and night,
Till it bore an apple bright;
And my foe beheld it shine,
And he knew that it was mine,

And into my garden stole
When the night had veiled the pole:
In the morning glad I see
My foe outstretched beneath the tree.

From MILTON

AND did those feet in ancient time
Walk upon England's mountains green?
And was the holy Lamb of God
On England's pleasant pastures seen?

And did the Countenance Divine
Shine forth upon our clouded hills?
And was Jerusalem builded here
Among these dark satanic mills?

Bring me my bow of burning gold!
Bring me my arrows of desire! .
Bring me my spear! O clouds unfold!
Bring me my chariot of fire!

I will not cease from mental fight,
Nor shall my sword sleep in my hand
Till we have built Jerusalem
In England's green and pleasant land.

ROBERT BURNS

O, MY LUVE's like a red, red rose,
   That's newly sprung in June:
O, my luve's like the melodie
   That's sweetly played in tune.

As fair art thou, my bonie lass,
   So deep in luve am I:
And I will luve thee still, my dear,
   Till a' the seas gang dry.   *all: go*

Till a' the seas gang dry, my dear,
   And the rocks melt wi' the sun:
I will luve thee still, my dear,
   While the sands o' life shall run.

And fare thee weel, my only luve,
　And fare thee weel awhile!
And I will come again, my luve,
　Tho' it were ten thousand mile.

Go FETCH to me a pint o' wine,
　An' fill it in a silver tassie;　　　　　　　　*goblet*
That I may drink before I go
　A service to my bonie lassie.　　　　　　　*toast*
The boat rocks at the pier o' Leith;
　Fu' loud the wind blaws frae the ferry;　*full: from*
The ship rides by the Berwick-law,
　And I maun leave my bonie Mary.　　　　*must*

The trumpets sound, the banners fly,
　The glittering spears are rankèd ready;
The shouts o' war are heard afar,
　The battle closes thick and bloody;
But it's no the roar o' sea or shore
　Wad mak me langer wish to tarry;
Nor shout o' war that's heard afar,
　It's leaving thee, my bonie Mary.

AE FOND KISS, and then we sever!　　　　　*One*
Ae fareweel, alas, for ever!
Deep in heart-wrung tears I'll pledge thee,
Warring sighs and groans I'll wage thee.
Who shall say that fortune grieves him
While the star of hope she leaves him?
Me, nae cheerfu' twinkle lights me,　　　　　*no*
Dark despair around benights me.

I'll ne'er blame my partial fancy,
Naething could resist my Nancy;
But to see her, was to love her;
Love but her, and love for ever.
Had we never loved sae kindly,　　　　　　　*so*

Had we never loved sae blindly,
Never met – or never parted,
We had ne'er been broken-hearted.

Fare thee weel, thou first and fairest!
Fare thee weel, thou best and dearest!
Thine be ilka joy and treasure,   *every*
Peace, enjoyment, love, and pleasure.
Ae fond kiss, and then we sever;
Ae fareweel, alas, for ever!
Deep in heart-wrung tears I pledge thee,
Warring sighs and groans I'll wage thee.

Is THERE, for honest poverty,
That hangs his head, and a' that?   *all*
The coward-slave, we pass him by,
We dare be poor for a' that!
For a' that, and a' that,
Our toils obscure, and a' that;
The rank is but the guinea stamp;
The man's the gowd for a' that.   *gold*

What tho' on hamely fare we dine,
Wear hodden-grey, and a' that;
Gie fools their silks, and knaves their wine,   *Give*
A man's a man for a' that.
For a' that, and a' that,
Their tinsel show, and a' that;
The honest man, tho' e'er sae poor   *so*
Is king o' men for a' that.

Ye see yon birkie, ca'd a lord,   *swaggerer: called*
Wha struts, and stares, and a' that;   *Who*
Tho' hundreds worship at his word,
He's but a coof for a' that: *fool*
For a' that, and a' that,
His riband, star, and a' that,
The man of independent mind,
He looks and laughs at a' that.

A prince can mak a belted knight,   *make*
  A marquis, duke, and a' that;
But an honest man's aboon his might,   *above*
  Guid faith he mauna fa' that!   *Good: must not: achieve*
    For a' that, and a' that,
      Their dignities, and a' that,
      The pith o' sense, and pride o' worth,
      Are higher rank than a' that.

Then let us pray that come it may,
  As come it will for a' that;
That sense and worth, o'er a' the earth,
  May bear the gree, and a' that.   *prize*
    For a' that, and a' that,
      It's coming yet, for a' that,
      That man to man, the warld o'er,
      Shall brothers be, for a' that.

WILLIAM WORDSWORTH

LINES

*Composed a Few Miles above Tintern Abbey, on Revisiting
the Banks of the Wye during a Tour. July 13, 1798*

FIVE years have passed; five summers, with the length
Of five long winters! and again I hear
These waters, rolling from their mountain-springs
With a soft inland murmur. – Once again
Do I behold these steep and lofty cliffs,
That on a wild secluded scene impress
Thoughts of more deep seclusion; and connect
The landscape with the quiet of the sky.
The day is come when I again repose
Here, under this dark sycamore, and view
These plots of cottage-ground, these orchard-tufts,
Which at this season, with their unripe fruits,
Are clad in one green hue, and lose themselves
'Mid groves and copses. Once again I see

These hedge-rows, hardly hedge-rows, little lines
Of sportive wood run wild: these pastoral farms,
Green to the very door; and wreaths of smoke
Sent up, in silence, from among the trees!
With some uncertain notice, as might seem
Of vagrant dwellers in the houseless woods,
Or of some Hermit's cave, where by his fire
The Hermit sits alone.
               These beauteous forms,
Through a long absence, have not been to me
As is a landscape to a blind man's eye:
But oft, in lonely rooms, and 'mid the din
Of towns and cities, I have owed to them
In hours of weariness, sensations sweet,
Felt in the blood, and felt along the heart;
And passing even into my purer mind,
With tranquil restoration – feelings too
Of unremembered pleasure: such, perhaps,
As have no slight or trivial influence
On that best portion of a good man's life,
His little, nameless, unremembered, acts
Of kindness and of love. Nor less, I trust,
To them I may have owed another gift,
Of aspect more sublime; that blessèd mood
In which the burden of the mystery,
In which the heavy and the weary weight
Of all this unintelligible world,
Is lightened: that serene and blessèd mood,
In which the affections gently lead us on –
Until, the breath of this corporeal frame
And even the motion of our human blood
Almost suspended, we are laid asleep
In body, and become a living soul:
While with an eye made quiet by the power
Of harmony, and the deep power of joy,
We see into the life of things.
                     If this
Be but a vain belief, yet, oh! how oft –
In darkness and amid the many shapes

Of joyless daylight: when the fretful stir
Unprofitable, and the fever of the world,
Have hung upon the beatings of my heart –
How oft, in spirit, have I turned to thee,
O sylvan Wye! thou wanderer through the woods,
How often has my spirit turned to thee!

And now, with gleams of half-extinguished thought,
With many recognitions dim and faint,
And somewhat of a sad perplexity,
The picture of the mind revives again:
While here I stand, not only with the sense
Of present pleasure, but with pleasing thoughts
That in this moment there is life and food
For future years. And so I dare to hope,
Though changed, no doubt, from what I was when first
I came among these hills; when like a roe
I bounded o'er the mountains, by the sides
Of the deep rivers, and the lonely streams,
Wherever nature led: more like a man
Flying from something that he dreads, than one
Who sought the thing he loved. For nature then
(The coarser pleasures of my boyish days,
And their glad animal movements all gone by)
To me was all in all. – I cannot paint
What then I was. The sounding cataract
Haunted me like a passion: the tall rock,
The mountain, and the deep and gloomy wood,
Their colours and their forms, were then to me
An appetite; a feeling and a love,
That had no need of a remoter charm,
By thought supplied, nor any interest
Unborrowed from the eye. – That time is past,
And all its aching joys are now no more,
And all its dizzy raptures. Not for this
Faint I, nor mourn nor murmur; other gifts
Have followed; for such loss, I would believe,
Abundant recompense. For I have learned
To look on nature, not as in the hour

Of thoughtless youth; but hearing oftentimes
The still, sad music of humanity,
Nor harsh nor grating, though of ample power
To chasten and subdue. And I have felt
A presence that disturbs me with the joy
Of elevated thoughts; a sense sublime
Of something far more deeply interfused,
Whose dwelling is the light of setting suns,
And the round ocean and the living air,
And the blue sky, and in the mind of man:
A motion and a spirit, that impels
All thinking things, all objects of all thought,
And rolls through all things. Therefore am I still
A lover of the meadows and the woods,
And mountains; and of all that we behold
From this green earth; of all the mighty world
Of eye, and ear – both what they half create,
And what perceive; well pleased to recognise
In nature and the language of the sense,
The anchor of my purest thoughts, the nurse,
The guide, the guardian of my heart, and soul
Of all my moral being.

       Nor perchance,
If I were not thus taught, should I the more
Suffer my genial spirits to decay:
For thou art with me here upon the banks
Of this fair river; thou my dearest Friend,
My dear, dear Friend; and in thy voice I catch
The language of my former heart, and read
My former pleasures in the shooting lights
Of thy wild eyes. Oh! yet a little while
May I behold in thee what I was once,
My dear, dear Sister! and this prayer I make,
Knowing that Nature never did betray
The heart that loved her; 'tis her privilege,
Through all the years of this our life, to lead
From joy to joy: for she can so inform
The mind that is within us, so impress
With quietness and beauty, and so feed

With lofty thoughts, that neither evil tongues,
Rash judgements, nor the sneers of selfish men,
Nor greetings where no kindness is, nor all
The dreary intercourse of daily life,
Shall e'er prevail against us, or disturb
Our cheerful faith, that all which we behold
Is full of blessings. Therefore let the moon
Shine on thee in thy solitary walk;
And let the misty mountain-winds be free
To blow against thee: and, in after years,
When these wild ecstasies shall be matured
Into a sober pleasure; when thy mind
Shall be a mansion for all lovely forms,
Thy memory be as a dwelling-place
For all sweet sounds and harmonies; oh! then,
If solitude, or fear, or pain, or grief,
Should be thy portion, with what healing thoughts
Of tender joy wilt thou remember me,
And these my exhortations! Nor, perchance –
If I should be where I no more can hear
Thy voice, nor catch from thy wild eyes these gleams
Of past existence – wilt thou then forget
That on the banks of this delightful stream
We stood together; and that I, so long
A worshipper of Nature, hither came
Unwearied in that service: rather say
With warmer love – oh! with far deeper zeal
Of holier love. Nor wilt thou then forget
That after many wanderings, many years
Of absence, these steep woods and lofty cliffs,
And this green pastoral landscape, were to me
More dear, both for themselves and for thy sake!

A SLUMBER did my spirit seal;
    I had no human fears:
She seemed a thing that could not feel
    The touch of earthly years.

No motion has she now, no force;
    She neither hears nor sees;
Rolled round in earth's diurnal course,
    With rocks, and stones, and trees.

SHE DWELT among the untrodden ways
    Beside the springs of Dove,
A Maid whom there were none to praise
    And very few to love:

A violet by a mossy stone
    Half hidden from the eye!
- Fair as a star, when only one
    Is shining in the sky.

She lived unknown, and few could know
    When Lucy ceased to be;
But she is in her grave, and, oh,
    The difference to me!

STRANGE fits of passion have I known:
And I will dare to tell,
But in the Lover's ear alone,
What once to me befell.

When she I loved looked every day
Fresh as a rose in June,
I to her cottage bent my way,
Beneath an evening moon.

Upon the moon I fixed my eye,
All over the wide lea;
With quickening pace my horse drew nigh
Those paths so dear to me.

And now we reached the orchard-plot;
And, as we climbed the hill,
The sinking moon to Lucy's cot
Came near, and nearer still.

In one of those sweet dreams I slept,
Kind Nature's gentlest boon!
And all the while my eyes I kept
On the descending moon.

My horse moved on; hoof after hoof
He raised, and never stopped:
When down behind the cottage roof,
At once, the bright moon dropped.

What fond and wayward thoughts will slide
Into a Lover's head!
'Oh mercy!' to myself I cried,
'If Lucy should be dead!'

THREE YEARS she grew in sun and shower,
Then Nature said, 'A lovelier flower
On earth was never sown;
This Child I to myself will take;
She shall be mine, and I will make
A Lady of my own.

'Myself will to my darling be
Both law and impulse: and with me
The Girl, in rock and plain,
In earth and heaven, in glade and bower,
Shall feel an overseeing power
To kindle or restrain.

'She shall be sportive as the fawn
That wild with glee across the lawn
Or up the mountain springs;
And hers shall be the breathing balm,
And hers the silence and the calm
Of mute insensate things.

'The floating clouds their state shall lend
To her; for her the willow bend;
Nor shall she fail to see

Even in the motions of the Storm
Grace that shall mould the Maiden's form
By silent sympathy.

'The stars of midnight shall be dear
To her; and she shall lean her ear
In many a secret place
Where rivulets dance their wayward round,
And beauty born of murmuring sound
Shall pass into her face.

'And vital feelings of delight
Shall rear her form to stately height,
Her virgin bosom swell;
Such thoughts to Lucy I will give
While she and I together live
Here in this happy dell.'

Thus Nature spake – The work was done –
How soon my Lucy's race was run!
She died, and left to me
This heath, this calm, and quiet scene;
The memory of what has been,
And never more will be.

I TRAVELLED among unknown men,
    In lands beyond the sea;
Nor, England! did I know till then
    What love I bore to thee.

'Tis past, that melancholy dream!
    Nor will I quit thy shore
A second time; for still I seem
    To love thee more and more.

Among thy mountains did I feel
    The joy of my desire;
And she I cherished turned her wheel
    Beside an English fire.

Thy mornings showed, thy nights concealed,
   The bowers where Lucy played;
And thine too is the last green field
   That Lucy's eyes surveyed.

MY HEART leaps up when I behold
   A rainbow in the sky:
So was it when my life began;
So is it now I am a man;
So be it when I shall grow old,
   Or let me die!
The Child is father of the Man;
And I could wish my days to be
Bound each to each by natural piety.

ODE

INTIMATIONS OF IMMORTALITY FROM
RECOLLECTIONS OF EARLY CHILDHOOD

THERE was a time when meadow, grove, and stream,
The earth, and every common sight,
   To me did seem
   Apparelled in celestial light,
The glory and the freshness of a dream.
It is not now as it hath been of yore;
   Turn wheresoe'er I may,
   By night or day,
The things which I have seen I now can see no more.

   The Rainbow comes and goes,
   And lovely is the Rose;
   The Moon doth with delight
Look round her when the heavens are bare;
   Waters on a starry night
   Are beautiful and fair;

The sunshine is a glorious birth;
But yet I know, where'er I go,
That there hath passed away a glory from the earth.

Now, while the birds thus sing a joyous song,
And while the young lambs bound
As to the tabor's sound,
To me alone there came a thought of grief:
A timely utterance gave that thought relief,
And I again am strong:
The cataracts blow their trumpets from the steep;
No more shall grief of mine the season wrong;
I hear the Echoes through the mountains throng,
The Winds come to me from the fields of sleep,
And all the earth is gay;
Land and sea
Give themselves up to jollity,
And with the heart of May
Doth every Beast keep holiday;
Thou Child of Joy,
Shout round me, let me hear thy shouts, thou happy
Shepherd-boy!

Ye blessèd Creatures, I have heard the call
Ye to each other make; I see
The heavens laugh with you in your jubilee;
My heart is at your festival,
My head hath its coronal,
The fullness of your bliss, I feel – I feel it all.
Oh, evil day! if I were sullen
While Earth herself is adorning,
This sweet May-morning,
And the Children are culling
On every side,
In a thousand valleys far and wide,
Fresh flowers; while the sun shines warm,
And the Babe leaps up on his Mother's arm –
I hear, I hear, with joy I hear!
– But there's a Tree, of many, one,

A single Field which I have looked upon,
Both of them speak of something that is gone:
         The Pansy at my feet
         Doth the same tale repeat:
Whither is fled the visionary gleam?
Where is it now, the glory and the dream?

Our birth is but a sleep and a forgetting:
The Soul that rises with us, our life's Star,
         Hath had elsewhere its setting,
            And cometh from afar:
         Not in entire forgetfulness,
         And not in utter nakedness,
But trailing clouds of glory do we come
         From God, who is our home:
Heaven lies about us in our infancy!
Shades of the prison-house begin to close
         Upon the growing Boy,
               But He
Beholds the light, and whence it flows,
         He sees it in his joy;
The Youth, who daily farther from the east
         Must travel, still is Nature's Priest,
         And by the vision splendid
         Is on his way attended;
At length the Man perceives it die away,
And fade into the light of common day.

Earth fills her lap with pleasures of her own;
Yearnings she hath in her own natural kind,
And, even with something of a Mother's mind,
         And no unworthy aim,
         The homely Nurse doth all she can
To make her Foster-child, her Inmate Man,
         Forget the glories he hath known,
And that imperial palace whence he came.

Behold the Child among his new-born blisses,
A six years' Darling of a pigmy size!
See, where 'mid work of his own hand he lies,

Fretted by sallies of his mother's kisses,
With light upon him from his father's eyes!
See, at his feet, some little plan or chart,
Some fragment from his dream of human life,
Shaped by himself with newly-learnèd art;

    A wedding or a festival,
    A mourning or a funeral;
      And this hath now his heart,
    And unto this he frames his song:
      Then will he fit his tongue
To dialogues of business, love, or strife;
    But it will not be long
    Ere this be thrown aside,
    And with new joy and pride
The little Actor cons another part;
Filling from time to time his 'humorous stage'
With all the Persons, down to palsied Age,
That Life brings with her in her equipage;
    As if his whole vocation
    Were endless imitation.

Thou, whose exterior semblance doth belie
    Thy Soul's immensity;
Thou best Philosopher, who yet dost keep
Thy heritage, thou Eye among the blind,
That, deaf and silent, read'st the eternal deep,
Haunted for ever by the eternal mind –
    Might Prophet! Seer blest!
    On whom those truths do rest,
Which we are toiling all our lives to find,
In darkness lost, the darkness of the grave;
Thou, over whom thy Immortality
Broods like the Day, a Master o'er a Slave,
A Presence which is not to be put by;
Thou little Child, yet glorious in the might
Of heaven-born freedom on thy being's height,
Why with such earnest pains dost thou provoke
The years to bring the inevitable yoke,

Thus blindly with thy blessedness at strife?
Full soon thy Soul shall have her earthly freight,
And custom lie upon thee with a weight,
Heavy as frost, and deep almost as life!

Oh, joy! that in our embers
Is something that doth live,
That nature yet remembers
What was so fugitive!
The thought of our past years in me doth breed
Perpetual benediction: not indeed
For that which is most worthy to be blessed;
Delight and liberty, the simple creed
Of Childhood, whether busy or at rest,
With new-fledged hope still fluttering in his breast –
Not for these I raise
The song of thanks and praise;
But for those obstinate questionings
Of sense and outward things,
Fallings from us, vanishings;
Blank misgivings of a Creature
Moving about in worlds not realised,
High instincts before which our mortal Nature
Did tremble like a guilty Thing surprised:
But for those first affections,
Those shadowy recollections,
Which, be they what they may,
Are yet the fountain light of all our day,
Are yet a master light of all our seeing;
Uphold us, cherish, and have power to make
Our noisy years seem moments in the being
Of the eternal Silence: truths that wake,
To perish never;
Which neither listlessness, nor mad endeavour,
Nor Man nor Boy,
Nor all that is at enmity with joy,
Can utterly abolish or destroy!
Hence in a season of calm weather

Though inland far we be,
Our Souls have sight of that immortal sea
Which brought us hither,
Can in a moment travel thither,
And see the Children sport upon the shore,
And hear the mighty water rolling evermore.

Then sing, ye Birds, sing, sing a joyous song!
And let the young Lambs bound
As to the tabor's sound!
We in thought will join your throng,
Ye that pipe and ye that play,
Ye that through your hearts today
Feel the gladness of the May!
What though the radiance which was once so bright
Be now for ever taken from my sight,
Though nothing can bring back the hour
Of splendour in the grass, of glory in the flower;
We will grieve not, rather find
Strength in what remains behind;
In the primal sympathy
Which having been must ever be;
In the soothing thoughts that spring
Out of human suffering;
In the faith that looks through death,
In years that bring the philosophic mind.

And O, ye Fountains, Meadows, Hills, and Groves,
Forebode not any severing of our loves!
Yet in my heart of hearts I feel your might;
I only have relinquished one delight
To live beneath your more habitual sway.
I love the Brooks which down their channels fret,
Even more than when I tripped lightly as they;
The innocent brightness of a new-born Day
Is lovely yet;
The Clouds that gather round the setting sun
Do take a sober colouring from an eye
That hath kept watch o'er man's mortality;
Another race hath been, and other palms are won.

Thanks to the human heart by which we live,
Thanks to its tenderness, its joys, and fears,
To me the meanest flower that blows can give
Thoughts that do often lie too deep for tears.

COMPOSED UPON WESTMINSTER BRIDGE, SEPTEMBER 3, 1802

EARTH has not anything to show more fair:
Dull would he be of soul who could pass by
A sight so touching in its majesty:
This City now doth, like a garment, wear
The beauty of the morning; silent, bare,
Ships, towers, domes, theatres, and temples lie
Open unto the fields, and to the sky;
All bright and glittering in the smokeless air.
Never did sun more beautifully steep
In his first splendour, valley, rock, or hill;
Ne'er saw I, never felt, a calm so deep!
The river glideth at his own sweet will:
Dear God! the very houses seem asleep;
And all that mighty heart is lying still!

I WANDERED lonely as a cloud
That floats on high o'er vales and hills,
When all at once I saw a crowd,
A host, of golden daffodils;
Beside the lake, beneath the trees,
Fluttering and dancing in the breeze.

Continuous as the stars that shine
And twinkle on the milky way,
They stretched in never-ending line
Along the margin of a bay:
Ten thousand saw I at a glance,
Tossing their heads in sprightly dance.

The waves beside them danced; but they
Out-did the sparkling waves in glee:

A poet could not but be gay,
In such a jocund company:
I gazed – and gazed – but little thought
What wealth the show to me had brought:

For oft, when on my couch I lie
In vacant or in pensive mood,
They flash upon that inward eye
Which is the bliss of solitude;
And then my heart with pleasure fills,
And dances with the daffodils.

From THE PRELUDE

THERE was a Boy: ye knew him well, ye cliffs
And islands of Winander! – many a time
At evening, when the earliest stars began
To move along the edges of the hills,
Rising or setting, would he stand alone
Beneath the trees or by the glimmering lake,
And there, with fingers interwoven, both hands
Pressed closely palm to palm, and to his mouth
Uplifted, he, as through an instrument,
Blew mimic hootings to the silent owls,
That they might answer him; and they would shout
Across the watery vale, and shout again,
Responsive to his call, with quivering peals,
And long halloos and screams, and echoes loud,
Redoubled and redoubled, concourse wild
Of jocund din; and, when a lengthened pause
Of silence came and baffled his best skill,
Then sometimes, in that silence while he hung
Listening, a gentle shock of mild surprise
Has carried far into his heart the voice
Of mountain torrents; or the visible scene
Would enter unawares into his mind,
With all its solemn imagery, its rocks,
Its woods, and that uncertain heaven, received
Into the bosom of the steady lake.

SAMUEL TAYLOR COLERIDGE

THE RIME OF THE ANCIENT MARINER

PART I

An ancient
Mariner meeteth
three Gallants
bidden to a
wedding-feast,
and detaineth
one.

IT IS an ancient Mariner,
And he stoppeth one of three.
'By thy long grey beard and glittering eye,
Now wherefore stopp'st thou me?

'The Bridegroom's doors are opened wide,
And I am next of kin;
The guests are met, the feast is set:
May'st hear the merry din.'

The Wedding
Guest is spell-
bound by the eye
of the old sea-
faring man, and
constrained to
hear his tale.

He holds him with his skinny hand,
'There was a ship,' quoth he.
'Hold off! Unhand me, grey-beard loon!'
Eftsoons his hand dropped he.

He holds him with his glittering eye –
The Wedding-Guest stood still,
And listens like a three years' child:
The Mariner hath his will.

The Wedding-Guest sat on a stone:
He cannot choose but hear;
And thus spake on that ancient man,
The bright-eyed Mariner.

The Mariner tells
how the ship
sailed southward
with a good
wind and fair
weather, till it
reached the Line.

'The ship was cheered, the harbour cleared,
Merrily did we drop
Below the kirk, below the hill,
Below the lighthouse top.

'The Sun came up upon the left,
Out of the sea came he!
And he shone bright, and on the right
Went down into the sea.

'Higher and higher every day,
Till over the mast at noon—'
The Wedding-Guest here beat his breast,
For he heard the loud bassoon.

The Wedding-
Guest heareth
the bridal music;
but the Mariner
continueth his
tale.

The bride hath paced into the hall,
Red as a rose is she;
Nodding their heads before her goes
The merry minstrelsy.

The Wedding-Guest he beat his breast,
Yet he cannot choose but hear;
And thus spake on that ancient man,
The bright-eyed Mariner.

The ship driven
by a storm
toward the
South Pole.

'And now the Storm-blast came, and he
Was tyrannous and strong:
He struck with his o'ertaking wings,
And chased us south along.

'With sloping masts and dipping prow,
As who pursued with yell and blow
Still treads the shadow of his foe,
And forward bends his head,
The ship drove fast, loud roared the blast,
And southward aye we fled.

'And now there came both mist and snow,
And it grew wondrous cold:
And ice, mast-high, came floating by,
As green as emerald.

The land of ice,
and of fearful
sounds where no
living thing was
to be seen.

'And through the drifts the snowy clifts
Did send a dismal sheen:
Nor shapes of men nor beasts we ken –
The ice was all between.

'The ice was here, the ice was there,
The ice was all around:
It cracked and growled, and roared and howled,
Like noises in a swound!

Till a great sea-bird, called the Albatross, came through the snow-fog, and was received with great joy and hospitality.

'At length did cross an Albatross,
Thorough the fog it came;
As if it had been a Christian soul,
We hailed it in God's name.

'It ate the food it ne'er had eat,
And round and round it flew.
The ice did split with a thunder-fit;
The helmsman steered us through!

And lo! the Albatross proveth a bird of good omen, and followeth the ship as it returned northward through fog and floating ice.

'And a good south wind sprung up behind;
The Albatross did follow,
And every day, for food or play,
Came to the mariners' hollo!

'In mist or cloud, on mast or shroud,
It perched for vespers nine;
Whiles all the night, through fog-smoke white,
Glimmered the white moonshine.'

The ancient Mariner inhospitably killeth the pious bird of good omen.

'God save thee, ancient Mariner,
From the fiends, that plague thee thus! –
Why look'st thou so?' – 'With my cross-bow
I shot the Albatross.

PART II

'The Sun now rose upon the right:
Out of the sea came he,
Still hid in mist, and on the left
Went down into the sea.

'And the good south wind still blew behind,
But no sweet bird did follow,
Nor any day for food or play
Came to the mariners' hollo!

His shipmates cry out against the ancient Mariner, for killing the bird of good luck.

'And I had done a hellish thing,
And it would work 'em woe:
For all averred, I had killed the bird
That made the breeze to blow.
Ah wretch! said they, the bird to slay,
That made the breeze to blow!

But when the
fog cleared off,
they justify the
same, and thus
make themselves
accomplices in
the crime.

'Nor dim nor red, like God's own head,
The glorious Sun uprist:
Then all averred I had killed the bird
That brought the fog and mist.
'Twas right, said they, such birds to slay,
That bring the fog and mist.

The fair breeze
continues; the
ship enters the
Pacific Ocean,
and sails north-
ward, even till it
reaches the Line.

'The fair breeze blew, the white foam flew,
The furrow followed free;
We were the first that ever burst
Into that silent sea.

'Down dropped the breeze, the sails dropped down,
'Twas sad as sad could be;
And we did speak only to break
The silence of the sea!

The ship hath
been suddenly
becalmed.

'All in a hot and copper sky,
The bloody Sun, at noon,
Right up above the mast did stand,
No bigger than the Moon.

'Day after day, day after day,
We stuck, nor breath nor motion;
As idle as a painted ship
Upon a painted ocean.

And the Alba-
tross begins to be
avenged.

'Water, water, everywhere,
And all the boards did shrink;
Water, water, everywhere,
Nor any drop to drink.

'The very deep did rot: O Christ!
That ever this should be!
Yea, slimy things did crawl with legs
Upon the slimy sea.

'About, about, in reel and rout
The death-fires danced at night;
The water, like a witch's oils,
Burnt green, and blue and white.

'And some in dreams assurèd were
Of the Spirit that plagued us so;
Nine fathom deep he had followed us
From the land of mist and snow.

A Spirit had followed them; one of the invisible inhabitants of this planet, neither departed souls nor angels; concerning whom the learned Jew, Josephus, and the Platonic Constantinopolitan, Michael Psellus, may be consulted. They are very numerous, and there is no climate or element without one or more.

'And every tongue, through utter drought,
Was withered at the root;
We could not speak, no more than if
We had been choked with soot.

The shipmates, in their sore distress, would fain throw the whole guilt on the ancient Mariner: in sign whereof they hang the dead sea-bird round his neck.

'Ah! well a-day! what evil looks
Had I from old and young!
Instead of the cross, the Albatross
About my neck was hung.

PART III

'There passed a weary time. Each throat
Was parched, and glazed each eye.
A weary time! a weary time!
How glazed each weary eye!

The ancient Mariner beholdeth a sign in the element afar off.

When looking westward, I beheld
A something in the sky.

'At first it seemed a little speck,
And then it seemed a mist;
It moved and moved, and took at last
A certain shape, I wist.

'A speck, a mist, a shape, I wist!
And still it neared and neared:
As if it dodged a water-sprite,
It plunged, and tacked, and veered.

At its nearer approach, it seemeth him to be a ship; and at a dear ransom he freeth his speech from the bonds of thirst.

'With throats unslaked, with black lips baked,
We could nor laugh nor wail;
Through utter drought all dumb we stood!
I bit my arm, I sucked the blood,
And cried, A sail! a sail!

'With throats unslaked, with black lips baked,
Agape they heard me call:
A flash of joy:
Gramercy! they for joy did grin,
And all at once their breath drew in,
As they were drinking all.

And horror follows. For can it be a ship that comes onward without wind or tide?

'See! see! (I cried) she tacks no more!
Hither to work us weal;
Without a breeze, without a tide,
She steadies with upright keel!

'The western wave was all aflame.
The day was well nigh done!
Almost upon the western wave
Rested the broad, bright Sun;
When that strange shape drove suddenly
Betwixt us and the Sun.

It seemeth him but the skeleton of a ship.

'And straight the Sun was flecked with bars
(Heaven's Mother send us grace!),
As if through a dungeon-grate he peered
With broad and burning face.

And its ribs are seen as bars on the face of the setting Sun. The Spectre-Woman and her Death-mate, and no other on board the skeleton ship.

'Alas! (thought I, and my heart beat loud)
How fast she nears and nears!
Are those *her* sails that glance in the Sun,
Like restless gossameres?

'Are those *her* ribs through which the Sun
Did peer, as through a grate?
And is that Woman all her crew?
Is that a Death? and are there two?
Is Death that Woman's mate?

Like vessel, like crew! Death and Life-in-Death have diced for the ship's crew, and she (the latter) winneth the ancient Mariner.

'*Her* lips were red, *her* looks were free,
Her locks were yellow as gold;
Her skin was as white as leprosy,
The Nightmare Life-in-Death was she,
Who thicks man's blood with cold.

'The naked hulk alongside came,
And the twain were casting dice;
"The game is done! I've won! I've won!"
Quoth she, and whistles thrice.

No twilight within the courts of the Sun.

'The Sun's rim dips; the stars rush out:
At one stride comes the dark;
With far-heard whisper, o'er the sea,
Off shot the spectre-bark.

At the rising of the Moon,

'We listened and looked sideways up!
Fear at my heart, as at a cup,
My life-blood seemed to sip!
The stars were dim, and thick the night,
The steersman's face by his lamp gleamed white;
From the sails the dew did drip –
Till clomb above the eastern bar
The hornèd Moon, with one bright star
Within the nether tip.

One after another,

'One after one, by the star-dogged Moon
Too quick for groan or sigh,
Each turned his face with a ghastly pang,
And cursed me with his eye.

His shipmates drop down dead.

'Four times fifty living men
(And I heard nor sigh nor groan),
With heavy thump, a lifeless lump,
They dropped down one by one.

But Life-in-Death begins her work on the ancient Mariner.

'The souls did from their bodies fly –
They fled to bliss or woe!
And every soul, it passed me by,
Like the whizz of my cross-bow!'

PART IV

The Wedding-
Guest feareth
that a Spirit is
talking to him;

'I fear thee, ancient Mariner!
I fear thy skinny hand!
And thou art long, and lank, and brown,
As is the ribbed sea-sand.

'I fear thee and thy glittering eye,
And thy skinny hand, so brown.' –

But the ancient
Mariner assureth
him of his bodily
life and pro-
ceedeth to relate
his horrible
penance.

'Fear not, fear not, thou Wedding-Guest!
This body dropped not down.

'Alone, alone, all, all alone,
Alone on a wide, wide sea!
And never a saint took pity on
My soul in agony.

'The many men, so beautiful!
And they all dead did lie:
And a thousand thousand slimy things
Lived on; and so did I.

And envieth
that *they* should
live and so many
lie dead.

'I looked upon the rotting sea,
And drew my eyes away;
I looked upon the rotting deck,
And there the dead men lay.

'I looked to heaven, and tried to pray;
But or ever a prayer had gushed,
A wicked whisper came, and made
My heart as dry as dust.

'I closed my lids, and kept them close,
And the balls like pulses beat;
For the sky and the sea, and the sea and the sky
Lay like a load on my weary eye,
And the dead were at my feet.

But the curse
liveth for him
in the eye of
the dead men.

'The cold sweat melted from their limbs,
Nor rot nor reek did they:
The look with which they looked on me
Had never passed away.

'An orphan's curse would drag to hell
A spirit from on high;
But oh! more horrible than that
Is the curse in a dead man's eye!
Seven days, seven nights, I saw that curse,
And yet I could not die.

In his loneliness
and fixedness he
yearneth towards
the journeying
Moon, and the
stars that still
sojourn, yet still
move onward;
and everywhere
the blue sky
belongs to them,
and is their
appointed rest,
and their native
country and their own natural homes, which they enter unannounced, as
lords that are certainly expected and yet there is a silent joy at their arrival.

'The moving Moon went up the sky,
And nowhere did abide;
Softly she was going up,
And a star or two beside –

'Her beams bemocked the sultry main,
Like April hoar-frost spread;
But where the ship's huge shadow lay,
The charmèd water burnt alway
A still and awful red.

By the light of
the Moon he
beholdeth God's
creatures of the
great calm.

'Beyond the shadow of the ship,
I watched the water-snakes:
They moved in tracks of shining white,
And when they reared, the elfish light
Fell off in hoary flakes.

'Within the shadow of the ship
I watched their rich attire:
Blue, glossy green, and velvet black,
They coiled and swam; and every track
Was a flash of golden fire.

Their beauty and
their happiness.

He blesseth
them in his
heart.

'O happy living things! no tongue
Their beauty might declare:
A spring of love gushed from my heart,
And I blessed them unaware:
Sure my kind saint took pity on me,
And I blessed them unaware.

The spell begins
to break.

'The self-same moment I could pray;
And from my neck so free
The Albatross fell off, and sank
Like lead into the sea.

PART V

'Oh sleep! it is a gentle thing,
Beloved from pole to pole!
To Mary Queen the praise be given!
She sent the gentle sleep from Heaven,
That slid into my soul.

By grace of the
holy Mother, the
ancient Mariner
is refreshed
with rain.

'The silly buckets on the deck,
That had so long remained,
I dreamt that they were filled with dew;
And when I awoke, it rained.

'My lips were wet, my throat was cold,
My garments all were dank;
Sure I had drunken in my dreams,
And still my body drank.

'I moved, and could not feel my limbs:
I was so light – almost
I thought that I had died in sleep,
And was a blessèd ghost.

He heareth
sounds and seeth
strange sights
and commotions
in the sky and
the element.

'And soon I heard a roaring wind:
It did not come anear;
But with its sound it shook the sails,
That were so thin and sere.

'The upper air burst into life!
And a hundred fire-flags sheen,
To and fro they were hurried about!
And to and fro, and in and out,
The wan stars danced between.

'And the coming wind did roar more loud,
And the sails did sigh like sedge;
And the rain poured down from one black cloud;
The Moon was at its edge.

'The thick black cloud was cleft, and still
The Moon was at its side:
Like water shot from some high crag,
The lightning fell with never a jag,
A river steep and wide.

The bodies of
the ship's crew
are inspirited,
and the ship
moves on;

'The loud wind never reached the ship,
Yet now the ship moved on!
Beneath the lightning and the Moon
The dead men gave a groan.

'They groaned, they stirred, they all uprose,
Nor spake, nor moved their eyes;
It had been strange, even in a dream,
To have seen those dead men rise.

'The helmsman steered, the ship moved on;
Yet never a breeze up-blew;
The mariners all 'gan work the ropes,
Where they were wont to do;
They raised their limbs like lifeless tools –
We were a ghastly crew.

'The body of my brother's son
Stood by me, knee to knee:
The body and I pulled at one rope,
But he said nought to me.'

But not by the
souls of the men,
nor by daemons
of earth or
middle air, but
by a blessed
troop of angelic
spirits, sent down
by the invocation
of the guardian
saint.

'I fear thee, ancient Mariner!'
'Be calm, thou Wedding-Guest!
'Twas not those souls that fled in pain,
Which to their corses came again,
But a troop of spirits blest:

'For when it dawned – they dropped their arms,
And clustered round the mast;
Sweet sounds rose slowly through their mouths,
And from their bodies passed.

'Around, around, flew each sweet sound,
Then darted to the Sun;
Slowly the sounds came back again,
Now mixed, now one by one.

'Sometimes a-dropping from the sky
I heard the skylark sing;
Sometimes all little birds that are,
How they seemed to fill the sea and air
With their sweet jargoning!

'And now 'twas like all instruments,
Now like a lonely flute;
And now it is an angel's song,
That makes the heavens be mute.

'It ceased; yet still the sails made on
A pleasant noise till noon,
A noise like of a hidden brook
In the leafy month of June,
That to the sleeping wood all night
Singeth a quiet tune.

'Till noon we quietly sailed on,
Yet never a breeze did breathe:
Slowly and smoothly went the ship,
Moved onward from beneath.

The lonesome
Spirit from the
South Pole
carries on the
ship as far as the
Line, in obedience
to the angelic
troop, but still
requireth
vengeance.

'Under the keel nine fathom deep,
From the land of mist and snow,
The Spirit slid: and it was he
That made the ship to go.
The sails at noon left off their tune,
And the ship stood still also.

'The Sun, right up above the mast,
Had fixed her to the ocean:
But in a minute she 'gan stir,
With a short uneasy motion –
Backwards and forwards half her length
With a short uneasy motion.

'Then like a pawing horse let go,
She made a sudden bound:
It flung the blood into my head,
And I fell down in a swound.

<table>
<tr><td>

The Polar Spirit's fellow-daemons, the invisible inhabitants of the element, take part in his wrong; and two of them relate, one to the other, that penance long and heavy for the ancient Mariner hath been accorded to the Polar Spirit, who returneth southward.

</td><td>

'How long in that same fit I lay,
I have not to declare;
But ere my living life returned,
I heard and in my soul discerned
Two voices in the air.

' "Is it he?" quoth one. "Is this the man?
By Him who died on cross
With his cruel bow he laid full low
The harmless Albatross.

' "The Spirit who bideth by himself
In the land of mist and snow,
He loved the bird that loved the man
Who shot him with his bow."

</td></tr>
</table>

'The other was a softer voice,
As soft as honey-dew:
Quoth he, "The man hath penance done,
And penance more will do."

PART VI
First Voice

' "But tell me, tell me! speak again,
Thy soft response renewing –
What makes that ship drive on so fast?
What is the Ocean doing?"

Second Voice

' "Still as a slave before his lord,
The Ocean hath no blast;
His great bright eye most silently
Up to the Moon is cast –

' "If he may know which way to go;
For she guides him smooth or grim.
See, brother, see! how graciously
She looketh down on him."

First Voice

The Mariner
hath been cast
into a trance;
for the angelic
power causeth
the vessel to
drive northward
faster than
human life
could endure.

' "But why drives on that ship so fast,
Without or wave or wind?"

Second Voice

' "The air is cut away before,
And closes from behind.

' "Fly, brother, fly! more high, more high!
Or we shall be belated:
For slow and slow that ship will go,
When the Mariner's trance is abated."

The super-
natural motion
is retarded; the
Mariner awakes,
and his penance
begins anew.

'I woke, and we were sailing on
As in a gentle weather:
'Twas night, calm night, the Moon was high;
The dead men stood together.

'All stood together on the deck,
For a charnel-dungeon fitter:
All fixed on me their stony eyes,
That in the Moon did glitter.

'The pang, the curse, with which they died,
Had never passed away:
I could not draw my eyes from theirs,
Nor turn them up to pray.

The curse is
finally expiated.

'And now this spell was snapped: once more
I viewed the ocean green,
And looked far forth, yet little saw
Of what had else been seen –

'Like one that on a lonesome road
Doth walk in fear and dread,
And having once turned round walks on,
And turns no more his head;
Because he knows, a frightful fiend
Doth close behind him tread.

'But soon there breathed a wind on me,
Nor sound nor motion made:
Its path was not upon the sea,
In ripple or in shade.

'It raised my hair, it fanned my cheek
Like a meadow-gale of spring –
It mingled strangely with my fears,
Yet it felt like a welcoming.

'Swiftly, swiftly flew the ship,
Yet she sailed softly too:
Sweetly, sweetly blew the breeze –
On me alone it blew.

And the ancient
Mariner behold-
eth his native
country.

'Oh! dream of joy! Is this indeed
The lighthouse top I see?
Is this the hill? Is this the kirk?
Is this mine own countree?

'We drifted o'er the harbour-bar,
And I with sobs did pray –
Oh, let me be awake, my God!
Or let me sleep alway.

'The harbour-bar was clear as glass,
So smoothly it was strewn!
And on the bay the moonlight lay,
And the shadow of the Moon.

'The rock shone bright, the kirk no less,
That stands above the rock:
The moonlight steeped in silentness
The steady weathercock.

The angelic
spirits leave the
dead bodies,

'And the bay was white with silent light,
Till rising from the same,
Full many shapes, that shadows were,
In crimson colours came.

And appear in
their own forms
of light.

'A little distance from the prow
Those crimson shadows were:
I turned my eyes upon the deck –
Oh, Christ! what saw I there!

'Each corse lay flat, lifeless and flat,
And, by the holy rood!
A man all light, a seraph-man,
On every corse there stood.

'This seraph-band, each waved his hand:
It was a heavenly sight!
They stood as signals to the land,
Each one a lovely light;

'This seraph-band, each waved his hand,
No voice did they impart –
No voice: but oh! the silence sank
Like music on my heart.

'But soon I heard the dash of oars,
I heard the Pilot's cheer;
My head was turned perforce away
And I saw a boat appear.

'The Pilot and the Pilot's boy,
I heard them coming fast:
Dear Lord in Heaven! it was a joy
The dead men could not blast.

'I saw a third – I heard his voice:
It is the Hermit good!
He singeth loud his godly hymns
That he makes in the wood.
He'll shrieve my soul, he'll wash away
The Albatross's blood.

PART VII

*The Hermit of
the Wood*

'This Hermit good lives in that wood
Which slopes down to the sea.
How loudly his sweet voice he rears!
He loves to talk with marineres
That come from a far countree.

'He kneels at morn, and noon, and eve –
He hath a cushion plump:
It is the moss that wholly hides
The rotted old oak-stump.

'The skiff-boat neared: I heard them talk,
"Why, this is strange, I trow!
Where are those lights so many and fair,
That signal made but now?"

*Approacheth
the ship with
wonder.*

' "Strange, by my faith!" the Hermit said –
"And they answered not our cheer!
The planks looked warped! and see those sails,
How thin they are and sere!
I never saw aught like to them,
Unless perchance it were

' "Brown skeletons of leaves that lag
My forest-brook along;
When the ivy-tod is heavy with snow,
And the owlet whoops to the wolf below,
That eats the she-wolf's young." '

' "Dear Lord! it hath a fiendish look –
(The Pilot made reply)
I am a-feared" – "Push on, push on!"
Said the Hermit cheerily.

'The boat came closer to the ship,
But I nor spake nor stirred;
The boat came close beneath the ship,
And straight a sound was heard.

The ship
suddenly sinketh.

'Under the water it rumbled on,
Still louder and more dread:
It reached the ship, it split the bay;
The ship went down like lead.

The ancient
Mariner is
saved in the
Pilot's boat.

'Stunned by that loud and dreadful sound,
Which sky and ocean smote,
Like one that hath been seven days drowned
My body lay afloat;
But swift as dreams, myself I found
Within the Pilot's boat.

'Upon the whirl, where sank the ship,
The boat spun round and round;
And all was still, save that the hill
Was telling of the sound.

'I moved my lips – the Pilot shrieked
And fell down in a fit;
The holy Hermit raised his eyes,
And prayed where he did sit.

'I took the oars: the Pilot's boy,
Who now doth crazy go,
Laughed loud and long, and all the while
His eyes went to and fro.
"Ha! ha!" quoth he, "full plain I see,
The Devil knows how to row."

'And now, all in my own countree,
I stood on the firm land!
The Hermit stepped forth from the boat,
And scarcely he could stand.

The ancient
Mariner earnest-
ly entreateth the
Hermit to
shrieve him; and
the penance of
life falls on him.

' "O shrieve me, shrieve me, holy man!"
The Hermit crossed his brow.
"Say quick," quoth he, "I bid thee say –
What manner of man art thou?"

'Forthwith this frame of mine was wrenched
With a woeful agony,
Which forced me to begin my tale;
And then it left me free.

'Since then, at an uncertain hour,
That agony returns:
And till my ghastly tale is told,
This heart within me burns.

'I pass, like night, from land to land;
I have strange power of speech;
That moment that his face I see,
I know the man that must hear me:
To him my tale I teach.

'What loud uproar bursts from that door!
The wedding-guests are there:
But in the garden-bower the bride
And bride-maids singing are:
And hark the little vesper bell,
Which biddeth me to prayer!

'O Wedding-Guest! this soul hath been
Alone on a wide, wide sea:
So lonely 'twas, that God himself
Scarce seemèd there to be.

'Oh, sweeter than the marriage-feast,
'Tis sweeter far to me,
To walk together to the kirk
With a goodly company! –

'To walk together to the kirk,
And all together pray,
While each to his great Father bends,
Old men, and babes, and loving friends
And youths and maidens gay!

And to teach,
by his own
example, love
and reverence to
all things that
God made and
loveth.

'Farewell, farewell! but this I tell
To thee, thou Wedding-Guest!
He prayeth well, who loveth well
Both man and bird and beast.

'He prayeth best, who loveth best
All things both great and small;
For the dear God who loveth us,
He made and loveth all.'

The Mariner, whose eye is bright,
Whose beard with age is hoar,
Is gone: and now the Wedding-Guest
Turned from the bridegroom's door.

He went like one that hath been stunned,
And is of sense forlorn:
A sadder and a wiser man,
He rose the morrow morn.

FROST AT MIDNIGHT

THE frost performs its secret ministry,
Unhelped by any wind. The owlet's cry
Came loud – and hark, again! loud as before.
The inmates of my cottage, all at rest,
Have left me to that solitude, which suits
Abstruser musings: save that at my side
My cradled infant slumbers peacefully.
'Tis calm indeed! so calm, that it disturbs
And vexes meditation with its strange
And extreme silentness. Sea, hill, and wood,
This populous village! Sea, and hill, and wood,
With all the numberless goings-on of life,
Inaudible as dreams! the thin blue flame
Lies on my low-burnt fire, and quivers not;
Only that film, which fluttered on the grate,
Still flutters there, the sole unquiet thing.

Methinks, its motion in this hush of nature
Gives it dim sympathies with me who live,
Making it a companionable form,
Whose puny flaps and freaks the idling spirit
By its own moods interprets, everywhere
Echo or mirror seeking of itself,
And makes a toy of thought.

                                 But oh! how oft,
How oft, at school, with most believing mind,
Presageful, have I gazed upon the bars,
To watch that fluttering *stranger*! and as oft
With unclosed lids, already had I dreamt
Of my sweet birthplace, and the old church-tower,
Whose bells, the poor man's only music, rang
From morn to evening, all the hot fair-day,
So sweetly, that they stirred and haunted me
With a wild pleasure, falling on mine ear
Most like articulate sounds of things to come!
So gazed I, till the soothing things, I dreamt,
Lulled me to sleep, and sleep prolonged my dreams!
And so I brooded all the following morn,
Awed by the stern preceptor's face, mine eye
Fixed with mock study on my swimming book:
Save if the door half opened, and I snatched
A hasty glance, and still my heart leaped up,
For still I hoped to see the *stranger's* face,
Townsman, or aunt, or sister more beloved,
My playmate when we both were clothed alike!

Dear Babe, that sleepest cradled by my side,
Whose gentle breathings, heard in this deep calm,
Fill up the interspersèd vacancies
And momentary pauses of the thought!
My babe so beautiful! it thrills my heart
With tender gladness, thus to look at thee,
And think that thou shalt learn far other lore,
And in far other scenes! For I was reared
In the great city, pent 'mid cloisters dim,
And saw nought lovely but the sky and stars.

But *thou*, my babe! shalt wander like a breeze
By lakes and sandy shores, beneath the crags
Of ancient mountain, and beneath the clouds,
Which image in their bulk both lakes and shores
And mountain crags: so shalt thou see and hear
The lovely shapes and sounds intelligible
Of that eternal language, which thy God
Utters, who from eternity doth teach
Himself in all, and all things in Himself.
Great universal Teacher! He shall mould
Thy spirit, and by giving make it ask.

Therefore all seasons shall be sweet to thee,
Whether the summer clothe the general earth
With greenness, or the redbreast sit and sing
Betwixt the tufts of snow on the bare branch
Of mossy apple-tree, while the nigh thatch
Smokes in the sun-thaw; whether the eave-drops fall
Heard only in the trances of the blast,
Or if the secret ministry of frost
Shall hang them up in silent icicles,
Quietly shining to the quiet moon.

KUBLA KHAN

Or a vision in a dream. A fragment

In XANADU did Kubla Khan
   A stately pleasure-dome decree:
Where Alph, the sacred river, ran
Through caverns measureless to man
   Down to a sunless sea.
So twice five miles of fertile ground
   With walls and towers were girdled round:
And there were gardens bright with sinuous rills
Where blossomed many an incense-bearing tree;
And here were forests ancient as the hills,
Enfolding sunny spots of greenery.

But oh, that deep romantic chasm which slanted
Down the green hill athwart a cedarn cover!
A savage place! as holy and enchanted
As e'er beneath a waning moon was haunted
By woman wailing for her demon-lover!
And from this chasm, with ceaseless turmoil seething,
As if this earth in fast thick pants were breathing,
A mighty fountain momently was forced;
Amid whose swift half-intermitted burst
Huge fragments vaulted like rebounding hail,
Or chaffy grain beneath the thresher's flail:
And 'mid these dancing rocks at once and ever
It flung up momently the sacred river.
Five miles meandering with a mazy motion
Through wood and dale the sacred river ran,
Then reached the caverns measureless to man,
And sank in tumult to a lifeless ocean:
And 'mid this tumult Kubla heard from far
Ancestral voices prophesying war!

The shadow of the dome of pleasure
    Floated midway on the waves;
Where was heard the mingled measure
    From the fountain and the caves.
It was a miracle of rare device,
A sunny pleasure-dome with caves of ice!

A damsel with a dulcimer
    In a vision once I saw:
It was an Abyssinian maid,
    And on her dulcimer she played,
Singing of Mount Abora.
    Could I revive within me,
    Her symphony and song,
To such a deep delight 'twould win me,
That with music loud and long,
I would build that dome in air,
That sunny dome! those caves of ice!
And all who heard should see them there,

And all should cry, Beware! Beware!
His flashing eyes, his floating hair!
Weave a circle round him thrice,
    And close your eyes with holy dread,
    For he on honey-dew hath fed,
And drunk the milk of Paradise.

WALTER SAVAGE LANDOR

IANTHE

PAST ruined Ilion Helen lives,
    Alcestis rises from the shades;
Verse calls them forth; 'tis verse that gives
    Immortal youth to mortal maids.

Soon shall Oblivion's deepening veil
    Hide all the peopled hills you see,
The gay, the proud, while lovers hail
    These many summers you and me.

ROSE AYLMER

AH, WHAT avails the sceptred race!
    Ah! what the form divine!
What every virtue, every grace!
    Rose Aylmer, all were thine.

Rose Aylmer, whom these wakeful eyes
    May weep, but never see,
A night of memories and of sighs
    I consecrate to thee.

I STROVE with none, for none was worth my strife.
Nature I loved and, next to Nature, Art:
I warmed both hands before the fire of Life;
It sinks, and I am ready to depart.

DIRCE

STAND close around, ye Stygian set,
    With Dirce in one boat conveyed!
Or Charon, seeing, may forget
    That he is old and she a shade.

LEIGH HUNT

THE NILE

IT FLOWS through old hushed Egypt and its sands,
    Like some grave mighty thought threading a dream,
    And times and things, as in that vision, seem
Keeping along it their eternal stands –
Caves, pillars, pyramids, the shepherd bands
    That roamed through the young world, the glory extreme
    Of high Sesostris, and that southern beam,
The laughing queen that caught the world's great hands.
Then comes a mightier silence, stern and strong,
As of a world left empty of its throng,
    And the void weighs on us; and then we wake,
And hear the fruitful stream lapsing along
    'Twixt villages, and think how we shall take
    Our own calm journey on for human sake.

RONDEAU

JENNY kissed me when we met,
    Jumping from the chair she sat in;
Time, you thief, who love to get
    Sweets into your list, put that in!
Say I'm weary, say I'm sad,
    Say that health and wealth have missed me,
Say I'm growing old, but add,
    Jenny kissed me.

LORD BYRON

SHE walks in beauty, like the night
 Of cloudless climes and starry skies;
And all that's best of dark and bright
 Meet in her aspect and her eyes:
Thus mellowed to that tender light
 Which heaven to gaudy day denies.

One shade the more, one ray the less,
 Had half impaired the nameless grace
Which waves in every raven tress,
 Or softly lightens o'er her face;
Where thoughts serenely sweet express
 How pure, how dear their dwelling-place.

And on that cheek, and o'er that brow,
 So soft, so calm, yet eloquent,
The smiles that win, the tints that glow,
 But tell of days in goodness spent,
A mind at peace with all below,
 A heart whose love is innocent!

From CHILDE HAROLD'S PILGRIMAGE

[THE EVE OF WATERLOO]

THERE was a sound of revelry by night,
And Belgium's Capital had gathered then
Her Beauty and her Chivalry, and bright
The lamps shone o'er fair women and brave men;
A thousand hearts beat happily; and when
Music arose with its voluptuous swell,
Soft eyes looked love to eyes which spake again,
And all went merry as a marriage bell;
But hush! hark! a deep sound strikes like a rising knell!

Did ye not hear it? – No; 'twas but the wind,
Or the car rattling o'er the stony street;
On with the dance! let joy be unconfined;
No sleep till morn, when Youth and Pleasure meet
To chase the glowing Hours with flying feet –
But hark! – that heavy sound breaks in once more,
As if the clouds its echo would repeat;
And nearer, clearer, deadlier than before!
Arm! Arm! it is – it is – the cannon's opening roar!

Within a windowed niche of that high hall
Sate Brunswick's fated chieftain; he did hear
That sound the first amidst the festival,
And caught its tone with Death's prophetic ear;
And when they smiled because he deemed it near,
His heart more truly knew that peal too well
Which stretched his father on a bloody bier,
And roused the vengeance blood alone could quell;
He rushed into the field, and, foremost fighting, fell.

Ah! then and there was hurrying to and fro,
And gathering tears, and tremblings of distress,
And cheeks all pale, which but an hour ago
Blushed at the praise of their own loveliness;
And there were sudden partings, such as press
The life from out young hearts, and choking sighs
Which ne'er might be repeated; who could guess
If evermore should meet those mutual eyes,
Since upon night so sweet such awful morn could rise!

And there was mounting in hot haste: the steed,
The mustering squadron, and the clattering car,
Went pouring forward with impetuous speed,
And swiftly forming in the ranks of war;
And the deep thunder peal on peal afar;
And near, the beat of the alarming drum
Roused up the soldiers ere the morning star;
While thronged the citizens with terror dumb,
Or whispering, with white lips – 'The foe! They come! they come!'

And wild and high the 'Cameron's Gathering' rose!
The war-note of Lochiel, which Albyn's hills
Have heard, and heard, too, have her Saxon foes:
How in the noon of night that pibroch thrills,
Savage and shrill! But with the breath which fills
Their mountain-pipe, so fill the mountaineers
With the fierce native daring which instils
The stirring memory of a thousand years,
And Evan's, and Donald's fame rings in each clansman's ears!

And Ardennes waves above them her green leaves,
Dewy with nature's tear-drops, as they pass,
Grieving, if aught inanimate e'er grieves,
Over the unreturning brave – alas!
Ere evening to be trodden like the grass
Which now beneath them, but above shall grow
In its next verdure, when this fiery mass
Of living valour, rolling on the foe
And burning with high hope, shall moulder cold and low.

Last noon beheld them full of lusty life,
Last eve in Beauty's circle proudly gay,
The midnight brought the signal-sound of strife,
The morn the marshalling in arms – the day
Battle's magnificently stern array!
The thunder-clouds close o'er it, which when rent
The earth is covered thick with other clay,
Which her own clay shall cover, heaped and pent,
Rider and horse – friend, foe – in one red burial blent!

    So, we'll go no more a-roving
      So late into the night,
    Though the heart be still as loving,
      And the moon be still as bright.

    For the sword outwears its sheath,
      And the soul wears out the breast,
    And the heart must pause to breathe,
      And love itself have rest.

Though the night was made for loving,
  And the day returns too soon,
Yet we'll go no more a-roving
  By the light of the moon.

From DON JUAN

THE isles of Greece, the isles of Greece!
  Where burning Sappho loved and sung,
Where grew the arts of war and peace,
  Where Delos rose, and Phoebus sprung,
Eternal summer gilds them yet,
But all, except their sun, is set.

The Scian and the Teian Muse,
  The hero's harp, the lover's lute
Have found the fame your shores refuse.
  Their place of birth alone is mute
To sounds which echo further west
Than your sires' 'Islands of the Blest'.

The mountains look on Marathon,
  And Marathon looks on the sea.
And musing there an hour alone,
  I dreamed that Greece might still be free,
For standing on the Persians' grave,
I could not deem myself a slave.

A king sate on the rocky brow
  Which looks o'er sea-born Salamis;
And ships by thousands lay below,
  And men in nations – all were his!
He counted them at break of day,
And when the sun set where were they?

And where are they? And where art thou,
  My country? On the voiceless shore
The heroic lay is tuneless now,

The heroic bosom beats no more!
And must thy lyre, so long divine,
Degenerate into hands like mine?

'Tis something in the dearth of fame,
    Though linked among a fettered race,
To feel at least a patriot's shame,
    Even as I sing, suffuse my face.
For what is left the poet here?
For Greeks a blush, for Greece a tear.

Must *we* but weep o'er days more blest?
    Must *we* but blush? Our fathers bled.
Earth! render back from out thy breast
    A remnant of our Spartan dead!
Of the three hundred grant but three,
To make a new Thermopylae!

What, silent still? And silent all?
    Ah no! The voices of the dead
Sound like a distant torrent's fall
    And answer, 'Let one living head,
But one arise – we come, we come!'
'Tis but the living who are dumb.

In vain – in vain – strike other chords.
    Fill high the cup with Samian wine!
Leave battles to the Turkish hordes,
    And shed the blood of Scio's vine!
Hark, rising to the ignoble call,
How answers each bold bacchanal!

You have the Pyrrhic dance as yet,
    Where is the Pyrrhic phalanx gone?
Of two such lessons, why forget
    The nobler and the manlier one?
You have the letters Cadmus gave;
Think ye he meant them for a slave?

Fill high the bowl with Samian wine!
  We will not think of themes like these.
It made Anacreon's song divine;
  He served, but served Polycrates,
A tyrant; but our masters then
Were still at least our countrymen.

The tyrant of the Chersonese
  Was freedom's best and bravest friend.
That tyrant was Miltiades.
  Oh, that the present hour would lend
Another despot of the kind!
Such chains as his were sure to bind.

Fill high the bowl with Samian wine!
  On Suli's rock and Parga's shore,
Exists the remnant of a line
  Such as the Doric mothers bore.
And there perhaps some seed is sown,
The Heracleidan blood might own.

Trust not for freedom to the Franks;
  They have a king who buys and sells.
In native words and native ranks
  The only hope of courage dwells,
But Turkish force and Latin fraud
Would break your shield, however broad.

Fill high the bowl with Samian wine!
  Our virgins dance beneath the shade.
I see their glorious black eyes shine,
  But gazing on each glowing maid,
My own the burning teardrop laves,
To think such breasts must suckle slaves.

Place me on Sunium's marbled steep,
  Where nothing, save the waves and I,
May hear our mutual murmurs sweep;
  There, swan-like, let me sing and die.
A land of slaves shall ne'er be mine –
Dash down yon cup of Samian wine!

PERCY BYSSHE SHELLEY

OZYMANDIAS

I MET a traveller from an antique land
Who said: 'Two vast and trunkless legs of stone
Stand in the desert. . . . Near them, on the sand,
Half sunk, a shattered visage lies, whose frown,
And wrinkled lip, and sneer of cold command,
Tell that its sculptor well those passions read
Which yet survive, stamped on these lifeless things,
The hand that mocked them, and the heart that fed:
And on the pedestal these words appear:
"My name is Ozymandias, king of kings:
Look on my works, ye Mighty, and despair!"
Nothing beside remains. Round the decay
Of that colossal wreck, boundless and bare
The lone and level sands stretch far away.'

ODE TO THE WEST WIND

I

O WILD West Wind, thou breath of Autumn's being,
Thou from whose unseen presence the leaves dead
Are driven like ghosts from an enchanter fleeing,

Yellow, and black, and pale, and hectic red,
Pestilence-stricken multitudes: O thou,
Who chariotest to their dark wintry bed

The wingèd seeds, where they lie cold and low,
Each like a corpse within its grave, until
Thine azure sister of the Spring shall blow

Her clarion o'er the dreaming earth, and fill
(Driving sweet buds like flocks to feed in air)
With living hues and odours plain and hill:

Wild Spirit, which art moving everywhere;
Destroyer and preserver; hear, O, hear!

II

Thou on whose stream, 'mid the deep sky's commotion,
Loose clouds like earth's decaying leaves are shed,
Shook from the tangled boughs of Heaven and Ocean,

Angels of rain and lightning: there are spread
On the blue surface of thine aëry surge,
Like the bright hair uplifted from the head

Of some fierce Maenad, even from the dim verge
Of the horizon to the zenith's height,
The locks of the approaching storm. Thou dirge

Of the dying year, to which this closing night
Will be the dome of a vast sepulchre,
Vaulted with all thy congregated might

Of vapours, from whose solid atmosphere
Black rain, and fire, and hail will burst: O, hear!

III

Thou who did'st waken from his summer dreams
The blue Mediterranean, where he lay,
Lulled by the coil of his crystalline streams,

Beside a pumice isle in Baiae's bay,
And saw in sleep old palaces and towers
Quivering within the wave's intenser day,

All overgrown with azure moss and flowers
So sweet, the sense faints picturing them! Thou
For whose path the Atlantic's level powers

Cleave themselves into chasms, while far below
The sea-blooms and the oozy woods which wear
The sapless foliage of the ocean, know

Thy voice, and suddenly grow grey with fear,
And tremble and despoil themselves: O, hear!

IV

If I were a dead leaf thou mightest bear;
If I were a swift cloud to fly with thee;
A wave to pant beneath thy power, and share

The impulse of thy strength, only less free
Than thou, O uncontrollable! If even
I were as in my boyhood, and could be

The comrade of thy wanderings over Heaven,
As then, when to outstrip thy skiey speed
Scarce seemed a vision; I would ne'er have striven

As thus with thee in prayer in my sore need.
Oh, lift me as a wave, a leaf, a cloud!
I fall upon the thorns of life! I bleed!

A heavy weight of hours has chained and bowed
One too like thee: tameless, and swift, and proud.

V

Make me thy lyre, even as the forest is:
What if my leaves are falling like its own!
The tumult of thy mighty harmonies

Will take from both a deep, autumnal tone,
Sweet though in sadness. Be thou, Spirit fierce,
My spirit! Be thou me, impetuous one!

Drive my dead thoughts over the universe
Like withered leaves to quicken a new birth!
And, by the incantation of this verse,

Scatter, as from an unextinguished hearth
Ashes and sparks, my words among mankind!
Be through my lips to unawakened earth

The trumpet of a prophecy! O Wind,
If Winter comes, can Spring be far behind?

TO A SKYLARK

Hail to thee, blithe Spirit!
  Bird thou never wert,
That from Heaven, or near it,
  Pourest thy full heart
In profuse strains of unpremeditated art.

Higher still and higher
  From the earth thou springest
Like a cloud of fire;
  The blue deep thou wingest,
And singing still dost soar, and soaring ever singest.

In the golden lightning
  Of the sunken sun,
O'er which clouds are bright'ning,
  Thou dost float and run;
Like an unbodied joy whose race is just begun.

The pale purple even
  Melts around thy flight;
Like a star of Heaven,
  In the broad daylight
Thou art unseen, but yet I hear thy shrill delight,

Keen as are the arrows
  Of that silver sphere,
Whose intense lamp narrows
  In the white dawn clear
Until we hardly see – we feel that it is there.

All the earth and air
  With thy voice is loud,
As, when night is bare,
  From one lonely cloud
The moon rains out her beams, and Heaven is
      overflowed.

What thou art we know not;
  What is most like thee?
From rainbow clouds there flow not
  Drops so bright to see
As from thy presence showers a rain of melody.

Like a Poet hidden
  In the light of thought,
Singing hymns unbidden,
  Till the world is wrought
To sympathy with hopes and fears it heeded not:

Like a high-born maiden
  In a palace-tower,
Soothing her love-laden
  Soul in secret hour
With music sweet as love, which overflows her bower:

Like a glow-worm golden
  In a dell of dew,
Scattering unbeholden
  Its aëreal hue
Among the flowers and grass, which screen it from the
    view!

Like a rose embowered
  In its own green leaves,
By warm winds deflowered,
  Till the scent it gives
Makes faint with too much sweet those heavy-wingèd
    thieves:

Sound of vernal showers
  On the twinkling grass,
Rain-awakened flowers,
  All that ever was
Joyous, and clear, and fresh, thy music doth surpass:

Teach us, Sprite or Bird,
  What sweet thoughts are thine:

I have never heard
   Praise of love or wine
That panted forth a flood of rapture so divine.

Chorus Hymeneal,
   Or triumphal chant,
Matched with thine would be all
   But an empty vaunt,
A thing wherein we feel there is some hidden want.

What objects are the fountains
   Of thy happy strain?
What fields, or waves, or mountains?
   What shapes of sky or plain?
What love of thine own kind? What ignorance of pain?

With thy clear keen joyance
   Languor cannot be:
Shadow of annoyance
   Never came near thee:
Thou lovest – but ne'er knew love's sad satiety.

Waking or asleep,
   Thou of death must deem
Things more true and deep
   Than we mortals dream,
Or how could thy notes flow in such a crystal stream?

We look before and after,
   And pine for what is not:
Our sincerest laughter
   With some pain is fraught;
Our sweetest songs are those that tell of saddest thought.

Yet if we could scorn
   Hate, and pride, and fear;
If we were things born
   Not to shed a tear,
I know not how thy joy we ever should come near.

Better than all measures
  Of delightful sound,
Better than all treasures
  That in books are found,
Thy skill to poet were, thou scorner of the ground!

Teach me half the gladness
  That thy brain must know,
Such harmonious madness
  From my lips would flow
The world should listen then – as I am listening now.

MUSIC, when soft voices die,
Vibrates in the memory;
Odours, when sweet violets sicken,
Live within the sense they quicken.

Rose leaves, when the rose is dead,
Are heaped for the belovèd's bed;
And so thy thoughts, when thou art gone,
Love itself shall slumber on.

WHEN the lamp is shattered
The light in the dust lies dead;
  When the cloud is scattered
The rainbow's glory is shed;
  When the lute is broken,
Sweet tones are remembered not;
  When the lips have spoken,
Loved accents are soon forgot.

  As music and splendour
Survive not the lamp and the lute,
  The heart's echoes render
No song when the spirit is mute –
  No song but sad dirges,
Like the wind through a ruined cell,
  Or the mournful surges
That ring the dead seaman's knell.

When hearts have once mingled
Love first leaves the well-built nest;
   The weak one is singled
To endure what it once possessed.
   O Love! who bewailest
The frailty of all things here,
   Why choose you the frailest
For your cradle, your home, and your bier?

   Its passions will rock thee
As the storms rock the ravens on high;
   Bright reason will mock thee,
Like the sun from a wintry sky.
   From thy nest every rafter
Will rot, and thine eagle home
   Leave thee naked to laughter,
When leaves fall and cold winds come.

From ADONAÏS

PEACE, peace! He is not dead, he doth not sleep –
He hath awakened from the dream of life –
'Tis we, who lost in stormy visions, keep
With phantoms an unprofitable strife,
And in mad trance, strike, with our spirit's knife
Invulnerable nothings. – *We* decay
Like corpses in a charnel; fear and grief
Convulse us and consume us day by day,
And cold hopes swarm like worms within our living clay.

He has outsoared the shadow of our night;
Envy and calumny and hate and pain,
And that unrest which men miscall delight,
Can touch him not and torture not again;
From the contagion of the world's slow stain
He is secure, and now can never mourn
A heart grown cold, a head grown grey in vain;
Nor, when the spirit's self has ceased to burn,
With sparkless ashes load an unlamented urn.

He lives, he wakes – 'tis Death is dead, not he;
Mourn not for Adonaïs. – Thou young Dawn,
Turn all thy dew to splendour, for from thee
The spirit thou lamentest is not gone;
Ye caverns and ye forests, cease to moan!
Cease, ye faint flowers and fountains, and thou Air,
Which like a mourning veil thy scarf had'st thrown
O'er the abandoned Earth, now leave it bare
Even to the joyous stars which smile on its despair!

He is made one with Nature: there is heard
His voice in all her music, from the moan
Of thunder, to the song of night's sweet bird;
He is a presence to be felt and known
In darkness and in light, from herb and stone,
Spreading itself where'er that Power may move
Which has withdrawn his being to its own;
Which wields the world with never-wearied love,
Sustains it from beneath, and kindles it above.

He is a portion of the loveliness
Which once he made more lovely: he doth bear
His part, while the one Spirit's plastic stress
Sweeps through the dull dense world, compelling there,
All new successions to the forms they wear;
Torturing th' unwilling dross that checks its flight
To its own likeness, as each mass may bear;
And bursting in its beauty and its might
From trees and beasts and men into the Heaven's light.

The splendours of the firmament of time
May be eclipsed, but are extinguished not;
Like stars to their appointed height they climb,
And death is a low mist which cannot blot
The brightness it may veil. When lofty thought
Lifts a young heart above its mortal lair,
And love and life contend in it, for what
Shall be its earthly doom, the dead live there
And move like winds of light on dark and stormy air.

The inheritors of unfulfilled renown
Rose from their thrones, built beyond mortal thought,
Far in the Unapparent. Chatterton
Rose pale – his solemn agony had not
Yet faded from him; Sidney, as he fought
And as he fell and as he lived and loved
Sublimely mild, a Spirit without spot,
Arose; and Lucan, by his death approved:
Oblivion as they rose shrank like a thing reproved.

And many more, whose names on Earth are dark,
But whose transmitted effluence cannot die
So long as fire outlives the parent spark,
Rose, robed in dazzling immortality.
'Thou art become as one of us,' they cry,
'It was for thee yon kingless sphere has long
Swung blind in unascended majesty,
Silent alone amid an Heaven of Song.
Assume thy wingèd throne, thou Vesper of our throng!'

Who mourns for Adonaïs? Oh, come forth,
Fond wretch! and know thyself and him aright.
Clasp with thy panting soul the pendulous Earth;
As from a centre, dart thy spirit's light
Beyond all worlds, until its spacious might
Satiate the void circumference: then shrink
Even to a point within our day and night;
And keep thy heart light lest it make thee sink
When hope has kindled hope, and lured thee to the brink.

Or go to Rome, which is the sepulchre,
Oh, not of him, but of our joy: 'tis nought
That ages, empires, and religions there
Lie buried in the ravage they have wrought;
For such as he can lend – they borrow not
Glory from those who made the world their prey;
And he is gathered to the kings of thought
Who waged contention with their time's decay,
And of the past are all that cannot pass away.

Go thou to Rome – at once the Paradise,
The grave, the city, and the wilderness;
And where its wrecks like shattered mountains rise,
And flowering weeds, and fragrant copses dress
The bones of Desolation's nakedness
Pass, till the spirit of the spot shall lead
Thy footsteps to a slope of green access
Where, like an infant's smile, over the dead
A light of laughing flowers along the grass is spread;

And grey walls moulder round, on which dull Time
Feeds, like slow fire upon a hoary brand;
And one keen pyramid with wedge sublime,
Pavilioning the dust of him who planned
This refuge for his memory, doth stand
Like flame transformed to marble; and beneath,
A field is spread, on which a newer band
Have pitched in Heaven's smile their camp of death,
Welcoming him we lose with scarce extinguished breath.

Here pause: these graves are all too young as yet
To have outgrown the sorrow which consigned
Its charge to each; and if the seal is set,
Here, on one fountain of a mourning mind,
Break it not thou! Too surely shalt thou find
Thine own well full, if thou returnest home,
Of tears and gall. From the world's bitter wind
Seek shelter in the shadow of the tomb.
What Adonaïs is, why fear we to become?

The One remains, the many change and pass;
Heaven's light forever shines, Earth's shadows fly;
Life, like a dome of many-coloured glass,
Stains the white radiance of Eternity,
Until Death tramples it to fragments. – Die,
If thou would'st be with that which thou dost seek!
Follow where all is fled! – Rome's azure sky,
Flowers, ruins, statues, music, words, are weak
The glory they transfuse with fitting truth to speak.

Why linger, why turn back, why shrink, my Heart?
Thy hopes are gone before: from all things here
They have departed; thou should'st now depart!
A light is passed from the revolving year,
And man, and woman; and what still is dear
Attracts to crush, repels to make thee wither.
The soft sky smiles – the low wind whispers near:
'Tis Adonaïs calls! oh, hasten thither,
No more let Life divide what Death can join together.

That Light whose smile kindles the Universe,
That Beauty in which all things work and move,
That Benediction which the eclipsing Curse
Of birth can quench not, that sustaining Love
Which through the web of being blindly wove
By man and beast and earth and air and sea,
Burns bright or dim, as each are mirrors of
The fire for which all thirst; now beams on me,
Consuming the last clouds of cold mortality.

The breath whose might I have invoked in song
Descends on me; my spirit's bark is driven,
Far from the shore, far from the trembling throng
Whose sails were never to the tempest given;
The massy earth and spherèd skies are riven!
I am borne darkly, fearfully, afar;
Whilst, burning through the inmost veil of Heaven,
The soul of Adonaïs, like a star,
Beacons from the abode where the Eternal are.

JOHN CLARE

SWORDY WELL

I'VE loved thee, Swordy Well, and love thee still.
Long was I with thee, tending sheep and cow,
In boyhood ramping up each steepy hill
To play at 'roly-poly' down; and now,
A man, I trifle on thee, cares to kill,
Haunting thy mossy steeps to botanise
And hunt the orchis tribes, where Nature's skill
Doth, like my thoughts, run into phantasies,
Spider and bee all mimicking at will,
Displaying powers that fool the proudly wise,
Showing the wonders of great Nature's plan
In trifles insignificant and small,
Puzzling the power of that great trifle, Man,
Who finds no reason to be proud at all.

I AM – yet what I am none cares or knows,
    My friends forsake me like a memory lost;
I am the self-communer of my woes,
    They rise and vanish in oblivions host,
Like shadows in love – frenzied stifled throes;
And yet I am, and live like vapours tossed

Into the nothingness of scorn and noise,
    Into the living sea of waking dreams,
Where there is neither sense of life or joys,
    But the vast shipwreck of my life's esteems;
And e'en the dearest – that I love the best –
Are strange – nay, rather stranger than the rest.

I long for scenes where man has never trod,
    A place where woman never smiled or wept;
There to abide with my Creator, God,
    And sleep as I in childhood sweetly slept:
Untroubling and untroubled where I lie,
The grass below – above the vaulted sky.

JOHN KEATS

ON FIRST LOOKING INTO CHAPMAN'S HOMER

MUCH have I travelled in the realms of gold,
   And many goodly states and kingdoms seen;
   Round many western islands have I been
Which bards in fealty to Apollo hold.
Oft of one wide expanse had I been told
   That deep-browed Homer ruled as his demesne;
   Yet did I never breathe its pure serene
Till I heard Chapman speak out loud and bold.
Then felt I like some watcher of the skies
   When a new planet swims into his ken;
Or like stout Cortez when with eagle eyes
   He stared at the Pacific – and all his men
Looked at each other with a wild surmise –
   Silent, upon a peak in Darien.

LA BELLE DAME SANS MERCI

OH, WHAT can ail thee, knight-at-arms,
   Alone and palely loitering?
The sedge has withered from the lake,
   And no birds sing!

Oh, what can ail thee, knight-at-arms,
   So haggard and so woe-begone?
The squirrel's granary is full,
   And the harvest's done.

I see a lily on thy brow,
   With anguish moist and fever-dew,
And on thy cheek a fading rose
   Fast withereth too.

'I met a lady in the meads
   Full beautiful, a faery's child,
Her hair was long, her foot was light,
   And her eyes were wild.

'I made a garland for her head,
　　And bracelets too, and fragrant zone;
She looked at me as she did love,
　　And made sweet moan.

'I set her on my pacing steed,
　　And nothing else saw all day long;
For sideways would she lean, and sing
　　A faery's song.

'She found me roots of relish sweet,
　　And honey wild, and manna dew;
And sure in language strange she said,
　　"I love thee true!"

'She took me to her elfin grot,
　　And there she wept, and sighed full sore,
And there I shut her wild, wild eyes
　　With kisses four.

'And there she lullèd me asleep,
　　And there I dreamed – ah! woe betide! –
The latest dream I ever dreamed
　　On the cold hill's side.

'I saw pale kings, and princes too,
　　Pale warriors, death-pale were they all;
Who cried – "La belle Dame sans merci
　　Hath thee in thrall!"

'I saw their starved lips in the gloam
　　With horrid warning gapèd wide,
And I awoke, and found me here
　　On the cold hill's side.

'And this is why I sojourn here,
　　Alone and palely loitering,
Though the sedge is withered from the lake,
　　And no birds sing.'

ODE TO A NIGHTINGALE

MY HEART aches, and a drowsy numbness pains
　My sense, as though of hemlock I had drunk,
Or emptied some dull opiate to the drains
　One minute past, and Lethe-wards had sunk.
'Tis not through envy of thy happy lot,
　But being too happy in thy happiness –
　　That thou, light-wingèd Dryad of the trees,
　　　In some melodious plot
　Of beechen green, and shadows numberless,
　　Singest of summer in full-throated ease.

Oh, for a draught of vintage! that hath been
　Cooled a long age in the deep-delvèd earth,
Tasting of Flora and the country green,
　Dance, and Provençal song, and sunburnt mirth!
Oh, for a beaker full of the warm South!
　Full of the true, the blushful Hippocrene,
　　With beaded bubbles winking at the brim,
　　　And purple-stainèd mouth;
　That I might drink, and leave the world unseen,
　　And with thee fade away into the forest dim –

Fade far away, dissolve, and quite forget
　What thou among the leaves hast never known,
The weariness, the fever, and the fret
　Here, where men sit and hear each other groan;
Where palsy shakes a few, sad, last grey hairs,
　Where youth grows pale, and spectre-thin, and dies;
　　Where but to think is to be full of sorrow
　　　And leaden-eyed despairs;
　Where Beauty cannot keep her lustrous eyes,
　　Or new Love pine at them beyond tomorrow.

Away! away! for I will fly to thee,
　Not charioted by Bacchus and his pards,
But on the viewless wings of Poesy,
　Though the dull brain perplexes and retards.

Already with thee! Tender is the night,
  And haply the Queen-Moon is on her throne,
    Clustered around by all her starry fays;
      But here there is no light,
  Save what from heaven is with the breezes blown
    Through verdurous glooms and winding mossy ways.

I cannot see what flowers are at my feet,
  Nor what soft incense hangs upon the boughs,
But, in embalmèd darkness, guess each sweet
  Wherewith the seasonable month endows
The grass, the thicket, and the fruit-tree wild –
  White hawthorn, and the pastoral eglantine;
    Fast-fading violets covered up in leaves;
      And mid-May's eldest child,
  The coming musk-rose, full of dewy wine,
    The murmurous haunt of flies on summer eves.

Darkling I listen; and for many a time
  I have been half in love with easeful Death,
Called him soft names in many a musèd rhyme,
  To take into the air my quiet breath;
Now more than ever seems it rich to die,
  To cease upon the midnight with no pain,
    While thou art pouring forth thy soul abroad
      In such an ecstasy!.
  Still would'st thou sing, and I have ears in vain –
    To thy high requiem become a sod.

Thou wast not born for death, immortal Bird!
  No hungry generations tread thee down;
The voice I hear this passing night was heard
  In ancient days by emperor and clown:
Perhaps the self-same song that found a path
  Through the sad heart of Ruth, when, sick for home,
    She stood in tears amid the alien corn;
      The same that oft-times hath
  Charmed magic casements, opening on the foam
    Of perilous seas in faery lands forlorn.

Forlorn! The very word is like a bell
  To toll me back from thee to my sole self!
Adieu! The fancy cannot cheat so well
  As she is famed to do, deceiving elf.
Adieu! Adieu! Thy plaintive anthem fades
  Past the near meadows, over the still stream,
    Up the hill-side; and now 'tis buried deep
      In the next valley-glades:
  Was it a vision, or a waking dream?
    Fled is that music. . . . Do I wake or sleep?

ODE ON A GRECIAN URN

THOU still unravished bride of quietness,
  Thou foster-child of Silence and slow Time,
Sylvan historian, who can'st thus express
  A flowery tale more sweetly than our rhyme!
What leaf-fringed legend haunts about thy shape
  Of deities or mortals, or of both,
    In Tempe or the dales of Arcady?
  What men or gods are these? What maidens loth?
What mad pursuit? What struggle to escape?
    What pipes and timbrels? What wild ecstasy?

Heard melodies are sweet, but those unheard
  Are sweeter; therefore, ye soft pipes, play on;
Not to the sensual ear, but, more endeared,
  Pipe to the spirit ditties of no tone.
Fair youth beneath the trees, thou can'st not leave
  Thy song, nor ever can those trees be bare;
    Bold Lover, never, never can'st thou kiss,
Though winning near the goal – yet do not grieve:
  She cannot fade, though thou hast not thy bliss,
    For ever wilt thou love, and she be fair!

Ah, happy, happy boughs! that cannot shed
  Your leaves, nor ever bid the spring adieu;
And, happy melodist, unwearièd,
  For ever piping songs for ever new!

More happy love! More happy, happy love!
   For ever warm and still to be enjoyed,
      For ever panting, and for ever young –
All breathing human passion far above,
   That leaves a heart high-sorrowful and cloyed,
      A burning forehead, and a parching tongue.

Who are these coming to the sacrifice?
   To what green altar, O mysterious priest,
Lead'st thou that heifer lowing at the skies,
   And all her silken flanks with garlands dressed?
What little town by river or sea-shore,
   Or mountain-built with peaceful citadel,
      Is emptied of this folk, this pious morn?
And, little town, thy streets for evermore
   Will silent be; and not a soul to tell
      Why thou art desolate can e'er return.

O Attic shape! fair attitude! with brede
   Of marble men and maidens overwrought,
With forest branches and the trodden weed –
   Thou, silent form! dost tease us out of thought
As doth eternity. Cold pastoral!
   When old age shall this generation waste,
      Thou shalt remain, in midst of other woe
Than ours, a friend to man, to whom thou say'st,
   'Beauty is truth, truth beauty – that is all
      Ye know on earth, and all ye need to know.'

ODE ON MELANCHOLY

No, NO, go not to Lethe, neither twist
   Wolf's-bane, tight-rooted, for its poisonous wine;
Nor suffer thy pale forehead to be kissed
   By nightshade, ruby grape of Proserpine;
Make not your rosary of yew-berries,
   Nor let the beetle, nor the death-moth be
     Your mournful Psyche, nor the downy owl
A partner in your sorrow's mysteries;
   For shade to shade will come too drowsily,
     And drown the wakeful anguish of the soul.

But when the melancholy fit shall fall
   Sudden from heaven like a weeping cloud,
That fosters the droop-headed flowers all,
   And hides the green hill in an April shroud;
Then glut thy sorrow on a morning rose,
   Or on the rainbow of the salt sand-wave,
     Or on the wealth of globèd peonies;
Or if thy mistress some rich anger shows,
   Imprison her soft hand, and let her rave,
     And feed deep, deep upon her peerless eyes.

She dwells with Beauty – Beauty that must die;
   And Joy, whose hand is ever at his lips
Bidding adieu; and aching Pleasure nigh,
   Turning to poison while the bee-mouth sips.
Aye, in the very temple of Delight
   Veiled Melancholy has her sovran shrine,
     Though seen of none save him whose strenuous tongue
Can burst Joy's grape against his palate fine;
   His soul shall taste the sadness of her might,
     And be among her cloudy trophies hung.

TO AUTUMN

SEASON of mists and mellow fruitfulness,
    Close bosom-friend of the maturing sun,
Conspiring with him how to load and bless
    With fruit the vines that round the thatch-eaves run;
To bend with apples the mossed cottage-trees,
    And fill all fruit with ripeness to the core;
        To swell the gourd, and plump the hazel shells
With a sweet kernel; to set budding more,
    And still more, later flowers for the bees,
    Until they think warm days will never cease,
        For summer has o'er-brimmed their clammy cells.

Who hath not seen thee oft amid thy store?
    Sometimes whoever seeks abroad may find
Thee sitting careless on a granary floor,
    Thy hair soft-lifted by the winnowing wind;
Or on a half-reaped furrow sound asleep,
    Drowsed with the fume of poppies, while thy hook
        Spares the next swath and all its twinèd flowers;
And sometimes like a gleaner thou dost keep
    Steady thy laden head across a brook;
Or by a cider-press, with patient look,
        Thou watchest the last oozings hours by hours.

Where are the songs of spring? Aye, where are they?
    Think not of them, thou hast thy music too –
While barred clouds bloom the soft-dying day,
    And touch the stubble-plains with rosy hue;
Then in a wailful choir the small gnats mourn
    Among the river sallows, borne aloft
        Or sinking as the light wind lives or dies;
And full-grown lambs loud bleat from hilly bourn;
    Hedge-crickets sing; and now with treble soft
The redbreast whistles from a garden-croft;
        And gathering swallows twitter in the skies.

BRIGHT STAR! would I were steadfast as thou art –
   Not in lone splendour hung aloft the night
And watching, with eternal lids apart,
   Like Nature's patient, sleepless eremite,
The moving waters at their priestlike task
   Of pure ablution round earth's human shores,
Or gazing on the new soft-fallen mask
   Of snow upon the mountains and the moors;
No – yet still steadfast, still unchangeable,
   Pillowed upon my fair love's ripening breast,
To feel for ever its soft fall and swell,
   Awake for ever in a sweet unrest,
Still, still to hear her tender-taken breath,
And so live ever – or else swoon to death.

WILLIAM BARNES

WOAK HILL

WHEN sycamore leaves wer a-spreaden,
    Green-ruddy, in hedges,
Bezide the red doust o' the ridges,
    A-dried at Woak Hill;

I packed up my goods all a-sheenen
    Wi' long years o' handlen
On dousty red wheels ov a waggon,
    To ride at Woak Hill.

The brown thatchen ruf o' the dwellen,
    I then wer a-leäven,
Had shelter'd the sleek head o' Meäry,
    My bride at Woak Hill.

But now vor zome years, her light voot-vall
    'S a-lost vrom the vlooren.
Too soon vor my jay an' my childern,
    She died at Woak Hill.

But still I do think that, in soul,
    She do hover about us;
To ho vor her motherless childern,
    Her pride at Woak Hill.

Zoo – lest she should tell me hereafter
    I stole off 'ithout her,
An' left her, uncall'd at house-ridden,
    To bide at Woak Hill –

I call'd her so fondly, wi' lippens
    All soundless to others,
An' took her wi' aïr-reachen hand,
    To my zide at Woak Hill.

On the road I did look round, a-talken
    To light at my shoulder,
An' then led her in at the door-way,
    Miles wide vrom Woak Hill.

An' that's why vo'k thought, vor a season,
    My mind wer a-wandren
Wi' sorrow, when I wer so sorely
    A-tried at Woak Hill.

But no; that my Meäry mid never
    Behold herzelf slighted,
I wanted to think that I guided
    My guide vrom Woak Hill.

THE GEÄTE A-VALLEN TO

In the zunsheen of our zummers
    Wi' the häytime now a-come,
How busy wer we out a-vield
    Wi' vew a-left at hwome,
When waggons rumbled out ov yard
    Red wheeled, wi' body blue,

And back behind 'em loudly slamm'd
   The geäte a-vallen to.

Drough day sheen ov how many years
   The geäte ha' now a-swung,
Behind the veet o' vull-grown men
   And vootsteps of the young.
Drough years o' days it swung to us
   Behind each little shoe,
As we tripped lightly on avore
   The geäte a-vallen to.

In evenen time o' starry night
   How mother zot at hwome
And kept her blazing vire bright
   Till father should ha' come,
And how she quicken'd up and smiled
   And stirred her vire anew,
To hear the trampen ho'ses' steps
   And geäte a-vallen to.

There's moon-sheen now in nights o' Fall
   When leaves be brown vrom green,
When to the slammen o' the geäte
   Our Jenny's ears be keen,
When the wold dog do wag his taïl,
   And Jeän could tell to who,
As he do come in drough the geäte,
   The geäte a-vallen to.

And oft do come a saddened hour
   When there must goo away
One well-beloved to our heart's core.
   Vor long, perhaps for aye:
And oh! it is a touchen thing
   The loven heart must rue
To hear behind his last farewell
   The geäte a-vallen to.

ELIZABETH BARRETT BROWNING

From SONNETS FROM THE PORTUGUESE

I THOUGHT once how Theocritus had sung
   Of the sweet years, the dear and wished-for years,
   Who each one in a gracious hand appears
To bear a gift for mortals, old or young:
And, as I mused it in his antique tongue,
   I saw, in gradual vision through my tears,
   The sweet, sad years, the melancholy years,
Those of my own life, who by turns had flung
A shadow across me. Straightway I was 'ware,
   So weeping, how a mystic Shape did move
Behind me, and drew me backward by the hair;
   And a voice said in mastery, while I strove,
'Guess now who holds thee?' – 'Death,' I said. But there
   The silver answer rang – 'Not Death, but Love.'

How DO I love thee? Let me count the ways.
   I love thee to the depth and breadth and height
   My soul can reach, when feeling out of sight
For the ends of Being and ideal Grace.
I love thee to the level of every day's
   Most quiet need, by sun and candlelight.
I love thee freely, as men strive for Right;
I love thee purely, as they turn from Praise.
I love thee with the passion put to use
   In my old griefs, and with my childhood's faith.
I love thee with a love I seemed to lose
   With my lost saints – I love thee with the breath,
Smiles, tears, of all my life! – and, if God choose,
   I shall but love thee better after death.

ALFRED, LORD TENNYSON

From THE LOTOS-EATERS

CHORIC SONG

THERE is sweet music here that softer falls
Than petals from blown roses on the grass,
Or night-dews on still waters between walls
Of shadowy granite, in a gleaming pass;
Music that gentlier on the spirit lies,
Than tired eyelids upon tired eyes;
Music that brings sweet sleep down from the blissful skies.
Here are cool mosses deep,
And through the moss the ivies creep,
And in the stream the long-leaved flowers weep,
And from the craggy ledge the poppy hangs in sleep.

Why are we weighed upon with heaviness,
And utterly consumed with sharp distress,
While all things else have rest from weariness?
All things have rest: why should we toil alone,
We only toil, who are the first of things,
And make perpetual moan,
Still from one sorrow to another thrown:
Nor ever fold our wings,
And cease from wanderings,
Nor steep our brows in slumber's holy balm;
Nor harken what the inner spirit sings,
'There is no joy but calm!'
Why should we only toil, the roof and crown of things?

Lo! in the middle of the wood,
The folded leaf is wooed from out the bud
With winds upon the branch, and there
Grows green and broad, and takes no care,
Sun-steeped at noon, and in the moon
Nightly dew-fed; and turning yellow
Falls, and floats adown the air.

Lo! sweetened with the summer light,
The full-juiced apple, waxing over-mellow,
Drops in a silent autumnal night.
All its allotted length of days,
The flower ripens in its place,
Ripens and fades, and falls, and hath no toil,
Fast-rooted in the fruitful soil.

Hateful is the dark-blue sky,
Vaulted o'er the dark-blue sea,
Death is the end of life; ah, why
Should life all labour be?
Let us alone. Time driveth onward fast,
And in a little while our lips are dumb.
Let us alone. What is it that will last?
All things are taken from us, and become
Portions and parcels of the dreadful Past.
Let us alone. What pleasure can we have
To war with evil? Is there any peace
In ever climbing up the climbing wave?
All things have rest, and ripen toward the grave
In silence; ripen, fall and cease:
Give us long rest or death, dark death, or dreamful ease.

How sweet it were, hearing the downward stream,
With half-shut eyes ever to seem
Falling asleep in a half-dream!
To dream and dream, like yonder amber light,
Which will not leave the myrrh-bush on the height;
To hear each other's whispered speech;
Eating the Lotos day by day,
To watch the crisping ripples on the beach,
And tender curving lines of creamy spray;
To lend our hearts and spirits wholly
To the influence of mild-minded melancholy;
To muse and brood and live again in memory,
With those old faces of our infancy
Heaped over with a mound of grass,
Two handfuls of white dust, shut in an urn of brass!

Dear is the memory of our wedded lives,
And dear the last embraces of our wives
And their warm tears: but all hath suffered change:
For surely now our household hearths are cold:
Our sons inherit us: our looks are strange:
And we should come like ghosts to trouble joy.
Or else the island princes over-bold
Have eat our substance, and the minstrel sings
Before them of the ten years' war in Troy,
And our great deeds, as half-forgotten things.
Is there confusion in the little isle?
Let what is broken so remain.
The Gods are hard to reconcile:
'Tis hard to settle order once again.
There *is* confusion worse than death,
Trouble on trouble, pain on pain,
Long labour unto agèd breath,
Sore tasks to hearts worn out by many wars
And eyes grown dim with gazing on the pilot-stars.

But, propped on beds of amaranth and moly,
How sweet (while warm airs lull us, blowing lowly)
With half-dropped eyelid still,
Beneath a heaven dark and holy,
To watch the long bright river drawing slowly
His waters from the purple hill –
To hear the dewy echoes calling
From cave to cave through the thick-twined vine –
To watch the emerald-coloured water falling
Through many a woven acanthus-wreath divine!
Only to hear and see the far-off sparkling brine,
Only to hear were sweet, stretched out beneath the pine.

The Lotos blooms below the barren peak:
The Lotos blows by every winding creek:
All day the wind breathes low with mellower tone:
Through every hollow cave and alley lone
Round and round the spicy downs the yellow Lotos-dust is
    blown.

We have had enough of action, and of motion we,
Rolled to starboard, rolled to larboard, when the surge was
    seething free,
Where the wallowing monster spouted his foam-fountains in
    the sea.
Let us swear an oath, and keep it with an equal mind,
In the hollow Lotos-land to live and lie reclined
On the hills like Gods together, careless of mankind.
For they lie beside their nectar, and the bolts are hurled
Far below them in the valleys, and the clouds are lightly
    curled
Round their golden houses, girdled with the gleaming world:
Where they smile in secret, looking over wasted lands,
Blight and famine, plague and earthquake, roaring deeps and
    fiery sands,
Clanging fights, and flaming towns, and sinking ships, and
    praying hands.
But they smile, they find a music centred in a doleful song
Steaming up, a lamentation and an ancient tale of wrong,
Like a tale of little meaning though the words are strong;
Chanted from an ill-used race of men that cleave the soil,
Sow the seed, and reap the harvest with enduring toil,
Storing yearly little dues of wheat, and wine and oil;
Till they perish and they suffer – some, 'tis whispered – down
    in hell
Suffer endless anguish, other in Elysian valleys dwell,
Resting weary limbs at last on beds of asphodel.
Surely, surely, slumber is more sweet than toil, the shore
Than labour in the deep mid-ocean, wind and wave and oar;
Oh, rest ye, brother mariners, we will not wander more.

ULYSSES

IT LITTLE profits that an idle king,
By this still hearth, among these barren crags,
Matched with an agèd wife, I mete and dole
Unequal laws unto a savage race,
That hoard, and sleep, and feed, and know not me.

I cannot rest from travel: I will drink
Life to the lees: all times I have enjoyed
Greatly, have suffered greatly, both with those
That loved me, and alone; on shore, and when
Through scudding drifts the rainy Hyades
Vexed the dim sea: I am become a name;
For always roaming with a hungry heart
Much have I seen and known; cities of men
And manners, climates, councils, governments,
Myself not least, but honoured of them all;
And drunk delight of battle with my peers,
Far on the ringing plains of windy Troy.
I am a part of all that I have met;
Yet all experience is an arch wherethrough
Gleams that untravelled world, whose margin fades
For ever and for ever when I move.
How dull it is to pause, to make an end,
To rust unburnished, not to shine in use!
As though to breathe were life. Life piled on life
Were all too little, and of one to me
Little remains: but every hour is saved
From that eternal silence, something more,
A bringer of new things: and vile it were
For some three suns to store and hoard myself,
And this grey spirit yearning in desire
To follow knowledge like a sinking star,
Beyond the utmost bound of human thought.
This is my son, mine own Telemachus,
To whom I leave the sceptre and the isle –
Well-loved of me, discerning to fulfil
This labour, by slow prudence to make mild
A rugged people, and through soft degrees
Subdue them to the useful and the good.
Most blameless is he, centred in the sphere
Of common duties, decent not to fail
In offices of tenderness, and pay
Meet adoration to my household gods,
When I am gone. He works his work, I mine.
There lies the port; the vessel puffs her sail:

There gloom the dark broad seas. My mariners,
Souls that have toiled, and wrought, and thought with me –
That ever with a frolic welcome took
The thunder and the sunshine, and opposed
Free hearts, free foreheads – and you and I are old;
Old age hath yet his honour and his toil;
Death closes all: but something ere the end,
Some work of noble note, may yet be done,
Not unbecoming men that strove with Gods.
The lights begin to twinkle from the rocks:
The long day wanes: the slow moon climbs: the deep
Moans round with many voices. Come, my friends,
'Tis not too late to seek a newer world.
Push off, and sitting well in order smite
The sounding furrows; for my purpose holds
To sail beyond the sunset, and the baths
Of all the western stars, until I die.
It may be that the gulfs will wash us down:
It may be we shall touch the Happy Isles,
And see the great Achilles, whom we knew.
Though much is taken, much abides; and though
We are not now that strength which in old days
Moved earth and heaven; that which we are, we are;
One equal temper of heroic hearts,
Made weak by time and fate, but strong in will
To strive, to seek, to find, and not to yield.

    BREAK, break, break,
       On thy cold grey stones, O Sea!
    And I would that my tongue could utter
       The thoughts that arise in me.

    Oh, well for the fisherman's boy,
       That he shouts with his sister at play!
    Oh, well for the sailor lad,
       That he sings in his boat on the bay!

And the stately ships go on
　　To their haven under the hill;
But, oh, for the touch of a vanished hand,
　　And the sound of a voice that is still!

Break, break, break,
　　At the foot of thy crags, O Sea!
But the tender grace of a day that is dead
　　Will never come back to me.

From THE PRINCESS

THE SPLENDOUR falls on castle walls
　　And snowy summits old in story:
The long light shakes across the lakes,
　　And the wild cataract leaps in glory.
Blow, bugle, blow, set the wild echoes flying,
Blow, bugle; answer, echoes, dying, dying, dying.

Oh, hark, oh, hear! how thin and clear,
　　And thinner, clearer, farther going!
Oh, sweet and far from cliff and scar
　　The horns of Elfland faintly blowing!
Blow, let us hear the purple glens replying:
Blow, bugle; answer, echoes, dying, dying, dying.

O love, they die in yon rich sky,
　　They faint on hill or field or river:
Our echoes roll from soul to soul,
　　And grow for ever and for ever.
Blow, bugle, blow, set the wild echoes flying,
And answer, echoes, answer, dying, dying, dying.

TEARS, idle tears, I know not what they mean,
Tears from the depth of some divine despair
Rise in the heart, and gather to the eyes,
In looking on the happy autumn fields,
And thinking on the days that are no more.

Fresh as the first beam glittering on a sail,
That brings our friends up from the underworld,
Sad as the last which reddens over one
That sinks with all we love below the verge;
So sad, so fresh, the days that are no more.

Ah, sad and strange as in dark summer dawns
The earliest pipe of half-awakened birds
To dying ears, when unto dying eyes
The casement slowly grows a glimmering square;
So sad, so strange, the days that are no more.

Dear as remembered kisses after death,
And sweet as those by hopeless fancy feigned
On lips that are for others; deep as love,
Deep as first love, and wild with all regret;
O Death in Life, the days that are no more.

From IN MEMORIAM

OLD YEW, which graspest at the stones
    That name the under-lying dead,
    Thy fibres net the dreamless head,
Thy roots are wrapped about the bones.

The seasons bring the flower again,
    And bring the firstling of the flock;
    And in the dusk of thee, the clock
Beats out the little lives of men.

Oh, not for thee the glow, the bloom,
    Who changest not in any gale,
    Nor branding summer suns avail
To touch thy thousand years of gloom:

And gazing on thee, sullen tree,
    Sick for thy stubborn hardihood,
    I seem to fail from out my blood
And grow incorporate into thee.

DARK HOUSE, by which once more I stand
   Here in the long unlovely street,
   Doors, where my heart was used to beat
So quickly, waiting for a hand,

A hand that can be clasped no more –
   Behold me, for I cannot sleep,
   And like a guilty thing I creep
At earliest morning to the door.

He is not here; but far away
   The noise of life begins again,
   And ghastly through the drizzling rain
On the bald street breaks the blank day.

CALM is the morn without a sound,
   Calm as to suit a calmer grief,
   And only through the faded leaf
The chestnut pattering to the ground:

Calm and deep peace on this high wold,
   And on these dews that drench the furze,
   And all the silvery gossamers
That twinkle into green and gold:

Calm and still light on yon great plain
   That sweeps with all its autumn bowers,
   And crowded farms and lessening towers,
To mingle with the bounding main:

Calm and deep peace in this wide air,
   These leaves that redden to the fall;
And in my heart, if calm at all,
If any calm, a calm despair:

Calm on the seas, and silver sleep,
   And waves that sway themselves in rest,
   And dead calm in that noble breast
Which heaves but with the heaving deep.

TONIGHT the winds begin to rise
   And roar from yonder dropping day:
   The last red leaf is whirled away,
The rooks are blown about the skies;

The forest cracked, the waters curled,
   The cattle huddled on the lea;
   And wildly dashed on tower and tree
The sunbeam strikes along the world:

And but for fancies, which aver
   That all thy motions gently pass
   Athwart a plane of molten glass,
I scarce could brook the strain and stir

That makes the barren branches loud;
   And but for fear it is not so,
   The wild unrest that lives in woe
Would dote and pore on yonder cloud

That rises upward always higher,
   And onward drags a labouring breast,
   And topples round the dreary west,
A looming bastion fringed with fire.

Now fades the last long streak of snow,
   Now burgeons every maze of quick
   About the flowering squares, and thick
By ashen roots the violets blow.

Now rings the woodland loud and long,
   The distance takes a lovelier hue,
   And drowned in yonder living blue
The lark becomes a sightless song.

Now dance the lights on lawn and lea,
   The flocks are whiter down the vale,
   And milkier every milky sail
On winding stream or distant sea;

Where now the seamew pipes, or dives
   In yonder greening gleam, and fly
   The happy birds, that change their sky
To build and brood; that live their lives

From land to land; and in my breast
   Spring wakens too; and my regret
   Becomes an April violet,
And buds and blossoms like the rest.

CROSSING THE BAR

Sunset and evening star,
   And one clear call for me!
And may there be no moaning of the bar,
   When I put out to sea,

But such a tide as moving seems asleep,
   Too full for sound and foam,
When that which drew from out the boundless deep
   Turns again home.

Twilight and evening bell,
   And after that the dark!
And may there be no sadness of farewell,
   When I embark;

For though from out our bourn of Time and Place
   The flood may bear me far,
I hope to see my Pilot face to face
   When I have crossed the bar.

ROBERT BROWNING

MEETING AT NIGHT

THE GREY SEA and the long black land;
And the yellow half-moon large and low;
And the startled little waves that leap
In fiery ringlets from their sleep,
As I gain the cove with pushing prow,
And quench its speed i' the slushy sand.

Then a mile of warm sea-scented beach;
Three fields to cross till a farm appears;
A tap at the pane, the quick sharp scratch
And blue spurt of a lighted match,
And a voice less loud, through its joys and fears,
Than the two hearts beating each to each!

PARTING AT MORNING

ROUND the cape of a sudden came the sea,
And the sun looked over the mountain's rim:
And straight was a path of gold for him,
And the need of a world of men for me.

HOME-THOUGHTS, FROM ABROAD

OH, TO BE in England
Now that April's there,
And whoever wakes in England
Sees, some morning, unaware,
That the lowest boughs and the brushwood sheaf
Round the elm-tree bole are in tiny leaf,
While the chaffinch sings on the orchard bough
In England – now!

And after April, when May follows,
And the whitethroat builds, and all the swallows!
Hark, where my blossomed pear-tree in the hedge
Leans to the field and scatters on the clover
Blossoms and dewdrops – at the bent spray's edge –
That's the wise thrush; he sings each song twice over,
Lest you should think he never could recapture
The first fine careless rapture!
And though the fields look rough with hoary dew,
All will be gay when noontide wakes anew
The buttercups, the little children's dower
– Far brighter than this gaudy melon-flower!

TWO IN THE CAMPAGNA

I WONDER do you feel today
  As I have felt since, hand in hand,
We sat down on the grass, to stray
  In spirit better through the land,
This morn of Rome and May?

For me, I touched a thought, I know,
  Has tantalised me many times
(Like turns of thread the spiders throw
  Mocking across our path), for rhymes
To catch at and let go.

Help me to hold it! First it left
  The yellowing fennel, run to seed
There, branching from the brickwork's cleft,
  Some old tomb's ruin: yonder weed
Took up the floating weft,

Where one small orange cup amassed
  Five beetles – blind and green they grope
Among the honey-meal: and last,
  Everywhere on the grassy slope
I traced it. Hold it fast!

The champaign with its endless fleece
 Of feathery grasses everywhere!
Silence and passion, joy and peace,
 An everlasting wash of air –
Rome's ghost since her decease.

Such life here, through such lengths of hours,
 Such miracles performed in play,
Such primal naked forms of flowers,
 Such letting nature have her way
While heaven looks from its towers!

How say you? Let us, O my dove,
 Let us be unashamed of soul,
As earth lies bare to heaven above!
 How is it under our control
To love or not to love?

I would that you were all to me,
 You that are just so much, no more.
Nor yours nor mine, nor slave nor free!
 Where does the fault lie? What the core
O' the wound, since wound must be?

I would I could adopt your will,
 See with your eyes, and set my heart
Beating by yours, and drink my fill
 At your soul's springs – your part my part
In life, for good and ill.

No. I yearn upward, touch you close,
 Then stand away. I kiss your cheek,
Catch your soul's warmth – I pluck the rose
 And love it more than tongue can speak –
Then the good minute goes.

Already how am I so far
 Out of that minute? Must I go
Still like the thistle-ball, no bar,
 Onward, whenever light winds blow,
Fixed by no friendly star?

Just when I seemed about to learn!
　　Where is the thread now? Off again!
The old trick! Only I discern –
　　Infinite passion, and the pain
Of finite hearts that yearn.

MY LAST DUCHESS

Ferrara

THAT's my last Duchess painted on the wall,
Looking as if she were alive. I call
That piece a wonder, now: Fra Pandolf's hands
Worked busily a day, and there she stands.
Will 't please you sit and look at her? I said
'Fra Pandolf' by design, for never read
Strangers like you that pictured countenance,
The depth and passion of its earnest glance,
But to myself they turned (since none puts by
The curtain I have drawn for you, but I)
And seemed as they would ask me, if they durst,
How such a glance came there; so, not the first
Are you to turn and ask thus. Sir, 'twas not
Her husband's presence only, called that spot
Of joy into the Duchess' cheek: perhaps
Fra Pandolf chanced to say 'Her mantle laps
Over my lady's wrist too much,' or 'Paint
Must never hope to reproduce the faint
Half-flush that dies along her throat': such stuff
Was courtesy, she thought, and cause enough
For calling up that spot of joy. She had
A heart – how shall I say? – too soon made glad,
Too easily impressed; she liked whate'er
She looked on, and her looks went everywhere.
Sir, 'twas all one! My favour at her breast,
The dropping of the daylight in the West,
The bough of cherries some officious fool
Broke in the orchard for her, the white mule
She rode with round the terrace – all and each

Would draw from her alike the approving speech,
Or blush, at least. She thanked men – good! but
   thanked
Somehow – I know not how – as if she ranked
My gift of a nine-hundred-years-old name
With anybody's gift. Who'd stoop to blame
This sort of trifling? Even had you skill
In speech – (which I have not) – to make your will
Quite clear to such an one, and say, 'Just this
Or that in you disgusts me; here you miss,
Or there exceed the mark' – and if she let
Herself be lessoned so, nor plainly set
Her wits to yours, forsooth, and made excuse,
– E'en then would be some stooping; and I choose
Never to stoop. Oh, sir, she smiled, no doubt,
Whene'er I passed her; but who passed without
Much the same smile? This grew; I gave commands;
Then all smiles stopped together. There she stands
As if alive. Will 't please you rise? We'll meet
The company below, then. I repeat,
The Count your master's known munificence
Is ample warrant that no just pretence
Of mine for dowry will be disallowed;
Though his fair daughter's self, as I avowed
At starting, is my object. Nay, we'll go
Together down, sir. Notice Neptune, though,
Taming a sea-horse, thought a rarity,
Which Claus of Innsbruck cast in bronze for me!

EMILY BRONTË

REMEMBRANCE

COLD in the earth – and the deep snow piled above thee,
Far, far removed, cold in the dreary grave!
Have I forgot, my only Love, to love thee,
Severed at last by Time's all-severing wave?

Now, when alone, do my thoughts no longer hover
Over the mountains, on that northern shore,
Resting their wings where heath and fern-leaves cover
Thy noble heart for ever, ever more?

Cold in the earth – and fifteen wild Decembers
From those brown hills have melted into spring:
Faithful, indeed, is the spirit that remembers
After such years of change and suffering!

Sweet Love of youth, forgive, if I forget thee,
While the world's tide is bearing me along:
Other desires and other hopes beset me,
Hopes which obscure, but cannot do thee wrong!

No later light has lightened up my heaven;
No second morn has ever shone for me;
All my life's bliss from thy dear life was given,
All my life's bliss is in the grave with thee.

But, when the days of golden dreams had perished,
And even Despair was powerless to destroy,
Then did I learn how existence could be cherished,
Strengthened, and fed without the aid of joy;

Then did I check the tears of useless passion,
Weaned my young soul from yearning after thine;
Sternly denied its burning wish to hasten
Down to that tomb already more than mine!

And, even yet, I dare not let it languish,
Dare not indulge in Memory's rapturous pain;
Once drinking deep of that divinest anguish,
How could I seek the empty world again?

[LAST LINES]

No COWARD SOUL is mine,
No trembler in the world's storm-troubled sphere;
I see Heaven's glories shine,
And faith shines equal, arming me from fear.

O God within my breast,
Almighty, ever-present Deity!
Life – that in me has rest,
As I, undying Life, have power in thee!

Vain are the thousand creeds
That move men's hearts, unutterably vain;
Worthless as withered weeds,
Or idlest froth amid the boundless main,

To waken doubt in one
Holding so fast by thine infinity;
So surely anchored on
The steadfast rock of immortality.

With wide-embracing love
Thy spirit animates eternal years,
Pervades and broods above,
Changes, sustains, dissolves, creates, and rears.

Though earth and man were gone,
And suns and universes ceased to be,
And thou were left alone,
Every existence would exist in thee.

There is not room for Death,
Nor atom that his might could render void:
Thou – Thou art Being and Breath,
And what Thou art may never be destroyed.

ARTHUR HUGH CLOUGH

SAY not, the struggle nought availeth,
　　The labour and the wounds are vain,
The enemy faints not, nor faileth,
　　And as things have been things remain.

If hopes were dupes, fears may be liars;
　　It may be, in yon smoke concealed,
Your comrades chase e'en now the fliers,
　　And, but for you, possess the field.

For while the tired waves, vainly breaking,
　　Seem here no painful inch to gain,
Far back, through creeks and inlets making,
　　Comes silent, flooding in, the main,

And not by eastern windows only,
　　When daylight comes, comes in the light,
In front the sun climbs slow, how slowly,
　　But westward, look, the land is bright.

MATTHEW ARNOLD

REQUIESCAT

STREW on her roses, roses,
　　And never a spray of yew!
In quiet she reposes;
　　Ah, would that I did too!

Her mirth the world required;
　　She bathed it in smiles of glee.
But her heart was tired, tired,
　　And now they let her be.

Her life was turning, turning,
　　In mazes of heat and sound.
But for peace her soul was yearning,
　　And now peace laps her round.

Her cabined, ample spirit,
    It fluttered and failed for breath.
Tonight it doth inherit
    The vasty hall of death.

TO MARGUERITE

Yes! In the sea of life enisled,
    With echoing straits between us thrown,
Dotting the shoreless watery wild,
    We mortal millions live *alone*.
The islands feel the enclasping flow,
And then their endless bounds they know.

But when the moon their hollow lights,
    And they are swept by balms of spring,
And in their glens, on starry nights,
    The nightingales divinely sing;
And lovely notes, from shore to shore,
Across the sounds and channels pour –

Oh! then a longing like despair
    Is to their farthest caverns sent;
For surely once, they feel, we were
    Parts of a single continent!
Now round us spreads the watery plain –
Oh, might our marges meet again!

Who ordered that their longing's fire
    Should be, as soon as kindled, cooled?
Who renders vain their deep desire? –
    A God, a God their severance ruled!
And bade betwixt their shores to be
The unplumbed, salt, estranging sea.

DOVER BEACH

The sea is calm tonight.
The tide is full, the moon lies fair
Upon the straits – on the French coast the light

Gleams and is gone; the cliffs of England stand,
Glimmering and vast, out in the tranquil bay.
Come to the window, sweet is the night air!
Only, from the long line of spray
Where the sea meets the moon-blanched land,
Listen! you hear the grating roar
Of pebbles which the waves draw back, and fling,
At their return, up the high strand,
Begin, and cease, and then again begin,
With tremulous cadence slow, and bring
The eternal note of sadness in.

Sophocles long ago
Heard it on the Ægæan, and it brought
Into his mind the turbid ebb and flow
Of human misery; we
Find also in the sound a thought,
Hearing it by this distant northern sea.

The Sea of Faith
Was once, too, at the full, and round earth's shore
Lay like the folds of a bright girdle furled.
But now I only hear
Its melancholy, long, withdrawing roar,
Retreating, to the breath
Of the night-wind, down the vast edges drear
And naked shingles of the world.

Ah, love, let us be true
To one another! for the world, which seems
To lie before us like a land of dreams,
So various, so beautiful, so new,
Hath really neither joy, nor love, nor light,
Nor certitude, nor peace, nor help for pain;
And we are here as on a darkling plain
Swept with confused alarms of struggle and flight,
Where ignorant armies clash by night.

DANTE GABRIEL ROSSETTI

THE BLESSÈD DAMOZEL

THE blessèd damozel leaned out
  From the gold bar of Heaven;
Her eyes were deeper than the depth
  Of waters stilled at even;
She had three lilies in her hand,
  And the stars in her hair were seven.

Her robe, ungirt from clasp to hem,
  No wrought flowers did adorn,
But a white rose of Mary's gift,
  For service meetly worn;
Her hair that lay along her back
  Was yellow like ripe corn.

Herseemed she scarce had been a day
  One of God's choristers;
The wonder was not yet quite gone
  From that still look of hers;
Albeit, to them she left, her day
  Had counted as ten years.

(To one, it is ten years of years.
  . . . Yet now, and in this place,
Surely she leaned o'er me – her hair
  Fell all about my face. . . .
Nothing: the autumn-fall of leaves.
  The whole year sets apace.)

It was the rampart of God's house
  That she was standing on;
By God built over the sheer depth
  The which is Space begun;
So high, that looking downward thence
  She scarce could see the sun.

It lies in Heaven, across the flood
   Of ether, as a bridge.
Beneath, the tides of day and night
   With flame and darkness ridge
The void, as low as where this earth
   Spins like a fretful midge.

Around her, lovers, newly met
   'Mid deathless love's acclaims,
Spoke evermore among themselves
   Their heart-remembered names;
And the souls mounting up to God
   Went by her like thin flames.

And still she bowed herself and stooped
   Out of the circling charm;
Until her bosom must have made
   The bar she leaned on warm,
And the lilies lay as if asleep
   Along her bended arm.

From the fixed place of Heaven she saw
   Time like a pulse shake fierce
Through all the worlds. Her gaze still strove
   Within the gulf to pierce
Its path; and now she spoke as when
   The stars sang in their spheres.

The sun was gone now; the curled moon
   Was like a little feather
Fluttering far down the gulf; and now
   She spoke through the still weather.
Her voice was like the voice the stars
   Had when they sang together.

(Ah sweet! Even now, in that bird's song,
   Strove not her accents there,
Fain to be hearkened? When those bells
   Possessed the mid-day air,
Strove not her steps to reach my side
   Down all the echoing stair?)

'I wish that he were come to me,
　For he will come,' she said.
'Have I not prayed in Heaven? – on earth,
　Lord, Lord, has he not prayed?
Are not two prayers a perfect strength?
　And shall I feel afraid?

'When round his head the aureole clings,
　And he is clothed in white,
I'll take his hand and go with him
　To the deep wells of light;
As unto a stream we will step down,
　And bathe there in God's sight.

'We two will stand beside that shrine,
　Occult, withheld, untrod,
Whose lamps are stirred continually
　With prayer sent up to God;
And see our old prayers, granted, melt
　Each like a little cloud.

'We two will lie i' the shadow of
　That living mystic tree
Within whose secret growth the Dove
　Is sometimes felt to be,
While every leaf that His plumes touch
　Saith His Name audibly.

'And I myself will teach to him,
　I myself, lying so,
The songs I sing here; which his voice
　Shall pause in, hushed and slow,
And find some knowledge at each pause,
　Or some new thing to know.'

(Alas! We two, we two, thou say'st!
　Yea, one wast thou with me
That once of old. But shall God lift
　To endless unity
The soul whose likeness with thy soul
　Was but its love for thee?)

'We two', she said, 'will seek the groves
   Where the lady Mary is,
With her five handmaidens, whose names
   Are five sweet symphonies,
Cecily, Gertrude, Magdalen,
   Margaret and Rosalys.

'Circlewise sit they, with bound locks
   And foreheads garlanded;
Into the fine cloth white like flame
   Weaving the golden thread,
To fashion the birth-robes for them
   Who are just born, being dead.

'He shall fear, haply, and be dumb:
   Then will I lay my cheek
To his, and tell about our love,
   Not once abashed or weak:
And the dear Mother will approve
   My pride, and let me speak.

'Herself shall bring us, hand in hand,
   To Him round whom all souls
Kneel, the clear-ranged unnumbered heads
   Bowed with their aureoles:
And angels meeting us shall sing
   To their citherns and citoles.

'There will I ask of Christ the Lord
   Thus much for him and me:
Only to live as once on earth
   With Love – only to be,
As then awhile, for ever now
   Together, I and he.'

She gazed and listened and then said,
   Less sad of speech than mild,
'All this is when he comes.' She ceased.
   The light thrilled towards her, filled
With angels in strong level flight.
   Her eyes prayed, and she smiled.

(I saw her smile.) But soon their path
   Was vague in distant spheres:
And then she cast her arms along
   The golden barriers,
And laid her face between her hands,
   And wept. (I heard her tears.)

CHRISTINA ROSSETTI

A BIRTHDAY

MY HEART is like a singing bird
   Whose nest is in a watered shoot;
My heart is like an apple-tree
   Whose boughs are bent with thick-set fruit;
My heart is like a rainbow shell
   That paddles in a halcyon sea;
My heart is gladder than all these
   Because my love is come to me.

Raise me a daïs of silk and down;
   Hang it with vair and purple dyes;
Carve it in doves and pomegranates,
   And peacocks with a hundred eyes;
Work it in gold and silver grapes,
   In leaves and silver fleur-de-lys;
Because the birthday of my life
   Is come, my love is come to me.

SONG

WHEN I am dead, my dearest,
   Sing no sad songs for me;
Plant thou no roses at my head,
   Nor shady cypress tree:
Be the green grass above me
   With showers and dewdrops wet;
And if thou wilt, remember,
   And if thou wilt, forget.

I shall not see the shadows,
　　I shall not feel the rain;
I shall not hear the nightingale
　　Sing on, as if in pain;
And dreaming through the twilight
　　That doth not rise nor set,
Haply I may remember,
　　And haply may forget.

ALGERNON CHARLES SWINBURNE

From ATALANTA IN CALYDON

WHEN the hounds of spring are on winter's traces,
　　The mother of months in meadow or plain
Fills the shadows and windy places
　　With lisp of leaves and ripple of rain;
And the brown bright nightingale amorous
Is half assuaged for Itylus,
For the Thracian ships and the foreign faces,
　　The tongueless vigil, and all the pain.

Come with bows bent and with emptying of quivers,
　　Maiden most perfect, lady of light,
With a noise of winds and many rivers,
　　With a clamour of waters, and with might;
Bind on thy sandals, O thou most fleet,
Over the splendour and speed of thy feet;
For the faint east quickens, the wan west shivers,
　　Round the feet of the day and the feet of the night.

Where shall we find her, how shall we sing to her,
　　Fold our hands round her knees, and cling?
Oh, that man's heart were as fire and could spring to her,
　　Fire, or the strength of the streams that spring!
For the stars and the winds are unto her
As raiment, as songs of the harp-player;
For the risen stars and the fallen cling to her,
　　And the southwest-wind and the west-wind sing.

For winter's rains and ruins are over,
   And all the season of snows and sins;
The days dividing lover and lover,
   The light that loses, the night that wins;
And time remembered is grief forgotten,
And frosts are slain and flowers begotten,
And in green underwood and cover
   Blossom by blossom the spring begins.

The full streams feed on flower of rushes,
   Ripe grasses trammel a travelling foot,
The faint fresh flame of the young year flushes
   From leaf to flower and flower to fruit;
And fruit and leaf are as gold and fire,
And the oat is heard above the lyre,
And the hoofèd heel of a satyr crushes
   The chestnut-husk at the chestnut-root.

And Pan by noon and Bacchus by night,
   Fleeter of foot than the fleet-foot kid,
Follows with dancing and fills with delight
   The Mænad and the Bassarid;
And soft as lips that laugh and hide
The laughing leaves of the trees divide,
And screen from seeing and leave in sight
   The god pursuing, the maiden hid.

The ivy falls with the Bacchanal's hair
   Over her eyebrows hiding her eyes;
The wild vine slipping down leaves bare
   Her bright breast shortening into sighs;
The wild vine slips with the weight of its leaves,
But the berried ivy catches and cleaves
To the limbs that glitter, the feet that scare
   The wolf that follows, the fawn that flies.

THOMAS HARDY

THE DARKLING THRUSH

I LEANT upon a coppice gate
  When Frost was spectre-grey,
And Winter's dregs made desolate
  The weakening eye of day.
The tangled bine-stems scored the sky
  Like strings of broken lyres,
And all mankind that haunted nigh
  Had sought their household fires.

The land's sharp features seemed to be
  The Century's corpse outleant,
His crypt the cloudy canopy,
  The wind his death-lament.
The ancient pulse of germ and birth
  Was shrunken hard and dry,
And every spirit upon earth
  Seemed fervourless as I.

At once a voice arose among
  The bleak twigs overhead
In a full-hearted evensong
  Of joy illimited;
An agèd thrush, frail, gaunt, and small,
  In blast-beruffled plume,
Had chosen thus to fling his soul
  Upon the growing gloom.

So little cause for carolings
  Of such ecstatic sound
Was written on terrestrial things
  Afar or nigh around,
That I could think there trembled through
  His happy good-night air
Some blessèd Hope, whereof he knew
  And I was unaware.

31 December 1900

THE GOING

WHY did you give no hint that night
That quickly after the morrow's dawn,
And calmly, as if indifferent quite,
You would close your term here, up and be gone
     Where I could not follow
     With wing of swallow
To gain one glimpse of you ever anon!

     Never to bid good-bye,
     Or lip me the softest call,
Or utter a wish for a word, while I
Saw morning harden upon the wall,
     Unmoved, unknowing
     That your great going
Had place that moment, and altered all.

Why do you make me leave the house
And think for a breath it is you I see
At the end of the alley of bending boughs
Where so often at dusk you used to be:
     Till in darkening dankness
     The yawning blankness
Of the perspective sickens me!

     You were she who abode
     By those red-veined rocks far West,
You were the swan-necked one who rode
Along the beetling Beeny Crest,
     And, reining nigh me,
     Would muse and eye me,
While Life unrolled us its very best.

Why, then, latterly did we not speak,
Did we not think of those days long dead,
And ere your vanishing strive to seek
That time's renewal? We might have said,
     'In this bright spring weather
     We'll visit together
Those places that once we visited.'

Well, well! All's past amend,
    Unchangeable. It must go.
I seem but a dead man held on end
To sink down soon. . . . O you could not know
    That such swift fleeing
    No soul foreseeing –
Not even I – would undo me so!

December 1912

BEENY CLIFF

March 1870–March 1913

I

O THE opal and the sapphire of that wandering western sea,
And the woman riding high above with bright hair flapping free –
The woman whom I loved so, and who loyally loved me.

II

The pale mews plained below us, and the waves seemed far away
In a nether sky, engrossed in saying their ceaseless babbling say,
As we laughed light-heartedly aloft on that clear-sunned March day.

III

A little cloud then cloaked us, and there flew an irised rain,
And the Atlantic dyed its levels with a dull misfeatured stain,
And then the sun burst out again, and purples prinked the main.

IV

– Still in all its chasmal beauty bulks old Beeny to the sky,
And shall she and I not go there once again now March is nigh,
And the sweet things said in that March say anew there by and by?

V

What if still in chasmal beauty looms that wild weird western shore,
The woman now is – elsewhere – whom the ambling pony bore,
And nor knows nor cares for Beeny, and will laugh there
    nevermore.

THE OXEN

CHRISTMAS EVE, and twelve of the clock.
   'Now they are all on their knees,'
An elder said as we sat in a flock
   By the embers in hearthside ease.

We pictured the meek mild creatures where
   They dwelt in their strawy pen,
Nor did it occur to one of us there
   To doubt they were kneeling then.

So fair a fancy few would weave
   In these years! Yet, I feel,
If someone said on Christmas Eve,
   'Come; see the oxen kneel

'In the lonely barton by yonder coomb
   Our childhood used to know,'
I should go with him in the gloom,
   Hoping it might be so.

1915

IN TIME OF 'THE BREAKING OF NATIONS'

I

ONLY a man harrowing clods
   In a slow silent walk
With an old horse that stumbles and nods
   Half asleep as they stalk.

II

Only thin smoke without flame
   From the heaps of couch-grass;
Yet this will go onward the same
   Though Dynasties pass.

III

Yonder a maid and her wight
    Come whispering by:
War's annals will cloud into night
    Ere their story die.

1915

AFTERWARDS

WHEN the Present has latched its postern behind my tremulous stay,
    And the May month flaps its glad green leaves like wings,
Delicate-filmed as new-spun silk, will the neighbours say,
    'He was a man who used to notice such things'?

If it be in the dusk when, like an eyelid's soundless blink,
    The dewfall-hawk comes crossing the shades to alight
Upon the wind-warped upland thorn, a gazer may think,
    'To him this must have been a familiar sight.'

If I pass during some nocturnal blackness, mothy and warm,
    When the hedgehog travels furtively over the lawn,
One may say, 'He strove that such innocent creatures should come
        to no harm,
    But he could do little for them: and now he is gone.'

If, when hearing that I have been stilled at last, they stand at the
        door,
    Watching the full-starred heavens that winter sees,
Will this thought rise on those who will meet my face no more,
    'He was one who had an eye for such mysteries'?

And will any say when my bell of quittance is heard in the gloom,
    And a crossing breeze cuts a pause in its outrollings,
Till they rise again, as they were a new bell's boom,
    'He hears it not now, but used to notice such things'?

GERARD MANLEY HOPKINS

THE WINDHOVER

To Christ our Lord

I CAUGHT this morning morning's minion, king-
 dom of daylight's dauphin, dapple-dawn-drawn Falcon, in his
  riding
 Of the rolling level underneath him steady air, and striding
High there, how he rung upon the rein of a wimpling wing
In his ecstasy! then off, off forth on swing,
 As a skate's heel sweeps smooth on a bow-bend: the hurl and
  gliding
 Rebuffed the big wind. My heart in hiding
Stirred for a bird, – the achieve of, the mastery of the thing!

Brute beauty and valour and act, oh, air, pride, plume, here
 Buckle! AND the fire that breaks from thee then, a billion
Times told lovelier, more dangerous, O my chevalier!

No wonder of it: shéer plód makes plough down sillion
Shine, and blue-bleak embers, ah my dear,
 Fall, gall themselves, and gash gold-vermilion.

PIED BEAUTY

GLORY be to God for dappled things –
 For skies of couple-colour as a brinded cow;
  For rose-moles all in stipple upon trout that swim;
Fresh-firecoal chestnut-falls; finches' wings;
 Landscape plotted and pieced – fold, fallow, and plough;
  And áll trádes, their gear and tackle and trim.
All things counter, original, spare, strange;
 Whatever is fickle, freckled (who knows how?)
  With swift, slow; sweet, sour; adazzle, dim;
He fathers-forth whose beauty is past change:
                    Praise him.

FELIX RANDAL

FELIX RANDAL the farrier, O is he dead then? my duty all ended,
Who have watched his mould of man, big-boned and hardy-
     handsome
Pining, pining, till time when reason rambled in it and some
Fatal four disorders, fleshed there, all contended?

Sickness broke him. Impatient, he cursed at first, but mended
Being anointed and all; though a heavenlier heart began some
Months earlier, since I had our sweet reprieve and ransom
Tendered to him. Ah well, God rest him all road ever he offended!

This seeing the sick endears them to us, us too it endears.
My tongue had taught thee comfort, touch had quenched thy tears,
Thy tears that touched my heart, child, Felix, poor Felix Randal;

How far from then forethought of, all thy more boisterous years,
When thou at the random grim forge, powerful amidst peers,
Didst fettle for the great grey drayhorse his bright and battering
     sandal!

NOT, I'll not, carrion comfort, Despair, not feast on thee;
Not untwist – slack they may be – these last strands of man
In me ór, most weary, cry *I can no more*. I can;
Can something, hope, wish day come, not choose not to be.

But ah, but O thou terrible, why wouldst thou rude on me
Thy wring-world right foot rock? lay a lionlimb against me? scan
With darksome devouring eyes my bruisèd bones? and fan,
O in turns of tempest, me heaped there; me frantic to avoid thee
     and flee?

Why? That my chaff might fly; my grain lie, sheer and clear,
Nay in all that toil, that coil, since (seems) I kissed the rod,
Hand rather, my heart lo! lapped strength, stole joy, would laugh,
     chéer.
Cheer whom though? The hero whose heaven-handling flung me,
     fóot tród

Me? or me that fought him? O which one? is it each one? That
   night, that year
Of now done darkness I wretch lay wrestling with (my God!) my
   God.

GOD'S GRANDEUR

THE world is charged with the grandeur of God.
   It will flame out, like shining from shook foil;
   It gathers to a greatness, like the ooze of oil
Crushed. Why do men then now not reck his rod?
Generations have trod, have trod, have trod;
   And all is seared with trade; bleared, smeared with toil;
   And wears man's smudge and shares man's smell: the soil
Is bare now, nor can foot feel, being shod.

And for all this, nature is never spent;
   There lives the dearest freshness deep down things;
And though the last lights off the black West went
   Oh, morning, at the brown brink eastward, springs –
Because the Holy Ghost over the bent
   World broods with warm breast and with ah! bright wings

ROBERT BRIDGES

LONDON SNOW

WHEN men were all asleep the snow came flying,
   In large white flakes falling on the city brown,
Stealthily and perpetually settling and loosely lying,
     Hushing the latest traffic of the drowsy town;
Deadening, muffling, stifling its murmurs failing;
Lazily and incessantly floating down and down:
     Silently sifting and veiling road, roof and railing;
Hiding difference, making unevenness even,
Into angles and crevices softly drifting and sailing.

All night it fell, and when full inches seven
It lay in the depth of its uncompacted lightness,
The clouds blew off from a high and frosty heaven;
    And all woke earlier for the unaccustomed brightness
Of the winter dawning, the strange unheavenly glare:
The eye marvelled – marvelled at the dazzling whiteness;
    The ear hearkened to the stillness of the solemn air;
No sound of wheel rumbling nor of foot falling,
And the busy morning cries came thin and spare.
    Then boys I heard, as they went to school, calling,
They gathered up the crystal manna to freeze
Their tongues with tasting, their hands with snowballing;
    Or rioted in a drift, plunging up to the knees;
Or peering up from under the white-mossed wonder,
'O look at the trees!' they cried, 'O look at the trees!'
    With lessened load a few carts creak and blunder,
Following along the white deserted way,
A country company long dispersed asunder:
    When now already the sun, in pale display
Standing by Paul's high dome, spread forth below
His sparkling beams, and awoke the stir of the day.
    For now doors open, and war is waged with the snow;
And trains of sombre men, past tale of number,
Tread long brown paths, as toward their toil they go:
    But even for them awhile no cares encumber
Their minds diverted; the daily word is unspoken,
The daily thoughts of labour and sorrow slumber
    At the sight of the beauty that greets them, for the charm
        they have broken.

NIGHTINGALES

BEAUTIFUL must be the mountains whence ye come,
  And bright in the fruitful valleys the streams, wherefrom
      Ye learn your song:
Where are those starry woods? O might I wander there,
  Among the flowers, which in that heavenly air
      Bloom the year long!

Nay, barren are those mountains and spent the streams:
Our song is the voice of desire, that haunts our dreams,
  A throe of the heart,
Whose pining visions dim, forbidden hopes profound,
 No dying cadence nor long sigh can sound,
  For all our art.

Alone, aloud in the raptured ear of men
We pour our dark nocturnal secret; and then,
  As night is withdrawn
From these sweet-springing meads and bursting boughs of May,
 Dream, while the innumerable choir of day
  Welcome the dawn.

A. E. HOUSMAN

From A SHROPSHIRE LAD

LOVELIEST of trees, the cherry now
Is hung with bloom along the bough,
And stands about the woodland ride
Wearing white for Eastertide.

Now, of my threescore years and ten,
Twenty will not come again,
And take from seventy springs a score,
It only leaves me fifty more.

And since to look at things in bloom
Fifty springs are little room,
About the woodlands I will go
To see the cherry hung with snow.

ON WENLOCK EDGE the wood's in trouble;
 His forest fleece the Wrekin heaves;
The gale, it plies the saplings double,
 And thick on Severn snow the leaves.

'Twould blow like this through holt and hanger
 When Uricon the city stood:
'Tis the old wind in the old anger,
 But then it threshed another wood.

Then, 'twas before my time, the Roman
 At yonder heaving hill would stare:
The blood that warms an English yeoman,
 The thoughts that hurt him, they were there.

There, like the wind through woods in riot,
 Through him the gale of life blew high;
The tree of man was never quiet:
 Then 'twas the Roman, now 'tis I.

The gale, it plies the saplings double,
 It blows so hard, 'twill soon be gone:
Today the Roman and his trouble
 Are ashes under Uricon.

  INTO my heart an air that kills
   From yon far country blows:
  What are those blue remembered hills,
   What spires, what farms are those?

  That is the land of lost content,
   I see it shining plain,
  The happy highways where I went
   And cannot come again.

RUDYARD KIPLING

RECESSIONAL

1897

GOD of our fathers, known of old,
   Lord of our far-flung battle-line,
Beneath whose awful Hand we hold
   Dominion over palm and pine –
Lord God of Hosts, be with us yet,
Lest we forget – lest we forget!

The tumult and the shouting dies;
   The Captains and the Kings depart:
Still stands Thine ancient sacrifice,
   An humble and a contrite heart.
Lord God of Hosts, be with us yet,
Lest we forget – lest we forget!

Far-called, our navies melt away;
   On dune and headland sinks the fire:
Lo, all our pomp of yesterday
   Is one with Nineveh and Tyre!
Judge of the Nations, spare us yet,
Lest we forget – lest we forget!

If, drunk with sight of power, we loose
   Wild tongues that have not Thee in awe
Such boastings as the Gentiles use,
   Or lesser breeds without the Law –
Lord God of Hosts, be with us yet,
Lest we forget – lest we forget!

For heathen heart that puts her trust
   In reeking tube and iron shard,
All valiant dust that builds on dust,
   And guarding, calls not Thee to guard,
For frantic boast and foolish word –
Thy mercy on Thy People, Lord!

DANNY DEEVER

'WHAT are the bugles blowin' for?' said Files-on-Parade.
'To turn you out, to turn you out,' the Colour-Sergeant said.
'What makes you look so white, so white?' said Files-on-Parade.
'I'm dreadin' what I've got to watch,' the Colour-Sergeant said.
 For they're hangin' Danny Deever, you can hear the Dead
   March play,
   The Regiment's in 'ollow square – they're hangin' him today;
   They've taken of his buttons off an' cut his stripes away,
   An' they're hangin' Danny Deever in the mornin'.

'What makes the rear-rank breathe so 'ard?' said Files-on-Parade.
'It's bitter cold, it's bitter cold,' the Colour-Sergeant said.
'What makes that front-rank man fall down?' said Files-on-Parade.
'A touch o' sun, a touch o' sun,' the Colour-Sergeant said.
 They are hangin' Danny Deever, they are marchin' of 'im round,
   They 'ave 'alted Danny Deever by 'is coffin on the ground;
   An' 'e'll swing in 'arf a minute for a sneakin' shootin' hound –
   O they're hangin' Danny Deever in the mornin'!

' 'Is cot was right-'and cot to mine,' said Files-on-Parade.
' 'E's sleepin' out an' far tonight,' the Colour-Sergeant said.
'I've drunk 'is beer a score o' times,' said Files-on-Parade.
' 'E's drinkin' bitter beer alone,' the Colour-Sergeant said.
 They are hangin' Danny Deever, you must mark 'im to 'is place,
   For 'e shot a comrade sleepin' – you must look 'im in the face;
   Nine 'undred of 'is county an' the Regiment's disgrace,
   While they're hangin' Danny Deever in the mornin'.

'What's that so black agin the sun?' said Files-on-Parade.
'It's Danny fightin' 'ard for life,' the Colour-Sergeant said.
'What's that that whimpers over'ead?' said Files-on-Parade.
'It's Danny's soul that's passin' now,' the Colour-Sergeant said.
 For they're done with Danny Deever, you can 'ear the quickstep
   play,
   The Regiment's in column, an' they're marchin' us away;
   Ho! the young recruits are shakin', an' they'll want their beer
   today,
   After hangin' Danny Deever in the mornin'!

CITIES and Thrones and Powers
  Stand in Time's eye,
Almost as long as flowers,
  Which daily die:
But, as new buds put forth
  To glad new men,
Out of the spent and unconsidered Earth
  The Cities rise again.

This season's Daffodil,
  She never hears
What change, what chance, what chill,
  Cut down last year's;
But with bold countenance,
  And knowledge small,
Esteems her seven days' continuance
  To be perpetual.

So Time that is o'er-kind
  To all that be,
Ordains us e'en as blind,
  As bold as she:
That in our very death,
  And burial sure,
Shadow to shadow, well persuaded, saith,
  'See how our works endure!'

THE WAY THROUGH THE WOODS

THEY shut the road through the woods
Seventy years ago.
Weather and rain have undone it again,
And now you would never know
There was once a road through the woods
Before they planted the trees.
It is underneath the coppice and heath
And the thin anemones.
Only the keeper sees

That, where the ring-dove broods,
And the badgers roll at ease,
There was once a road through the woods.

Yet, if you enter the woods
Of a summer evening late,
When the night-air cools on the trout-ringed pools
Where the otter whistles his mate,
(They fear not men in the woods,
Because they see so few.)
You will hear the beat of a horse's feet,
And the swish of a skirt in the dew,
Steadily cantering through
The misty solitudes,
As though they perfectly knew
The old lost road through the woods. . . .
But there is no road through the woods.

W. B. YEATS

THE SECOND COMING

TURNING and turning in the widening gyre
The falcon cannot hear the falconer;
Things fall apart; the centre cannot hold;
Mere anarchy is loosed upon the world,
The blood-dimmed tide is loosed, and everywhere
The ceremony of innocence is drowned;
The best lack all conviction, while the worst
Are full of passionate intensity.

Surely some revelation is at hand;
Surely the Second Coming is at hand.
The Second Coming! Hardly are those words out
When a vast image out of *Spiritus Mundi*
Troubles my sight: somewhere in sands of the desert
A shape with lion body and the head of a man,
A gaze blank and pitiless as the sun,

Is moving its slow thighs, while all about it
Reel shadows of the indignant desert birds.
The darkness drops again; but now I know
That twenty centuries of stony sleep
Were vexed to nightmare by a rocking cradle,
And what rough beast, its hour come round at last,
Slouches towards Bethlehem to be born?

SAILING TO BYZANTIUM

I

THAT is no country for old men. The young
In one another's arms, birds in the trees
– Those dying generations – at their song,
The salmon-falls, the mackerel-crowded seas,
Fish, flesh, or fowl, commend all summer long
Whatever is begotten, born, and dies.
Caught in that sensual music all neglect
Monuments of unageing intellect.

II

An agèd man is but a paltry thing,
A tattered coat upon a stick, unless
Soul clap its hands and sing, and louder sing
For every tatter in its mortal dress,
Nor is there singing school but studying
Monuments of its own magnificence;
And therefore I have sailed the seas and come
To the holy city of Byzantium.

III

O sages standing in God's holy fire
As in the gold mosaic of a wall,
Come from the holy fire, perne in a gyre,
And be the singing-masters of my soul.
Consume my heart away; sick with desire
And fastened to a dying animal
It knows not what it is; and gathers me
Into the artifice of eternity.

IV

Once out of nature I shall never take
My bodily form from any natural thing,
But such a form as Grecian goldsmiths make
Of hammered gold and gold enamelling
To keep a drowsy Emperor awake;
Or set upon a golden bough to sing
To lords and ladies of Byzantium
Of what is past, or passing, or to come.

1927

AMONG SCHOOL CHILDREN

I

I WALK through the long schoolroom questioning;
A kind old nun in a white hood replies;
The children learn to cipher and to sing,
To study reading-books and history,
To cut and sew, be neat in everything
In the best modern way – the children's eyes
In momentary wonder stare upon
A sixty-year-old smiling public man.

II

I dream of a Ledaean body, bent
Above a sinking fire, a tale that she
Told of a harsh reproof, or trivial event
That changed some childish day to tragedy –
Told, and it seemed that our two natures blent
Into a sphere from youthful sympathy,
Or else, to alter Plato's parable,
Into the yolk and white of the one shell.

III

And thinking of that fit of grief or rage
I look upon one child or t'other there
And wonder if she stood so at that age –
For even daughters of the swan can share
Something of every paddler's heritage –
And had that colour upon cheek or hair,

And thereupon my heart is driven wild:
She stands before me as a living child.

IV

Her present image floats into the mind –
Did Quattrocento finger fashion it
Hollow of cheek as though it drank the wind
And took a mess of shadows for its meat?
And I though never of Ledaean kind
Had pretty plumage once – enough of that,
Better to smile on all that smile, and show
There is a comfortable kind of old scarecrow.

V

What youthful mother, a shape upon her lap
Honey of generation had betrayed,
And that must sleep, shriek, struggle to escape
As recollection or the drug decide,
Would think her son, did she but see that shape
With sixty or more winters on its head,
A compensation for the pang of his birth,
Or the uncertainty of his setting forth?

VI

Plato thought nature but a spume that plays
Upon a ghostly paradigm of things;
Solider Aristotle played the taws
Upon the bottom of a king of kings;
World-famous golden-thighed Pythagoras
Fingered upon a fiddle-stick or strings
What a star sang and careless Muses heard:
Old clothes upon old sticks to scare a bird.

VII

Both nuns and mothers worship images,
But those the candles light are not as those
That animate a mother's reveries,
But keep a marble or a bronze repose.
And yet they too break hearts – O Presences
That passion, piety or affection knows,
And that all heavenly glory symbolise –
O self-born mockers of man's enterprise;

VIII

Labour is blossoming or dancing where
The body is not bruised to pleasure soul,
Nor beauty born out of its own despair,
Nor blear-eyed wisdom out of midnight oil.
O chestnut-tree, great-rooted blossomer,
Are you the leaf, the blossom or the bole?
O body swayed to music, O brightening glance,
How can we know the dancer from the dance?

BYZANTIUM

THE unpurged images of day recede;
The Emperor's drunken soldiery are abed;
Night resonance recedes, night-walkers' song
After great cathedral gong;
A starlit or a moonlit dome disdains
All that man is,
All mere complexities,
The fury and the mire of human veins.

Before me floats an image, man or shade,
Shade more than man, more image than a shade;
For Hades' bobbin bound in mummy-cloth
May unwind the winding path;
A mouth that has no moisture and no breath
Breathless mouths may summon;
I hail the superhuman;
I call it death-in-life and life-in-death.

Miracle, bird or golden handiwork,
More miracle than bird or handiwork,
Planted in the star-lit golden bough,
Can like the cocks of Hades crow,
Or, by the moon embittered, scorn aloud
In glory of changeless metal
Common bird or petal
And all complexities of mire or blood.

At midnight on the Emperor's pavement flit
Flames that no faggot feeds, nor steel has lit,
Nor storm disturbs, flames begotten of flame,
Where blood-begotten spirits come
And all complexities of fury leave,
Dying into a dance,
An agony of trance,
An agony of flame that cannot singe a sleeve.

Astraddle on the dolphin's mire and blood,
Spirit after spirit! The smithies break the flood,
The golden smithies of the Emperor!
Marbles of the dancing floor
Break bitter furies of complexity,
Those images that yet
Fresh images beget,
That dolphin-torn, that gong-tormented sea.

1930

ERNEST DOWSON

NON SUM QUALIS ERAM BONAE SUB REGNO CYNARAE

Last night, ah, yesternight, betwixt her lips and mine
There fell thy shadow, Cynara! thy breath was shed
Upon my soul between the kisses and the wine;
And I was desolate and sick of an old passion,
    Yea, I was desolate and bowed my head:
I have been faithful to thee, Cynara! in my fashion.

All night upon mine heart I felt her warm heart beat,
Night-long within mine arms in love and sleep she lay;
Surely the kisses of her bought red mouth were sweet;
But I was desolate and sick of an old passion,
    When I awoke and found the dawn was grey:
I have been faithful to thee, Cynara! in my fashion.

I have forgot much, Cynara! gone with the wind,
Flung roses, roses riotously with the throng,
Dancing, to put thy pale, lost lilies out of mind;
But I was desolate and sick of an old passion,
   Yea, all the time, because the dance was long:
I have been faithful to thee, Cynara! in my fashion.

I cried for madder music and for stronger wine,
But when the feast is finished and the lamps expire,
Then falls thy shadow, Cynara! the night is thine;
And I am desolate and sick of an old passion,
   Yea, hungry for the lips of my desire:
I have been faithful to thee, Cynara! in my fashion.

WALTER DE LA MARE

ALL THAT'S PAST

VERY old are the woods;
   And the buds that break
Out of the brier's boughs,
   When March winds wake,
So old with their beauty are –
   Oh, no man knows
Through what wild centuries
   Roves back the rose.

Very old are the brooks;
   And the rills that rise
Where snow sleeps cold beneath
   The azure skies
Sing such a history
   Of come and gone,
Their every drop is as wise
   As Solomon.

Very old are we men;
   Our dreams are tales
Told in dim Eden
   By Eve's nightingales;
We wake and whisper awhile,
   But, the day gone by,
Silence and sleep like fields
   Of amaranth lie.

THE LISTENERS

'Is THERE anybody there?' said the Traveller,
   Knocking on the moonlit door;
And his horse in the silence champed the grasses
   Of the forest's ferny floor:
And a bird flew up out of the turret,
   Above the Traveller's head:
And he smote upon the door again a second time;
   'Is there anybody there?' he said.
But no one descended to the Traveller;
   No head from the leaf-fringed sill
Leaned over and looked into his grey eyes,
   Where he stood perplexed and still.
But only a host of phantom listeners
   That dwelt in the lone house then
Stood listening in the quiet of the moonlight
   To that voice from the world of men:
Stood thronging the faint moonbeams on the dark stair,
   That goes down to the empty hall,
Hearkening in an air stirred and shaken
   By the lonely Traveller's call.
And he felt in his heart their strangeness,
   Their stillness answering his cry,
While his horse moved, cropping the dark turf,
   'Neath the starred and leafy sky;
For he suddenly smote on the door, even
   Louder, and lifted his head: –
'Tell them I came, and no one answered,
   That I kept my word,' he said.

Never the least stir made the listeners,
    Though every word he spake
Fell echoing through the shadowiness of the still house
    From the one man left awake:
Ay, they heard his foot upon the stirrup,
    And the sound of iron on stone,
And how the silence surged softly backward,
    When the plunging hoofs were gone.

THE RAILWAY JUNCTION

From here through tunnelled gloom the track
Forks into two; and one of these
Wheels onward into darkening hills,
And one toward distant seas.

How still it is; the signal light
At set of sun shines palely green;
A thrush sings; other sound there's none,
Nor traveller to be seen –

Where late there was a throng. And now,
In peace awhile, I sit alone;
Though soon, at the appointed hour,
I shall myself be gone.

But not their way: the bow-legged groom,
The parson in black, the widow and son,
The sailor with his cage, the gaunt
Gamekeeper with his gun,

That fair one, too, discreetly veiled –
All, who so mutely came, and went,
Will reach those far nocturnal hills,
Or shores, ere night is spent.

I nothing know why thus we met –
Their thoughts, their longings, hopes, their fate:
And what shall I remember, except –
The evening growing late –

That here through tunnelled gloom the track
Forks into two; of these
One into darkening hills leads on,
And one toward distant seas?

JOHN MASEFIELD

CARGOES

QUINQUIREME of Nineveh from distant Ophir
Rowing home to haven in sunny Palestine
With a cargo of ivory,
And apes and peacocks,
Sandalwood, cedarwood, and sweet white wine.

Stately Spanish galleon coming from the Isthmus,
Dipping through the Tropics by the palm-green shores,
With a cargo of diamonds,
Emeralds, amethysts,
Topazes, and cinnamon, and gold moidores.

Dirty British coaster with a salt-caked smoke stack
Butting through the Channel in the mad March days,
With a cargo of Tyne coal,
Road-rail, pig-lead,
Firewood, iron-ware, and cheap tin trays.

SEA-FEVER

I MUST go down to the seas again, to the lonely sea and the sky,
And all I ask is a tall ship and a star to steer her by,
And the wheel's kick and the wind's song and the white sail's
    shaking,
And a grey mist on the sea's face and a grey dawn breaking.

I must go down to the seas again, for the call of the running tide
Is a wild call and a clear call that may not be denied;
And all I ask is a windy day with the white clouds flying,
And the flung spray and the blown spume, and the sea-gulls crying.

I must go down to the seas again, to the vagrant gypsy life,
To the gull's way and the whale's way where the wind's like
  a whetted knife;
And all I ask is a merry yarn from a laughing fellow-rover,
And quiet sleep and a sweet dream when the long trick's over.

EDWARD THOMAS

ADLESTROP

YES. I remember Adlestrop –
The name, because one afternoon
Of heat the express-train drew up there
Unwontedly. It was late June.

The steam hissed. Someone cleared his throat.
No one left and no one came
On the bare platform. What I saw
Was Adlestrop – only the name

And willows, willow-herb, and grass,
And meadowsweet, and haycocks dry,
No whit less still and lonely fair
Than the high cloudlets in the sky.

And for that minute a blackbird sang
Close by, and round him, mistier,
Farther and farther, all the birds
Of Oxfordshire and Gloucestershire.

COCK-CROW

OUT of the wood of thoughts that grows by night
To be cut down by the sharp axe of light, –
Out of the night, two cocks together crow,
Cleaving the darkness with a silver blow:
And bright before my eyes twin trumpeters stand,
Heralds of splendour, one at either hand,
Each facing each as in a coat of arms:
The milkers lace their boots up at the farms.

LAURENCE BINYON

FOR THE FALLEN

September 1914

WITH proud thanksgiving, a mother for her children,
England mourns for her dead across the sea.
Flesh of her flesh they were, spirit of her spirit,
Fallen in the cause of the free.

Solemn the drums thrill: Death august and royal
Sings sorrow up into immortal spheres.
There is music in the midst of desolation
And a glory that shines upon our tears.

They went with songs to the battle, they were young,
Straight of limb, true of eye, steady and aglow.
They were staunch to the end against odds uncounted,
They fell with their faces to the foe.

They shall grow not old, as we that are left grow old:
Age shall not weary them, nor the years condemn.
At the going down of the sun and in the morning
We will remember them.

They mingle not with their laughing comrades again;
They sit no more at familiar tables of home;
They have no lot in our labour of the day-time;
They sleep beyond England's foam.

But where our desires are and our hopes profound,
Felt as a well-spring that is hidden from sight,
To the innermost heart of their own land they are known
As the stars are known to the Night;

As the stars that shall be bright when we are dust,
Moving in marches upon the heavenly plain,
As the stars that are starry in the time of our darkness,
To the end, to the end, they remain.

From THE BURNING OF THE LEAVES

Now is the time for the burning of the leaves.
They go to the fire; the nostril pricks with smoke
Wandering slowly into a weeping mist.
Brittle and blotched, ragged and rotten sheaves!
A flame seizes the smouldering ruin and bites
On stubborn stalks that crackle as they resist.

The last hollyhock's fallen tower is dust;
All the spices of June are a bitter reek,
All the extravagant riches spent and mean.
All burns! The reddest rose is a ghost;
Sparks whirl up, to expire in the mist: the wild
Fingers of fire are making corruption clean.

Now is the time for stripping the spirit bare,
Time for the burning of days ended and done,
Idle solace of things that have gone before:
Rootless hope and fruitless desire are there;
Let them go to the fire, with never a look behind.
The world that was ours is a world that is ours no more.

They will come again, the leaf and the flower, to arise
From squalor of rottenness into the old splendour,
And magical scents to a wondering memory bring;
The same glory, to shine upon different eyes.
Earth cares for her own ruins, naught for ours.
Nothing is certain, only the certain spring.

SIEGFRIED SASSOON

ATTACK

AT DAWN the ridge emerges massed and dun
In the wild purple of the glow'ring sun,
Smouldering through spouts of drifting smoke that shroud
The menacing scarred slope; and, one by one,

Tanks creep and topple forward to the wire.
The barrage roars and lifts. Then, clumsily bowed
With bombs and guns and shovels and battle-gear,
Men jostle and climb to meet the bristling fire.
Lines of grey, muttering faces, masked with fear,
They leave their trenches, going over the top,
While time ticks blank and busy on their wrists,
And hope, with furtive eyes and grappling fists,
Flounders in mud. O Jesus, make it stop!

EVERYONE SANG

EVERYONE suddenly burst out singing;
And I was filled with such delight
As prisoned birds must find in freedom,
Winging wildly across the white
Orchards and dark-green fields; on – on – and out of sight.

Everyone's voice was suddenly lifted;
And beauty came like the setting sun:
My heart was shaken with tears; and horror
Drifted away . . . O, but Everyone
Was a bird; and the song was wordless; the singing will never be
done.

RUPERT BROOKE

THE SOLDIER

IF I SHOULD DIE, think only this of me:
    That there's some corner of a foreign field
That is for ever England. There shall be
    In that rich earth a richer dust concealed;
A dust whom England bore, shaped, made aware,
    Gave, once, her flowers to love, her ways to roam,
A body of England's, breathing English air,
    Washed by the rivers, blest by suns of home.

And think, this heart, all evil shed away,
   A pulse in the eternal mind, no less
      Gives somewhere back the thoughts by England given;
Her sights and sounds; dreams happy as her day;
      And laughter, learnt of friends; and gentleness,
      In hearts at peace, under an English heaven.

THE OLD VICARAGE, GRANTCHESTER

(CAFÉ DES WESTENS, BERLIN, MAY 1912)

JUST now the lilac is in bloom,
All before my little room;
And in my flower-beds, I think,
Smile the carnation and the pink;
And down the borders, well I know,
The poppy and the pansy blow . . .
Oh! there the chestnuts, summer through,
Beside the river make for you
A tunnel of green gloom, and sleep
Deeply above; and green and deep
The stream mysterious glides beneath,
Green as a dream and deep as death.
– Oh, damn! I know it! and I know
How the May fields all golden show,
And when the day is young and sweet,
Gild gloriously the bare feet
That run to bathe . . .
              Du lieber Gott!

Here am I, sweating, sick, and hot,
And there the shadowed waters fresh
Lean up to embrace the naked flesh.
Temperamentvoll German Jews
Drink beer around; – and *there* the dews
Are soft beneath a morn of gold.
Here tulips bloom as they are told;
Unkempt about those hedges blows
An English unofficial rose;

And there the unregulated sun
Slopes down to rest when day is done,
And wakes a vague unpunctual star,
A slippered Hesper; and there are
Meads towards Haslingfield and Coton
Where *das Betreten*'s not *verboten*.

ετθε γενοίμην ... would I were
In Grantchester, in Grantchester! –
Some, it may be, can get in touch
With Nature there, or Earth, or such.
And clever modern men have seen
A Faun a-peeping through the green,
And felt the Classics were not dead,
To glimpse a Naiad's reedy head,
Or hear the Goat-foot piping low:
But these are things I do not know.
I only know that you may lie
Day long and watch the Cambridge sky,
And, flower-lulled in sleepy grass,
Hear the cool lapse of hours pass,
Until the centuries blend and blur
In Grantchester, in Grantchester. . . .
Still in the dawnlit waters cool
His ghostly Lordship swims his pool,
And tries the strokes, essays the tricks,
Long learnt on Hellespont, or Styx.
Dan Chaucer hears his river still
Chatter beneath a phantom mill.
Tennyson notes, with studious eye,
How Cambridge waters hurry by . . .
And in that garden, black and white,
Creep whispers through the grass all night;
And spectral dance, before the dawn,
A hundred Vicars down the lawn;
Curates, long dust, will come and go
On lissom, clerical, printless toe;
And oft between the boughs is seen
The sly shade of a Rural Dean . . .

Till, at a shiver in the skies,
Vanishing with Satanic cries,
The prim ecclesiastic rout
Leaves but a startled sleeper-out,
Grey heavens, the first bird's drowsy calls,
The falling house that never falls.

God! I will pack, and take a train,
And get me to England once again!
For England's the one land, I know
Where men with Splendid Hearts may go;
And Cambridgeshire, of all England,
The shire for Men who Understand;
And of *that* district I prefer
The lovely hamlet Grantchester.
For Cambridge people rarely smile,
Being urban, squat, and packed with guile;
And Royston men in the far South
Are black and fierce and strange of mouth;
At Over they fling oaths at one,
And worse than oaths at Trumpington,
And Ditton girls are mean and dirty,
And there's none in Harston under thirty,
And folks in Shelford and those parts
Have twisted lips and twisted hearts,
And Barton men make Cockney rhymes,
And Coton's full of nameless crimes,
And things are done you'd not believe
At Madingley, on Christmas Eve.
Strong men have run for miles and miles,
When one from Cherry Hinton smiles;
Strong men have blanched, and shot their wives,
Rather than send them to St Ives;
Strong men have cried like babes, bydam,
To hear what happened at Babraham.
But Grantchester! ah, Grantchester!
There's peace and holy quiet there,
Great clouds along pacific skies,
And men and women with straight eyes,

Lithe children lovelier than a dream,
A bosky wood, a slumbrous stream,
And little kindly winds that creep
Round twilight corners, half asleep.
In Grantchester their skins are white;
They bathe by day, they bathe by night;
The women there do all they ought;
The men observe the Rules of Thought.
They love the Good; they worship Truth;
They laugh uproariously in youth;
(And when they get to feeling old,
They up and shoot themselves, I'm told) . . .
   Ah God! to see the branches stir
Across the moon at Grantchester!
To smell the thrilling-sweet and rotten
Unforgettable, unforgotten
River-smell, and hear the breeze
Sobbing in the little trees.
Say, do the elm-clumps greatly stand
Still guardians of that holy land?
The chestnuts shade, in reverend dream,
The yet unacademic stream?
Is dawn a secret shy and cold
Anadyomene, silver-gold?
And sunset still a golden sea
From Haslingfield to Madingley?
And after, ere the night is born,
Do hares come out about the corn?
Oh, is the water sweet and cool,
Gentle and brown, above the pool?
And laughs the immortal river still
Under the mill, under the mill?
Say, is there Beauty yet to find?
And Certainty? and Quiet kind?
Deep meadows yet, for to forget
The lies, and truths, and pain? . . . oh! yet
Stands the Church clock at ten to three?
And is there honey still for tea?

JULIAN GRENFELL

INTO BATTLE

The naked earth is warm with Spring,
  And with green grass and bursting trees
Leans to the sun's gaze glorying,
  And quivers in the sunny breeze;

And life is colour and warmth and light,
  And a striving evermore for these;
And he is dead who will not fight;
  And who dies fighting has increase.

The fighting man shall from the sun
  Take warmth, and life from the glowing earth;
Speed with the light-foot winds to run,
  And with the trees to newer birth;
And find, when fighting shall be done,
  Great rest, and fullness after dearth.

All the bright company of Heaven
  Hold him in their high comradeship,
The Dog-Star, and the Sisters Seven,
  Orion's belt and sworded hip.

The woodland trees that stand together,
  They stand to him each one a friend;
They gently speak in the windy weather;
  They guide to valley and ridge's end.

The kestrel hovering by day,
  And the little owls that call by night,
Bid him be swift and keen as they,
  As keen of ear, as swift of sight.

The blackbird sings to him, 'Brother, brother,
  If this be the last song you shall sing,
Sing well, for you may not sing another;
  Brother, sing.'

In dreary, doubtful waiting hours,
  Before the brazen frenzy starts,
The horses show him nobler powers;
  O patient eyes, courageous hearts!

And when the burning moment breaks,
  And all things else are out of mind,
And only joy of battle takes
  Him by the throat, and makes him blind,

Through joy and blindness he shall know,
  Not caring much to know, that still
Nor lead nor steel shall reach him, so
  That it be not the Destined Will.

The thundering line of battle stands,
  And in the air Death moans and sings;
But Day shall clasp him with strong hands,
  And Night shall fold him in soft wings.

ISAAC ROSENBERG

BREAK OF DAY IN THE TRENCHES

THE darkness crumbles away.
It is the same old druid Time as ever,
Only a live thing leaps my hand,
A queer sardonic rat,
As I pull the parapet's poppy
To stick behind my ear.
Droll rat, they would shoot you if they knew
Your cosmopolitan sympathies.
Now you have touched this English hand
You will do the same to a German
Soon, no doubt, if it be your pleasure
To cross the sleeping green between.
It seems you inwardly grin as you pass
Strong eyes, fine limbs, haughty athletes,

Less chanced than you for life,
Bonds to the whims of murder,
Sprawled in the bowels of the earth,
The torn fields of France.
What do you see in our eyes
At the shrieking iron and flame
Hurled through still heavens?
What quaver – what heart aghast?
Poppies whose roots are in man's veins
Drop, and are ever dropping;
But mine in my ear is safe –
Just a little white with the dust.

June 1916

LOUSE HUNTING

NUDES – stark and glistening,
Yelling in lurid glee. Grinning faces
And raging limbs
Whirl over the floor one fire.
For a shirt verminously busy
Yon soldier tore from his throat, with oaths
Godhead might shrink at, but not the lice.
And soon the shirt was aflare
Over the candle he'd lit while we lay.

Then we all sprang up and stript
To hunt the verminous brood.
Soon like a demons' pantomime
The place was raging.
See the silhouettes agape,
See the gibbering shadows
Mixed with the battled arms on the wall.
See gargantuan hooked fingers
Pluck in supreme flesh
To smutch supreme littleness.
See the merry limbs in hot Highland fling
Because some wizard vermin

Charmed from the quiet this revel
When our ears were half lulled
By the dark music
Blown from Sleep's trumpet.

1917

WILFRED OWEN

STRANGE MEETING

IT SEEMED that out of battle I escaped
Down some profound dull tunnel, long since scooped
Through granites which titanic wars had groined.
Yet also there encumbered sleepers groaned,
Too fast in thought or death to be bestirred.
Then, as I probed them, one sprang up, and stared
With piteous recognition in fixed eyes,
Lifting distressful hands as if to bless.
And by his smile, I knew that sullen hall,
By his dead smile I knew we stood in Hell.
With a thousand pains that vision's face was grained;
Yet no blood reached there from the upper ground,
And no guns thumped, or down the flues made moan.
'Strange friend,' I said, 'here is no cause to mourn.'
'None,' said the other, 'save the undone years,
The hopelessness. Whatever hope is yours,
Was my life also; I went hunting wild
After the wildest beauty in the world,
Which lies not calm in eyes, or braided hair,
But mocks the steady running of the hour,
And if it grieves, grieves richlier than here.
For of my glee might many men have laughed,
And of my weeping something had been left,
Which must die now. I mean the truth untold,
The pity of war, the pity war distilled.
Now men will go content with what we spoiled,
Or, discontent, boil bloody, and be spilled.
They will be swift with swiftness of the tigress.

None will break ranks, though nations trek from progress.
Courage was mine, and I had mystery,
Wisdom was mine, and I had mastery:
To miss the march of this retreating world
Into vain citadels that are not walled.
Then, when much blood had clogged their chariot-wheels,
I would go up and wash them from sweet wells,
Even with truths that lie too deep for taint.
I would have poured my spirit without stint
But not through wounds; not on the cess of war.
Foreheads of men have bled where no wounds were.
I am the enemy you killed, my friend.
I knew you in this dark: for so you frowned
Yesterday through me as you jabbed and killed.
I parried; but my hands were loath and cold.
Let us sleep now. . . .'

ANTHEM FOR DOOMED YOUTH

WHAT passing-bells for these who die as cattle?
  Only the monstrous anger of the guns.
  Only the stuttering rifles' rapid rattle
Can patter out their hasty orisons.
No mockeries now for them; no prayers nor bells,
  Nor any voice of mourning save the choirs, –
The shrill, demented choirs of wailing shells;
  And bugles calling for them from sad shires.

What candles may be held to speed them all?
  Not in the hands of boys, but in their eyes
Shall shine the holy glimmers of good-byes.
  The pallor of girls' brows shall be their pall;
Their flowers the tenderness of patient minds,
And each slow dusk a drawing-down of blinds.

ROBERT GRAVES

THE BARDS

THE bards falter in shame, their running verse
Stumbles, with marrow-bones the drunken diners
Pelt them for their delay.
It is a something fearful in the song
Plagues them – an unknown grief that like a churl
Goes commonplace in cowskin
And bursts unheralded, crowing and coughing,
An unpilled holly-club twirled in his hand,
Into their many-shielded, samite-curtained,
Jewel-bright hall where twelve kings sit at chess
Over the white-bronze pieces and the gold;
And by a gross enchantment
Flails down the rafters and leads off the queens –
The wild-swan-breasted, the rose-ruddy-cheeked
Raven-haired daughters of their admiration –
To stir his black pots and to bed on straw.

WELSH INCIDENT

'BUT that was nothing to what things came out
From the sea-caves of Criccieth yonder.'
'What were they? Mermaids? dragons? ghosts?'
'Nothing at all of any things like that.'
'What were they, then?'
                              'All sorts of queer things,
Things never seen or heard or written about,
Very strange, un-Welsh, utterly peculiar
Things. Oh, solid enough they seemed to touch,
Had anyone dared it. Marvellous creation,
All various shapes and sizes, and no sizes,
All new, each perfectly unlike his neighbour,
Though all came moving slowly out together.'
'Describe just one of them.'
                              'I am unable.'

'What were their colours?'
                              'Mostly nameless colours,
Colours you'd like to see; but one was puce
Or perhaps more like crimson, but not purplish.
Some had no colour.'
                        'Tell me, had they legs?'
'Not a leg nor foot among them that I saw.'
'But did these things come out in any order?
What o'clock was it? What was the day of the week?
Who else was present? How was the weather?'
'I was coming to that. It was half-past three
On Easter Tuesday last. The sun was shining.
The Harlech Silver Band played *Marchog Jesu*
On thirty-seven shimmering instruments,
Collecting for Carnarvon's (Fever) Hospital Fund.
The populations of Pwllheli, Criccieth,
Portmadoc, Borth, Tremadoc, Penrhyndeudraeth,
Were all assembled. Criccieth's mayor addressed them
First in good Welsh and then in fluent English,
Twisting his fingers in his chain of office,
Welcoming the things. They came out on the sand,
Not keeping time to the band, moving seaward
Silently at a snail's pace. But at last
The most odd, indescribable thing of all,
Which hardly one man there could see for wonder
Did something recognizably a something.'
'Well, what?'
              'It made a noise.'
                                    'A frightening noise?'
'No, no.'
          'A musical noise? A noise of scuffling?'
'No, but a very loud, respectable noise –
Like groaning to oneself on Sunday morning
In Chapel, close before the second psalm.'
'What did the mayor do?'
                          'I was coming to that.'

THE FACE IN THE MIRROR

GREY haunted eyes, absent-mindedly glaring
From wide, uneven orbits; one brow drooping
Somewhat over the eye
Because of a missile fragment still inhering,
Skin deep, as a foolish record of old-world fighting.

Crookedly broken nose – low tackling caused it;
Cheeks, furrowed; coarse grey hair, flying frenetic;
Forehead, wrinkled and high;
Jowls, prominent; ears, large; jaw, pugilistic;
Teeth, few; lips, full and ruddy; mouth, ascetic.

I pause with razor poised, scowling derision
At the mirrored man whose beard needs my attention,
And once more ask him why
He still stands ready, with a boy's presumption,
To court the queen in her high silk pavilion.

EDMUND BLUNDEN

REPORT ON EXPERIENCE

I HAVE been young, and now am not too old;
And I have seen the righteous forsaken,
His health, his honour and his quality taken.
   This is not what we were formerly told.

I have seen a green country, useful to the race,
Knocked silly with guns and mines, its villages vanished,
Even the last rat and last kestrel banished –
   God bless us all, this was peculiar grace.

I knew Seraphina; Nature gave her hue,
Glance, sympathy, note, like one from Eden.
I saw her smile warp, heard her lyric deaden;
   She turned to harlotry; – this I took to be new.

Say what you will, our God sees how they run.
These disillusions are His curious proving
That He loves humanity and will go on loving;
    Over there are faith, life, virtue in the sun.

T. S. ELIOT

THE LOVE SONG OF J. ALFRED PRUFROCK

> *S'io credessi che mia risposta fosse*
> *a persona che mai tornasse al mondo,*
> *questa fiamma staria senza più scosse.*
> *Ma per ciò che giammai di questo fondo*
> *non tornò vivo alcun, s'i'odo il vero,*
> *senza tema d'infamia ti rispondo.*

LET US go then, you and I,
When the evening is spread out against the sky
Like a patient etherised upon a table;
Let us go, through certain half-deserted streets,
The muttering retreats
Of restless nights in one-night cheap hotels
And sawdust restaurants with oyster-shells:
Streets that follow like a tedious argument
Of insidious intent
To lead you to an overwhelming question . . .
Oh, do not ask, 'What is it?'
Let us go and make our visit.

In the room the women come and go
Talking of Michelangelo.

The yellow fog that rubs its back upon the window-panes,
The yellow smoke that rubs its muzzle on the window-panes,
Licked its tongue into the corners of the evening,
Lingered upon the pools that stand in drains,
Let fall upon its back the soot that falls from chimneys,
Slipped by the terrace, made a sudden leap,
And seeing that it was a soft October night,
Curled once about the house, and fell asleep.

And indeed there will be time
For the yellow smoke that slides along the street
Rubbing its back upon the window-panes;
There will be time, there will be time
To prepare a face to meet the faces that you meet;
There will be time to murder and create,
And time for all the works and days of hands
That lift and drop a question on your plate;
Time for you and time for me,
And time yet for a hundred indecisions,
And for a hundred visions and revisions,
Before the taking of a toast and tea.

In the room the women come and go
Talking of Michelangelo.

And indeed there will be time
To wonder, 'Do I dare?' and, 'Do I dare?'
Time to turn back and descend the stair,
With a bald spot in the middle of my hair –
(They will say: 'How his hair is growing thin!')
My morning coat, my collar mounting firmly to the chin,
My necktie rich and modest, but asserted by a simple pin –
(They will say: 'But how his arms and legs are thin!')
Do I dare
Disturb the universe?
In a minute there is time
For decisions and revisions which a minute will reverse.

For I have known them all already, known them all –
Have known the evenings, mornings, afternoons,
I have measured out my life with coffee spoons;
I know the voices dying with a dying fall
Beneath the music from a farther room.
So how should I presume?

And I have known the eyes already, known them all –
The eyes that fix you in a formulated phrase,
And when I am formulated, sprawling on a pin,

When I am pinned and wriggling on the wall,
Then how should I begin
To spit out all the butt-ends of my days and ways?
  And how should I presume?

And I have known the arms already, known them all –
Arms that are braceleted and white and bare
(But in the lamplight, downed with light brown hair!)
Is it perfume from a dress
That makes me so digress?
Arms that lie along a table, or wrap about a shawl.
  And should I then presume?
  And how should I begin?

.   .   .

Shall I say, I have gone at dusk through narrow streets
And watched the smoke that rises from the pipes
Of lonely men in shirt-sleeves, leaning out of windows? . . .

I should have been a pair of ragged claws
Scuttling across the floors of silent seas.

.   .   .

And the afternoon, the evening, sleeps so peacefully!
Smoothed by long fingers,
Asleep . . . tired . . . or it malingers,
Stretched on the floor, here beside you and me.
Should I, after tea and cakes and ices,
Have the strength to force the moment to its crisis?
But though I have wept and fasted, wept and prayed,
Though I have seen my head (grown slightly bald) brought
    in upon a platter,
I am no prophet – and here's no great matter;
I have seen the moment of my greatness flicker,
And I have seen the eternal Footman hold my coat, and
    snicker,
And in short, I was afraid.

And would it have been worth it, after all,
After the cups, the marmalade, the tea,
Among the porcelain, among some talk of you and me,
Would it have been worth while,
To have bitten off the matter with a smile,
To have squeezed the universe into a ball
To roll it towards some overwhelming question,
To say: 'I am Lazarus, come from the dead,
Come back to tell you all, I shall tell you all' –
If one, settling a pillow by her head,
      Should say: 'That is not what I meant at all.
      That is not it, at all.'

And would it have been worth it, after all,
Would it have been worth while,
After the sunsets and the dooryards and the sprinkled streets,
After the novels, after the teacups, after the skirts that trail
      along the floor –
And this, and so much more? –
It is impossible to say just what I mean!
But as if a magic lantern threw the nerves in patterns on a
      screen:
Would it have been worth while
If one, settling a pillow or throwing off a shawl,
And turning toward the window, should say:
      'That is not it at all,
      That is not what I meant, at all.'

·   ·   ·

No! I am not Prince Hamlet, nor was meant to be;
Am an attendant lord, one that will do
To swell a progress, start a scene or two,
Advise the prince; no doubt, an easy tool,
Deferential, glad to be of use,
Politic, cautious, and meticulous;
Full of high sentence, but a bit obtuse;
At times, indeed, almost ridiculous –
Almost, at times, the Fool.

I grow old . . . I grow old . . .
I shall wear the bottoms of my trousers rolled.

Shall I part my hair behind? Do I dare to eat a peach?
I shall wear white flannel trousers, and walk upon the beach.
I have heard the mermaids singing, each to each.

I do not think that they will sing to me.

I have seen them riding seaward on the waves
Combing the white hair of the waves blown back
When the wind blows the water white and black.

We have lingered in the chambers of the sea
By sea-girls wreathed with seaweed red and brown
Till human voices wake us, and we drown.

THE WASTE LAND

'Nam Sibyllam quidem Cumis ego ipse oculis meis
vidi in ampulla pendere, et cum illi pueri dicerent:
Σίβυλλα τί θέλειζ; respondebat illa: ἀποθανεῖυ θέλω.'

For Ezra Pound
il miglior fabbro

I. THE BURIAL OF THE DEAD
APRIL is the cruellest month, breeding
Lilacs out of the dead land, mixing
Memory and desire, stirring
Dull roots with spring rain.
Winter kept us warm, covering
Earth in forgetful snow, feeding
A little life with dried tubers.
Summer surprised us, coming over the Starnbergersee
With a shower of rain; we stopped in the colonnade,
And went on in sunlight, into the Hofgarten,
And drank coffee, and talked for an hour.
Bin gar keine Russin, stamm' aus Litauen, echt deutsch.
And when we were children, staying at the arch-duke's,

My cousin's, he took me out on a sled,
And I was frightened. He said, Marie,
Marie, hold on tight. And down we went.
In the mountains, there you feel free.
I read, much of the night, and go south in the winter.

What are the roots that clutch, what branches grow
Out of this stony rubbish? Son of man,
You cannot say, or guess, for you know only
A heap of broken images, where the sun beats,
And the dead tree gives no shelter, the cricket no relief,
And the dry stone no sound of water. Only
There is shadow under this red rock,
(Come in under the shadow of this red rock),
And I will show you something different from either
Your shadow at morning striding behind you
Or your shadow at evening rising to meet you;
I will show you fear in a handful of dust.
                    Frisch weht der Wind
                    Der Heimat zu
                    Mein Irisch Kind,
                    Wo weilest du?
'You gave me hyacinths first a year ago;
'They called me the hyacinth girl.'
– Yet when we came back, late, from the hyacinth garden,
Your arms full, and your hair wet, I could not
Speak, and my eyes failed, I was neither
Living nor dead, and I knew nothing,
Looking into the heart of light, the silence.
Oed' und leer das Meer.

Madame Sosostris, famous clairvoyante,
Had a bad cold, nevertheless
Is known to be the wisest woman in Europe,
With a wicked pack of cards. Here, said she,
Is your card, the drowned Phoenician Sailor,
(Those are pearls that were his eyes. Look!)
Here is Belladonna, the Lady of the Rocks,
The lady of situations.

Here is the man with three staves, and here the Wheel,
And here is the one-eyed merchant, and this card,
Which is blank, is something he carries on his back,
Which I am forbidden to see. I do not find
The Hanged Man. Fear death by water.
I see crowds of people, walking round in a ring.
Thank you. If you see dear Mrs Equitone,
Tell her I bring the horoscope myself:
One must be so careful these days.

   Unreal City,
Under the brown fog of a winter dawn,
A crowd flowed over London Bridge, so many,
I had not thought death had undone so many.
Sighs, short and infrequent, were exhaled,
And each man fixed his eyes before his feet.
Flowed up the hill and down King William Street,
To where Saint Mary Woolnoth kept the hours
With a dead sound on the final stroke of nine.
There I saw one I knew, and stopped him, crying: 'Stetson!
'You who were with me in the ships at Mylae!
'That corpse you planted last year in your garden,
'Has it begun to sprout? Will it bloom this year?
'Or has the sudden frost disturbed its bed?
'O keep the Dog far hence, that's friend to men,
'Or with his nails he'll dig it up again!
'You! hypocrite lecteur – mon semblable, – mon frère!'

II. A GAME OF CHESS

   The Chair she sat in, like a burnished throne,
Glowed on the marble, where the glass
Held up by standards wrought with fruited vines
From which a golden Cupidon peeped out
(Another hid his eyes behind his wing)
Doubled the flames of sevenbranched candelabra
Reflecting light upon the table as
The glitter of her jewels rose to meet it,
From satin cases poured in rich profusion.
In vials of ivory and coloured glass
Unstoppered, lurked her strange synthetic perfumes,

Unguent, powdered, or liquid – troubled, confused
And drowned the sense in odours; stirred by the air
That freshened from the window, these ascended
In fattening the prolonged candle-flames,
Flung their smoke into the laquearia,
Stirring the pattern on the coffered ceiling.
Huge sea-wood fed with copper
Burned green and orange, framed by the coloured stone,
In which sad light a carvèd dolphin swam.
Above the antique mantel was displayed
As though a window gave upon the sylvan scene
The change of Philomel, by the barbarous king
So rudely forced; yet there the nightingale
Filled all the desert with inviolable voice
And still she cried, and still the world pursues,
'Jug Jug' to dirty ears.
And other withered stumps of time
Were told upon the walls; staring forms
Leaned out, leaning, hushing the room enclosed.
Footsteps shuffled on the stair.
Under the firelight, under the brush, her hair
Spread out in fiery points
Glowed into words, then would be savagely still.

'My nerves are bad tonight. Yes, bad. Stay with me.
'Speak to me. Why do you never speak. Speak.
　'What are you thinking of? What thinking? What?
'I never know what you are thinking. Think.'

　I think we are in rats' alley
Where the dead men lost their bones.

　'What is that noise?'
　　　　　　The wind under the door.
'What is that noise now? What is the wind doing?'
　　　　　　Nothing again nothing.
　　　　　　　　　　　　　　　　　'Do
'You know nothing? Do you see nothing? Do you remember
'Nothing?'

  I remember
Those are pearls that were his eyes.
'Are you alive, or not? Is there nothing in your head?'
              But

O O O O that Shakespeherian Rag –
It's so elegant
So intelligent
'What shall I do now? What shall I do?'
'I shall rush out as I am, and walk the street
'With my hair down, so. What shall we do tomorrow?
'What shall we ever do?'
           The hot water at ten.
And if it rains, a closed car at four.
And we shall play a game of chess,
Pressing lidless eyes and waiting for a knock upon the door.

  When Lil's husband got demobbed, I said –
I didn't mince my words, I said to her myself,
HURRY UP PLEASE IT'S TIME
Now Albert's coming back, make yourself a bit smart.
He'll want to know what you done with that money he
  gave you
To get yourself some teeth. He did, I was there.
You have them all out, Lil, and get a nice set,
He said, I swear, I can't bear to look at you.
And no more can't I, I said, and think of poor Albert,
He's been in the army four years, he wants a good time,
And if you don't give it him, there's others will, I said.
Oh is there, she said. Something o' that, I said.
Then I'll know who to thank, she said, and give me a
  straight look.
HURRY UP PLEASE IT'S TIME
If you don't like it you can get on with it, I said.
Others can pick and choose if you can't.
But if Albert makes off, it won't be for lack of telling.
You ought to be ashamed, I said, to look so antique.
(And her only thirty-one.)
I can't help it, she said, pulling a long face,
It's them pills I took, to bring it off, she said.

(She's had five already, and nearly died of young George.)
The chemist said it would be all right, but I've never been
    the same.
You *are* a proper fool, I said.
Well, if Albert won't leave you alone, there it is, I said,
What you get married for if you don't want children?
HURRY UP PLEASE IT'S TIME
Well, that Sunday Albert was home, they had a hot
    gammon,
And they asked me in to dinner, to get the beauty of it
    hot –
HURRY UP PLEASE IT'S TIME
HURRY UP PLEASE IT'S TIME
Goonight Bill. Goonight Lou. Goonight May. Goonight.
Ta ta. Goonight. Goonight.
Good night, ladies, good night, sweet ladies, good night,
    good night.

III. THE FIRE SERMON

    The river's tent is broken; the last fingers of leaf
Clutch and sink into the wet bank. The wind
Crosses the brown land, unheard. The nymphs are departed.
Sweet Thames, run softly, till I end my song.
The river bears no empty bottles, sandwich papers,
Silk handkerchiefs, cardboard boxes, cigarette ends
Or other testimony of summer nights. The nymphs are
    departed.
And their friends, the loitering heirs of City directors;
Departed, have left no addresses.
By the waters of Leman I sat down and wept . . .
Sweet Thames, run softly till I end my song,
Sweet Thames, run softly, for I speak not loud or long.
But at my back in a cold blast I hear
The rattle of the bones, and chuckle spread from ear to ear.

A rat crept softly through the vegetation
Dragging its slimy belly on the bank
While I was fishing in the dull canal
On a winter evening round behind the gashouse
Musing upon the king my brother's wreck

And on the king my father's death before him.
White bodies naked on the low damp ground
And bones cast in a little low dry garret,
Rattled by the rat's foot only, year to year.
But at my back from time to time I hear
The sound of horns and motors, which shall bring
Sweeney to Mrs Porter in the spring.

O the moon shone bright on Mrs Porter
And on her daughter
They wash their feet in soda water
Et O ces voix d'enfants, chantant dans la coupole!

Twit twit twit
Jug jug jug jug jug jug
So rudely forc'd.
Tereu

   Unreal City
Under the brown fog of a winter noon
Mr Eugenides, the Smyrna merchant
Unshaven, with a pocket full of currants
C.i.f. London: documents at sight,
Asked me in demotic French
To luncheon at the Cannon Street Hotel
Followed by a weekend at the Metropole.

   At the violet hour, when the eyes and back
Turn upward from the desk, when the human engine waits
Like a taxi throbbing waiting,
I Tiresias, though blind, throbbing between two lives,
Old man with wrinkled female breasts, can see
At the violet hour, the evening hour that strives
Homeward, and brings the sailor home from sea,
The typist home at teatime, clears her breakfast, lights
Her stove, and lays out food in tins.
Out of the window perilously spread
Her drying combinations touched by the sun's last rays,
On the divan are piled (at night her bed)

Stockings, slippers, camisoles, and stays.
I Tiresias, old man with wrinkled dugs
Perceived the scene, and foretold the rest –
I too awaited the expected guest.
He, the young man carbuncular, arrives,
A small house agent's clerk, with one bold stare,
One of the low on whom assurance sits
As a silk hat on a Bradford millionaire.
The time is now propitious, as he guesses,
The meal is ended, she is bored and tired,
Endeavours to engage her in caresses
Which still are unreproved, if undesired.
Flushed and decided, he assaults at once;
Exploring hands encounter no defence;
His vanity requires no response,
And makes a welcome of indifference.
(And I Tiresias have foresuffered all
Enacted on this same divan or bed;
I who have sat by Thebes below the wall
And walked among the lowest of the dead.)
Bestows one final patronising kiss,
And gropes his way, finding the stairs unlit . . .

She turns and looks a moment in the glass,
Hardly aware of her departed lover;
Her brain allows one half-formed thought to pass:
'Well now that's done: and I'm glad it's over.'
When lovely woman stoops to folly and
Paces about her room again, alone,
She smoothes her hair with automatic hand,
And puts a record on the gramophone.

'This music crept by me upon the waters'

And along the Strand, up Queen Victoria Street.
O City city, I can sometimes hear
Beside a public bar in Lower Thames Street,
The pleasant whining of a mandoline
And a clatter and a chatter from within

Where fishmen lounge at noon: where the walls
Of Magnus Martyr hold
Inexplicable splendour of Ionian white and gold.

> The river sweats
> Oil and tar
> The barges drift
> With the turning tide
> Red sails
> Wide
> To leeward, swing on the heavy spar.
> The barges wash
> Drifting logs
> Down Greenwich reach
> Past the Isle of Dogs.
> > Weialala leia
> > Wallala leialala

> Elizabeth and Leicester
> Beating oars
> The stern was formed
> A gilded shell
> Red and gold
> The brisk swell
> Rippled both shores
> Southwest wind
> Carried down stream
> The peal of bells
> White towers
> > Weialala leia
> > Wallala leialala

'Trams and dusty trees.
Highbury bore me. Richmond and Kew
Undid me. By Richmond I raised my knees
Supine on the floor of a narrow canoe.'

'My feet are at Moorgate, and my heart
Under my feet. After the event

He wept. He promised "a new start".
I made no comment. What should I resent?'

'On Margate Sands.
I can connect
Nothing with nothing.
The broken fingernails of dirty hands.
My people humble people who expect
Nothing.'
                    la la

To Carthage then I came

Burning burning burning burning
O Lord Thou pluckest me out
O Lord Thou pluckest

burning

IV. DEATH BY WATER

Phlebas the Phoenician, a fortnight dead,
Forgot the cry of gulls, and the deep sea swell
And the profit and loss.
                    A current under sea
Picked his bones in whispers. As he rose and fell
He passed the stages of his age and youth
Entering the whirlpool.
                    Gentile or Jew
O you who turn the wheel and look to windward,
Consider Phlebas, who was once handsome and tall as you.

V. WHAT THE THUNDER SAID

After the torchlight red on sweaty faces
After the frosty silence in the gardens
After the agony in stony places
The shouting and the crying
Prison and palace and reverberation
Of thunder of spring over distant mountains
He who was living is now dead
We who were living are now dying
With a little patience

Here is no water but only rock
Rock and no water and the sandy road
The road winding above among the mountains
Which are mountains of rock without water
If there were water we should stop and drink
Amongst the rock one cannot stop or think
Sweat is dry and feet are in the sand
If there were only water amongst the rock
Dead mountain mouth of carious teeth that cannot spit
Here one can neither stand nor lie nor sit
There is not even silence in the mountains
But dry sterile thunder without rain
There is not even solitude in the mountains
But red sullen faces sneer and snarl
From doors of mudcracked houses
                                    If there were water

    And no rock
    If there were rock
    And also water
    And water
    A spring
    A pool among the rock
    If there were the sound of water only
    Not the cicada
    And dry grass singing
    But sound of water over a rock
    Where the hermit-thrush sings in the pine trees
    Drip drop drip drop drop drop drop
    But there is no water

Who is the third who walks always beside you?
When I count, there are only you and I together
But when I look ahead up the white road
There is always another one walking beside you
Gliding wrapt in a brown mantle, hooded
I do not know whether a man or a woman
– But who is that on the other side of you?

What is that sound high in the air
Murmur of maternal lamentation
Who are those hooded hordes swarming
Over endless plains, stumbling in cracked earth
Ringed by the flat horizon only
What is the city over the mountains
Cracks and reforms and bursts in the violet air
Falling towers
Jerusalem Athens Alexandria
Vienna London
Unreal

A woman drew her long black hair out tight
And fiddled whisper music on those strings
And bats with baby faces in the violet light
Whistled, and beat their wings
And crawled head downward down a blackened wall
And upside down in air were towers
Tolling reminiscent bells, that kept the hours
And voices singing out of empty cisterns and exhausted
   wells.

In this decayed hole among the mountains
In the faint moonlight, the grass is singing
Over the tumbled graves, about the chapel
There is the empty chapel, only the wind's home.
It has no windows, and the door swings,
Dry bones can harm no one.
Only a cock stood on the rooftree
Co co rico co co rico
In a flash of lightning. Then a damp gust
Bringing rain

Ganga was sunken, and the limp leaves
Waited for rain, while the black clouds
Gathered far distant, over Himavant.
The jungle crouched, humped in silence.
Then spoke the thunder
Da

Datta: what have we given?
My friend, blood shaking my heart
The awful daring of a moment's surrender
Which an age of prudence can never retract
By this, and this only, we have existed
Which is not to be found in our obituaries
Or in memories draped by the beneficent spider
Or under seals broken by the lean solicitor
In our empty rooms
DA
Dayadhvam: I have heard the key
Turn in the door once and turn once only
We think of the key, each in his prison
Thinking of the key, each confirms a prison
Only at nightfall, aethereal rumours
Revive for a moment a broken Coriolanus
DA
Damyata: The boat responded
Gaily, to the hand expert with sail and oar
The sea was calm, your heart would have responded
Gaily, when invited, beating obedient
To controlling hands

                              I sat upon the shore
Fishing, with the arid plain behind me
Shall I at least set my lands in order?
London Bridge is falling down falling down falling down
Poi s'ascose nel foco che gli affina
Quando fiam uti chelidon – O swallow swallow
Le Prince d'Aquitaine à la tour abolie
These fragments I have shored against my ruins
Why then Ile fit you. Hieronymo's mad againe.
Datta. Dayadhvam. Damyata.
                    Shantih shantih shantih

JOURNEY OF THE MAGI

'A COLD COMING we had of it,
Just the worst time of the year
For a journey, and such a long journey:
The ways deep and the weather sharp,
The very dead of winter.'
And the camels galled, sore-footed, refractory,
Lying down in the melting snow.
There were times we regretted
The summer palaces on slopes, the terraces,
And the silken girls bringing sherbet.
Then the camel men cursing and grumbling
And running away, and wanting their liquor and women,
And the night-fires going out, and the lack of shelters,
And the cities hostile and the towns unfriendly
And the villages dirty and charging high prices:
A hard time we had of it.
At the end we preferred to travel all night,
Sleeping in snatches,
With the voices singing in our ears, saying
That this was all folly.

Then at dawn we came down to a temperate valley,
Wet, below the snow line, smelling of vegetation,
With a running stream and a water-mill beating the darkness,
And three trees on the low sky.
And an old white horse galloped away in the meadow.
Then we came to a tavern with vine-leaves over the lintel,
Six hands at an open door dicing for pieces of silver,
And feet kicking the empty wine-skins.
But there was no information, and so we continued
And arrived at evening, not a moment too soon
Finding the place; it was (you may say) satisfactory.

All this was a long time ago, I remember,
And I would do it again, but set down
This set down
This: were we led all that way for
Birth or Death? There was a Birth, certainly,

We had evidence and no doubt. I had seen birth and death,
But had thought they were different; this Birth was
Hard and bitter agony for us, like Death, our death.
We returned to our places, these Kingdoms,
But no longer at ease here, in the old dispensation,
With an alien people clutching their gods.
I should be glad of another death.

LITTLE GIDDING

I

MIDWINTER spring is its own season
Sempiternal though sodden towards sundown,
Suspended in time, between pole and tropic.
When the short day is brightest, with frost and fire,
The brief sun flames the ice, on pond and ditches,
In windless cold that is the heart's heat,
Reflecting in a watery mirror
A glare that is blindness in the early afternoon.
And glow more intense than blaze of branch, or brazier,
Stirs the dumb spirit: no wind, but pentecostal fire
In the dark time of the year. Between melting and freezing
The soul's sap quivers. There is no earth smell
Or smell of living thing. This is the spring time
But not in time's covenant. Now the hedgerow
Is blanched for an hour with transitory blossom
Of snow, a bloom more sudden
Than that of summer, neither budding nor fading,
Not in the scheme of generation.
Where is the summer, the unimaginable
Zero summer?

             If you came this way,
Taking the route you would be likely to take
From the place you would be likely to come from,
If you came this way in may time, you would find the hedges
White again, in May, with voluptuary sweetness.
It would be the same at the end of the journey,
If you came at night like a broken king,

If you came by day not knowing what you came for,
It would be the same, when you leave the rough road
And turn behind the pig-sty to the dull façade
And the tombstone. And what you thought you came for
Is only a shell, a husk of meaning
From which the purpose breaks only when it is fulfilled
If at all. Either you had no purpose
Or the purpose is beyond the end you figured
And is altered in fulfilment. There are other places
Which also are the world's end, some at the sea jaws,
Or over a dark lake, in a desert or a city –
But this is the nearest, in place and time,
Now and in England.

                    If you came this way,
Taking any route, starting from anywhere,
At any time or at any season,
It would always be the same: you would have to put off
Sense and notion. You are not here to verify,
Instruct yourself, or inform curiosity
Or carry report. You are here to kneel
Where prayer has been valid. And prayer is more
Than an order of words, the conscious occupation
Of the praying mind, or the sound of the voice praying.
And what the dead had no speech for, when living,
They can tell you, being dead: the communication
Of the dead is tongued with fire beyond the language of the
   living.
Here, the intersection of the timeless moment
Is England and nowhere. Never and always.

II

Ash on an old man's sleeve
Is all the ash the burnt roses leave.
Dust in the air suspended
Marks the place where a story ended.
Dust inbreathed was a house –
The wall, the wainscot and the mouse.
The death of hope and despair,
    This is the death of air.

There are flood and drouth
Over the eyes and in the mouth,
Dead water and dead sand
Contending for the upper hand.
The parched eviscerate soil
Gapes at the vanity of toil,
Laughs without mirth.
  This is the death of earth.

Water and fire succeed
The town, the pasture and the weed.
Water and fire deride
The sacrifice that we denied.
Water and fire shall rot
The marred foundations we forgot,
Of sanctuary and choir.
  This is the death of water and fire.

In the uncertain hour before the morning
  Near the ending of interminable night
  At the recurrent end of the unending
After the dark dove with the flickering tongue
  Had passed below the horizon of his homing
  While the dead leaves still rattled on like tin
Over the asphalt where no other sound was
  Between three districts whence the smoke arose
  I met one walking, loitering and hurried
As if blown towards me like the metal leaves
  Before the urban dawn wind unresisting.
  And as I fixed upon the down-turned face
That pointed scrutiny with which we challenge
  The first-met stranger in the waning dusk
  I caught the sudden look of some dead master
Whom I had known, forgotten, half recalled
  Both one and many; in the brown baked features
  The eyes of a familiar compound ghost
Both intimate and unidentifiable.
  So I assumed a double part, and cried
  And heard another's voice cry: 'What! are *you* here?'

Although we were not. I was still the same,
   Knowing myself yet being someone other –
   And he a face still forming; yet the words sufficed
To compel the recognition they preceded.
   And so, compliant to the common wind,
   Too strange to each other for misunderstanding,
In concord at this intersection time
   Of meeting nowhere, no before and after,
   We trod the pavement in a dead patrol.
I said: 'The wonder that I feel is easy,
   Yet ease is cause of wonder. Therefore speak:
   I may not comprehend, may not remember.'
And he: 'I am not eager to rehearse
   My thoughts and theory which you have forgotten.
   These things have served their purpose: let them be.
So with your own, and pray they be forgiven
   By others, as I pray you to forgive
   Both bad and good. Last season's fruit is eaten
And the fullfed beast shall kick the empty pail.
   For last year's words belong to last year's language
   And next year's words await another voice.
But, as the passage now presents no hindrance
   To the spirit unappeased and peregrine
   Between two worlds become much like each other.
So I find words I never thought to speak
   In streets I never thought I should revisit
   When I left my body on a distant shore.
Since our concern was speech, and speech impelled us
   To purify the dialect of the tribe
   And urge the mind to aftersight and foresight,
Let me disclose the gifts reserved for age
   To set a crown upon your lifetime's effort.
   First, the cold friction of expiring sense
Without enchantment, offering no promise
   But bitter tastelessness of shadow fruit
   As body and soul begin to fall asunder.
Second, the conscious impotence of rage
   At human folly, and the laceration
   Of laughter at what ceases to amuse.

And last, the rending pain of re-enactment
  Of all that you have done, and been; the shame
  Of motives late revealed, and the awareness
Of things ill done and done to others' harm
  Which once you took for exercise of virtue.
  Then fools' approval stings, and honour stains.
From wrong to wrong the exasperated spirit
  Proceeds, unless restored by that refining fire
  Where you must move in measure, like a dancer.'
The day was breaking. In the disfigured street
  He left me, with a kind of valediction,
  And faded on the blowing of the horn.

III

There are three conditions which often look alike
Yet differ completely, flourish in the same hedgerow:
Attachment to self and to things and to persons, detachment
From self and from things and from persons; and, growing
  between them, indifference
Which resembles the others as death resembles life,
Being between two lives – unflowering, between
The live and the dead nettle. This is the use of memory:
For liberation – not less of love but expanding
Of love beyond desire, and so liberation
From the future as well as the past. Thus, love of a country
Begins as attachment to our own field of action
And comes to find that action of little importance
Though never indifferent. History may be servitude,
History may be freedom. See, now they vanish,
The faces and places, with the self which, as it could, loved
  them,
To become renewed, transfigured, in another pattern.
Sin is Behovely, but
All shall be well, and
All manner of thing shall be well.
If I think, again, of this place,
And of people, not wholly commendable,
Of no immediate kin or kindness,
But some of peculiar genius,
All touched by a common genius,

United in the strife which divided them;
If I think of a king at nightfall,
Of three men, and more, on the scaffold
And a few who died forgotten
In other places, here and abroad,
And of one who died blind and quiet,
Why should we celebrate
These dead men more than the dying?
It is not to ring the bell backward
Nor is it an incantation
To summon the spectre of a Rose.
We cannot revive old factions
We cannot restore old policies
Or follow an antique drum.
These men, and those who opposed them
And those whom they opposed
Accept the constitution of silence
And are folded in a single party.
Whatever we inherit from the fortunate
We have taken from the defeated
What they had to leave us – a symbol:
A symbol perfected in death.
And all shall be well and
All manner of thing shall be well
By the purification of the motive
In the ground of our beseeching.

IV

The dove descending breaks the air
With flame of incandescent terror
Of which the tongues declare
The one discharge from sin and error.
The only hope, or else despair
   Lies in the choice of pyre or pyre –
   To be redeemed from fire by fire.

Who then devised the torment? Love.
Love is the unfamiliar Name
Behind the hands that wove
The intolerable shirt of flame

Which human power cannot remove.
  We only live, only suspire
  Consumed by either fire or fire.

v

What we call the beginning is often the end
And to make an end is to make a beginning.
The end is where we start from. And every phrase
And sentence that is right (where every word is at home,
Taking its place to support the others,
The word neither diffident nor ostentatious,
An easy commerce of the old and the new,
The common word exact without vulgarity,
The formal word precise but not pedantic,
The complete consort dancing together)
Every phrase and every sentence is an end and a beginning,
Every poem an epitaph. And any action
Is a step to the block, to the fire, down the sea's throat
Or to an illegible stone: and that is where we start.
We die with the dying:
See, they depart, and we go with them.
We are born with the dead:
See, they return, and bring us with them.
The moment of the rose and the moment of the yew-tree
Are of equal duration. A people without history
Is not redeemed from time, for history is a pattern
Of timeless moments. So, while the light fails
On a winter's afternoon, in a secluded chapel
History is now and England.

With the drawing of this Love and the voice of this Calling

We shall not cease from exploration
And the end of all our exploring
Will be to arrive where we started
And know the place for the first time.
Through the unknown, remembered gate
When the last of earth left to discover
Is that which was the beginning;
At the source of the longest river

The voice of the hidden waterfall
And the children in the apple-tree
Not known, because not looked for
But heard, half-heard, in the stillness
Between two waves of the sea.
Quick now, here, now, always –
A condition of complete simplicity
(Costing not less than everything)
And all shall be well and
All manner of thing shall be well
When the tongues of flame are in-folded
Into the crowned knot of fire
And the fire and the rose are one.

T. E. HULME

AUTUMN

A TOUCH of cold in the Autumn night –
I walked abroad,
And saw the ruddy moon lean over a hedge
Like a red-faced farmer.
I did not stop to speak, but nodded,
And round about were the wistful stars
With white faces like town children.

ABOVE THE DOCK

ABOVE the quiet dock in mid night,
Tangled in the tall mast's corded height,
Hangs the moon. What seemed so far away
Is but a child's balloon, forgotten after play.

D. H. LAWRENCE

SNAKE

A SNAKE came to my water-trough
On a hot, hot day, and I in pyjamas for the heat,
To drink there.

In the deep, strange-scented shade of the great dark carob-tree
I came down the steps with my pitcher
And must wait, must stand and wait, for there he was at the trough
    before me.

He reached down from a fissure in the earth-wall in the gloom
And trailed his yellow-brown slackness soft-bellied down, over the
    edge of the stone trough
And rested his throat upon the stone bottom,
And where the water had dripped from the tap, in a small clearness,
He sipped with his straight mouth,
Softly drank through his straight gums, into his slack long body,
Silently.

Someone was before me at my water-trough,
And I, like a second comer, waiting.

He lifted his head from his drinking, as cattle do,
And looked at me vaguely, as drinking cattle do,
And flickered his two-forked tongue from his lips, and mused a
    moment,
And stooped and drank a little more,
Being earth-brown, earth-golden from the burning bowels of the
    earth
On the day of Sicilian July, with Etna smoking.

The voice of my education said to me
He must be killed,
For in Sicily the black, black snakes are innocent, the gold are
    venomous.

And voices in me said, If you were a man
You would take a stick and break him now, and finish him off.

But must I confess how I liked him,
How glad I was he had come like a guest in quiet, to drink at my
    water-trough
And depart peaceful, pacified, and thankless,
Into the burning bowels of this earth?

Was it cowardice, that I dared not kill him?
Was it perversity, that I longed to talk to him?
Was it humility, to feel so honoured?
I felt so honoured.

And yet those voices:
If you were not afraid, you would kill him!

And truly I was afraid, I was most afraid,
But even so, honoured still more
That he should seek my hospitality
From out the dark door of the secret earth.

He drank enough
And lifted his head, dreamily, as one who has drunken,
And flickered his tongue like a forked night on the air, so black;
Seeming to lick his lips,
And looked around like a god, unseeing, into the air,
And slowly turned his head,
And slowly, very slowly, as if thrice adream,
Proceeded to draw his slow length curving round
And climb again the broken bank of my wall-face.
And as he put his head into that dreadful hole,
And as he slowly drew up, snake-easing his shoulders, and entered
    farther,
A sort of horror, a sort of protest against his withdrawing into that
    horrid black hole,
Deliberately going into the blackness, and slowly drawing himself
    after,
Overcame me now his back was turned.

I looked round, I put down my pitcher,
I picked up a clumsy log
And threw it at the water-trough with a clatter.

I think it did not hit him,
But suddenly that part of him that was left behind convulsed in
    undignified haste,
Writhed like lightning, and was gone
Into the black hole, the earth-lipped fissure in the wall-front,
At which, in the intense still noon, I stared with fascination.

And immediately I regretted it.
I thought how paltry, how vulgar, what a mean act!
I despised myself and the voices of my accursèd human education.

And I thought of the albatross,
And I wished he would come back, my snake.

For he seemed to me again like a king,
Like a king in exile, uncrowned in the underworld,
Now due to be crowned again.

And so, I missed my chance with one of the lords
Of life.
And I have something to expiate;
A pettiness.

   Taormina

BAVARIAN GENTIANS

NOT every man has gentians in his house
in Soft September, at slow, Sad Michaelmas.

Bavarian gentians, big and dark, only dark
darkening the day-time, torch-like with the smoking blueness of
    Pluto's gloom,
ribbed and torch-like, with their blaze of darkness spread blue
down flattening into points, flattened under the sweep of white day

torch-flower of the blue-smoking darkness, Pluto's dark-blue daze,
black lamps from the halls of Dis, burning dark blue,
giving off darkness, blue darkness, as Demeter's pale lamps give off
    light,
lead me then, lead the way.

Reach me a gentian, give me a torch!
let me guide myself with the blue, forked torch of this flower
down the darker and darker stairs, where blue is darkened on
    blueness
even where Persephone goes, just now, from the frosted September
to the sightless realm where darkness is awake upon the dark
and Persephone herself is but a voice
or a darkness invisible enfolded in the deeper dark
of the arms Plutonic, and pierced with the passion of dense gloom,
among the splendour of torches of darkness, shedding darkness on
    the lost bride and her groom.

EDWIN MUIR

SUBURBAN DREAM

WALKING the suburbs in the afternoon
In summer when the idle doors stand open
    And the air flows through the rooms
    Fanning the curtain hems,

You wander through a cool elysium
Of women, schoolgirls, children, garden talks,
    With a schoolboy here and there
    Conning his history book.

The men are all away in offices,
Committee-rooms, laboratories, banks,
    Or pushing cotton goods
    In Wick or Ilfracombe.

The massed unanimous absence liberates
The light keys of the piano and sets free
  Chopin and everlasting youth,
    Now, with the masters gone.

And all things turn to images of peace,
The boy curled over his book, the young girl poised
  On the path as if beguiled
    By the silence of a wood.

It is a child's dream of a grown-up world.
But soon the brazen evening clocks will bring
  The tramp of feet and brisk
    Fanfare of motor horns
      And the masters come.

DAME EDITH SITWELL

STILL FALLS THE RAIN

The Raids, 1940. Night and Dawn

STILL falls the Rain –
Dark as the world of man, black as our loss –
Blind as the nineteen hundred and forty nails
Upon the Cross.

Still falls the Rain
With a sound like the pulse of the heart that is changed to the
  hammer-beat
In the Potter's Field, and the sound of the impious feet

On the Tomb:
          Still falls the Rain
In the Field of Blood where the small hopes breed and the human
  brain
Nurtures its greed, that worm with the brow of Cain.

Still falls the Rain
At the feet of the Starved Man hung upon the Cross.
Christ that each day, each night, nails there, have mercy on us –
On Dives and on Lazarus:
Under the Rain the sore and the gold are as one.

Still falls the Rain –
Still falls the Blood from the Starved Man's wounded Side:
He bears in His Heart all wounds, – those of the light that died,
The last faint spark
In the self-murdered heart, the wounds of the sad uncomprehending
  dark,
The wounds of the baited bear, –
The blind and weeping bear whom the keepers beat
On his helpless flesh . . . the tears of the hunted hare.

Still falls the Rain –
Then – O Ile leape up to my God: who pulles me doune –
See, see where Christ's blood streames in the firmament:
It flows from the Brow we nailed upon the tree
Deep to the dying, to the thirsting heart
That holds the fires of the world, – dark-smirched with pain
As Caesar's laurel crown.

Then sounds the voice of One who like the heart of man
Was once a child who among beasts has lain –
'Still do I love, still shed my innocent light, my Blood, for thee.'

HUGH MACDIARMID

From A DRUNK MAN LOOKS AT THE THISTLE

THE FEMININE PRINCIPLE

I AM like Burns, and ony wench	*any*
Can ser' me for a time.	*serve*
Licht's in them a' – in some a sun,	*all*
In some the merest skime.	*gleam*

I'm no' like Burns, and weel I ken,   *not: know*
Tho' ony wench can ser',
It's no' through mony but through yin   *himself*
That ony man wuns fer. . . .   *wins: far*

I wedded thee frae fause love, lass,
To free thee and to free mysel';
But man and wumman tied for life
True can be and truth can tell.

Pit ony couple in a knot   *Put*
They canna lowse and needna try,   *loose*
And mair o' love at last they'll ken
– If ocht! – than joy'll alane descry.   *aught*

For them as for the beasts, my wife,
A's fer frae dune when pleesure's owre, *All's: done: over*
And coontless difficulties gar   *cause*
Ilk hert discover a' its power.   *Each*

I dinna say that bairns alane
Are true love's task – a sairer task
Is aiblins to create oorsels   *perhaps*
As we can be – it's that I ask.

Create oorsels, syne bairns, syne race.   *thereafter*
Sae on the cod I see't in you   *pillow*
Wi' Maidenkirk to John o' Groats
The bosom that you draw me to.

And nae Scot wi' a wumman lies,
But I am he and ken as 'twere
A stage I've passed as he maun pass't,   *must*
Gin he grows up, his way wi' her! . . .   *By the time*

A'thing wi' which a man   *Anything*
Can intromit's a wumman,
And can, and s'ud, become
As intimate and human.

And Jean's nae mair my wife
Than whisky is at times,
Or munelicht or a thistle   *moonlicht*
Or kittle thochts or rhymes.   *ticklish*

He's no' a man ava',   *at all*
And lacks a proper pride,
Gin less than a' the warld   *By*
Can ser' him for a bride!

MY QUARREL WITH ENGLAND

AND let me pit in guid set terms
My quarrel wi' th'owre sonsy rose,   *over: comely*
That roond about its devotees
A fair fat cast o' aureole throws
That blinds them, in its mirlygoes,   *dazzle*
To the necessity o' foes.

Upon their King and system I
Glower as on things that whiles in pairt
I may admire (at least for them),
But wi' nae claim upon my hert,
While a' their pleasure and their pride   *all*
Ootside me lies – and there maun bide.   *must*

Ootside me lies – and mair than that,
For I stand still for forces which
Were subjugated to mak' way
For England's poo'er, and to enrich
The kinds o' English, and o' Scots,
The least congenial to my thoughts.

Hauf his soul a Scot maun use   *Half*
Indulgin' in illusions,
And hauf in gettin' rid o' them
And comin' to conclusions
Wi' the demoralisin' dearth
O' onything worth while on Earth. ....

W. H. AUDEN

LAY your sleeping head, my love,
Human on my faithless arm;
Time and fevers burn away
Individual beauty from
Thoughtful children, and the grave
Proves the child ephemeral:
But in my arms till break of day
Let the living creature lie,
Mortal, guilty, but to me
The entirely beautiful.

Soul and body have no bounds:
To lovers as they lie upon
Her tolerant enchanted slope
In their ordinary swoon,
Grave the vision Venus sends
Of supernatural sympathy,
Universal love and hope;
While an abstract insight wakes
Among the glaciers and the rocks
The hermit's sensual ecstasy.

Certainty, fidelity
On the stroke of midnight pass
Like vibrations of a bell,
And fashionable madmen raise
Their pedantic boring cry:
Every farthing of the cost,
All the dreaded cards foretell,
Shall be paid, but from this night
Not a whisper, not a thought,
Not a kiss nor look be lost.

Beauty, midnight, vision dies:
Let the winds of dawn that blow
Softly round your dreaming head
Such a day of sweetness show

Eye and knocking heart may bless,
Find the mortal world enough;
Noons of dryness see you fed
By the involuntary powers,
Nights of insult let you pass
Watched by every human love.

MUSÉE DES BEAUX ARTS

ABOUT suffering they were never wrong,
The Old Masters: how well they understood
Its human position; how it takes place
While someone else is eating or opening a window or just walking
  dully along:
How, when the aged are reverently, passionately waiting
For the miraculous birth, there always must be
Children who did not specially want it to happen, skating
On a pond at the edge of the wood:
They never forgot
That even the dreadful martyrdom must run its course
Anyhow in a corner, some untidy spot
Where the dogs go on with their doggy life and the torturer's
  horse
Scratches its innocent behind on a tree.
In Brueghel's *Icarus*, for instance: how everything turns away
Quite leisurely from the disaster; the ploughman may
Have heard the splash, the forsaken cry,
But for him it was not an important failure; the sun shone
As it had to on the white legs disappearing into the green
Water; and the expensive delicate ship that must have seen
Something amazing, a boy falling out of the sky,
Had somewhere to get to and sailed calmly on.

IN MEMORY OF W. B. YEATS

(d. January 1939)

I

HE DISAPPEARED in the dead of winter:
The brooks were frozen, the airports almost deserted,
And snow disfigured the public statues;
The mercury sank in the mouth of the dying day.
O all the instruments agree
The day of his death was a dark cold day.

Far from his illness
The wolves ran on through the evergreen forests,
The peasant river was untempted by the fashionable quays;
By mourning tongues
The death of the poet was kept from his poems.

But for him it was his last afternoon as himself,
An afternoon of nurses and rumours;
The provinces of his body revolted,
The squares of his mind were empty,
Silence invaded the suburbs,
The current of his feeling failed: he became his admirers.

Now he is scattered among a hundred cities
And wholly given over to unfamiliar affections;
To find his happiness in another kind of wood
And be punished under a foreign code of conscience.
The words of a dead man
Are modified in the guts of the living.

But in the importance and noise of tomorrow
When the brokers are roaring like beasts on the floor of the Bourse,
And the poor have the sufferings to which they are fairly
   accustomed,
And each in the cell of himself is almost convinced of his freedom,
A few thousand will think of this day
As one thinks of a day when one did something slightly unusual.

O all the instruments agree
The day of his death was a dark cold day.

II

You were silly like us: your gift survived it all:
The parish of rich women, physical decay,
Yourself; mad Ireland hurt you into poetry.
Now Ireland has her madness and her weather still,
For poetry makes nothing happen: it survives
In the valley of its saying where executives
Would never want to tamper; it flows south
From ranches of isolation and the busy griefs,
Raw towns that we believe and die in; it survives,
A way of happening, a mouth.

III

Earth, receive an honoured guest;
William Yeats is laid to rest:
Let the Irish vessel lie
Emptied of its poetry.

Time that is intolerant
Of the brave and innocent,
And indifferent in a week
To a beautiful physique,

Worships language and forgives
Everyone by whom it lives:
Pardons cowardice, conceit,
Lays its honours at their feet.

Time that with this strange excuse
Pardoned Kipling and his views,
And will pardon Paul Claudel,
Pardons him for writing well.

In the nightmare of the dark
All the dogs of Europe bark,
And the living nations wait,
Each sequestered in its hate;

Follow, poet, follow right
To the bottom of the night,
With your unconstraining voice
Still persuade us to rejoice;

With the farming of a verse
Make a vineyard of the curse,
Sing of human unsuccess
In a rapture of distress;

In the deserts of the heart
Let the healing fountain start,
In the prison of his days
Teach the free man how to praise.

THE SHIELD OF ACHILLES

SHE looked over his shoulder
    For vines and olive trees,
Marble well-governed cities,
    And ships upon untamed seas,
But there on the shining metal
    His hands had put instead
An artificial wilderness
    And a sky like lead.

A plain without a feature, bare and brown,
    No blade of grass, no sign of neighbourhood,
Nothing to eat and nowhere to sit down,
    Yet, congregated on its blankness, stood
    An unintelligible multitude,
A million eyes, a million boots in line,
Without expression, waiting for a sign.

Out of the air a voice without a face
    Proved by statistics that some cause was just
In tones as dry and level as the place:
    No one was cheered and nothing was discussed;

Column by column in a cloud of dust
They marched away enduring a belief
Whose logic brought them, somewhere else, to grief.

　　She looked over his shoulder
　　　　For ritual pieties,
　　White flower-garlanded heifers,
　　　　Libation and sacrifice,
　　But there on the shining metal
　　　　Where the altar should have been,
　　She saw by his flickering forge-light
　　　　Quite another scene.

Barbed wire enclosed an arbitrary spot
　　Where bored officials lounged (one cracked a joke)
And sentries sweated, for the day was hot:
　　A crowd of ordinary decent folk
　　Watched from without and neither moved nor spoke
As three pale figures were led forth and bound
To three posts driven upright in the ground.

The mass and majesty of this world, all
　　That carries weight and always weighs the same,
Lay in the hands of others; they were small
　　And could not hope for help and no help came:
　　What their foes liked to do was done, their shame
Was all the worst could wish; they lost their pride
And died as men before their bodies died.

　　She looked over his shoulder
　　　　For athletes at their games,
　　Men and women in a dance
　　　　Moving their sweet limbs
　　Quick, quick, to music.
　　　　But there on the shining shield
　　His hands had set no dancing-floor
　　　　But a weed-choked field.

A ragged urchin, aimless and alone,
   Loitered about that vacancy; a bird
Flew up to safety from his well-aimed stone;
   That girls are raped, that two boys knife a third,
   Were axioms to him, who'd never heard
Of any world where promises were kept
Or one could weep because another wept.

    The thin-lipped armourer,
      Hephaestos, hobbled away;
    Thetis of the shining breasts
      Cried out in dismay
    At what the god had wrought
      To please her son, the strong
    Iron-hearted man-slaying Achilles
      Who would not live long.

AUGUST 1968

    THE OGRE does what ogres can,
    Deeds quite impossible for Man,
    But one prize is beyond his reach,
    The Ogre cannot master Speech:
    About a subjugated plain,
    Among its desperate and slain,
    The Ogre stalks with hands on hips,
    While drivel gushes from his lips.

LOUIS MACNEICE

SUNDAY MORNING

DOWN the road someone is practising scales,
The notes like little fishes vanish with a wink of tails,
Man's heart expands to tinker with his car
For this is Sunday morning, Fate's great bazaar;
Regard these means as ends, concentrate on this Now,

And you may grow to music or drive beyond Hindhead anyhow,
Take corners on two wheels until you go so fast
That you can clutch a fringe or two of the windy past,
That you can abstract this day and make it to the week of time
A small eternity, a sonnet self-contained in rhyme.

But listen, up the road, something gulps, the church spire
Open its eight bells out, skulls' mouths which will not tire
To tell how there is no music or movement which secures
Escape from the weekday time. Which deadens and endures.

SNOW

THE ROOM was suddenly rich and the great bay-window was
Spawning snow and pink roses against it
Soundlessly collateral and incompatible:
World is suddener than we fancy it.

World is crazier and more of it than we think,
Incorrigibly plural. I peel and portion
A tangerine and spit the pips and feel
The drunkenness of things being various.

And the fire flames with a bubbling sound for world
Is more spiteful and gay than one supposes –
On the tongue on the eyes on the ears in the palms of one's hands -
There is more than glass between the snow and the huge roses.

BAGPIPE MUSIC

IT'S NO GO the merrygoround, it's no go the rickshaw,
All we want is a limousine and a ticket for the peepshow.
Their knickers are made of crêpe-de-chine, their shoes are made of
   python,
Their halls are lined with tiger rugs and their walls with heads of
   bison.

John MacDonald found a corpse, put it under the sofa,
Waited till it came to life and hit it with a poker,
Sold its eyes for souvenirs, sold its blood for whisky,
Kept its bones for dumb-bells to use when he was fifty.

It's no go the Yogi-Man, it's no go Blavatsky,
All we want is a bank balance and a bit of skirt in a taxi.

Annie MacDougall went to milk, caught her foot in the heather,
Woke to hear a dance record playing of Old Vienna.
It's no go your maidenheads, it's no go your culture,
All we want is a Dunlop tyre and the devil mend the puncture.

The Laird o' Phelps spent Hogmanay declaring he was sober,
Counted his feet to prove the fact and found he had one foot over.
Mrs Carmichael had her fifth, looked at the job with repulsion,
Said to the midwife 'Take it away; I'm through with over-
    production'.

It's no go the gossip column, it's no go the ceilidh,
All we want is a mother's help and a sugar-stick for the baby.

Willie Murray cut his thumb, couldn't count the damage,
Took the hide of an Ayrshire cow and used it for a bandage.
His brother caught three hundred cran when the seas were lavish,
Threw the bleeders back in the sea and went upon the parish.

It's no go the Herring Board, it's no go the Bible,
All we want is a packet of fags when our hands are idle.

It's no go the picture palace, it's no go the stadium,
It's no go the country cot with a pot of pink geraniums,
It's no go the Government grants, it's no go the elections,
Sit on your arse for fifty years and hang your hat on a pension.

It's no go my honey love, it's no go my poppet;
Work your hands from day to day, the winds will blow the profit.
The glass is falling hour by hour, the glass will fall for ever,
But if you break the bloody glass you won't hold up the weather.

MEETING POINT

TIME was away and somewhere else,
There were two glasses and two chairs
And two people with the one pulse
(Somebody stopped the moving stairs):
Time was away and somewhere else.

And they were neither up nor down;
The stream's music did not stop
Flowing through heather, limpid brown,
Although they sat in a coffee shop
And they were neither up nor down.

The bell was silent in the air
Holding its inverted poise –
Between the clang and clang a flower,
A brazen calyx of no noise:
The bell was silent in the air.

The camels crossed the miles of sand
That stretched around the cups and plates;
The desert was their own, they planned
To portion out the stars and dates:
The camels crossed the miles of sand.

Time was away and somewhere else.
The waiter did not come, the clock
Forgot them and the radio waltz
Came out like water from a rock:
Time was away and somewhere else.

Her fingers flicked away the ash
That bloomed again in tropic trees:
Not caring if the markets crash
When they had forests such as these,
Her fingers flicked away the ash.

God or whatever means the Good
Be praised that time can stop like this,
That what the heart has understood
Can verify in the body's peace
God or whatever means the Good.

Time was away and she was here
And life no longer what it was,
The bell was silent in the air
And all the room one glow because
Time was away and she was here.

STEPHEN SPENDER

I THINK continually of those who were truly great.
Who, from the womb, remembered the soul's history
Through corridors of light where the hours are suns,
Endless and singing. Whose lovely ambition
Was that their lips, still touched with fire,
Should tell of the Spirit, clothed from head to foot in song.
And who hoarded from the Spring branches
The desires falling across their bodies like blossoms.

What is precious, is never to forget
The essential delight of the blood drawn from ageless springs
Breaking through rocks in worlds before our earth.
Never to deny its pleasure in the morning simple light
Nor its grave evening demand for love.
Never to allow gradually the traffic to smother
With noise and fog, the flowering of the Spirit.

Near the snow, near the sun, in the highest fields,
See how these names are fêted by the waving grass
And by the streamers of white cloud
And whispers of wind in the listening sky.
The names of those who in their lives fought for life,
Who wore at their hearts the fire's centre.
Born of the sun, they travelled a short while toward the sun
And left the vivid air signed with their honour.

ROY FULLER

TRANSLATION

Now that the barbarians have got as far as Picra,
And all the new music is written in the twelve-tone scale,
And I am anyway approaching my fortieth birthday,
    I will dissemble no longer.

I will stop expressing my belief in the rosy
Future of man, and accept the evidence
Of a couple of wretched wars and innumerable
    Abortive revolutions.

I will cease to blame the stupidity of the slaves
Upon their masters and nurture, and will say,
Plainly, that they are enemies to culture,
    Advancement and cleanliness.

From progressive organisations, from quarterlies
Devoted to daring verse, from membership of
Committees, from letters of various protest
    I shall withdraw forthwith.

When they call me reactionary I shall smile,
Secure in another dimension. When they say
'Cinna has ceased to matter' I shall know
    How well I reflect the times.

The ruling class will think I am on their side
And make friendly overtures, but I shall retire
To the side farther from Picra and write some poems
    About the doom of the whole boiling.

Anyone happy in this age and place
Is daft or corrupt. Better to abdicate
From a material and spiritual terrain
    Fit only for barbarians.

CECIL DAY LEWIS

WILL IT BE SO AGAIN?

WILL it be so again
That the brave, the gifted are lost from view,
And empty, scheming men
Are left in peace their lunatic age to renew?
Will it be so again?

Must it be always so
That the best are chosen to fall and sleep
Like seeds, and we too slow
In claiming the earth they quicken, and the old usurpers reap
What they could not sow?

Will it be so again –
The jungle code and the hypocrite gesture?
A poppy wreath for the slain
And a cut-throat world for the living? that stale imposture
Played on us once again?

Will it be as before –
Peace, with no heart or mind to ensue it,
Guttering down to war
Like a libertine to his grave? We should not be surprised:
 we knew it
Happen before.

Shall it be so again?
Call not upon the glorious dead
To be your witnesses then.
The living alone can nail to their promise the ones who said
It shall not be so again.

WILLIAM EMPSON

TO AN OLD LADY

RIPENESS is all; her in her cooling planet
Revere; do not presume to think her wasted.
Project her no projectile, plan nor man it;
Gods cool in turn, by the sun long outlasted.

Our earth alone given no name of god
Gives, too, no hold for such a leap to aid her;
Landing, you break some palace and seem odd;
Bees sting their need, the keeper's queen invader.

No, to your telescope; spy out the land;
Watch while her ritual is still to see,
Still stand her temples emptying in the sand
Whose waves o'erthrew their crumbled tracery;

Still stand uncalled-on her soul's appanage;
Much social detail whose successor fades,
Wit used to run a house and to play Bridge,
And tragic fervour, to dismiss her maids.

Years her precession do not throw from gear.
She reads a compass certain of her pole;
Confident, finds no confines on her sphere,
Whose failing crops are in her sole control.

Stars how much further from me fill my night.
Strange that she too should be inaccessible,
Who shares my sun. He curtains her from sight,
And but in darkness is she visible.

MISSING DATES

SLOWLY the poison the whole blood stream fills.
It is not the effort nor the failure tires.
The waste remains, the waste remains and kills.

It is not your system or clear sight that mills
Down small to the consequence a life requires;
Slowly the poison the whole blood stream fills.

They bled an old dog dry yet the exchange rills
Of young dog blood gave but a month's desires.
The waste remains, the waste remains and kills.

It is the Chinese tombs and the slag hills
Usurp the soil, and not the soil retires.
Slowly the poison the whole blood stream fills.

Not to have fire is to be a skin that shrills.
The complete fire is death. From partial fires
The waste remains, the waste remains and kills.

It is the poems you have lost, the ills
From missing dates, at which the heart expires.
Slowly the poison the whole blood stream fills.
The waste remains, the waste remains and kills.

DYLAN THOMAS

AND death shall have no dominion.
Dead men naked they shall be one
With the man in the wind and the west moon;
When their bones are picked clean and the clean bones gone,
They shall have stars at elbow and foot;
Though they go mad they shall be sane,
Though they sink through the sea they shall rise again;
Though lovers be lost love shall not;
And death shall have no dominion.

And death shall have no dominion.
Under the windings of the sea
They lying long shall not die windily;
Twisting on racks when sinews give way,
Strapped to a wheel, yet they shall not break;

Faith in their hands shall snap in two,
And the unicorn evils run them through;
Split all ends up they shan't crack;
And death shall have no dominion.

And death shall have no dominion.
No more may gulls cry at their ears
Or waves break loud on the seashores;
Where blew a flower may a flower no more
Lift its head to the blows of the rain;
Though they be mad and dead as nails,
Heads of the characters hammer through daisies;
Break in the sun till the sun breaks down,
And death shall have no dominion.

Do NOT go gentle into that good night,
Old age should burn and rave at close of day;
Rage, rage against the dying of the light.

Though wise men at their end know dark is right,
Because their words had forked no lightning they
Do not go gentle into that good night.

Good men, the last wave by, crying how bright
Their frail deeds might have danced in a green bay,
Rage, rage against the dying of the light.

Wild men who caught and sang the sun in flight,
And learn, too late, they grieved it on its way,
Do not go gentle into that good night.

Grave men, near death, who see with blinding sight
Blind eyes could blaze like meteors and be gay,
Rage, rage against the dying of the light.

And you, my father, there on the sad height,
Curse, bless, me now with your fierce tears, I pray.
Do not go gentle into that good night.
Rage, rage against the dying of the light.

FERN HILL

Now as I was young and easy under the apple boughs
About the lilting house and happy as the grass was green,
     The night above the dingle starry,
       Time let me hail and climb
     Golden in the heydays of his eyes,
And honoured among wagons I was prince of the apple towns
And once below a time I lordly had the trees and leaves
       Trail with daisies and barley
     Down the rivers of the windfall light.

And as I was green and carefree, famous among the barns
About the happy yard and singing as the farm was home,
     In the sun that is young once only,
       Time let me play and be
     Golden in the mercy of his means,
And green and golden I was huntsman and herdsman, the calves
Sang to my horn, the foxes on the hills barked clear and cold,
       And the sabbath rang slowly
     In the pebbles of the holy streams.

All the sun long it was running, it was lovely, the hay
Fields high as the house, the tunes from the chimneys, it was air
     And playing, lovely and watery
       And fire green as grass.
     And nightly under the simple stars
As I rode to sleep the owls were bearing the farm away,
All the moon long I heard, blessed among stables, the nightjars
       Flying with the ricks, and the horses
        Flashing into the dark.

And then to awake, and the farm, like a wanderer white
With the dew, come back, the cock on his shoulder: it was all
     Shining, it was Adam and maiden,
       The sky gathered again
     And the sun grew round that very day.
So it must have been after the birth of the simple light
In the first, spinning place, the spellbound horses walking warm
       Out of the whinnying green stable
        On to the fields of praise.

And honoured among foxes and pheasants by the gay house
Under the new made clouds and happy as the heart was long,
    In the sun born over and over,
        I ran my heedless ways,
    My wishes raced through the house high hay
And nothing I cared, at my sky blue trades, that time allows
In all his tuneful turning so few and such morning songs
    Before the children green and golden
        Follow him out of grace,

Nothing I cared, in the lamb white days, that time would take me
Up to the swallow thronged loft by the shadow of my hand,
    In the moon that is always rising,
        Nor that riding to sleep
    I should hear him fly with high fields
And wake to the farm forever fled from the childless land.
Oh as I was young and easy in the mercy of his means,
        Time held me green and dying
    Though I sang in my chains like the sea.

HENRY REED

From LESSONS OF THE WAR

NAMING OF PARTS

TODAY we have naming of parts. Yesterday,
We had daily cleaning. And tomorrow morning,
We shall have what to do after firing. But today,
Today we have naming of parts. Japonica
Glistens like coral in all of the neighbouring gardens,
    And today we have naming of parts.

This is the lower sling swivel. And this
Is the upper sling swivel, whose use you will see,
When you are given your slings. And this is the piling swivel,
Which in your case you have not got. The branches
Hold in the gardens their silent, eloquent gestures,
    Which in our case we have not got.

This is the safety-catch, which is always released
With an easy flick of the thumb. And please do not let me
See anyone using his finger. You can do it quite easy
If you have any strength in your thumb. The blossoms
Are fragile and motionless, never letting anyone see
    Any of them using their finger.

And this you can see is the bolt. The purpose of this
Is to open the breech, as you see. We can slide it
Rapidly backwards and forwards: we call this
Easing the spring. And rapidly backwards and forwards
The early bees are assaulting and fumbling the flowers:
    They call it easing the Spring.

They call it easing the Spring: it is perfectly easy
If you have any strength in your thumb: like the bolt,
And the breech, and the cocking-piece, and the point of balance,
Which in our case we have not got; and the almond-blossom
Silent in all of the gardens and the bees going backwards and
    forwards,
    For today we have naming of parts.

JUDGING DISTANCES

NOT ONLY how far away, but the way that you say it
Is very important. Perhaps you may never get
The knack of judging a distance, but at least you know
How to report on a landscape: the central sector,
The right of arc and that, which we had last Tuesday,
    And at least you know

That maps are of time, not place, so far as the army
Happens to be concerned – the reason being,
Is one which need not delay us. Again, you know
There are three kinds of tree, three only, the fir and the poplar,
And those which have bushy tops to; and lastly
    That things only seem to be things.

A barn is not called a barn, to put it more plainly,
Or a field in the distance, where sheep may be safely grazing.
You must never be over-sure. You must say, when reporting:
At five o'clock in the central sector is a dozen
Of what appear to be animals; whatever you do,
    Don't call the bleeders *sheep*.

I am sure that's quite clear; and suppose, for the sake of example,
The one at the end, asleep, endeavours to tell us
What he sees over there to the west, and how far away,
After first having come to attention. There to the west,
On the fields of summer the sun and the shadows bestow
    Vestments of purple and gold.

The still white dwellings are like a mirage in the heat,
And under the swaying elms a man and a woman
Lie gently together. Which is, perhaps, only to say
That there is a row of houses to the left of arc,
And that under some poplars a pair of what appear to be humans
    Appear to be loving.

Well that, for an answer, is what we might rightly call
Moderately satisfactory only, the reason being,
Is that two things have been omitted, and those are important.
The human beings, now: in what direction are they,
And how far away, would you say? And do not forget
    There may be dead ground in between.

There may be dead ground in between; and I may not have got
The knack of judging a distance; I will only venture
A guess that perhaps between me and the apparent lovers,
(Who, incidentally, appear by now to have finished,)
At seven o'clock from the houses, is roughly a distance
    Of about one year and a half.

ALUN LEWIS

ALL DAY it has rained, and we on the edge of the moors
Have sprawled in our bell-tents, moody and dull as boors,
Groundsheets and blankets spread on the muddy ground
And from the first grey wakening we have found
No refuge from the skirmishing fine rain
And the wind that made the canvas heave and flap
And the taut wet guy-ropes ravel out and snap.
All day the rain has glided, wave and mist and dream,
Drenching the gorse and heather, a gossamer stream
Too light to stir the acorns that suddenly
Snatched from their cups by the wild south-westerly
Pattered against the tent and our upturned dreaming faces.
And we stretched out, unbuttoning our braces,
Smoking a Woodbine, darning dirty socks,
Reading the Sunday papers – I saw a fox
And mentioned it in the note I scribbled home; –
And we talked of girls, and dropping bombs on Rome,
And thought of the quiet dead and the loud celebrities
Exhorting us to slaughter, and the herded refugees;
– Yet thought softly, morosely of them, and as indifferently
As of ourselves or those whom we
For years have loved, and will again
Tomorrow maybe love; but now it is the rain
Possesses us entirely, the twilight and the rain.

And I can remember nothing dearer or more to my heart
Than the children I watched in the woods on Saturday
Shaking down burning chestnuts for the schoolyard's merry play,
Or the shaggy patient dog who followed me
By Sheet and Steep and up the wooded scree
To the Shoulder o' Mutton where Edward Thomas brooded long
On death and beauty – till a bullet stopped his song.

KEITH DOUGLAS

SIMPLIFY ME WHEN I'M DEAD

REMEMBER me when I am dead
and simplify me when I'm dead.

As the processes of earth
strip off the colour and the skin.
take the brown hair and blue eye

and leave me simpler than at birth,
when hairless I came howling in
as the moon entered the cold sky.

Of my skeleton perhaps,
so stripped, a learned man will say
'He was of such a type and intelligence,' no more.

Thus when in a year collapse
particular memories, you may
deduce, from the long pain I bore

the opinions I held, who was my foe
and what I left, even my appearance
but incidents will be no guide.

Time's wrong-way telescope will show
a minute man ten years hence
and by distance simplified.

Through that lens see if I seem
substance or nothing: of the world
deserving mention or charitable oblivion,

not by momentary spleen
or love into decision hurled,
leisurely arrive at an opinion.

Remember me when I am dead
and simplify me when I'm dead.

HOW TO KILL

UNDER the parabola of a ball,
a child turning into a man,
I looked into the air too long.
The ball fell in my hand, it sang
in the closed fist: *Open Open
Behold a gift designed to kill.*

Now in my dial of glass appears
the soldier who is going to die.
He smiles, and moves about in ways
his mother knows, habits of his.
The wires touch his face: I cry
NOW. Death, like a familiar, hears

and look, has made a man of dust
of a man of flesh. This sorcery
I do. Being damned, I am amused
to see the centre of love diffused
and the waves of love travel into vacancy.
How easy it is to make a ghost.

The weightless mosquito touches
her tiny shadow on the stone,
and with how like, how infinite
a lightness, man and shadow meet.
They fuse. A shadow is a man
when the mosquito death approaches.

Tunisia-Cairo, 1943

SIR JOHN BETJEMAN

A SUBALTERN'S LOVE-SONG

MISS J. HUNTER DUNN, Miss J. Hunter Dunn,
Furnish'd and burnish'd by Aldershot sun,
What strenuous singles we played after tea,
We in the tournament – you against me!

Love-thirty, love-forty, oh! weakness of joy,
The speed of a swallow, the grace of a boy,
With carefullest carelessness, gaily you won,
I am weak from your loveliness, Joan Hunter Dunn.

Miss Joan Hunter Dunn, Miss Joan Hunter Dunn,
How mad I am, sad I am, glad that you won.
The warm-handled racket is back in its press,
But my shock-headed victor, she loves me no less.

Her father's euonymus shines as we walk,
And swing past the summer-house, buried in talk,
And cool the verandah that welcomes us in
To the six-o'clock news and a lime-juice and gin.

The scent of the conifers, sound of the bath,
The view from my bedroom of moss-dappled path,
As I struggle with double-end evening tie,
For we dance at the Golf Club, my victor and I.

On the floor of her bedroom lie blazer and shorts
And the cream-coloured walls are be-trophied with sports,
And westering, questioning settles the sun
On your low-leaded window, Miss Joan Hunter Dunn.

The Hillman is waiting, the light's in the hall,
The pictures of Egypt are bright on the wall,
My sweet, I am standing beside the oak stair
And there on the landing's the light on your hair.

By roads 'not adopted', by woodlanded ways,
She drove to the club in the late summer haze,
Into nine-o'clock Camberley, heavy with bells
And mushroomy, pine-woody, evergreen smells.

Miss Joan Hunter Dunn, Miss Joan Hunter Dunn,
I can hear from the car-park the dance has begun.
Oh! full Surrey twilight! importunate band!
Oh! strongly adorable tennis-girl's hand!

Around us are Rovers and Austins afar,
Above us, the intimate roof of the car,
And here on my right is the girl of my choice,
With the tilt of her nose and the chime of her voice,

And the scent of her wrap, and the words never said,
And the ominous, ominous dancing ahead.
We sat in the car-park till twenty to one
And now I'm engaged to Miss Joan Hunter Dunn.

IN WESTMINSTER ABBEY

LET me take this other glove off
    As the *vox humana* swells,
And the beauteous fields of Eden
    Bask beneath the Abbey bells.
Here, where England's statesmen lie,
Listen to a lady's cry.

Gracious Lord, oh bomb the Germans.
    Spare their women for Thy Sake,
And if that is not too easy
    We will pardon Thy Mistake.
But, gracious Lord, whate'er shall be,
Don't let anyone bomb me.

Keep our Empire undismembered
  Guide our Forces by Thy Hand,
Gallant blacks from far Jamaica,
  Honduras and Togoland;
Protect them Lord in all their fights,
And, even more, protect the whites.

Think of what our Nation stands for,
  Books from Boots' and country lanes,
Free speech, free passes, class distinction,
  Democracy and proper drains.
Lord, put beneath Thy special care
One-eighty-nine Cadogan Square.

Although dear Lord I am a sinner,
  I have done no major crime;
Now I'll come to Evening Service
  Whensoever I have the time.
So, Lord, reserve for me a crown,
And do not let my shares go down.

I will labour for Thy Kingdom,
  Help our lads to win the war,
Send white feathers to the cowards
  Join the Women's Army Corps,
Then wash the Steps around Thy Throne
In the Eternal Safety Zone.

Now I feel a little better,
  What a treat to hear Thy Word,
Where the bones of leading statesmen,
  Have so often been interr'd.
And now, dear Lord, I cannot wait
Because I have a luncheon date.

PHILIP LARKIN

TOADS

WHY should I let the toad *work*
   Squat on my life?
Can't I use my wit as a pitchfork
   And drive the brute off?

Six days of the week it soils
   With its sickening poison –
Just for paying a few bills!
   That's out of proportion.

Lots of folk live on their wits:
   Lecturers, lispers,
Losels, loblolly-men, louts –
   They don't end as paupers;

Lots of folk live up lanes
   With fires in a bucket,
Eat windfalls and tinned sardines –
   They seem to like it.

Their nippers have got bare feet,
   Their unspeakable wives
Are skinny as whippets – and yet
   No one actually *starves*.

Ah, were I courageous enough
   To shout *Stuff your pension!*
But I know, all too well, that's the stuff
   That dreams are made on:

For something sufficiently toad-like
   Squats in me, too;
Its hunkers are heavy as hard luck,
   And cold as snow,

And will never allow me to blarney
  My way to getting
The fame and the girl and the money
  All at one sitting.

I don't say, one bodies the other
  One's spiritual truth;
But I do say it's hard to lose either,
  When you have both.

THE WHITSUN WEDDINGS

THAT Whitsun, I was late getting away:
  Not till about
One-twenty on the sunlit Saturday
Did my three-quarters-empty train pull out,
All windows down, all cushions hot, all sense
Of being in a hurry gone. We ran
Behind the backs of houses, crossed a street
Of blinding windscreens, smelt the fish-dock; thence
The river's level drifting breadth began,
Where sky and Lincolnshire and water meet.

All afternoon, through the tall heat that slept
  For miles inland,
A slow and stopping curve southwards we kept.
Wide farms went by, short-shadowed cattle, and
Canals with floatings of industrial froth;
A hothouse flashed uniquely: hedges dipped
And rose: and now and then a smell of grass
Displaced the reek of buttoned carriage-cloth
Until the next town, new and nondescript,
Approached with acres of dismantled cars.

At first, I didn't notice what a noise
  The weddings made
Each station that we stopped at: sun destroys
The interest of what's happening in the shade,

And down the long cool platforms whoops and skirls
I took for porters larking with the mails,
And went on reading. Once we started, though,
We passed them, grinning and pomaded, girls
In parodies of fashion, heels and veils,
All posed irresolutely, watching us go,

As if out on the end of an event
   Waving goodbye
To something that survived it. Struck, I leant
More promptly out next time, more curiously,
And saw it all again in different terms:
The fathers with broad belts under their suits
And seamy foreheads; mothers loud and fat;
An uncle shouting smut; and then the perms,
The nylon gloves and jewellery-substitutes,
The lemons, mauves, and olive-ochres that

Marked off the girls unreally from the rest.
   Yes, from cafés
And banquet-halls up yards, and bunting-dressed
Coach-party annexes, the wedding-days
Were coming to an end. All down the line
Fresh couples climbed aboard: the rest stood round;
The last confetti and advice were thrown,
And, as we moved, each face seemed to define
Just what it saw departing: children frowned
At something dull; fathers had never known

Success so huge and wholly farcical;
   The women shared
The secret like a happy funeral;
While girls, gripping their handbags tighter, stared
At a religious wounding. Free at last,
And loaded with the sum of all they saw,
We hurried towards London, shuffling gouts of steam.
Now fields were building-plots, and poplars cast
Long shadows over major roads, and for
Some fifty minutes, that in time would seem

Just long enough to settle hats and say
   I nearly died,
A dozen marriages got under way.
They watched the landscape, sitting side by side
– An Odeon went past, a cooling tower,
And someone running up to bowl – and none
Thought of the others they would never meet
Or how their lives would all contain this hour.
I thought of London spread out in the sun,
Its postal districts packed like squares of wheat:

There we were aimed. And as we raced across
   Bright knots of rail
Past standing Pullmans, walls of blackened moss
Came close, and it was nearly done, this frail
Travelling coincidence; and what it held
Stood ready to be loosed with all the power
That being changed can give. We slowed again,
And as the tightened brakes took hold, there swelled
A sense of falling, like an arrow-shower
Sent out of sight, somewhere becoming rain.

DOCKERY AND SON

'DOCKERY was junior to you,
Wasn't he?' said the Dean. 'His son's here now.'
Death-suited, visitant, I nod. 'And do
You keep in touch with—' Or remember how
Black-gowned, unbreakfasted, and still half-tight
We used to stand before that desk, to give
'Our version' of 'these incidents last night'?
I try the door of where I used to live:

Locked. The lawn spreads dazzlingly wide.
A known bell chimes. I catch my train, ignored.
Canal and clouds and colleges subside
Slowly from view. But Dockery, good Lord,
Anyone up today must have been born

In '43, when I was twenty-one.
If he was younger, did he get this son
At nineteen, twenty? Was he that withdrawn

High-collared public-schoolboy, sharing rooms
With Cartwright who was killed? Well, it just shows
How much . . . How little . . . Yawning, I suppose
I fell asleep, waking at the fumes
And furnace-glares of Sheffield, where I changed,
And ate an awful pie, and walked along
The platform to its end to see the ranged
Joining and parting lines reflect a strong

Unhindered moon. To have no son, no wife,
No house or land still seemed quite natural.
Only a numbness registered the shock
Of finding out how much had gone of life,
How widely from the others. Dockery, now:
Only nineteen, he must have taken stock
Of what he wanted, and been capable
Of . . . No, that's not the difference: rather, how

Convinced he was he should be added to!
Why did he think adding meant increase?
To me it was dilution. Where do these
Innate assumptions come from? Not from what
We think truest, or most want to do:
Those warp tight-shut, like doors. They're more a style
Our lives bring with them: habit for a while,
Suddenly they harden into all we've got

And how we got it; looked back on, they rear
Like sand-clouds, thick and close, embodying
For Dockery a son, for me nothing,
Nothing with all a son's harsh patronage.
Life is first boredom, then fear.
Whether or not we use it, it goes,
And leaves what something hidden from us chose,
And age, and then the only end of age.

THOM GUNN

IN SANTA MARIA DEL POPOLO

WAITING for when the sun an hour or less
Conveniently oblique makes visible
The painting on one wall of this recess
By Caravaggio, of the Roman School,
I see how shadow in the painting brims
With a real shadow, drowning all shapes out
But a dim horse's haunch and various limbs,
Until the very subject is in doubt.

But evening gives the act, beneath the horse
And one indifferent groom, I see him sprawl,
Foreshortened from the head, with hidden face,
Where he has fallen, Saul becoming Paul.
O wily painter, limiting the scene
From a cacophony of dusty forms
To the one convulsion, what is it you mean
In that wide gesture of the lifting arms?

No Ananias croons a mystery yet,
Casting the pain out under name of sin.
The painter saw what was, an alternate
Candour and secrecy inside the skin.
He painted, elsewhere, that firm insolent
Young whore in Venus' clothes, those pudgy cheats,
Those sharpers; and was strangled, as things went,
For money, by one such picked off the streets.

I turn, hardly enlightened, from the chapel
To the dim interior of the church instead,
In which there kneel already several people,
Mostly old women: each head closeted
In tiny fists holds comfort as it can.
Their poor arms are too tired for more than this
– For the large gesture of solitary man,
Resisting, by embracing, nothingness.

RITES OF PASSAGE

SOMETHING is taking place.
Horns bud bright in my hair.
My feet are turning hoof.
And Father, see my face
– Skin that was damp and fair
Is barklike and, feel, rough.

See Greytop how I shine.
I rear, break loose, I neigh
Snuffing the air, and harden
Toward a completion, mine.
And next I make my way
Adventuring through your garden.

My play is earnest now.
I canter to and fro.
My blood, it is like light.
Behind an almond bough,
Horns gaudy with its snow,
I wait live, out of sight.

All planned before my birth
For you, Old Man, no other,
Whom your groin's trembling warns.
I stamp upon the earth
A message to my mother.
And then I lower my horns.

TED HUGHES

HAWK ROOSTING

I SIT in the top of the wood, my eyes closed.
Inaction, no falsifying dream
Between my hooked head and hooked feet:
Or in sleep rehearse perfect kills and eat.

The convenience of the high trees!
The air's buoyancy and the sun's ray
Are of advantage to me;
And the earth's face upward for my inspection.

My feet are locked upon the rough bark.
It took the whole of Creation
To produce my foot, my each feather:
Now I hold Creation in my foot

Or fly up, and revolve it all slowly –
I kill where I please because it is all mine.
There is no sophistry in my body:
My manners are tearing off heads –

The allotment of death.
For the one path of my flight is direct
Through the bones of the living.
No arguments assert my right:

The sun is behind me.
Nothing has changed since I began.
My eye has permitted no change.
I am going to keep things like this.

PIKE

PIKE, three inches long, perfect
Pike in all parts, green tigering the gold.
Killers from the egg: the malevolent aged grin.
They dance on the surface among the flies.

Or move, stunned by their own grandeur,
Over a bed of emerald, silhouette
Of submarine delicacy and horror.
A hundred feet long in their world.

In ponds, under the heat-struck lily pads –
Gloom of their stillness:
Logged on last year's black leaves, watching upwards.
Or hung in an amber cavern of weeds

The jaws' hooked clamp and fangs
Not to be changed at this date;
A life subdued to its instrument;
The gills kneading quietly, and the pectorals.

Three we kept behind glass,
Jungled in weed: three inches, four,
And four and a half: fed fry to them –
Suddenly there were two. Finally one

With a sag belly and the grin it was born with.
And indeed they spare nobody.
Two, six pounds each, over two feet long,
High and dry and dead in the willow-herb –

One jammed past its gills down the other's gullet:
The outside eye stared: as a vice locks –
The same iron in this eye
Though its film shrank in death.

A pond I fished, fifty yards across,
Whose lilies and muscular tench
Had outlasted every visible stone
Of the monastery that planted them –

Stilled legendary depth:
It was as deep as England. It held
Pike too immense to stir, so immense and old
That past nightfall I dared not cast

But silently cast and fished
With the hair frozen on my head
For what might move, for what eye might move.
The still splashes on the dark pond,

Owls hushing the floating woods
Frail on my ear against the dream
Darkness beneath night's darkness had freed,
That rose slowly towards me, watching.

CROW ALIGHTS

Crow saw the herded mountains, steaming in the morning.
And he saw the sea
Dark-spined, with the whole earth in its coils.
He saw the stars, fuming away into the black, mushrooms of the
   nothing forest, clouding their spores, the virus of God.

And he shivered with the horror of Creation.

In the hallucination of the horror
He saw this shoe, with no sole, rain-sodden,
Lying on a moor.
And there was this garbage can, bottom rusted away,
A playing place for the wind, in a waste of puddles.

There was this coat, in the dark cupboard, in the silent room, in the
   silent house.
There was this face, smoking its cigarette between the dusk window
   and the fire's embers.

Near the face, this hand, motionless.

Near the hand, this cup.

Crow blinked. He blinked. Nothing faded.

He stared at the evidence.

Nothing escaped him. (Nothing could escape.)

INDEX OF POETS

INDEX OF FIRST LINES